Responsible Strategic Thinking for Business and Society

A Practical Guide

Edited by Olivia Ramsbottom

Routledge
Taylor & Francis Group
LONDON AND NEW YORK

Designed cover image: Inspiretta / Getty Images

First published 2026
by Routledge
4 Park Square, Milton Park, Abingdon, Oxon OX14 4RN

and by Routledge
605 Third Avenue, New York, NY 10158

Routledge is an imprint of the Taylor & Francis Group, an informa business

British Library Cataloguing-in-Publication Data
A catalogue record for this book is available from the British Library

ISBN: 978-1-032-75764-3 (hbk)
ISBN: 978-1-032-75762-9 (pbk)
ISBN: 978-1-003-47554-5 (ebk)

DOI: 10.4324/9781003475545

Typeset in Berling
by Deanta Global Publishing Services, Chennai, India

Access the Support Material: www.routledge.com/9781032757629

Contents

Responsible Strategic Thinking for Business and Society

This exciting new text investigates the true essence of strategic thinking, and explores the need for alternative, responsible approaches in a complex global environment.

Existing definitions of strategy and strategic management and leadership are examined, challenging previous ways of thinking that no longer relate to the way private, public, and third-sector organisations operate. Enriched by a diverse and experienced panel of contributors, chapters characterise the global systems which influence strategic thinking by spanning themes of politics, economics, society, technology, the legal framework, leveraging Generation Z's values, environmental sustainability, and ethics. Supported by detailed global case studies from well-known and smaller brands, examples show how business and organisation leaders have thought differently to bring about change. The work concludes by providing a 'systems view toolkit', which shows what can be done to optimise strategic thinking for change and longevity. To aid comprehension, each chapter includes a clear Outline and Key Points, as well as a Summary.

Written in an accessible style, this title is intended as introductory and recommended reading for advanced undergraduate and postgraduate students of Strategic Management and Leadership, who are interested in how strategic thinking relates to the global political, economic, and social environment.

Online supplementary resources include PowerPoint slides, as well as recommendations for further reading within each chapter.

Olivia Ramsbottom is a Senior Lecturer at Sheffield Hallam University, UK, who specialises in strategic thinking.

"This is a timely text that provides an overview of current practices and sets out an ambitious roadmap for the future. Drawing upon inspirational examples from different sectors, it will be of equal value in the classroom and the boardroom."

Laura Steele, *PhD, Reader of Business Ethics and Sustainability Education, Queen's Business School, UK*

Contributors

Marc Duffy is a former practitioner with international management experience in heavy industry, aluminium, iron, and steelmaking. In 2015, he returned to academia, specialising in strategic management and sustainability. Now at Ulster University in the UK, he focuses on degree apprenticeships, online courses, and leads the Principles of Responsible Management Education (PRME) team.

Nick Lawrence is a Senior Lecturer at Southampton Solent Business School, UK, and brings 35+ years' industry experience in IT, R&D funding, and leadership to his teaching and research. He has an MSc in Psychology and is particularly passionate about the use of technology (especially Artificial Intelligence) in developing organisational strategies.

Caroline Linhares is a Senior Lecturer at Sheffield Business School, UK, and specialises in Social and Environmental Accounting. With a decade of industry experience, her research explores accounting's role in sustainable development, focusing on embedding social and environmental impacts into decision-making and assessing sustainability reporting's effectiveness in fostering accountability.

Jules O'dor, Associate Head of Global Academic Partnerships at Sheffield Business School, UK, oversees international collaborations across Europe, Asia, and Africa. With a diverse career spanning IT, education, and government, he teaches and researches strategic management, organisational change, and sustainable leadership, focusing on social enterprise, student experience, and education for sustainable development.

Helen Pollard is a Senior Lecturer at Ulster University Business School, UK, and directs the MSc Business in Technology (MBT) and PG Cert Businesses Analysis and Consulting. With 20+ years' experience, she specialises in strategy, consulting and curriculum design. Her research focuses on leadership in tech, course co-design, integrated curriculum development, and microlearning.

Olivia Ramsbottom, a Senior Lecturer at Sheffield Hallam University, UK, specialises in strategic thinking. With 16 years of managerial experience, a PhD, MSc, and teaching qualifications, she focuses on creating teaching tools for professionals, emphasising the practical application of theories to embed knowledge effectively.

Jo Watts, a Senior Lecturer at Sheffield Hallam University, UK, draws on a 30-year career in learning, development, and leadership across private, public, and third sectors. Her teaching focuses on ethical management, consultancy, and research methods. She holds a PhD and MSc and researches Civil Society Infrastructure in a Department for Media Culture-supported project.

Peter Wells, Professor of Public Policy Analysis and Evaluation at Sheffield Hallam University, UK, has led over 50 projects and authored over 100 publications. He directs research for a range of public, private, and voluntary sector funders. He has held advisory roles for government departments, the European Commission, and local authorities.

Nichola Williams is a Lecturer in Economics at Sheffield Hallam University, UK, and holds an MSc, MBA, and a PhD in Economics. With expertise in macroeconomics, microeconomics, econometrics, and development economics, she combines global academic experience with a passion for teaching, inspiring students in economic principles.

Drew Woodhouse is a Senior Lecturer in Economics at Sheffield Hallam University, UK. He has a special interest in socioeconomic matters at both a local and national scale, engaging with place-based policy debates through a variety of academic and civic channels. He contributes to public discussions on structural reform, fiscal policy, and monetary issues, influencing global institutions.

Anne Wylie, Senior Lecturer in Business and Management at the University of Derby, UK, leads the BA (Hons) Business Management programme at the University of Derby and emphasises sustainability in all aspects of her teaching. A Fellow of the Higher Education Academy and doctoral candidate with over 30 years' experience of teaching, her focus is on social enterprise and sustainable entrepreneurship education.

Preface

Embarking on the journey of writing a book is a significant and time-consuming endeavour and must therefore be driven by a deep conviction that there is something important to convey. This book was motivated by experiences gained from teaching strategic management and leadership in a rapidly changing world, where traditional theories often fall short when facing current economic, social, and environmental challenges and where the key current economic, social, and environmental challenges are difficult to decipher. It was also motivated by the belief that strategic thinkers in all types of businesses and organisations have the potential to shape the future and, while the scale of the challenges we face can seem overwhelming, it is crucial to remember that even small changes made by strategic thinkers can lead to significant impacts. By examining the current state of external factors impacting on strategic thinking and showing where and how people can think differently for positive impact, this book aims to advance strategic thought for the twenty-first century. It serves as both a guide to evaluate current strategic practices and a platform to explore new theories and concepts. Ultimately, it is a call to action for responsible strategic thinking that can drive meaningful change in both business and society.

A RAPIDLY CHANGING WORLD

Our understanding of managing and leading businesses has evolved significantly over the past two centuries as our society evolves. Today, we face a complex environment that challenges traditional strategies focused on competition and shareholder value, which have contributed to an inequitable and unsustainable society in an increasingly volatile world. We must evolve our understanding to face the current environment. Certainly, we have seen wars, instability, inflation, recession, trade disagreements, and societal and technological change over the years, but the current combination of those factors and the speed of change (largely caused by globalisation and the speed of technological change) have created a uniquely complex environment. This complexity has led to various challenges. We are encouraged to be rational economic individuals yet feel the pang of loneliness and need for social support. We have an economic system focused on neoclassical economics where consumption and the dominance of capitalism have led to economic and social inequalities, unethical practices, and business failures. Population growth and climate change have led to environmental inequalities, with the poorest in society contributing just 10 per cent of the carbon in the atmosphere while the richest 10 per cent in society contribute more than 40 times the poorest 10 per cent. We live in a globalised economy, yet the impact of economic success in the developed world tends to have a negative impact on the developing world, and we have a new generation of workers and customers with quite different needs having ridden the wave of Covid at key formative points in their existence, which has affected their attitude towards life and work, and they have seen what damage their predecessors have done to the environment.

Based on these challenges, this book calls for a critical reimagining of strategic management and leadership and encourages a refocus on strategic thinking and systems thinking, with a new model for strategy-making incorporating sustainability, a focus on absolute value, consideration for people's needs, and a hybrid approach of prescriptive and emergent strategies with a long-term perspective, but with a critical requirement to look outside of the insular view to also look at society and life and the external factors which influence and can be influenced by businesses and organisations, and which, when acting together, strategic thinkers can change to improve the sustainability of our ecosystem.

A GUIDE TO THIS BOOK

This book has been designed around the systems thinking approach, and the need to look outside of the strategic thinker's individual position and the organisation of which they are a part, to the external system. The book starts with two chapters setting the scene and ends with a guide in the final chapter to show how a strategic thinker can act and the questions they should ask, but the core chapters 3 to 9 are an assessment of the Political, Economic, Social, Technological, Legal, and Environmental issues affecting the world and of which a strategic thinker needs to be aware.

Each chapter is organised with a Chapter Outline and Key Points at the start, and a Chapter Summary at the end. Each chapter is split into clear sections and sub-sections, with figures and tables used to demonstrate points. We know how busy strategic thinkers are, and as we invite you to take a small bite from the challenge of responsible strategic thinking, we also invite you to digest this book in small chunks.

SMALL CHANGES EQUAL BIG IMPACT

When we list the current social, economic, and environmental challenges, the size of the challenge can seem daunting and overwhelming, and the result of this can often be passivity. This book gives tips throughout of what strategic thinkers can do differently and gives examples showing how business and organisation leaders have thought differently to bring about change. There are case studies throughout and a guide at the end to suggest some actions and questions that strategic thinkers can employ. We as individuals cannot hope to tackle all the issues, but if we each take a small bite, we can. Actions, however small, can have an impact. Good behaviour, if not directly balanced out by bad, can incrementally cause change. For example, if I find a way to work with partners to recycle the waste from my business effectively, I can reduce the business', region's, and world's carbon footprint. This book simply asks you, as a senior leader, to consider responsible strategic thinking, and that a better balance of the social, economic, and environmental responsibilities of our organisations, every day, can make a difference. Take the examples of small businesses in Chapter 3 who have joined together in advocacy groups to influence policy-making. See in Chapter 4 how Marks & Spencer incorporated insights from Institutional Theory into its strategic decision-making processes to provide valuable guidance for navigating the complex institutional contexts of various countries. In Chapter 5 examples of social enterprise are spotlighted as alternative ways of doing business. In Chapter 6 find out how to embrace Generation Z, and in Chapter 7 how organisations are embracing the benefits and risks of technology. In Chapter 8 recognise that ethical behaviour is required to avoid the pitfalls caused by limiting one's outlook to what is required legally. In Chapter 9, Miele, Patagonia, and Toast are just three examples of finding ways to slow or close the sustainability loop to use fewer environmental resources. Case studies at key points show how real-world senior leaders have used strategic thinking in their professional lives and how organisations of various types have exercised different approaches to business.

THE AUTHORS

This book is the result of a collaborative effort, with each author contributing their unique expertise and perspective to the shared goal of promoting a holistic, systems-based approach to responsible strategic thinking. Together, they explore various dimensions of management, leadership, and contemporary societal challenges, offering insights into how we arrived at our current position and where we might head in the future. Through their collective knowledge, the authors aim to inspire new thinking and practical solutions for navigating the complexities ahead.

THANKS

We are grateful to the organisations who are doing things differently and who we use as examples throughout this book. We are also grateful for the insight from the following strategic leaders who gave their time to discuss the challenges of strategic thinking:

Adam Parsons – Consultant from a Big Four Consultancy.

Jayne Sowerby-Warrington – Founder, Director of Kudos Leadership Solutions Ltd and a previous Senior Leader at Lincolnshire County Council.

Sarah Webster – Acting Parks and Green Spaces Manager within the Climate and Environment Department at Derby City Council.

HOW TO USE THIS BOOK: A CALL TO ACTION

We do not expect you to read this book from cover to cover. The book has been designed for the busy strategic leader, who, seeking continuous learning and inspiration, and sharing our discomfort with traditional theories that often fall short when facing current economic, social, and environmental challenges, will 'dip into' the book for ideas, and we hope that it is thought-provoking. As you read you may ask 'so what, what if, and what now'.

This book is dedicated to those who persist in thinking differently despite the challenges!

CHAPTER 1

Defining Strategic Thinking

Olivia Ramsbottom

CHAPTER OUTLINE

This chapter explains how our world has changed since we started to think about how best to manage and lead our businesses and organisations 200 years ago. More traditional literature on strategy-making emphasises beating the competition and providing value for the shareholder. This has led to an inequitable and unsustainable society in an increasingly volatile, uncertain, complex, and ambiguous (VUCA) world (Bennett & Lemoine, 2014). In the early twenty-first century, we are in a more complex environment than ever before (Haslam & Shenoy, 2018). It is timely therefore to criticise and reimagine how we think about strategic management and leadership in preparation for the challenges we face, and which are to come.

In this chapter, vocabulary is clarified and defined starting with strategy-making and strategy. The traditionally relevant key terms and characteristics of strategy-making, including sustainability; competitive advantage and value; stakeholders; change; processes and approaches; and the long-term nature of strategy are debated and reframed in the light of our complex environment.

A model for strategy-making that combines sustainability, concern for absolute value, people's needs, change, prescriptive and emergent strategy (a hybrid approach), and a long-term view is proposed.

The skills for strategy-making are then confirmed, combining strategic management and leadership skills into strategic thinking. Strategic thinking should be at the centre of an outlook where a strategic thinker pays attention to the larger system (society/life) of which we as individuals, and businesses and organisations, are a part. This system can be represented by the PESTLE acronym, and this forms the framework for chapters 3 to 9 of this book.

DOI: 10.4324/9781003475545-1

KEY POINTS

- Management styles have always changed with changes in society, and it is time for a new look at strategy-making and the creation of a new strategy-making style.
- A model for strategy-making which combines sustainability, absolute value, people, change, a hybrid approach, and long-term thinking should help focus strategic thinkers on responsible approaches.
- Strategic thinking (combining strategic management and leadership) is appropriate for the current VUCA situation.
- Strategic thinkers need to look 'outside' to society and life and consider the PESTLE changes to which they need to respond.

THE COMPLEX ENVIRONMENT

Political, economic, sociocultural, and technological (PEST) (Aguilar, 1967) environmental features have impacted on management and leadership thought and practice over the last 200 years, and as the external environment changed, different management styles became more appropriate or rose to significance. This can be seen in Table 1.1.

We are now tasked with developing the appropriate methods of management and leadership for the modern era. The early twenty-first century presents a more complex and volatile environment than ever before (Haslam & Shenoy, 2018). As Raworth (2017) describes, our world is 'dynamic, unstable, and unpredictable' (p. 130), while Nonaka and Zhu (2012) assert that it is a world 'turning upside down' (p. 4). Since the introduction of the PEST model in 1967, the model has evolved to incorporate legal and environmental (or ecological) factors, recognising the influence these elements also exert on management and leadership and thus complicating the management and leadership environment further.

Today's business landscape is one of unprecedented change and uncertainty, shaped by several key factors:

- The collapse of shareholder capitalism, with governments stepping in to bail out the private sector following the 2008 financial crisis.
- Shifting economic gravity, where the 2008 crisis was concentrated in the West, while China and India continue to grow at a rapid pace.
- China's growing dominance in the global economy.
- The rise of BRIC (Brazil, Russia, India, and China) and MINT (Mexico, Indonesia, Nigeria, and Turkey) countries as emerging economic powers.
- A fluctuating attitude towards globalisation: it is embraced when convenient but met with protectionism when national interests are threatened. Events like the COVID-19 pandemic, the Russian invasion of Ukraine, and ensuing supply chain disruptions have underscored the interconnectedness of the global economy.
- Heightened concern for the ecological environment, despite a fragmented global response: while the UN advocates for sustainability, many governments hesitate or backtrack on their commitments.

TABLE 1.1 Different Management Styles and their PEST Influences

Period	Workplace situation informed by political, economic, technological, and sociocultural issues	Management styles
Pre-industrial revolution	Hierarchical structures. Landowners have rights over agricultural labour.	Apprenticeships and business schools exist.
Nineteenth century, *after* the industrial revolution (1760–1840)	Significant wealth generation for the ruling classes driven by major innovations such as steam engines, textile equipment, and tool-making. High production and mechanisation and European imperialism, with its resulting human tragedies. Increased workers' rights and representation towards the end of the period. Economic migration.	Scientific management school, 1850 to early 1900s.
1920s–1960s	Inter-World War economic decline and depression in 1930s. Technologies developed because of warfare. WWI challenged people's perceptions of humanity following the great loss of life and bloodshed. This is a changing period, with citizens gaining more power and – at the same time – being used as 'cannon fodder' in two World Wars. Western imperialism diminishes and certain societies become more liberal (e.g. women have an increased role in the workplace following the wars).	Human relations/ psychology management school.
1950s	Post-war period – austerity. Beginning of Cold War. Economic migration Vietnam war spans 1950s and 1960s and into 1970s.	Management science (and overlap with the human relations school and the integrating perspectives/systems school).
1950s		Integrating perspectives/ systems (and overlap with the human relations school and the management science school).
1970s	Emergence of the service sector as a key player in the market. High inflation.	Contingency.

(Continued)

TABLE 1.1 Continued

Period	Workplace situation informed by political, economic, technological, and sociocultural issues	Management styles
1990s	Following a period of boom in the 1980s, the 1990s brought recession to much of the Western world. The Soviet Union collapses.	Learning organisation.
2000s	The rise of the internet. Iraq War. A period of relative economic stability until 2008 when 'the great recession' hits, with the banks as the main losers having invested in sub-prime mortgages. Creates uncertainty and a long period of austerity. China rises as a superpower. 9/11 in the USA creates a decade of fear of terrorism.	Postmodernism.
2010s	Economies emerge from recession. The internet is a key feature of everyday life. Debate around AI and robots taking jobs formerly held by people. The 'gig' economy and casualisation of labour are trends in the job market. Widespread political change – Brexit, increased terrorism, Trump in power in the USA.	Triangular management approach.
2020s	Covid-19 pandemic. Ukraine v. Russian war. Israel vs. Hamas war. Global inflation, mental health and well-being are matters of widespread discussion. Brexit affects UK–Europe relations. China clashes with the USA. Certain countries (e.g. Japan and Sri Lanka) suffer considerably from reduction in tourism because of pandemic. Possible global recession. Climate change.	Modern day ?

This volatile, unpredictable landscape is aptly described by the acronym VUCA – Volatile, Uncertain, Complex, and Ambiguous (Bennett & Lemoine, 2014). In this environment, businesses are increasingly confronted with "wicked" problems: complex challenges that are difficult to define, with no clear solutions and ambiguous criteria for what is right or wrong, good or bad (Rittel & Webber, 1973; Haslam & Shenoy, 2018). These problems are further complicated by their evolving nature, with solutions often generating unintended, far-reaching consequences due to their interconnectedness with other issues.

The world today is more complex than ever before due to the convergence of numerous challenges and the accelerating pace of change. While humanity has always faced wars, economic instability, inflation, recessions, trade conflicts, and rapid technological shifts, the way these factors now intersect makes the current landscape particularly difficult to navigate.

For instance, technological advancements are occurring at an exponential rate, reshaping entire industries in a very short time. However, it is not just the speed of this change that increases complexity. Traditional boundaries between industries are dissolving. Technology now drives transformation across diverse sectors, such as transportation (e.g. Uber), accommodation (e.g. Airbnb), and healthcare (e.g. robotic surgery and fitness apps).

This merging of sectors, coupled with the effects of globalisation and evolving societal values such as the blending of public and private sector practices and a heightened emphasis on social responsibility, adds further layers of complexity. Additionally, the climate crisis stands out as a critical challenge. Despite widespread recognition of environmental threats, global responses remain inconsistent and fraught with political disagreement. As Neugebauer et al. (2015) point out, the pursuit of environmental sustainability is an inherently wicked problem, complicating efforts to address it.

What does this all mean? It does not mean that we should give up in the face of overwhelming challenges. While a PESTLE analysis might seem like the 'Four Horsemen of the Apocalypse' – Death, Disease, War, and Famine – it is a call to engage in a deeper, more holistic analysis of the environment in which we operate. We must recognise the interplay of these factors and use this understanding to make informed, strategic decisions. This also requires that we revisit and challenge some of the traditional concepts and processes that have shaped strategic management in the past, adapting them to the complexities of today's world to think strategically for the future.

STRATEGY-MAKING

Challenging concepts and processes can begin with looking at some vocabulary, and in this book 'strategy-making' will be used as an overarching term for the whole area. This highlights the active (making) nature of the field, encouraging strategy-makers of the future to be active in their decision-making processes. Active decision-making is essential to respond to the inevitable change we all experience. The term 'strategy-making' also shows that there is a product (we have made a strategy) from a process (the making).

STRATEGY

This work does *not* begin with a definition of strategy linked to its ancient beginnings in war as do many other books. The use of such analogies outside of history and war is unhelpful and can do a lot of damage, as the implication of beating and subjugating others and its rather violent intonations is distasteful in the current environment. This position will be expanded on below in the competitive advantage and value section, but for now the position is that general management theory and practice is not about war but about the management of businesses and organisations, and therefore definitions of strategy that are appropriate to current management practice are more useful.

Within the field of management theory and practice, 'strategy' is a term much misused and overused and therefore its meaning has become confused. In teaching classes and workshops there are frequently stories about how someone in an organisation makes themselves and something they are doing sound important by adding 'strategy' or 'strategic' to the title of their work, even when they are suggesting a simple task, a change in day-to-day operational process or the activities to achieve a strategy. Ritson (2016) bemoans exactly this regarding his field of marketing: 'One of the great problems of the new marketing world we live in is that all these dreary marketers ... simply do not understand the difference between strategy and tactics.'

Ritson (2016) says: 'Can I ... remind the reader of the difference between strategy, in this case working out what the stages are and which one to focus on in order to increase sales, and tactics, the various actions I will invest in to execute the strategy.' But strategy is a noun, not a verb. A name, not a doing word. It is an abstract noun. Strategy is surely therefore the product of something, rather than the process of creating that product. This is what leads many to define strategy as a plan. Unfortunately, this is still somewhat confusing in current business and society as, by defining strategy as a plan, we appear to have jumped straight to the endpoint, with little concentration on how we got there. Where did this plan come from, on what is it based? How do we know it is the right plan? In Ritson's complaint, the strategy (the endpoint) is to increase sales, yet the emphasis in his definition appears to be on the *stages* to reach the endpoint and those stages appear to involve some judgement on which is the right way forward.

In line with this debate, the definitions of strategy from key thinkers differ. Chandler's (1963) definition of strategy is 'the determination of the long-run goals and objectives of an enterprise and the adoption of a course of action and the allocation of resources necessary for carrying out these goals' (Chandler, 1963). Here there is a process to decide/determine the goals, the goals, *and* a process to put into action. Whittington et al. (2021) define strategy as 'the long-term direction of an organisation' (Whittington et al., 2021, p. 2). The careful use of the word 'direction' suggests the endpoint *and* the process of getting there. Nonaka and Zhu (2012) state that 'every strategy can be seen as ... an interactive process and contingent accomplishment' (Nonaka & Zhu, 2012, p. 80). However, Mintzberg's (2007) definition is 'a pattern in a stream of decisions' and appears to be about process, whereas Porter's (1996) and Drucker's (1994) definitions seem to be about the endpoint or the deliverable: 'competitive strategy is about being different. It means deliberately choosing a different set of activities to deliver a unique mix of value' (Porter, 1996) and 'a firm's theory about how to gain competitive advantages' (Drucker, 1994). But Liedtka argued against these definitions: 'It is no longer the products alone – the plans themselves – that are dominant, it is the process that we must concern ourselves with' (Liedtka, 1998, p. 124).

Subtly different are Haslam and Shenoy's (2018) definitions. Strategy 'is deploying resources, generating value and doing this with a degree of intent' (Haslam & Shenoy, 2018, p. 37) and 'strategy remains the simultaneous consideration of purpose (what the organisation seeks to achieve), world (what external stakeholders value and prioritise) and self (the capabilities the organisation can mobilise in pursuit of its goals)' (Haslam

& Shenoy, 2018, p. 201). While they also incorporate process and endpoint, there is also more recognition of the external in the second definition. Strategy as a response to the external is also included in 'a cohesive response to an important challenge' (Rumelt, 2011) where strategy appears to be the endpoint, the plan, although the idea of strategy as 'process' could be reflected here in its need to respond (be flexible, change, and follow a procedure) to develop the final response.

We can agree that existing definitions of strategy differ. There are definitions that refer to strategy as the process (the way to get there), strategy as an endpoint (the goal), and strategy as both process and endpoint. This can be confusing when making sense of the subject and in this book the proposal is that **strategy** is the end goal, and **strategy-making** is the process to decide on the appropriate goal.

CASE STUDY 1.1

The Importance of Process

Adam Parsons is a Consultant from a Big Four Consultancy with a focus on the energy and natural resources sector. As such, he advises a wide range of clients on navigating the strategic opportunities and challenges associated with the energy transition and the move towards a net zero society. In the following case study, he considers the importance of process in strategy-making.

'We're all very busy and the clients I work with are very busy. We're often working with senior people whose time is at a premium. While some of the academic tools can provide a framework for thinking, making the time to work through those tools in practise can be challenging, particularly when strategic decisions are having to be made at pace and while navigating a lot of uncertainty. Having a robust process and way of thinking is in many ways as important as working through specific tools or practises. You need to:

- Get an understanding of the baseline – where is your organisation today? Ask: what has been done to date? Find out how successful that has been. Draw from this learning.
- Move into objective setting – set that 'North Star', the guiding light for what the organisation wants to achieve. That's the overarching aim that consensus can be collectively built around. Here you need to talk to people at different levels and in different departments to bring together a diverse range of perspectives to inform the overarching aim.
- Build in other stakeholder views to define sub-objectives and sub-milestones that you want to achieve along the way.
- Define at a more granular level exactly what you want your strategy to look like, what targets you're going to set, what KPIs are going to hang off the back of that, and how that can be monitored going forward as you move into implementation.

It's a process, a flow. Having a consistent process for working through how you tackle a strategic problem, how you tackle complexity, in many respects is as important as having specific tools that you can apply on a day-to-day basis.'

The world is complex, dynamic, unstable, and presents us with wicked problems, the like we have not seen before, and this leads us to new ways of thinking about strategy and strategy-making. Strategy is an endpoint, and strategy-making a way to achieve that endpoint, but what is the endpoint intended to achieve? How will we know that it is 'good'? Several terms have been used previously in this discussion, and each will be examined to determine what strategy should achieve. The terms we will consider are sustainability, competitive advantage and value, stakeholders, change, strategy-making approaches, and the long term.

STRATEGY: KEY TERMS AND CHARACTERISTICS

Sustainability

Sustainable competitive advantage means keeping the business going successfully, relative to competitors. This is a comparatively insular view of sustainable strategy-making (when we compare it to later definitions of sustainability in this section), with a concentration on the business or organisation and the industry of which it is a part. Porter's (1996) generic strategies of differentiation, cost-leadership, and focus/niche are enduring in terms of solutions for businesses or organisations benchmarking themselves against others operating in their field, and the aim is to find ways of attracting customers (more than your competitor) to ensure profit and market share for financial survival and growth: sustainability. There is nothing wrong with trying to ensure financial success to sustain a business or organisation. This means that the bills and the people are paid. The degree to which it is beneficial to grow at the expense of others is questionable however, and there are two perspectives on this question.

The first is the company or organisation perspective: that the constant jostling for superior financial performance based on competitive rivalry will result in a 'red ocean': shark-infested waters where competitors take chunks out of each other and all are negatively impacted (Chan Kim & Mauborgne, 2005). This is because it is considered that cost will eventually be the prime decision-maker (Chan Kim & Mauborgne, 2005) and that companies offering similar items will eventually have to drive down costs to pass savings on to the customer so that they can compete on price, and this will inevitably shave off the profit margin. This in turn can lead to an extreme pressure on resources (e.g. using cheaper, non-sustainable resources or leading to cutting of staff) and this links to the second perspective on sustainability that is the wider picture. In this case, growth at the expense of others is detrimental. We might go further: 'Growth is one of the stupidest purposes ever invented by any culture, we've got to have an enough' (Meadows, cited in Raworth, 2017, p. 40). 'In response to the constant call for more growth', she argued, we should always ask: 'growth of what, and why, and for whom, and who pays the cost, and how long can it last, and what's the cost to the planet, and how much is enough?' (Raworth, 2017, p. 40). Consequently, an effort to keep the business going with a focus on competition can lead to hazards for the company's sustainability, *and* for the wider society's sustainability.

The wider meaning of sustainability is as concerning 'intra- and intergenerational justice as well as ecological limitations' (WCED, 1987, cited in Neugebauer et al., 2015) and considering 'the needs of the present without compromising the ability of future generations to meet their own needs' (WCED, 1991, cited in Higgins, 2015, p. 2). Sustainability is not 'just' about the environment or ecology as is often misunderstood:

> [M]any companies don't have a clear or agreed to view on sustainability. Some define it narrowly regarding environmental performance: their greenhouse gas emissions, energy use, waste management, and the like. Interestingly, those that take it seriously typically have a more expansive and integrative perspective that links environmental, societal and governance (ESG) responsibilities together into an overall sustainability agenda (sometimes joined under the names of corporate responsibility, social responsibility, or corporate citizenship).
>
> *(Mirvis et al., 2010, p. 316)*

While Porter's external view of sustainability focused on competitors and the industry, this definition of sustainability includes a much wider group of people and organisations, in fact, if we accept this term, then discussions about sustainability and sustainable competitive advantage put the business or organisation at the centre of a much more complex system. This moves the perspective, where the focus is first on context and contingency as opposed to on the insular entity. There is a supposed trade-off between sustainability and profit-making, with some considering that the two are incompatible, but you will find many examples in this book where sustainability is not only the ethical approach but a way to prosper.

A strategy should achieve sustainability for the organisation and for the wider community. Unsustainable strategy will be detrimental to both organisation and community.

Competitive Advantage and Value

This leads us on to discuss the second key term or characteristic of strategy: 'competitive advantage'. This overlaps with some of the above discussions.

One of the criticisms of a lot of strategy work is that it tends to apply the private sector perspective to all strategy-making, and ideas like 'competitive advantage' seem irrelevant if an organisation does not consider itself to be competitive or to have competitors. For example, a health service or a school may not be led by trying to be better than others operating in the same industry. Contrary to this non-competitive view, in many countries these organisations are regulated and there are standards (special measures, good, outstanding) and league tables which customers can access, and which may influence their decisions to work with or use those services, which creates a competitive environment as each organisation seeks to impress or meet the needs of a customer better than another. Still, it is fair to say that competitiveness is not the *leading* criteria in such an organisation's planning. Nevertheless, the strategy literature tends to talk about competitive advantage and the body of work on strategy for public sector or third-sector organisations that replaces the idea of competitor analysis and competitive advantage with benchmarking is relatively low profile (Courtney, 2013; Flynn & Asquer, 2017; Alford, 1993–2017) and the strategy literature for all audiences is dominated by more commercial works.

The first thing we can say therefore is that competitive advantage might not apply to all strategy. Where competitive advantage might apply, we can use a competitor analysis to assess strengths and weaknesses of a competitor and then plan an approach to maximise our strengths and minimise our weaknesses, relative to the competitor. An alternative perspective is that of Barney (1991) who launched the VRIO tool, which asks us to consider the resources and capabilities of an organisation and which could be valuable (V), rare (R), inimitable (I) – which means difficult or impossible to imitate and organisationally embedded (O) (Barney, 1991). If we answer yes to the questions 'is it valuable, is it rare, is it inimitable, is it organisationally embedded', then we have resources and capabilities, or a combination, that set us apart from our competitors. Answering yes to all four questions achieves sustainable competitive advantage, something we can maintain, as it is embedded, and difficult to copy. If a competitor could copy it, and it is not embedded or fully organisationally utilised, then we have only got temporary competitive advantage, and another organisation could beat us. While this is an 'inside-out' view, concentrating on the organisation primarily as a source of strength, the tool is used in relation to competitors, asking if they can copy, if any other competitor has the resources. It is therefore from the same stable of thought as the Porter views considered above.

Let us reframe the discussion. If we discard this need to beat the competition and compete over scarce resources, what might the driving force of our business be in terms of our customers, and wanting, perfectly naturally, them to buy or use what we have to offer? Haslam and Shenoy (2018) highlight that a forgotten intention of strategy should be for value creation. Of course, we must follow that up by saying that value can be different things to different people.

Imagine a whiteboard, and on that whiteboard I have drawn a line from left to right.

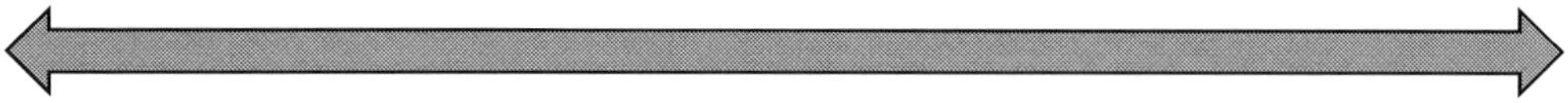

I am interested in what 'value' looks like. And I know that value may look different if I work in the private sector compared to the public sector. So, I write those terms under my line.

Private Sector **Public Sector**

I then ask what 'value' is for each of those areas. Let us go back to a dictionary definition of value first, and Merriam-Webster tells us that it is the worth of something (Merriam-Webster, 2023).

What does 'value' look like in the private sector? And what does 'value' look like in the public sector?

On the left-hand side, we are likely to see words or symbols appearing as follows:

Private Sector	**Public Sector**
£ $ %	
Profit	
Shareholder dividends	
Output	

Whereas on the right we may see words or symbols as follows:

Private Sector	**Public Sector**
£ $ %	☺
Profit	User Satisfaction
Shareholder dividends	Impact
Output	

On what is value on the left dependent? And on the right? How is it measured?

This results in the following words being added:

Private Sector	**Public Sector**
£ $ %	☺
Profit	User Satisfaction
Shareholder dividends	Impact
Commercial	Social

Private Sector	Public Sector
Quantitative	Qualitative
Competition	Stakeholders
Relative	Absolute
Costs and margin	Costs and quality

What we end up with here are different views of what is valuable, what is worthy and therefore worthwhile. We can recognise that, in the public sector, an organisation's value is not measured by whether it makes more money for its shareholders than a competitor, but rather whether it achieves a quality of life for its users. In fact, the public sector is often expected to fix the wrongs of the market, and to promote equity in society (Flynn & Asquer, 2017) where the private sector's pursuit of competition would judge success by increased market share and therefore the diminution of another. If we are in an organisation that does not judge value by the criteria of competitive advantage, then how useful is a model that has been designed to judge its achievement of that, such as the VRIO model or competitor analysis? And while the model above was intended to see extremes (private sector and public sector) as that is easiest to demonstrate, we can see situations where organisations do not sit at those extremes and have a mixture of what they consider to be valuable, and many ways to measure success. In fact, public sector organisations are increasingly impacted by costs and income streams, and private sector organisations are more impacted by social responsibility (to be discussed further throughout this book and in Chapter 5 particularly when we enhance the spectrum above), so while the private sector organisation may move more to the right, so too does the public sector move more to the left.

A definition of strategy which relies on achieving sustainable competitive advantage may just not be relevant any more as value is interpreted differently, and an organisation may have many aspects of value that it needs to reflect. It is surely our understanding of what value we are trying to achieve that affects the likelihood of good strategy. If we also combine the discussion of value with sustainability, the need to maintain the health of our environment and our people, then strategy looks different. Instead of competition or *relative* value we need absolute value, a business or organisation that is confident that what it supplies is worthwhile, that it contributes to society in such a way as to be viewed as valuable in whatever form that takes.

This approach could help organisations where there are dangers in judging value relatively in changeable, complex times. McGrath (2013) and Haslam and Shenoy (2018) raise the problem of looking at competitors when it is increasingly difficult to determine the industry a business or organisation is in and where an existing competitive advantage is now most likely to be disrupted by the emergence of something totally different, not from current competitors but from a new entrant to the sector: a disruptor or innovator. This reflects the characteristics of the VUCA world, its transience, and therefore that competitor advantage may be transient. Add to this what was discussed previously about the dangers of existing in the 'red ocean'.

The answer would presumably be to determine one's effort in a more absolute value approach because the competitive environment is so complex that any assessment linked to a measure affected by this complexity is likely to be unhelpful and confusing. Raworth's view on this is that there is a need for 'regenerative enterprise' which 'needs the support of financial partners seeking to invest long-term in generating *multiple* kinds of value – human, social, ecological, cultural and physical – along with a fair financial return' (Raworth, 2017, p. 234).

If we return to the blue versus red ocean theory mentioned in the previous section, there is precedence for concentrating on value: 'In sharp contrast to companies playing by traditional rules, the creators of blue oceans never used the competition as their benchmark. Instead, they made it irrelevant by creating a leap in value for both buyers and the company itself' (Chan Kim & Mauborgne, 2005). The problem the authors highlight is that business leaders are more likely to go to the tools they know (which are more relevant to competitive strategy). We need new tools and/or to think differently. Planning tools are discussed in more detail in Chapter 2 and this book offers a new systems thinking approach to strategy-making in Chapter 10.

Strategy is no longer about competitive advantage. It is about creating absolute value for customers and community, and this will support sustainability.

Stakeholders: Who Is Strategy For?

No business or organisation would be *in existence* if it were not for the people who buy from it or use its services, who work for it or with it, or who set it up in the first place. Businesses or organisations are dependent on people. In management literature we call these people stakeholders. Stakeholders are any individuals or groups that affect or are affected by a business or organisation's decisions, and consequently could be owners, employees, customers, community, suppliers, government. All of us. We have various tools to understand the power/influence and interest/attention (Mendelow,1991; Eden & Ackerman, 1998; Whittington et al., 2021) of these stakeholders, to prioritise them by importance, and to decide on our communication or collaboration with those stakeholders. Stakeholders are discussed in more detail in Chapter 6.

The impact of not recognising these connections is considerable and these people are at the heart of the wider sustainability requirement previously discussed. Friedman (1970) believed that the responsibility of a business could stop at making profit which would trickle down to others. He would be right if the rules of competitive advantage, relative value, and the dominance of shareholder benefit did *not* exist. If businesses and organisations allow the latter to dominate the stakeholder matrix, then the wider impact can be catastrophic. Consider the decision of Kraft's takeover of Cadbury, who then shut down the plant in Keynsham, United Kingdom, resulting in job losses. The impact on that community was significant and long-lasting.

Traditionally the planning of strategy has been the role of the senior managers at the top of their organisations. Middle managers and lower managers have always needed to understand the strategy so that they can understand their place and role in that strategy, and they in turn need to be able to explain the strategy to others. While the 'top-down' approach to strategy is traditional (and the domain of more prescriptive strategy – see the section below on 'Strategy-making Approaches') it has been more commonly accepted in modern times that strategy can be made by those lower down the hierarchies of power, considering they are at the forefront of business and organisation action and are therefore best placed to comment on impact and in fact on the needs and gaps of an organisation's product or service in society. Haslam and Shenoy (2018) refer to this as the 'middle out' approach 'where different parts of the organisation operate in different modes with more local discretion' (Haslam & Shenoy, 2018, p. 9). Haslam and Shenoy (2018) would argue that orderly, top-down guidelines are no longer relevant in a complex environment and that an iterative and non-linear approach (see emergent strategy-making) using experimentation, scaling, and framing is more appropriate. The importance of employees and colleagues as stakeholders is supported in the success of companies which are still seen to be doing something different by giving their stakeholders (employees in these cases) other than shareholders more power, such as Richer Sounds, John Lewis, and Timpson. In fact, some of these are where stakeholders have become shareholders through employee/colleague ownership. More of these examples are used throughout this book.

Outside of the organisation, there is also a movement towards co-creation, co-production (and many other words being with 'co' such as collaboration and cooperation) in strategy-making. This approach involves customers, suppliers, the community in the design of goods and services (a term often used here is 'prosumer' (a consumer who is proactively involved in the process). In fact, stakeholder relationship strategy (Kull et al., 2016) can be the source of 'competitive advantage' (or value in our redefined framework).

There are risks in stakeholder involvement, however. 'The challenges of satisfying the conflicting needs of different stakeholders lead to a situation where there is no "correct" answer on the way to proceed' (Haslam & Shenoy, 2018, p. 68). Hence the 'wickedness' of problems facing all organisations.

What do we need to do? Break the emphasis on perpetual growth and concentrate on sufficiency and consider sustainability involving human beings as a mark of success as opposed to shareholder dividends being a key measure. Multiple perspectives are required, and these can be obtained through collaboration and dialogue (Liedtka, 1998) 'based on multiple perspectives' (Nonaka & Zhu, 2012, p. 225).

Strategy is about people, and responsible strategic thinking recognises the multiplicity of people involved in any business or organisation.

CASE STUDY 1.2

Stakeholder Communication

Sarah Webster is Acting Parks and Green Spaces Manager within the Climate and Environment Department at Derby City Council. The following case study shows the challenges of turning strategy, influenced by multiple stakeholders/influencers, into projects and gives Sarah's guidance on managing projects with stakeholders and communication as key.

> *'You have this huge wealth of different groups that want to use parks in so many ways. And that's the challenge – parks are so many things to all people.'*

The users of the parks are many and varied, from the football player to the business employee, but the way strategy is set is also challenging as the parks department is influenced by a variety of bodies and interested stakeholders. There are international strategies on climate change and biodiversity; wider government strategies such as the Environment Act provide the national context (and can be changed depending on who has political power). The Council's overarching strategies, taking the international and national influences into account, feed down to more local action plans (such as the biodiversity action plan). And locally, planning laws must be considered, as parks are public open spaces. This umbrella of challenges, targets, and overall goals filters down to the departmental strategy, which is then implemented through projects or plans for, for example, nature reserve management, encouragement of biodiversity, and community engagement: 'one piece of open space must cover all these demands.'

'The main thing is thinking about who the stakeholders are, who the key people we need to talk to are, the local ward councillors, the neighbourhood team, the friends' groups. So, we have that baseline of people to talk to and then there will be additional stakeholders for projects such as contractors and ecologists. We collaborate on projects, we basically sit down with friends' groups who represent various members of the community, residents, interest groups, people who are just generally interested in the parks and open spaces, councillors. We are influenced by the individuals within the room as well as the wider community, with a lot of ideas for projects. Consultation is undertaken in line with Council's Consultation Policy. A lot of success comes with time and experience in a role, knowing who to talk to, finding new contacts as role holders change. And it could all change, you know. The Council, the government, if they have different priorities, then that comes down to us. Communication is important, whether it's just a poster on site and messaging out through the networks or a press release. It's about explaining why you're doing things.'

Change

Strategy-making is carried out to respond to change, and strategy will bring about change in a business or organisation. In responding to change, strategy-makers scan the external horizon, its Political, Economic, Sociological, Technological (PEST) (Aguilar, 1967) Legal and Environmental (PESTLE) challenges and look for opportunities and threats that will demand a response. 'With change comes opportunity, and much of strategy relates to the risks that come with uncertainty and how these can best be handled in the pursuit of value' (Haslam & Shenoy, 2018, p. 13). As all these aspects change, and as they change in combination, as considered in 'The Complex Environment' section of this chapter, a business or organisation will need to change accordingly to ensure sustainability and that it continues to provide value to its stakeholders. The concept that the external horizon is always and naturally subject to change means that a business or organisation should always be future-focused and dynamic, trying to respond in an evolutionary and adaptable rather than a revolutionary way, and while the changes that impact on a business or organisation may not be favourable, one hopes that the change instigated in response will be beneficial (APM, 2021; Creasey, 2021). Sustainable, valuable, people-focused change in a turbulent environment will require change to filter down through the organisation and will involve change at every level of an organisation. There is more about change management in Chapter 2.

Strategy will always incorporate change.

Strategy-making Approaches

There are two frameworks for drawing up strategy. As with the value spectrum they appear at either end of a spectrum and are called prescriptive (or planned, intended, rational, and analytic) and emergent. The reality, and an approach to be incorporated into the strategy-making process, is to combine the approaches as appropriate to the complex environment in which we operate and in line with the context in which we operate.

Prescriptive
Planned
Intended
Rational
Analytic

Emergent

Whichever approach is taken, it is always the case that strategy-making will incorporate the ideas of Analysis (A) – where are we, where do we want to be, what are our options? Formulation (F) – what could we do and what should we do that best suits our options and intentions? And Implementation (I) – what is the best way to put this into action? This is Rothaermel's (2020) AFI framework but there are many other versions that include the same stages. This does reflect the 'stages' that Ritson (2016) refers to, and the idea of seeing the process in stages can be helpful to ensure that they are covered and that a systematic approach is taken. However, the strategy-maker should be aware of the risk of strategic frameworks limiting rather than fostering creativity and, given the conversation thus far, the stages need to incorporate some key issues and questions regarding sustainability, value, consideration of people, and change.

Prescriptive Strategy

Prescriptive strategy has been described as a 'grand plan' (Johnson et al., 2014) determined by top management. This is in keeping with a more traditional and classical perspective of management as 'top-down'. Those at the top of the organisation are responsible for setting the direction of the organisation. However, we have already seen that this approach has been challenged by bottom-up and middle-out theories of who should be involved in organisational decision-making.

When following a prescriptive approach, the systematic process is as follows:

1. Set objective – goals deduced from vision.
2. Analyse the environment.
3. Reconsider objective.
4. Develop strategy options.
5. Select appropriate option.
6. Implement chosen strategy option.

The key characteristics of the prescriptive strategy-making approach are as follows (with any counter points noted in brackets):

- The objective is defined in advance (which assumes a stable environment in which an objective can be defined in advance, and the ability to think long term).
- The main elements of the strategy have been developed before implementation (which may be overly simplistic and need revision and reiteration).
- It is suited to stable, straightforward, and controllable environments (and we have already confirmed that we are performing in an increasingly complex, wicked environment where predictions are increasingly difficult to make).
- A dispassionate and logical approach is needed (which contrasts with the strategic leadership characteristics of being instinctive, creative, and imaginative).

(Hart, 1992; Regnér, 2003; Lynch, 2015; Neugebauer et al., 2015)

Emergent Strategy

Emergent strategy is less deliberate. It emerges, as the name suggests, from a series of decisions, in a pattern that becomes clear over time, rather than as a deliberate result of a 'grand plan' (Johnson et al., 2014).

This approach follows these steps:

1. Analyse the environment (macro).
2. Consider capabilities.
3. Consider objectives.
4. Develop strategy options.
5. Try options.
6. Correct/amend.

The key characteristics of the emergent strategy-making approach are as follows (with any counter points noted in brackets):

- It is more experimental. Ideas are tested through implementation as the strategy is formulated and the tests/implementation modify the strategy (this can feel like 'muddling along' and those trying to operationalise a strategy need more of a definite plan).
- Rather than having an objective or endpoint set in advance, the objective emerges out of the analysis of the situation or the process of strategy-making. The process is continuous and incremental (again this can feel indefinite, and people need a vision or objective).
- This approach is seen as more natural, human, and responsive.
- It supports a contextualised and timely approach to management, where no situation can be the same and all management challenges need to be dealt with separately using the best knowledge/experience that can be brought to bear on a situation.
- It is suited for wicked problems.

(Idenburg, 1993; Mintzberg, 1978, 1994; Whittington, 1996; Hendry, 2000; Regnér, 2003; Jarzabkowski, 2004; By, 2005; Lynch, 2015; Neugebauer et al., 2015)

Considering all of the above, an emergent approach should be more appropriate for the VUCA environment in which we are operating. However, it is more likely that we combine the skills of emergent and planned strategy-making as required. There may be some situations in which we can reliably predict the future and have a clear sense of our objective, where we can make some rational and planned decisions and take the risks that an incorrect decision would entail. But there will be others where the unknown does require us to take tentative, trial steps in a certain direction.

Strategy-making should take a hybrid approach, combining the planned and the emergent as appropriate to context.

Long-term

Another term used to describe strategy is 'long-term' or 'long-run'. This sets strategy apart from the short-term operational management decisions, crisis management, or project management, all important aspects of management and leadership, but that are not strategy-making or strategic thinking. These more short-term activities are discussed as complements to strategic thinking in Chapter 2.

Why does strategy-making need to be long-term, and can it be long-term in our current VUCA environment? Particularly good questions, that can only be answered by referring to the inevitability of an organisation's place in a complex system, and in a historical timeline, as well as the recognition that strategy-making should be sustainable (meaning not impacting negatively on future generations), as previously discussed. Businesses and organisations are part of time, history, and legacy and strategy-making will reflect always where we have come from, where we want to go and what we will leave behind.

There are challenges in thinking long-term:

1. Our systems are not set up for the long-term. Political systems of most countries expect elections every few years, and the emphasis of political parties is often on re-election

rather than sustainability. Organisations that are at the mercy of changes in elected officials can struggle with long-term planning out of fear that they will be forced to change. This can lead to stagnation. The issue of whether our systems are prepared for strategic thinking, or how they can be altered to be so, is discussed throughout this book.

2. There is also the difficulty of predicting what will happen in the long-term and therefore planning strategy without knowing what the situation will be (we have already talked about the VUCA environment, the speed of change, and the transience of competitive advantage).
3. As human beings, we are naturally predisposed towards short-term thinking (Higgins, 2015).

Strategy being long-term does not mean it is slow, or that decisions can be put off; for example, climate change requires tackling: that is a plan for now **and** for future generations.

Strategy is future focused; its impacts will affect generations. Strategy is long-term.

CASE STUDY 1.3

Long-term Strategy-making

Adam Parsons is a Consultant from a Big Four Consultancy with a focus on the energy and natural resources sector. As such, he advises a wide range of clients on navigating the strategic opportunities and challenges associated with the energy transition and the move towards a net zero society. In the following case study, he gives advice for senior leaders on how they might improve their chances of achieving the balance between economic, social, and environmental responsibility.

'Strategic thinkers need to own the strategy; own the overarching aims that they set. For example, the energy transition; moving towards a decarbonised decentralised energy system is challenging and it's in many ways a complete overhaul of the way that energy has worked in the UK and around the world for many, many years. And so that is challenging. That's complex. That's not something that can be achieved overnight. It is tricky. Owning a path and making sure that you trust and believe in that path and sticking to it is key because it's all too easy to waver when faced with such complexity, such uncertainties, such a volatile environment.

Off the back of the pandemic, we saw waves of organisations really boosting their investments in low carbon technologies: electric vehicles, renewables, heat pumps; then over the last couple of years, net zero momentum has started to stall. We've seen organisations dial back on some of those commitments as well. Really having ownership and not being passive is key because in what is a very volatile sector and a very volatile world it is critical to have a sense of what you're trying to achieve and stick to that path.

There is a need to be comfortable with uncertainty. Nobody knows what getting to net zero looks like. We haven't been there before. Nobody knows what a fully decarbonised world looks like: the technologies; the commercial models; the delivery models; the impacts on consumers. There are going to be unintended consequences of strategies that are set today that may happen in the next two to three years, they may happen by 2050, but there will be challenges. There may well be new opportunities to capitalise on as well but being comfortable with that uncertainty and not knowing necessarily all the outcomes and scenarios right now is key.

It's important for organisations to be able to take a long-term view. So often we have a very transactional and short-term tactical view of the world. Whether that's driven by political cycles, whether that's driven by short-term business planning periods both in the public and private sector, there is an inherent tendency to just focus on the here and now and on meeting our short-term aims. But to do something significant and tangible like delivering this energy transition, and capitalising on the opportunities that can come from that, will take a longer term outlook. It takes being comfortable with navigating potentially changing and fluid scenarios, but being ready, underneath that overarching objective of what you want your organisation to achieve, to adapt and be flexible where needed.'

The characteristics of good strategy are therefore as follows:

- It is **sustainable.**
- It is designed to give **absolute value.**
- It is for **people.**
- It will inevitably respond to **change** and bring about **change.**
- A flexible, **hybrid** approach to strategy-making is most likely to be able to respond to changeable, complex times.
- Strategy is **long-term**.

FIGURE 1.1 The Characteristics of Responsible Strategy

THE SKILLS FOR STRATEGY-MAKING

Our next step is to consider which skills are needed to accomplish good strategy-making. The argument will be that strategy-making includes **strategic management** (which incorporates strategic planning) and **strategic leadership** which combine to create balanced **strategic thinking**.

Strategic Management (Incorporating Planning)

As we have already seen in 'The Complex Environment' section above, management has been around for nearly 200 years in practice, and the discipline of management (as an area of study) emerged at the end of the nineteenth century, following the industrial revolution (1760–1840) and with the introduction of larger organisations in greater need of organisation, supervision, and control (Witzel, 2009). The earliest recognised thinkers in management were Taylor (1911) and Fayol (1949), representatives of the Scientific Management School whose views and practices are still very much a part of management today. Fayol's five functions of management were to plan, organise, command, coordinate, and control. Fayol's (and subsequent thinkers') emphasis on planning as part of the management toolkit has led to the incorporation of strategic planning (sometimes referred to separately) *within* the definition of strategic management in this book. This incorporation of planning is supported by other definitions of management, which use synonyms of planning such as guiding and creating or designing process. Managers guide organisations towards goals using resources (Certo & Certo, 2015) and there is an emphasis on terms such as 'process' (ongoing and interrelated activities); 'efficiency' (maximum productivity with minimum wasted effort or expense); and 'effectiveness' (achieving goals) (Robbins et al., 2013; Certo & Certo, 2015) as part of management.

Kotter (1991, cited in Armstrong, 2009, p. 9) gives the following management roles:

- Focusing on managing complexity by planning and budgeting with the aim of producing orderly results.
- Developing the capacity to achieve plans by creating an organisation structure and staffing it – developing human systems that can implement plans as precisely and efficiently as possible.
- Ensuring plan accomplishment by controlling and problem-solving – formally and informally comparing results to the plan, identifying deviations and then planning and organising to solve problems.

Mullins (1999, p. 255) shows how managers view situations:

- Managers adopt more impersonal or passive attitudes towards goals.
- To get people to accept solutions, the manager needs to continually coordinate and balance to enable compromise between conflicting values.

- In their relationship with others, managers maintain a low level of emotional involvement.
- Managers see themselves more as conservators and regulators of the existing order of affairs which they identify and from which they gain rewards.
- Management may be viewed more in terms of planning, organising, directing, and controlling the activities of subordinate staff.

Certo and Certo (2015, p. 338) claim that a manager's characteristics are dominated by the mind rather than the soul. They are rational, consultative, persistent, problem-solving, tough-minded, analytical, structure, deliberate, authoritative, and stabilising. A manager is more centred on the task rather than on people. While the mind versus soul comparison may work, there is also a separation between the active/doing (management) and the reflective/thinking (leadership).

These management characteristics can be seen in strategic management, or what is often called traditional, old, or classical strategy-making, and they separate this concept from that of strategic leadership which will be considered below. Mintzberg (1994, cited in Liedtka, 1998) argued that strategic planning 'is an analytical process aimed at programming already identified strategies. Its outcome is a plan.' Hamel and Prahalad (1994, cited in Liedtka, 1998) describe 'traditional' strategic management as 'strategy as form filling'. Strategic management is data-driven, analytical, information processing, a 'hardline' approach (Nasi, 1991; Raimond, 1996, cited in Liedtka, 1998) and is rational and economics-based (McGrath, 2013; Haslam & Shenoy, 2018).

Strategic Leadership

Now consider the more recent challenge to 'management' of 'leadership'. It could be argued that leadership emerged and evolved from the 1930s onwards, with significant growth in the 1950s and 1960s as human relations were recognised as more important in the world of business and work. Leadership emerged as more important following the Hawthorne experiments of the 1930s and later developed into the motivational theories of the 1950s and 1960s.

Kotter (1991, cited in Armstrong, 2009, p. 9) gives the following leadership roles:

- Focusing on producing change by developing a vision for the future along with the strategies for bringing about the changes needed to achieve that vision.
- Aligning people by communicating the new direction and creating coalitions that understand the vision and are committed to its achievement.
- Using motivation to engage people, not by pushing them in the right direction as control mechanisms do, but by satisfying basic human needs for achievement, a sense of belonging, recognition, self-esteem, a feeling of control over one's life, and the ability to live up to one's ideals.

Mullins (1999, p. 255) shows how leaders view situations:

- Leaders adopt a more personal and active attitude towards goals.
- The leader creates excitement in work and develops choices that give substance to images that excite people.
- Leaders have empathy with other people and give attention to what events and actions mean.
- Leaders work in – but do not belong to – the organisation. Their sense of identity does not depend upon membership or work roles, and they search out opportunities for change.
- Leadership is concerned more with communicating with, motivating, encouraging, and involving people.

Certo and Certo (2015, p. 338) claim that a leader's characteristics are dominated by the soul rather than the mind. They are visionary, passionate, creative, flexible, inspirational, innovative, courageous, imaginative, experimental, and independent.

It is clear then that strategic leadership emphasises the soft skills in contrast with the hard skills of management.

A Combination of Strategic Management and Strategic Leadership: Strategic Thinking

The best managers and leaders combine management and leadership skills. The balance of management and leadership is where strength lies. Strategic thinking 'is a synthesizing process, utilizing intuition and creativity, whose outcome is "an integrated perspective of the enterprise"' (Mintzberg, 1994, cited in Liedtka, 1998, p. 121).

Strategic thinking utilises intuition, creativity, dialogue, and collaboration to bring in diverse perspectives and co-production leading to ideas generation (Mintzberg, 1994; Liedtka, 1998). It is creative, explorative, and experimental (Hamel & Prahalad, 1994; Liedtka, 1998) and about learning, analogies, scenario, and hypotheses (Stacey, 1992; Liedtka, 1998). New strategy should incorporate innovation, transience, and implications for all (including staff) (McGrath, 2013; Haslam & Shenoy, 2018). As opposed to being data-driven, analytical, and information processing, strategic thinking calls on the creative imagination, and rather than being 'hardline' it is 'softline' and concerned with values and culture (Nasi, 1991; Liedtka 1998). However, it is important to say that the more hardline or analytical tools associated with management form a good framework for strategic thinking (Liedtka, 1998).

FIGURE 1.2 The Combination of Strategic Management and Strategic Leadership in Strategic Thinking

STRATEGIC THINKING AS SYSTEMS THINKING

Yet, the story does not stop there. While management and leadership skills are combined in strategic thinking, strategic thinking then needs to take a further step. Liedtka (1998) talks about the need for leaders to have a 'systems perspective' which implies a grasp of the 'bigger picture' (Haslam & Shenoy, 2018). 'One of the prevailing trends in management is the reducing emphasis on the insular entity, and the rise in the permeability of organisational boundaries, connection, rather than independence, is the new order' (Haslam and Shenoy, 2018). There is a need to not look simply at the organisation but to understand the connection of the manager and management function with the organisation and then beyond and to plan, manage, inspire, and motivate *in context*. Strategy-making needs to reflect life experience, and life experience is a 'dynamic web of relations' (Nonaka & Zhu, 2012, p. 171).

FIGURE 1.3 A Strategic Thinker's Context

CHAPTER SUMMARY

In effective strategy-making we combine process and content, management and leadership, deliberate and emergent strategy-making processes and different types of 'value'. A hybrid approach is essential. Strategy-making is impacted by everything and is a multiple-layered, complex thing. It is holistic and pragmatic. The reason we must think like this? Because the world is more complex than a singular focus can handle! We need to take a contingent approach (Haslam & Shenoy, 2018; Nonaka & Zhu, 2012), recognising that there is unpredictability in the environment and a strategic thinker needs to be prepared, using their combination of skills, to meet those challenges.

Strategy-making needs to result in an endpoint, a strategy that is sustainable, holds absolute value, and is for people. It will inevitably respond to change, bring about change, and a flexible, hybrid approach to strategy-making is most likely to be able to respond to changeable, complex times. Strategy is future focused. The most effective way to reflect the necessary characteristics of strategy is therefore to practice strategic

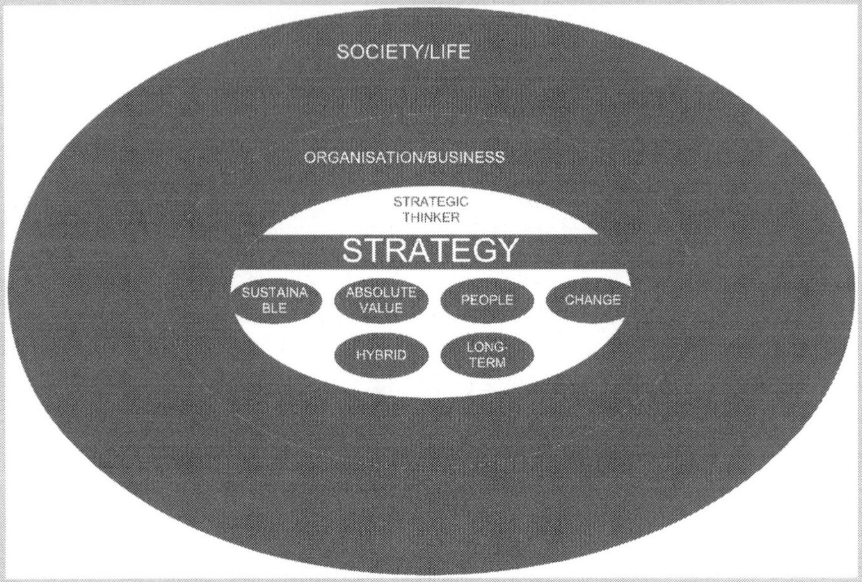

FIGURE 1.4 Strategy-making in Context

thinking, where strategic management and strategic leadership are combined. This will result in a good balance of the analytical and the creative, the hard and the soft line, and it is this hybrid, holistic, systems approach that is required for the complexity of the environment we face. The world has changed. It is complex. Everything is interrelated, and we cannot look at anything independently. Independent or individual as opposed to holistic thinking will not result in the necessary cohesive approach and will not cater for sustainable future-focused change. Strategy is everything and a multiple-layered, complex thing. Our response to it must be to address that complexity.

Chapter 2 introduces complements to strategic thinking, while chapters 3 to 9 provide perspectives on navigating this complex environment and practical advice for adopting a systems-thinking approach.

RECOMMENDED READING

Raworth, K. (2017) *Doughnut Economics: Seven Ways to Think Like a 21st Century Economist*. Random House Business Books.

REFERENCES

Aguilar, F. (1967) *Scanning the Business Environment*. New York: Macmillan.

Alford, J. (1993–2017) For a list of John Alford's public sector strategy publications see https://www.researchgate.net/profile/John-Alford-5.

APM (2021) *Change Management*. Retrieved February 15, 2021 from https://www.apm.org.uk/resources/what-is-project-management/what-is-change-management/.

Armstrong, M. (2019) *How to Manage People: Fast, Effective Management Skills That Really Get Results*. London: Kogan Page.

Barney, J. (1991). Firm resources and sustained competitive advantage. *Journal of Management*, 17(1), 99–120. doi:10.1177/014920639101700108.

Bennett, N. & Lemoine, G.J. (2014) What VUCA really means for you. *Harvard Business Review*, January/February. https://hbr.org/2014/01/what-vuca-really-means-for-you.

By, R.T. (2005) Organisational change management: A critical review. *Journal of Change Management*. 5(4), 369–380.

Certo, S. & Certo. S. (2015) *Modern Management: Concepts and Skills*. Harlow: Pearson Education.

Chandler, A.D. (1963) *Strategy and Structure: Chapters in the History of American Enterprise*. Cambridge, MA: MIT Press.

Chan Kim, W. & Mauborgne, R. (2005) Blue ocean strategy: From theory to practice. *Californian Management Review*, 47(3),103–121.

Courtney, R. (2013) *Strategic Management in the Third Sector*. Basingstoke: Palgrave Macmillan.

Creasey, T. (2021) Project management and change management: A side-by-side comparison. Retrieved February 15, 2021 from https://Blog.Prosci.Com/Project-management-and-change-management-comparison.

Drucker, P.F. (1994) The theory of business. *Harvard Business Review*, September/October.

Eden, C. & Ackermann, F. (1998) *Making Strategy: The Journey of Strategic Management*. London: Sage.

Fayol, H. (1949) *General and Industrial Management*. London: Pitman.

Flynn, N. & Asquer, A. (2017) *Public Sector Management*. London: Sage.

Friedman, M. (1970) The social responsibility of business is to increase its profits. *New York Times Magazine*, September 13, 122–126.

Hamel, G. & Prahalad, C.K. (1994) *Competing for the Future*. Boston, MA: Harvard School Press.

Hart, S.L. (1992) An integrative framework for strategy-making processes. *Academy of Management Review*, 17(2), 327–351.

Haslam, S. & Shenoy, B. (2018) *Strategic Decision Making: A Discovery-led Approach to Critical Choices in Turbulent Times*. London: Kogan Page.

Hendry, J. (2000) Strategic decision making, discourse, and strategy as social practice. *Journal of Management Studies*, 37, 955–978.

Higgins, K. (2015). *Economic Growth and Sustainability: Systems Thinking for a Complex World*. London: Academic Press.

Idenburg, P.J. (1993) Four styles of strategy development. *Long Range Planning* 26(6), 132–137.

Jarzabkowski, P. (2004) Strategy as practice: Recursiveness, adaptation, and practices-in-use. *Organization Studies*, 25, 529–560.

Johnson, G., Whittington, R., Scholes, K., Angwin, D. & Regner, P. (2014) *Exploring Strategy: Text & Cases* (10th ed.). Harlow: Pearson Education.

Kull, A.J., Mena, J.A. & Korschun, D. (2016) A resource-based view of stakeholder marketing. *Journal of Business Research*, 69, 5553–5560.

Liedtka, J.M. (1998) Strategic thinking: Can it be taught? *Long Range Planning*, February.

Lynch, R. (2015) *Strategic Management* (7th ed.). Harlow: Pearson Education.

McGrath, R.G. (2013) *The End of Competitive Advantage: How to Keep Your Strategy Moving as Fast as Your Business*. Cambridge, MA: Harvard Business Review Press.

Mendelow, A. (1991). Stakeholder mapping. *Proceedings of the 2nd International Conference on Information Systems*. Cambridge, MA.

Merriam-Webster (2023) *Value Definition & Meaning*. Retrieved February 23, 2024, from https://www.merriam-webster.com/dictionary/value.

Mintzberg, H. (1978) Patterns in strategy formation. *Management Science*, 24, 934–948.

Mintzberg, H. (1994) *The Rise and Fall of Strategic Planning*. New York: The Free Press.

Mintzberg, H. (2007) *Tracking Strategies: Towards a General Theory*. Oxford: Oxford University Press.

Mirvis, P., Googins, B. & Kinnicutt, S. (2010) Vision, mission, values: Guideposts to sustainability. *Organizational Dynamics*, 39, 316–324. doi:10.1016/j.orgdyn.2010.07.006.

Mullins, L.J. (1999) *Management and Organisational Behaviour* (5th ed.). Harlow: Financial Times/Prentice Hall.

Nasi, J. (Ed.) (1991) *Arenas of Strategic Thinking*. Helsinki, Finland: Foundation for Economic Education.

Neugebauer, F., Figge, F. & Hahn, T. (2015) *Planned or Emergent Strategy making? Exploring the Formation of Corporate Sustainability Strategies*. Chichester: John Wiley & Sons and ERP Environment.

Nonaka, I. & Zhu, Z. (2012) *Pragmatic Strategy: Eastern Wisdom, Global Success*. Cambridge: Cambridge University Press.

Porter, M.E. (1996) What is strategy? *Harvard Business Review*, November – December.

Raimond, P. (1996) Two styles of foresight. *Long Range Planning*, April, 208–214.

Raworth, K. (2017) *Doughnut Economics: Seven Ways to Think Like a 21st Century Economist*. New York: Random House Business Books.

Regnér, P. (2003) Strategy creation in the periphery: Inductive versus deductive strategy making. *Journal of Management Studies*, 40(1), 57–82.

Ritson, M. (2016) If you think the sales funnel is dead, you've mistaken tactics for strategy. *Marketing Week*, April 6. Retrieved July 18, 2023, from https://www.marketingweek.com/mark-ritson-if-you-think-the-sales-funnel-is-dead-youve-mistaken-tactics-for-strategy/.

Rittel, H.W.J. & Webber, M.M. (1973) Dilemmas in a general theory of planning. *Policy Sciences*, 4(2), 155–169.

Robbins, S.P., DeCenzo, D.A. & Coulter, M. (2013) *Fundamentals of Management: Essential Concepts and Applications* (8th ed.). Harlow: Pearson Education.

Rothaermel, F.T. (2020) *Strategic Management* (5th ed.). New York: McGraw Hill Education.

Rumelt, R. (2011) *Good Strategy, Bad Strategy: The Difference and Why it Matters*. New York: Crown.

Stacey, R. (1992) *Managing the Unknowable*. San Francisco, CA: Jossey-Bass.

Taylor, F.W. (1911) *The Principles of Scientific Management*. Monograph published by Taylor.

WCED (World Commission on Environment and Development) (1987) *Our Common Future. The Report of the World Commission on Environment and Development*. Chapter 2: Towards sustainable development. Retrieved August 14, 2014, from http://www.un-documents.net/ocf-02.htm.

WCED (World Commission on Environment and Development) (1991) *Our Common Future*. Oxford: Oxford University Press.

Whittington, R. (1996) Strategy as practice. *Long Range Planning*, 29, 731–735.

Whittington, R., Regner, P., Angwin, D., Johnson, G. & Scholes, K. (2021) *Fundamentals of Strategy* (5th ed.). Harlow: Pearson Education.

Witzel, M. (2009) *Management History: Text and Cases*. Abingdon, Oxon: Routledge.

CHAPTER 2

The Complements to Strategic Thinking

Olivia Ramsbottom

CHAPTER OUTLINE

This chapter explores the complements to strategic thinking: ideas and tools that enhance the development of effective strategy and ensure its successful implementation.

It highlights the critical role of operational management in strategy execution and emphasises the importance of strategic thinkers engaging with operational experts to create strategies that are not only visionary but also feasible. By incorporating operational perspectives, strategies can be better crafted to ensure practical applicability.

The chapter examines project and change management as essential tools for implementing strategy, each with its own set of characteristics and value. Projects must be directly aligned with the organisation's strategic goals, and those managing them must fully understand this connection for maximum impact. Similarly, understanding the necessity and nature of change is vital for those leading its implementation to optimise success.

While crisis management is not a direct form of strategic thinking, it provides a foundation for developing strategic agility and resilience, making it an important element in strategic thinking. The chapter also addresses a broad array of traditional tools and frameworks that support strategic decision-making, including Vision, Mission, and Values (VMV) and PESTLE analysis. These well-established tools have long been integral to strategy discussions, and their value in providing clarity and direction to strategic thinking is reinforced.

Risk management is explored as a crucial component at all levels of an organisation. The chapter examines how risk management practices, from operational to strategic levels, are interconnected, demonstrating how tools and steps used at one level can be adapted and scaled to others.

DOI: 10.4324/9781003475545-2

To conclude, the chapter presents a model illustrating how operational management, project management, change management, crisis management, planning tools, and risk management all interlink with and support the strategy-making process. This comprehensive view underscores the importance of integrating these complementary tools to create a cohesive and effective strategy.

KEY POINTS

- A strategic thinker needs to be aware of the complementary fields of management study from operational management to planning tools, as they can bring powerful knowledge, skills, and behaviours to the strategic thinker's toolkit.
- The complements to strategic thinking can be used to ensure effective implementation of strategy, potentially taking out some of the risk and uncertainty of effective strategy-making.

OPERATIONAL MANAGEMENT

To describe the different types of management and leadership, we often put 'Strategic' at the top of a pyramid and 'Operational' at the bottom (Figure 2.1).

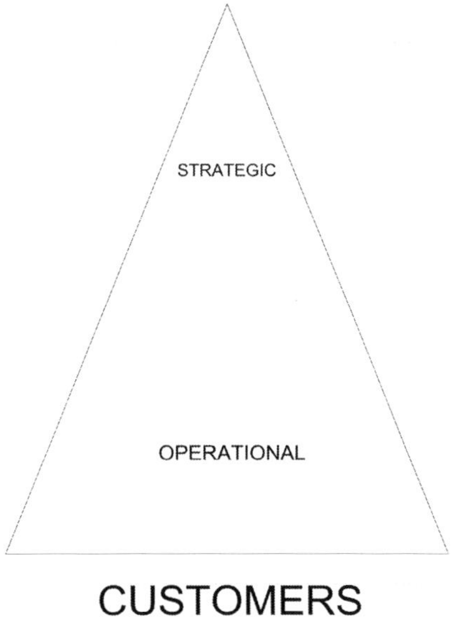

FIGURE 2.1 The Pyramid of Management

This has been useful in explaining that strategic thinking has often been the domain of those at the top of an organisation: the senior management or leadership, and the job of a few (the thinner top of the triangle), while operational management or leadership is the job of the many: team leaders and their staff (the fatter bottom of the pyramid). However, over time our thinking has changed, with some organisations recognising the power of those closer to the business being practised (those closer to the customers) to contribute to strategic thinking.

Strategic thinking is about why (the philosophy and meaning, the why of the organisation), and operational management is about the how and the what (the 'doing' or the actions and behaviours that demonstrate and achieve the why).

BOX 2.1 STRATEGIC COMPARED TO OPERATIONAL

STRATEGIC – Why – Philosophy and Meaning – Thinking

OPERATIONAL – How and What – Actions and Behaviours – Doing

The use of the pyramid (Figure 2.1) could suggest that strategic thinking is more important than the operational because it is higher up the pyramid or hierarchy. Certainly, those at the top of an organisation get paid more and are accountable at a high level for the organisation, but operational management should never be denigrated, as it is extremely important in any organisation. Operational management is the 'getting things done' in an organisation, the short-term jobs and activities, the tactics and actions. It is the domain of objectives, of processes and projects, and the interface with the customer. If we consider an example of a supermarket, it is the stocking of shelves, the baking of the bread, the checkout assistant scanning the customer's shopping, the scheduling of staff. All these things are essential to the success of the organisation.

The difference between strategic thinking and operational management can also be demonstrated with the SOSTAC tool (Smith, 1998) that presents a process of developing a strategy and breaking it down into its smaller components: tactics, that can then be put into action and controlled (monitored and measured). If we align the Pyramid of Management to the SOSTAC tool, we can see that strategy is the higher view, and operational thinking is the domain of tactics, action, and control or the smaller steps or objectives to achieve that higher view (Figure 2.2).

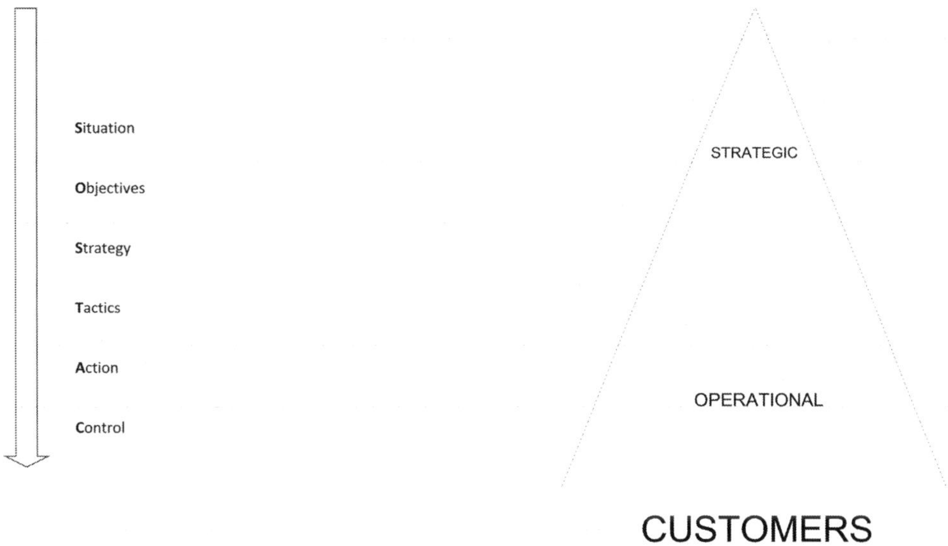

FIGURE 2.2 The SOSTAC Model Aligned with the Pyramid of Management

Operational management and leadership are concerned with getting the job done, with operationalising or implementing the strategy made by strategic thinkers. What we should not do is strategise our operations! Continuing the use of the supermarket as an example, cleaning the supermarket at the end of the day is not a strategy, nor is stock replenishment, but each task *does* contribute to a stakeholder relationship strategy that sees quality of service as key to the value offer of the organisation. When considering whether to call something a strategy, or to judge whether you are involved in strategic thinking, consider whether your discussions meet the criteria we have already discussed as a model for strategy-making, as shown in Figure 2.3.

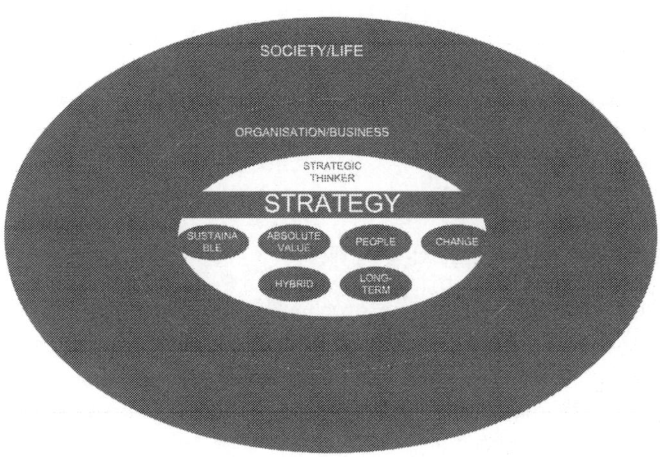

FIGURE 2.3 Strategy-making in Context

There are different approaches to strategy-making, as discussed in Chapter 1, among other things called prescriptive and emergent, and we agreed that a hybrid approach was likely to be the most successful in the current challenging environment, where implementation may not follow strategy-making in a linear fashion but may be something done *while* strategy-making and to inform a strategy being developed. Consequently, those simple tasks or tactics to operationalise or implement a strategy are important, but so are discussions *during* the strategy-making process about what those tasks or tactics might be to ensure effective operationalisation. These are the discussions about whether resources, capabilities, systems, and structures are in place, and whether there are risks to effective operationalisation. The SAF evaluation analysis (Whittington et al., 2020) and the use of McKinsey's 7-S framework (Peters & Waterman, 1982) are examples of testing a strategy for its likely effective implementation. Both models recognise the need to judge whether a strategy is aligned to the operational functions and abilities of the organisation. The 'Feasibility' criterion of the SAF model tests whether a strategy is achievable.

BOX 2.2 THE SAF EVALUATION ANALYSIS

Suitability – Does a proposed strategy address the key opportunities and threats an organisation faces?

Acceptability – Does a proposed strategy meet the expectations of the stakeholders? Is the level of risk acceptable? Is the likely return acceptable? Will stakeholder reactions be positive?

Feasibility – Would a proposed strategy work in practice? Can the strategy be financed? Do people and their skills exist, or can they be obtained? Can the required resources be obtained and integrated?

Whittington et al. (2020, p. 377)

The 7-S framework asks managers to consider the barriers and supporters to the implementation of a strategy by asking questions on Structure, Systems, Styles, Staff, Skills, and Shared Values.

BOX 2.3 THE 7-S FRAMEWORK

- *Structure*: How is the organisation structured? Who does what? Who reports to who? Who has authority? Do those authority relations work/or not? Does the structure align with the shared values? Will the structure allow your strategy to be put into action? Are there barriers in place and what can be done about these to ease the transition? What checks and controls are in place to ensure good governance and accountability?

- *Systems*: Systems refer to the overarching, central procedures that run a business. In organisations, systems are the methods, rules, or processes that guide and direct the activities of the many departments in an organisation. They ensure that all the departments and divisions inside an organisation are operating smoothly and efficiently. Systems might include inventory management, information systems, sales information, and more.
- *Styles*: An organisation's culture is made up of elements such as the way its employees interact with one another and its core beliefs. This is an intangible resource which can be difficult to understand but is essential to facilitate the successful implementation of strategy.
- *Staff*: The organisation's human resource management methods and accomplishments. or otherwise. Includes recruiting, training, deploying, measuring, rewarding performance, retention, and talent management. Where are the strengths and weaknesses and what needs to be done to ease the implementation of your strategy? How does the staffing align with other aspects of the organisation?
- *Skills*: Individual and organisational skills. Do you have the skills to manage the implementation of your strategy? Do skills need to be acquired or developed?
- *Shared values*: To create shared values, one must understand the organisation's position on economic benefit (for the company) and social value (for the community) at the same time as the larger society, or its position on profit, people, and planet. These shared values will include the organisation's position on social purpose and responsibility as well as stakeholder relationships. The shared values are those qualities, beliefs, and priorities that all staff should be able to agree are important. These are the overarching objectives that all staff will support.

Adapted from Peters & Waterman (1982)

Importantly, the strategy needs to align with the six other Ss for effective implementation. If there is a disjoint or misalignment, then the strategy will not work or will be short-lived.

Another aspect of operational management is the monitoring and measurement of tasks and activities daily, ensuring that the organisation is going in the right direction. This monitoring and measurement provide the data and information, and the knowledge, to reassure an organisation that its strategy is working, and is also the source of the warning data if things are going wrong. These measurements are not strategic in themselves but are essential to assess good strategy health. They are also a useful tool in encouraging people's buy-in and in rewarding success by highlighting the relationship between strategic thinking and operational measures that is normally hidden. They help employees understand the connection between what they are doing and the strategic plans of an organisation (Sneyd & Rowley, 2004). So, it is important to operationalise, but also to make sure that those operational tactics and actions are monitored and measured via mechanisms such as Key Performance Indicators (KPIs). This makes the operational actions 'live' by measuring them but there is also recognition that if not operationalised fully, openly, and monitored, the meaning of strategy for the operational layer might be lost or hidden. We will revisit these ideas about encouraging commitment when discussing change management, another management subject that interlinks with strategy-making.

The relationship of strategic and operational management is consequently not one-way (top to bottom or vice versa) and we can be more imaginative than using the standard pyramid! Instead imagine an elevator, with operational management and strategic management riding up and down the elevator and getting off at different floors to input, advise, connect, measure, and monitor.

Summary

Operational Management contributes to Strategic Thinking and Strategy-making by ensuring consideration of how a strategy will be implemented before it is introduced. Can it be achieved, and do the various resources and capabilities exist within the organisation, and align with the strategy, to ensure it will not be a failure? Operational Management then implements the strategy via tactics and actions and provides feedback as to its achievement against targets, and its eventual success.

CASE STUDY 2.1

Balancing the Strategic and Operational

Adam Parsons is a Consultant from a Big Four Consultancy with a focus on the energy and natural resources sector. As such, he advises a wide range of clients on navigating the strategic opportunities and challenges associated with the energy transition and the move towards a net zero society. In the following case study, he considers the challenges there are in operationalising strategy.

'The biggest challenge is bridging the dichotomy between headline strategic, blue sky thinking and what can be operationalised in practise and bringing those perspectives and views together. Often the strategy part of the business is a distinct unit that works very closely with the C-Suite and with the execs. It doesn't necessarily have that breadth of exposure to and experience of operational perspectives across the business.

'Strategy-making is about bringing together perspectives across an organisation. Ultimately too much strategy-making is done by executives in isolation without bringing the organisation on the journey and without really getting into that deeper level as to what the organisation needs, what can bring opportunities, and how the risks can be integrated for that organisation. A strategy shouldn't just sit on a shelf but should be very tangible, very actionable, and can be progressed. Getting buy-in at all levels in an organisation is key to making that happen.

'What works well is where strategic business partners are embedded in lots of different business units getting a grasp of that working level and the needs of the business that can then flow through into an overarching strategy. It's essential to have a kind of North Star that the whole organisation is working towards. But I think embedding strategy more into the day-to-day of what organisations are doing is key.'

PROJECT MANAGEMENT

Strategic change will lead to some incremental business changes (changes to processes and procedures) and some *projects*, the latter defined as time-defined, time-constrained, temporary combinations of resources to achieve something new and unique (Slack, 2009; Turner, 2014; Meredith et al., 2016; Schelini et al., 2017). In fact, strategy-making is likely to lead to a *portfolio or programme* of projects (PMI, 2017), with each project bringing about a change to contribute to the overall strategy.

A project can be instigated to develop a product or to investigate a market and plan a marketing campaign. Projects can also be used to construct a building, implement an IT system, or carry out research and development. All these things are clearly important to the future of organisations but getting the mechanism for making a strategy work (the how and what) mixed up with the strategy itself is not helpful. There are a set of project management skills and behaviours that have the right to be seen as separate, unique, and valuable when compared to strategic thinking and strategy-making, much as we have argued so far for recognition of a particular process and ingredients for strategy-making. Project management skills can be classified into five process groups: Initiating; Planning; Executing; Monitoring and Controlling, and Closing (PMI, 2017), and you can see some overlaps with operational management and strategic management skills here, but it is valid to say, much as with operational management, that project management is operating on a different level from strategy-making and is more about the how and the what.

Much like the debate regarding operational management, however, we must also say that projects should be linked to the strategy of the organisation (Cooke-Davies et al., 2009) (otherwise why are you spending time and money – precious resources – on them?). Successful projects start with a definition of objectives and strategies (Schelini et al., 2017). Strategy is needed to give projects purpose, focus, and coherence and projects are needed to implement the change required by strategy-making. If a strategy is not clear, then a project will lose its focus. I remember reading the following comment in the i newspaper in 2019:

> There is no doubt that the UK has fallen well behind other countries in terms of investment in improved railway infrastructure. However, what distinguishes these other countries is that their investment plans are based on an overall strategy for their entire rail network and not a piecemeal project-led approach.
>
> *(Ian Lawson, Milngavie, Glasgow) (i, 2019)*

The view that there has been a lack of strategic thinking and strategy-making as a foundation of the HS2 project has been borne out by its later failure (UK Parliament, 2024).

High-level skills in project management or project management maturity (Schelini et al., 2017) can be the source of advanced resources and capabilities and competencies and as such need to be considered when planning strategy, as they are likely to be essential for the effective implementation of strategy. Project management skills within an organisation are part of the 7-S framework, represented by staff, systems, skills and therefore the provision or otherwise of these in an organisation can lead to strategy implementation success or failure.

Summary

Projects are essential for implementing strategy. While project management operates differently from strategy-making, both must be aligned. Effective strategy provides project focus, while project management skills are crucial for execution, influencing strategic success.

SURVIVAL AND CRISIS MANAGEMENT

Survival mechanisms such as retrenchment, consolidation and divestment, while not necessarily focused on growth, may all be appropriate responses to certain conditions, and lead to sustainable organisations. However, there are some conditions that are less easy to respond to because of their surprising appearance in the organisation's environment. During the Covid-19 pandemic in the years from 2020 to 2021, all countries of the world and therefore all businesses and organisations had to manage their lives. Prior to Covid-19, other issues struck the global community, such as the global recession of 2008. After Covid-19, the global community had to deal with the wide impact of the Russian invasion of Ukraine. These events caused 'crises' which demanded a response. Are these responses strategic decisions or are they reactive, short-term, and therefore more operational decisions?

Certainly, emergent versus prescriptive strategy-making approaches were discussed in Chapter 1 and it was decided that a hybrid approach to strategy-making would be favourable in the VUCA and wicked global environment in which we are currently operating. Volatility and uncertainty suggest that events can occur, causing issues to which we must respond, and, despite our best efforts in planning for a sustainable future, these events may summon a more reactive rather than proactive response mode to deal with the unexpected. This flexibility or agility should, it is implied by the hybrid strategy-making approach, be built into our systems so that we do not persist with a strategy that has been thrown off course.

However, a demanded rather than planned change is more likely to lead to short-term decisions and therefore counters the sustainable and future-focused characteristics of strategy-making. There may be a time to respond to short-term demands, but we must keep a focus on the long-term. Whittington et al. (2023) discuss turnaround strategies: 'Situations calling for turnarounds include economic recessions, the failure of major investment projects or the sudden collapse of important markets' (p. 492) and while recognising the need for crisis stabilisation they warn that 'there is a danger of cutting long-term investments in research and development, training or brand-building, with negative implications for the long-term future of the organisation' (p. 494).

Le and Phi (2021) saw that Covid, as a crisis, was able to instigate strategic thought, particularly in the use of technology. Crises can therefore be the instigators of strategy and once crises have occurred they widen the parameters of the known versus the unknown and consequently should enhance the strategy-making process in future. Drucker (1966) required that we change our mindset from one that is focused primarily on 'crises' to be solved to opportunities to be pursued. Crises must be solved but there is a difference between a mindset that is primarily searching for opportunities, and a mindset that is primarily focused on problem-solving (the latter being the realm of crisis, project, and operational management level).

Summary

Crisis management, while being short-term, can be the source of change and opportunity that will lead to long-term change. The danger in short-term crisis management is that the characteristics of good strategy-making are abandoned and cause later distress.

CHANGE MANAGEMENT

'Change...is about *moving* from a current state, through a *transition* state to *arrive* at a *new future* state' (Creasey, 2022).

We discussed change on a few levels in Chapter 1. We discussed the VUCA environment in which we are operating (the nature of change and the speed of change contribute to the volatility, uncertainty, complexity, and ambiguity of the environment in which we must operate). We recognised that the need to respond to changes in the environment has led to changes in management and leadership practice through the centuries. We concluded that change is a key characteristic of strategy-making.

Figure 2.4 shows the relationship between strategy and change. As we equip ourselves to respond to change to create sustainable futures for our organisations and for society, the strategies that result from the strategy-making process will bring about change. We hope for positive, beneficial change through our strategies, or at least change that best responds to the changes we have identified.

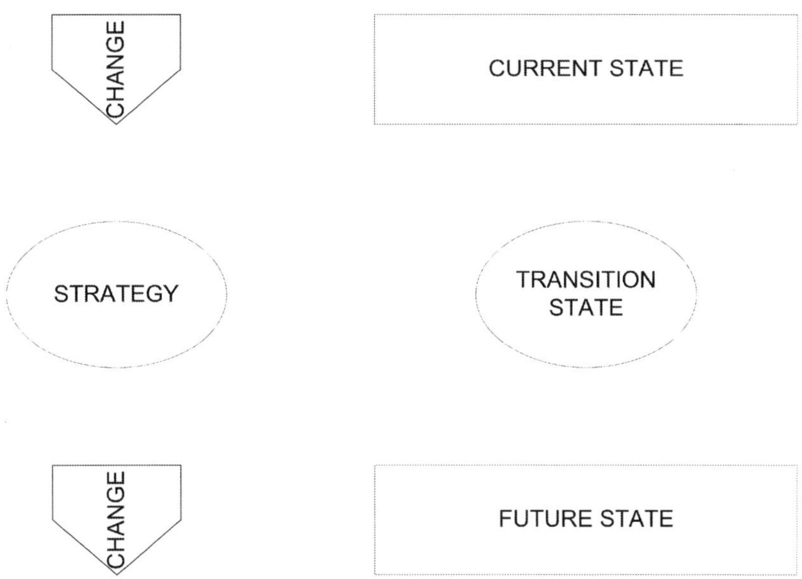

FIGURE 2.4 The Relationship between Strategy and Change

A strategy will foresee and respond to change and bring about change. Thus strategy-making and strategic thinking are inextricably linked with change management. Implementation of strategy (with operationalisation including projects) will require change management. Change management is, as with operational management and project management, a distinct area with particular skills and techniques.

Change management is, as is the case with strategy-making and project management, a structured approach, but whereas projects may close with the delivery of a new product, building, system, market research plan, and a strategy-making process will conclude with a future-focused plan for a sustainable, valued outcome for people, society and so on, it is the job of change management to get those deliverables embedded, embraced, and adopted.

Also, as we confirmed earlier, all business and organisational activities involve people (all our stakeholders, and especially our employees), and change management is concerned with ensuring particularly that people are moved from one state to another, that people are 'carried along'. Successful change occurs when the new state/the future is accepted and is adopted as what will now be.

Change management uses more of the soft skills we encountered in Chapter 1 when discussing leadership.

BOX 2.4 THE SKILLS OF STRATEGIC LEADERSHIP

Develop a vision, produce change, communicate, create coalitions, motivate, engage, satisfy, build recognition, self-esteem, be personal, be active, create excitement, have empathy, understand and give meaning, search out opportunities, encourage, involve, dominated by the soul, be passionate, be creative, be flexible, inspire, innovate, be courageous, be imaginative, be experimental, be independent, reflection.

The change manager also takes a view of the individual and the team within an organisation (and, by connection, the community and society) and they recognise that change can be difficult and the transition from one state to another tough (Bridges, 1992; Carnall, 1995; Cope, 2010). The change manager recognises the supporting and constraining forces in change: the Leaders, Focus, Supporters, and Laggards (Cope, 2010) and adapts their styles accordingly. We cannot just tell people what to do, but they will need to be persuaded to support us (if we are to gain their commitment and for the change to be adopted successfully).

There are two very well-known models we can consider when thinking about a systematic, structured approach to change management. Lewin (1947) is the first. He talked about a three-stage model of unfreezing, changing, and then refreezing or CATS (Change as Three Steps) and while this model has been criticised as simplistic and relatively static for today's complex working environment, others explain that this was one model taken from Lewin's work, and he also discussed field theory, group dynamics, and action research (Burnes, 2004a, 2004b; Cummings et al., 2015). Another model is Kotter's Eight-step Process (Kotter, 1996), which has been more recently updated to the

'Accelerate' model (Kotter, 2014), recognising that in modern management functions we work in a quicker, more agile way. But in all models, it is fair to recognise that communication is key, and involvement, collaboration, and co-creation are likely to be methods of working that result in greater degrees of stakeholder engagement for effective support for and embedding of change (Homans, 1950; Granovetter, 1973; Chan Kim & Mauborgne, 2024). The message is therefore to follow a change management approach when implementing strategy.

Summary

Strategy and change management are interlinked, with strategy requiring structured approaches to change management to achieve successful adoption and embedding of a strategy. Models like Lewin's and Kotter's emphasise communication, collaboration, and stakeholder engagement to embed change effectively.

VISION, MISSION, AND VALUES AND OTHER PLANNING TOOLS

Vision, Mission, and Values (VMV) statements are popularly seen as requirements for strategy-making. They tend to be the subject of key sections in strategy and strategic management books, and parts of business development workshops. However, the usefulness of these items has been questioned, and this section summarises the difficulties with the tools. However, it is important to ask whether it is the tools themselves that present difficulties, or whether, over time and in application, we have not understood the key principles of those tools, or have applied them incorrectly, causing the difficulties. If this is the case, and we were to revert to the key principles, could we apply these ideas in a more meaningful way? We will therefore look at the tools' principles, assess their intention, and take from our discussion what we should be considering in strategy-making.

This section will also revisit some strategic planning tools used for strategic management (discussed in Chapter 1 and that was argued should be combined with strategic leadership and result in strategic thinking) and we will discuss their pros and cons. Indeed, it will be appropriate to ask once again, as with VMV, whether they are useful for their key principles, which if applied will guide us appropriately to effective strategy-making.

We started to talk about VMV in the 1980s and developed ideas of VMV from then on (Peters & Waterman, 1982; Jaffe et al.,1993). These are still, in the mid 2020s, used in management situations. From a review of the literature, and from experience, the key difficulties and principles are as follows.

Difficulties with VMV Tools

There is uncertainty in the *definition* of the tools, and in discerning the *differences* between them (Kantabutra & Avery, 2010; Spear, 2017). This is not helped by the grouping of

VMV (Chun & Davies, 2001; Verma, 2009–2010; Spear, 2017) as indeed has been done here, so it can be difficult to be specific about the use and usefulness of each. However, here they have been grouped together *because* it is difficult to discern their difference, and there is undoubtedly linkage between them (Keller et al., 2010; Dowling & Moran, 2012; Spear, 2017). Here each of the VMV ideas is discussed.

The **Vision** statement is intended as a description of the future, where an organisation is going, where it wants to be, what it intends to become. It defines and guides the purpose and long-term direction of an organisation (Davies et al., 2003; Desmidt & Prinzie, 2008; Hirota et al., 2010; Kantabutra & Avery, 2010; Verma, 2009–2010; Spear, 2017; Rosen, 2023). It is aspirational (Gregory, 2016, cited in Haslam & Shenoy, 2018; Hinton, 2022: Rosen, 2023). However, a vision without an environmental scan examining how an organisation might respond to the needs of community and society (the system of which the organisation is a part) seems to be unrealistic, so how is the vision *different* from a strategy? And what comes first: the vision or the strategy? Here we could argue that a vision is intended to be broad in outlook rather than a more detailed plan (Hinton, 2022) but one might again argue that a broad outlook of where the organisation wants to be is the job of a strategy, and the detail will be in the operationalisation. However, it is likely that an organisation will have several different strategies that all contribute to the overall aim of the organisation, as we found that several projects might constitute a programme to achieve a strategy. Hence, we can understand that, in the discussions about strategy, one still needs an 'umbrella' or 'helicopter' view of where we want to be. We could also just call this the aim of the business, or the purpose.

However, the **Mission** is intended to encapsulate why the organisation exists and what its purpose is or what it is intended to achieve, its value proposition or rationale (Gregory, 2016, cited in Haslam & Shenoy, 2018; Hinton, 2022; Rosen, 2023). In comparing the mission and the vision, if the mission is the why, then presumably the vision would be the what. This is a difficult distinction, as the two (vision and mission) seem to be intertwined, let alone this clashing with our previous discussion in 'Operational Management' . One cannot set the what if the why has not been considered. If the idea of setting a vision and mission is tested on a hypothetical organisation, we might get something like the scenario in Box 2.5.

BOX 2.5 APPLYING PRINCIPLES OF VISION AND MISSION

SNW is a wood-burning stove-fitting company. Its vision is to offer the most reliable, well-fitted and well-engineered heating solutions in its local area.

If we asked 'why', we might go round in circles to a certain extent, but we could see that asking these questions would at least refine the vision.

The answer to 'why' might be because it is important to offer a quality service, and the purpose is twofold: to offer support to the customers and communities around a basic human need for warmth, but also to offer a solution that counters any less experienced and less well-intentioned organisation. But the organisation also wants to be profitable and to train and employ people.

Two problems have emerged. One is the similarity of the ideas, and the other is that we cannot just dream up a vision and mission without some idea of what is going on in the external environment. Vision and Mission then become not necessarily a starting point, but a set of questions to ask along the route of strategy-making. And rather than a linear process, a very circular and reiterative process (much like the emergent strategy-making approach considered in Chapter 1) would result, or at least some sort of filtering process where ideas are tested against a core set of VMV.

If we turn to **Values**, we are looking at what we believe and the ideals that guide action (Rosen, 2023); the distinctive or fundamental beliefs an organisation stands for (Quigley, 1994, cited in Spear, 2017). Again, it might be difficult to separate these from any simultaneous considerations of the vision and the mission as a person's and organisation's beliefs and ideals will have driven their aim and their reasoning behind wanting to achieve that aim. The idea of values does reflect the importance of considering the culture of an organisation which can be defined as 'the way we do things round here' (Bower,1966), the way staff interact with each other and the way they get things done. Every organisation is unique in this way because it is made up of people, who are each unique, and the combination of those individuals will also be unique. It is the product of years of history, of who was recruited, when and why, and what decisions were made. It does make sense to consider values (or culture) while formulating strategy, but again these sorts of considerations will be regarded as part of what is viewed as important (or not) to achieve and the appropriate (or not) approaches to achieving the aim. There must also be alignment (it is difficult to implement a strategy that works against what is expected/accepted and how an organisation has developed over time).

So, instead of compartmentalising the questions and labelling them, can we accept the principles and ask a series of questions to determine 'what and how we do things round here'?:

1. What are we doing?
2. Why are we doing it?
3. How do we do it?
4. What is important to us?

One might go further to look at the other side of the question (Box 2.6).

BOX 2.6 QUESTIONS ON 'WHAT AND HOW WE DO THINGS ROUND HERE'

1. What are we doing? AND What are we not doing/what wouldn't we do?
2. Why are we doing it? AND Why aren't we doing something different?
3. How do we do it? AND What would we not do to achieve our aim?
4. What is important to us? AND What is not important to us?

Issues, in addition to the difficulty in discerning the difference between VMV as explained above, include:

- VMV may 'seem 'old hat' or a 'been there, done that' exercise' (Mirvis et al., 2010, p. 316).
- The tools are not universally used (Spear, 2017), and if they are not always used, how essential can they be?
- The tools can be used inappropriately, with too much discussion, no agreement, and results that are too wordy, lengthy, and indeterminate, which render them unworkable (Hinton, 2022; Rosen, 2023). The longer and more indeterminate the results of discussions are, mission creep can set in.
- The process of developing VMV is too time-consuming.
- It is difficult to know who should be involved in VMV articulation. Traditionally it would be top-down but in keeping with other management and leadership developments we are moving to an increasingly bottom-up approach (Rosen, 2023). VMV articulation must involve all levels to 'close the gap between high-minded statements of vision, mission, and values and everyday ground-level practices' (Mirvis et al., 2010, p. 322). But involving all stakeholders is time-consuming and the likelihood of concluding with something succinct and determinate would be limited.
- How often should an organisation be looking at their VMV? If it is too often, then work could become about producing VMV rather than getting anything done!
- These are marketing tools rather than strategy-making tools. They are sloganeering, window dressing, image burnishing, and public relations (Mirvis et al., 2010) prone to greenwashing or carewashing. They risk being demonstrative and ingratiating and surface level rather than indicating true intentions and strategic change.
- They can be damaging if an organisation's actions do not fit with what it said it would do.
- Seeing them as separate exercises within strategy-making is problematic and they cannot be divided from the other work that needs to go on in strategy-making/strategic thinking such as environmental scanning.
- Organisations are not using V&M statements effectively as corporate identity cues (Ingenhoff & Fuhrer, 2010; Abdullah et al., 2013; Spear, 2017), despite this being one of their intentions.
- VMV are not unique, and they do not make organisations stand out (Spear, 2017).
- VMV do not pay sufficient attention to employees as key stakeholders (Spear, 2017).
- VMV do not sufficiently align with an organisation's corporate personality (or culture).
- VMV often get conflated with strategic planning and tactic implementation rather than focusing on the overarching principles that guide the organisation (Rosen, 2023).

Principles of VMV Tools

Despite the issues discussed above, VMV tools were developed and have been used over several years, and we are still using them and talking about them. It may be worth looking at what they were intended to do, and as previously noted, consider how to take these principles into our contemporary practice while mitigating the risks of poor application.

- VMV can help recruit, retain and motivate employees (Verschoor, 2005).
- VMV provide a foundation and guide to an organisation of where it wants to be and what it stands for, and this guide is needed to ensure that subsequent actions are in keeping with or aligned with the intention of the organisation (Jaffe et al., 1993; Mirvis et al., 2010; Hinton; 2022).
- It is possible to keep the process and the outcome short: 'This is what we are here to do' (Hinton, 2022; Rosen, 2023).
- As VMV are not always used, and the working world is not perfect, perhaps if we did all use VMV, strategy-making would be easier, more effective, and the results would be more understood by stakeholders.
- VMV supply an opportunity to address issues of ethics, culture, and social purpose/responsibility that might otherwise be overlooked.
- VMV supply the organisation with a personality with which stakeholders can relate and they differentiate the organisation from others (Chun & Davies, 2001; de Chernatony & Segal-Horn, 2003; de Chernatony et al., 2006; Desmidt & Prinzie, 2008; Hou et al., 2009; Verma, 2009–2010; Hirota et al., 2010; Ingenhoff & Fuhrer, 2010; Kantabutra & Avery, 2010; Dowling & Moran, 2012; Spear, 2017; Rosen, 2023).
- VMV are part of an organisation's communication tools, telling stakeholders what it is and what it stands for (Suvatjis & de Chernatony, 2005; Otubanjo & Melewar, 2007; Otubanjo, 2012,cited in Spear, 2017).
- Values are only window dressing if they are *not acted upon*. A good organisation would examine its practices regularly to ensure that there was alignment with the values they had recognised.

Considering all the above, is there a better way to place VMV as a part of the strategy-making process (Figure 2.5)?

Rather than *starting* with VMV discussions, we should take a strategic systems thinking view of how the organisation may go forward and then use the VMV discussions as checkpoints or alignments. This also echoes McKinsey's 7-S framework for implementation as discussed in 'Operational Management', as it would check that our strategy is in line with our Shared Values and Styles (at least).

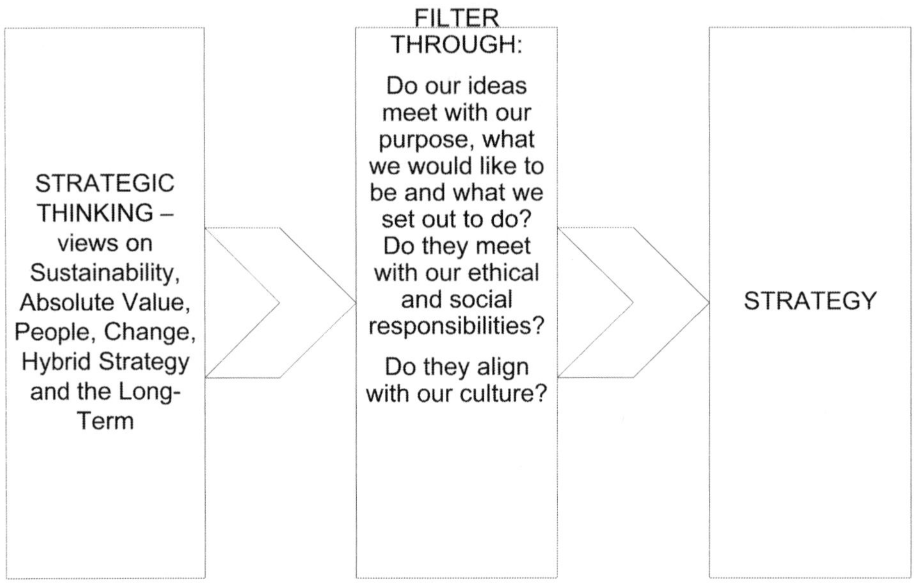

FIGURE 2.5 The Principles of VMV in Strategic Thinking and Strategy-making

OTHER PLANNING TOOLS

When discussing strategic planning or management, an important ingredient of strategic thinking, you will be asked to consider the following models. Each of these models has been in existence for some time and has been used extensively in a range of different contexts. It is now common practice to argue that classical strategy models are only partially helpful (Haslam & Shenoy, 2018) and that they are a conventional process-focused approach (Nonaka & Zhu, 2012) that needs some refinement for the twenty-first century. However, it is also argued that they offer a starting point (Liedtka, 1998) and that strategic thinkers can be creative and dynamic in using any model.

As with VMV, each model has its recognised benefits, and risks to bear in mind in its application, and these are summarised in tables 2.1 to 2.9.

The PESTLE tool has been used for the structure of this book, and you will see that all criteria are examined further in Chapters 3 to 9. In fact, the book responds to the criticism of the PESTLE model that the relationship is one-way and looks at ways businesses and organisations can impact on the wider environment.

Evidently there are a large number of models and tools linked to strategy-making and strategic thinking. Strategic thinkers are likely to use a range and contextualise them for their needs, as Case Study 2.2. shows.

TABLE 2.1 PESTLE Summary

What it is	PESTLE is an acronym which stands for Political, Economic, Sociological, Technological, Legal, and Environmental. It was developed from the smaller PEST. The idea is to use it as a macro-environmental scanning tool assessing factors or trends in each area that are likely to impact on an organisation. The trends should be assessed as either opportunities or threats, and these can form the basis for strategy-making.
Benefits	• It is a good, understandable place to start. • It recognises an organisation's place in the wider macro-environment. • It recognises that there may be some issues out of an organisation's control that, nevertheless, it needs to be aware of. • It keeps strategic thinkers up to date with trends. • It is essential to understand the system of which an organisation is part to plan sustainable strategies. PESTLE is a tool that helps understand that system.
Risks to be mitigated	• It is a static tool and will always be a snapshot in time, so will become out of date quickly. • It can result in an extensive list of daunting threats unless it is used selectively and to prioritise the most critical issues. • If not properly utilised, criteria are considered individually and it is more important to see where criteria interrelate and interact to form more pressing issues. • It should always be used in combination with other models such as Five Forces and competitor analysis to give more detail and meaning to individual organisations. • It entails a lot of work and is time-consuming and can lead to 'paralysis by analysis' (see Chapter 3 for a further explanation of this). • It can be subjective. To be useful, involve other people in the analysis. • It needs to be combined with internal analysis to be useful. • An effective PESTLE analysis relies on good data and information being used. If 'garbage in', then 'garbage out'. • It tends to concentrate on what is known rather than on future possibilities, so it is not useful for future trends and predictions. • If not used in an intelligent and thoughtful way and discussed as part of a strategy-making exercise, it can be seen and used simply as a tick-box exercise: something that has to be done and loses its meaning by doing it. • It is one-way. Businesses and organisations *can* impact on these 'external' criteria (this impact that businesses and organisations can have on the 'system' is discussed throughout this book).

TABLE 2.2 Five Forces Summary

What it is	Five Forces is a model developed by Porter (1985) to assess the size and impact of five forces that operate in an organisation's industry. It is an industry assessment tool rather than an individual organisation tool but should assess an organisation's role and strength in the industrial system of which it is part (its competitiveness). This is a different layer of analysis than that dealt with by the PESTLE, with the organisation in the centre, its industry surrounding it, and the macro-environment surrounding that, the latter represented by PESTLE analysis. The five forces are Competitive Rivalry (an assessment of the competition), Suppliers, Buyers, New Entrants, and Substitutes.
Benefits	• It is a well-recognised and much-used model that has resulted in useful insight into industries. • It contributes useful information to an analysis.

Risks to be mitigated	• It is a static tool and will always be a snapshot in time, so it will become out of date quickly.
	• It cannot be as detailed as is required to really understand a business. It should be used in combination with other tools (PESTLE and competitor analysis) for full coverage.
	• If not properly utilised criteria are considered individually and it is more important to see where criteria interrelate and interact to form pressing issues.
	• Criteria should be prioritised.
	• Criteria should be applied specifically and contextualised for individual businesses.
	• The model needs to be applied regularly to keep aware of change.
	• The difference between industries has become increasingly blurred.
	• Competition is potentially global and unknown.
	• What are considered substitutes has become less clear over time (this is linked to the blurring of boundaries between products and industries).
	• Newer models would add other forces to reflect the VUCA environment, including:
	  • The competitor's level of innovativeness
	  • Exposure to globalisation
	  • Threat of digitalisation
	  • Industry exposure to de/regulation activities (Isabelle et al., 2020)
	  • Complementors (Johnson et al., 2017)
	  • Coopetition (Crick & Crick, 2020).

TABLE 2.3 Competitor Analysis Summary

What it is	A tool to compare an organisation with its direct competitors to understand strengths and weaknesses according to the critical success factors any customer might expect from an organisation operating in that competitive field.
Benefits	• This can be a simple tool, systematically assessing an organisation and its competitors against certain criteria. • Statistics, reviews, and other evidence that is available publicly can be used to assess the organisations' performance. • The results show a clear comparison between competitors, and it is easy to recognise the gaps in an organisation's offering. • The results enable an organisation to identify its strengths in comparison to a competitor, and to build on those strengths.
Risks to be mitigated	• While a lot of information is available openly, there will always be information that is less accessible that could be essential to a detailed and reliable comparison and assessment. • It may be difficult to identify critical success factors, although market research and readily available review sites can be useful sources of these factors. • It might be difficult to identify competitors in increasingly blurred industries and in the globalised economies of which we are part. • The analysis is current and may not look to the future, although when carried out as part of a suite of analyses (including Five Forces and PESTLE analysis) it should be possible to obtain a holistic assessment. • One must ask oneself, in line with the debate about competitive advantage in Chapter 1, whether relative value will lead to sustainability, or whether absolute value should be sought.

TABLE 2.4 Resources and Capabilities Analysis

What it is	This analysis tool is part of the internal analysis of an organisation and details the assets an organisation owns and its abilities to use those assets well that then combine to create clear competencies in an organisation. These can be the source of strength for an organisation and can be built on in strategy-making. This tool can also examine an organisation for gaps, showing where assets are not used effectively, and these constitute weaknesses, which need to be worked on for success. There are specific resources and capabilities analysis tools (such as Value Chain and VRIO) but a simple table can be used to list resources and capabilities to start recognising what a company owns and what it does with what it owns. Resources can be categorised under headings such as financial resources, human resources, physical resources, and technological resources. They can also be split into tangible and intangible resources.
Benefits	• A straightforward way of listing and appreciating what the organisation has. • Information should be readily available to anyone working in the organisation, and someone working outside should be able to access a lot of the relevant information from the organisation's website, public records (if applicable), and sometimes from business comment on organisations (such as industry articles/media reports). • It provides a snapshot from which to base future developments.
Risks to be mitigated	• There is the potential for this assessment to be subjective when it comes to assessing the way an organisation uses its assets. For example, different departments in an organisation may criticise other departments, especially if they do not have full understanding of their operations. However, this can be useful too, as it shows internal perceptions of issues which are useful at this stage to examine and either support or dismiss with evidence. • While useful as a stand-alone piece, this work will be most helpful when understanding how resources and capabilities in an organisation compare to others and/or the requirements of the external environment, so, as with other models, this tool should be used in conjunction with others to make a holistic assessment.

TABLE 2.5 Value Chain Summary

What it is	Porter (1985) developed the value chain as an assessment of the strengths and weaknesses of each primary and supporting function of an organisation and its contribution to the final value of a product or service. Each function should be assessed by its cost compared to the value it brings to the final product or service. Overall price minus overall cost of the sum of these functions will equal profit margin. The primary functions in the original model were inbound logistics, operations, outbound logistics, marketing and sales; and service and the supporting functions were firm infrastructure, human resource management, technology development, and procurement. Over time, versions of the model have been developed, including a sustainability value chain which considers the environmental impact of each function in the value chain (Soosay et al., 2012) or a social value chain which, as the name suggests, would look at societal impact.
Benefits	The value chain analysis provides a high level of detail, looking at each function's contribution to the overall value of a product or service. This means that strengths and weaknesses can be focused on specifically, rather than looking at the organisation as a whole. This tool identifies how and where an organisation provides value.
Risks to be mitigated	• Historically this tool has been perceived as most applicable to a manufacturing business, but this tends to show a lack of imagination and the tool can be applied to services. • Given the discussion in this book about sustainability, a value chain that looked at the full picture of environmental, social and economic impact would be most beneficial to an organisation.

TABLE 2.6 VRIO Summary

What it is	VRIO stands for Valuable, Rare, Inimitable, and Organisationally Embedded. It started out life as VRIN (Valuable, Rare, Inimitable, and Non-substitutable) but the N was thought to be too like the meaning of Rare. This is Barney's (1991, 1997) model and represents his emphasis on the resource-based view of competitive advantage, as it is a tool to assess the strengths (or weaknesses) of internal resources and capabilities. The tool asks strategic thinkers to consider an identified resource (let us say its brand, for example) and ask questions: Does it bring value to the organisation and to our customers? Do only we own this resource? Is it difficult to copy by our competitors? Do we have the systems and processes in place in the organisation to fully exploit the value of the resource? If we answer 'Yes' to each of these questions, then the resource holds sustainable competitive advantage. If the resource or capability you are assessing has none of these characteristics, then there is no advantage, and in fact your organisation is likely to be at a competitive disadvantage. If the resource or capability has value but nothing else, then your organisation is likely to have competitive parity. If Valuable, Rare, not inimitable or organisationally embedded, then Temporary Competitive Advantage, and if the resource or capability has all four characteristics, then this represents Sustainable Competitive Advantage. This tool allows a strategic thinker to identify what are threshold resources and capabilities (anyone operating in the same area will have them), compared to what are distinctive resources and capabilities (they set the organisation apart from others).
Benefits	Rather than just identifying resources and capabilities in a list or table, the VRIO tool evaluates those resources and capabilities to see which represents a strength or weakness, and this added information can allow a strategic thinker to think of options for the future.
Risks to be mitigated	As identified in Chapter 1, the idea of competitive advantage may be less useful now, in the VUCA environment, than it was previously. McGrath (2013) said that with the speed of change and with the blurring of product, service, and industry boundaries, as has been discussed already on numerous occasions, the tool is likely to be of use, but a strategic thinker needs to recognise the limits to its use.

TABLE 2.7 SWOT Summary

What it is	The origins of the SWOT tool are difficult to define. It has been attributed to a few Harvard professors working in the 1950s and 1960s. It is ubiquitous in strategic thinking. It is an acronym and stands for Strengths, Weaknesses, Opportunities, and Threats and users are invited to create a checklist of these items for the organisation on which it is focused. It can therefore form a summary tool from which to develop strategic ideas. Also see TOWS which takes the SWOT summary and then asks the users to match Strengths and Weaknesses with Opportunities and Threats to formulate strategic plans.
Benefits	• SWOT is very well known and is a powerful summary tool to list points all in one place. • SWOT is a good assessment of where an organisation is now and what options may be available to it. • A SWOT takes the external analysis from PESTLE, Five Forces, and the competitor analysis tools to complete the Opportunities and Threats criteria, and it takes the internal analysis from the Resources and Capabilities analysis to populate the Strength and Weaknesses criteria.
Risks to be mitigated	• At times, the SWOT is used as the only tool rather than a summary tool, and if this happens it can be limited in depth. The previous stages of external and internal analysis will increase the depth and therefore usefulness of this tool.

TABLE 2.8 TOWS Summary

What it is	Weihrich (1982) took the SWOT tool and made it work to develop strategic futures. The TOWS tool looks like the SWOT tool in that it is a matrix and the Threats, Opportunities, Weakness, and Strengths are listed, but the point of the TOWS is to ask how a threat can be minimised and an opportunity maximised through effective use of strengths. Weihrich listed the various options as: • Maxi-Maxi: strategies that make the most use of strengths to capitalise on opportunities. • Maxi-Mini: use its strengths to minimise or neutralise threats. • Mini-Maxi: make the most of any new opportunity to overcome weakness. • Mini-Mini: a defensive strategy to minimise internal weaknesses and avoid external threats.
Benefits	• It is a systematic ending to a strategy-making process, taking the results of the process so far and slotting them into a tool that can help plan the future. • Strengths, Weaknesses, Opportunities, and Threats are prioritised and matched so that strategic thinkers can see the connection of internal resources and capabilities to the environmental possibilities presented by the business/social/global environment.
Risks to be mitigated	• It can be confused with SWOT, with users not taking the opportunity to match the internal and the external.

TABLE 2.9 SAF and other Business Case Models Summary

What it is	A strategic proposal will be considered for its viability prior to implementation, and an argument put to senior members of staff to approve implementation. SAF stands for Suitability, Acceptability, and Feasibility, and it has already been used in this chapter in the section on Operational Management (Box 2.2). A strategic thinker must justify their ideas, explaining how their strategy faces the opportunities and threats presented by the business environment (Suitability) and how it maintains the organisation's value and purpose. Acceptability is a consideration of stakeholder support and the potential risks the strategy presents. Are those risks acceptable? Feasibility considers whether the resources and capabilities are in place for the strategy to go ahead. Thus we see that the work done on analysis using other tools will be useful at this stage of the strategy-making process. Other business case models can be used and may be more suitable depending on context. For example, a five-case model (APM, 2019) considers Strategic Case, Financial Case, Management Case, Economic Case, and Commercial Case. Or a cost-benefit analysis (but including wider benefits and costs than just financial) may be suitable.
Benefits	• All strategies need to be discussed and presented in some way to gain approval. Putting forward the business case for something to happen benefits once again from the use of a systematic process of considering all the criteria of a successful strategy.
Risks to be mitigated	• These tools need to reflect the context of the organisation for which they are used. A tool that reflects the model of strategy-making discussed in Chapter 1 may be a useful tool in strategic thinking assessment. Is the strategy Sustainable (balancing environmental, societal, and economic responsibilities); of Absolute Value (not depending on transient competitive advantage); cognisant of the role of People, responding appropriately to Change, recognising the value of Hybrid, and Long-Term?

CASE STUDY 2.2

An Application of Planning Tools

Jayne Sowerby-Warrington is the Founder, Director of Kudos Leadership Solutions Ltd and was a previous Senior Leader at Lincolnshire County Council and here considers the use of tools and processes for strategic thinking, the contrast between the strategic and the operational, and the need to embed strategic direction across departments through effective communication.

To get to grips with her department's future, Jayne carried out a diagnostic piece of work: finding out as much information in terms of actually 'where are we now?' and then mapping out 'where do we need to get to?'. As a result, Jayne re-modelled her department's activities under four pillars: culture and vision, resources, leadership and policies, processes and systems.

Jayne also used a model with the acronym VMOST and asked: What's the Vision? What's the Mission? What are the Objectives? And then distilled these down to Strategies and Tactics and then made the tactics into smart objectives for the team with the appropriate level of ownership.

'We review the tactics every month and we're starting to review them for the next couple of years...trying to embed strategy across the department is important. Strategic thinking is great, but if you were working for me, you would need me to communicate that and you would need me to distil it in terms of what does it mean. We've worked hard to get out the key messages. We've had online sessions and awaydays, team meetings at every level. It's constantly talked about and it's translated into the kinds of activities that people can really relate to because I do think sometimes high-level strategies that are not really communicated well and distilled are probably not that effective. As a strategic leader, you've got to learn to balance the strategic and the operational.'

SUMMARY

Planning tools are critical to strategic management and therefore form a part of strategic thinking as discussed in Chapter 1. They should be used creatively and imaginatively, however, and an understanding of their principles, risks, and benefits will allow for a more informed use of them.

RISK MANAGEMENT

There are many layers of risk and risk management is applicable for operational management, project management, and strategic thinking.

At the operational level, we use the risk assessment and management process as part of everyday business and the implementation of this can be seen in health and safety assessments, the institution of standard operating procedures to reduce risk of physical or emotional injury, death and trauma or, less seriously, to reduce the risk of wastage or to institute appropriate cleaning or caring protocols in line with regulations. We carry out a risk assessment for projects to understand the risks to the completion of the project and use the same risk assessment and management tools, assessing the likelihood and impact of factors such as supply delays, cost increases, staff and expertise shortage, client changes as well as operational risks and external environmental risks that we may foresee or not (note the overlap with crisis management).

There will always be risk at all levels because there will always be uncertainty, and that uncertainty is a key feature of the VUCA environment in which we operate (see Chapter 1 for a discussion of 'The Complex Environment'). As the size and complexity of what we are doing grows, so does the risk. And as size and complexity grows, from operational to project to strategic thinking, so does the impact if a risk turns into an issue (Figure 2.6).

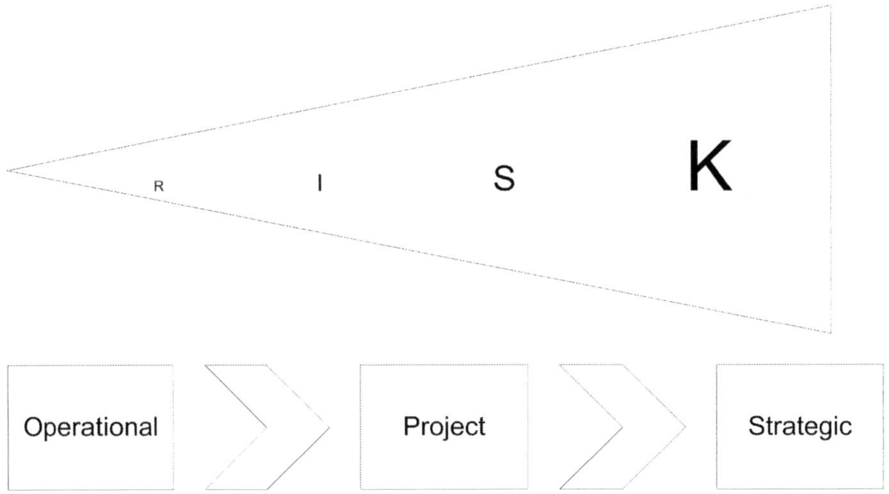

FIGURE 2.6 The Scale of Risk Related to Operational, Project, and Strategic Management

A risk is a prediction, the issue is the reality, and the risk assessment and management approach is intended to try to foresee and have a plan to handle the issues should they arise. At least this is risk management in its more reactive sense. At the strategic level, risk is slightly different. It is twofold. We hope that risk can be foreseen and labelled as a potential threat and that proactive actions can be planned to reduce that threat or to equip the organisation to deal with that threat. So, strategy-making can be seen as a pre-emptive strike against risk, threat, or challenge, a way to embrace it as opposed to deal with it. On the other hand, risk must also be factored into the implementation of a strategy once it is designed, and, with project and operational risk assessment and management, strategic thinkers must consider the potential issues that could arise in the implementation of their strategies and plan actions to handle them.

Nevertheless, the process is mostly the same, as demonstrated in Table 2.10.

TABLE 2.10 The Process of Risk Assessment and Management at Operational, Project, and Strategic Levels

Operational	Project	Strategy-making
Identify the risk • Technical • Financial • People • Environment	Identify the risk • Financial • Technical • Commercial • Execution • Legal • People/stakeholders/ environmental/ social	Identify the threat or challenge: P E S T L E
Assess/evaluate it	Assess/evaluate it	Assess/evaluate it
• Probability of the risk occurring (the likelihood of a particular outcome actually happening). • The impact of it occurring (the effect or result of a particular outcome actually happening). There are a number of risk assessment tools available, including assigning 'low, medium, or high' to probability and impact, or assigning numbers to show degrees of probability and impact.		
Plan ways to minimise or eradicate the risk	Plan ways to minimise or eradicate the risk	Plan ways to embrace the threat or challenge
Choose an appropriate response	Choose an appropriate response	Choose an appropriate strategic response
Build this response into the plan	Build this response into the plan	Implement the strategy
Monitor	Monitor	Monitor

CASE STUDY 2.3

An Assessment of Strategic Risks

Adam Parsons is Consultant from a Big Four Consultancy with a focus on the energy and natural resources sector. As such, he advises a wide range of clients on navigating the strategic opportunities and challenges associated with the energy transition and the move towards a net zero society. In the following case study, he talks about risk in strategy-making.

'Risk and strategy are too often conflated, and good strategies are often put aside because of what in many ways are more practical risks that could be worked through and shouldn't inhibit the development of the overarching plans. Yes, implementation needs to be part of strategy, but there does also need to be that distinction between what is your overarching aim and what are the kinds of modular steps to getting to that.

'In terms of risk appetite, we're in a very uncertain world right now. And we've seen lots of commitments to invest in perhaps some of the riskier elements of that world in the renewables and low carbon space being dialled back by some of the biggest players in the energy sector, and that is concerning. These things need to happen, these changes will have a material impact on the ability of societies to operate in this world in a safe and secure way, and the energy sector is critical to making that happen. That overarching risk aversion is a concern.

'However, I would say that some of the organisations that I've seen to be successful are those that have embraced risk. For example, look at some of the players that in the 1990s, early 2000s were rooted as oil and gas majors in the energy sector, but made a bold decision that they were going to make a complete pivot in strategy. They got their business behind it, recognised that it would require a lot of hard work, engagement with policy-makers, development of new skills and capabilities at pace, an appreciation of new commercial models and new ways of doing things, new ways of treating projects and approving projects. These organisations made that jump early, the risk that they took was very significant and they were in fact in many ways bolder than many organisations would like to be. They were early movers, but ultimately you look at some of those organisations now and they are the largest wind developers in the world and they're the most resistant to some of the shocks and volatile energy prices that we've seen around the world. They saw the opportunities and are now capitalising and building on that.

'This comes back to the point that strategic thinkers need to own a decision, own the overarching goal. Be confident, trust the decisions you're making and not flip-flop every few years in response to changing external conditions.

'There are different types of risk. Strategic risks are:

- How are you going to deliver the strategy that you're setting?
- What are the barriers to entry to delivery: skills barriers, external perceptions, political risks, technical constraints?
- Are there commercial risks and are those risks too big?

'These strategic risks need to be distinguished from the practical, day-to-day risks and it is often those practical risks that inhibit people from pursuing perhaps some of the bolder, more ambitious strategies because people too often get distracted by some of the more practical and the easier-to-think-about risks because they are more straightforward to understand and it is easier to recognise the impact of them, but ultimately those are practical project-based risks, not ones that should inhibit development of overarching strategies. For those practical risks, mitigations can be implemented down the line and don't need to be answered at the upfront point that you're developing a strategy.'

When considering risk, there are also some overarching challenges to consider, of prediction, a collaborative approach, and reputation.

Prediction

Prediction of what might happen is difficult and uncertain: 'Forecasts aren't facts: they're the best predictions experts have' (Coulter, 2013, p. 81). We are always operating in an unknown environment, and we cannot possibly know the future. We tend to do our best within the parameters of what has happened before and what we know to predict what might happen next, although some creative thinkers can imagine beyond those boundaries (Steve Jobs used to question why Apple would ask its customers what they wanted, as *they* couldn't possibly imagine the possibilities, whereas he could).

There is also the issue of optimism bias 'which drives us to favor (sic) information that supports our positions (typically successes) and suppress information that contradicts them (typically failures). When events depart from our expectations, we tend to escalate commitment, irrationally directing even more resources to our failed course of action – throwing good money after bad' (Kaplan & Mikes, 2012, pp. 51–52). Hence the point from Maylor that the only people who give reliable estimates are depressed (Maylor, 2010).

Collaborative Approach

We can accept that operational management is different from project management is different from strategic thinking, but all of these levels of management, leadership, and thinking have a small system going on around them, including people, the environment, the organisation, and as with the size of the risk due to complexity and size, the size of the system also changes. But the approach should be the same. Given that systems thinking is relevant at all levels, it makes sense to collect views from the variety of perspectives operating within that system to draw out as much information as possible. This also reduces the risk of subjectivity, and the inability to imagine the possibilities (and restrictions) on practice.

Reputation

Finally, a point on reputation. An inability to assess and manage risk appropriately at all levels can be damaging to an organisation in terms of its reputation. Reputation is a valuable, intangible asset that, when good can meet the VRIO criteria (Valuable, Rare, Inimitable, or Organisationally embedded) and its inimitability (its inability to be copied) is likely to make it a strong resource (Kull et al., 2016).

Summary

Risk Management is relevant at all levels of an organisation and should be used at operational management, project management and in strategy-making. The tools for consideration of risks are largely the same at each level, although the impact of a strategic decision, given its wide-reaching consequences for the system of which it is a part, is likely to be large.

CHAPTER SUMMARY

This chapter has considered the management and leadership subjects of operational management, project management, survival and crisis management, change management, VMV and planning tools, and risk management, showing how these subjects complement strategic thinking and strategy-making. Figure 2.7 shows the interplay of these subjects with strategy, its development, and its implementation.

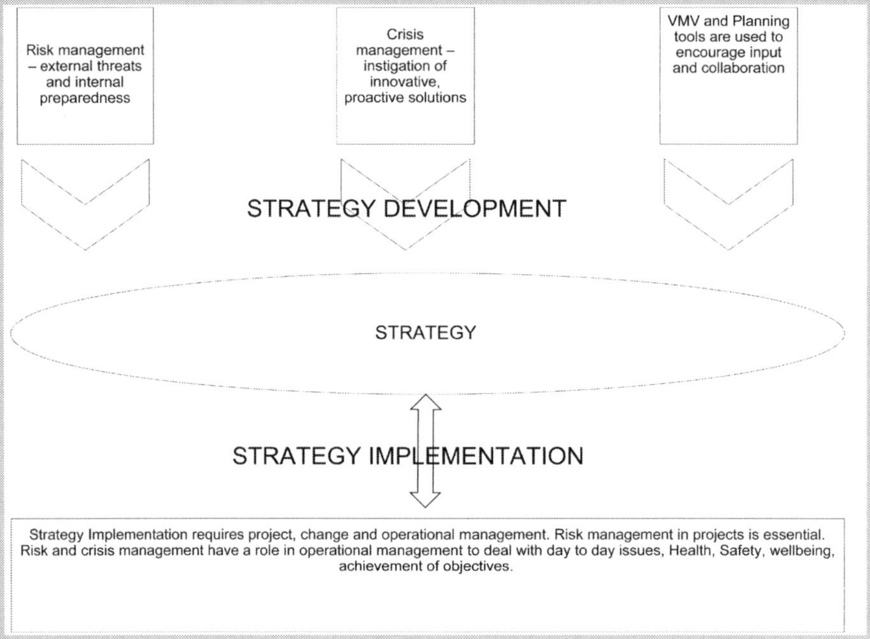

FIGURE 2.7 The Complements to Strategic Thinking

RECOMMENDED READING

Whittington, R., Angwin, D., Regner, P., Johnson, G. & Scholes, K. (2023) *Exploring Strategy* (13th ed.). Harlow: Pearson Education.

REFERENCES

Abdullah, Z., Nordin, S.M. & Aziz Y.A. (2013) Building a unique online corporate identity. *Marketing Intelligence & Planning,* 31(5), 451–471. doi:10.1108/mip-04-2013-0057.

Ansoff, H. I. (1965) *Corporate Strategy*. London: Penguin.

APM (2019) *Business Case*. Retrieved February 1, 2019 from https://www.apm.org.uk/body-of-knowledge/delivery/integrative-management/business-case/.

Barney, J. (1991). Firm resources and sustained competitive advantage. *Journal of Management*, 17(1), 99–120.

Barney, J.B. (1997). *Gaining and Sustaining Competitive Advantage*. Reading, MA: Addison Wesley.

Bower, M. (1966) *The Will to Manage: Corporate Success Through Programmed Management*. New York: McGraw-Hill.

Bridges, W. (1992) *Managing Transitions*. London: Nicholas Brealey Publishing.

Burnes, B. (2004a) Kurt Lewin and the planned approach to change: A re-appraisal. *Journal of*
Management Studies, 41(6), 977–1002.

Burnes, B. (2004b) Kurt Lewin and complexity theories: Back to the future? *Journal of Change*
Management, 4(4), 309–325.

Carnall, C.A. (1995) *Managing Change in Organisations* (2nd ed.). London: Prentice-Hall International, UK.

Chan Kim, W. & Mauborgne, R. (2024) *Fair Process*. Retrieved January 9, 2024 from https://www.blueoceanstrategy.com/tools/fair-process/.

Chun, R. & Davies, G. (2001) E-reputation: The role of mission and vision statements in positioning strategy. *Journal of Brand Management*, 8(4/5), 315–333. doi:10.1057/palgrave.bm.2540031.

Cooke-Davies, T.J., Crawford, L.H. & Lechler, T.G. (2009) Project management systems: Moving project management from an operational to a strategic discipline. *Project Management Journal*, March, 110–123. Wiley InterScience. doi: 10.1002/pmj.

Cope, M. (2010) *The Seven Cs of Consultancy* (3rd ed.). London: Financial Times Publishing.

Coulter, M.K. (2013). *Strategic Management in Action* (6th ed.). Harlow: Pearson Education.

Creasey, T. (2022) *Project Management and Change Management: A Side-by-side Comparison*. Retrieved September 29, 2022 from https://www.prosci.com/blog/change-management-and-project-management-comparison.

Crick, J.M. & Crick, D. (2020) Coopetition and COVID-19: Collaborative business-to-business marketing strategies in a pandemic crisis. *Industrial Marketing Management*, 88, 206–213. https://doi.org/10.1016/j.indmarman.2020.05.016.

Cummings, S., Bridgman, T. & Brown, K.G. (2015) Unfreezing change as three steps: Rethinking Kurt Lewin's legacy for change management. *Human Relations*, 69(1), 33–60. doi: 10.1177/0018726715577707.

Davies, G., Chun, R., da Silva, V. & Roper, S. (2003) *Corporate Reputation and Competitiveness*. London: Routledge.

de Chernatony, L., Cottam, S. & Segal-Horn, S. (2006) Communicating services brands' values internally and externally. *Service Industries Journal*, 26(8), 819–836. doi:10.1080/02642060601011616.

de Chernatony, L. & Segal-Horn, S. (2003) The criteria for successful services brands. *European Journal of Marketing*, 37(7/8), 1095–1118. doi:10.1108/03090560310477681.

Desmidt, S. & Prinzi, A.A. (2008) The impact of mission statements: An empirical analysis from a sense-making perspective. *Academy of Management Proceedings*, 55, 1–6. doi:10.5465/ambpp.2008.33716826.

Dowling, G. & Moran, P. (2012) Corporate reputation: Built in or bolted on? *California Management Review*, 54(2), 25–34. doi:10.1525/cmr.2012.54.2.25.

Drucker, P.F. (1966) *The Effective Executive*. New York: Harper & Row.

Granovetter, M.S. (1973) The strength of weak ties. *American Journal of Sociology*, 78(6), 1360–1380. http://www.jstor.org/stable/2776392.

Gregory, L. (2016) Amazon.com Inc's vision and mission statement (an analysis). *Business Management* (Panmore Institute), July 21.

Haslam, S. & Shenoy, B. (2018) *Strategic Decision Making: A Discovery-led Approach to Critical Choices in Turbulent Times*. London: Kogan Page.

Hinton, K.E. (2022) Components of a strategic plan align institutional mission, vision, and values through the strategic planning process. Book excerpt. *Planning for Higher Education* V50N4 July–September, 30–33. The Society for College and University Planning. taken from SCUP's recently released *Second Edition of A Practical Guide to Strategic Planning in Higher Education*.

Hirota, S., Kubo, K., Miyajima, H. P. & Young Won, P. (2010) Corporate mission, corporate policies and business outcomes: Evidence from Japan. *Management Decision*, 48(7), 1134–1153. doi:10.1108/00251741011068815.

Homans, G. (1950) *The Human Group*. New York: Harcourt, Brace & World.

Hou, J., Du, L. & Tian, Z. (2009) The effects of non-profit brand equity on individual giving intention: Mediating by the self-concept of individual donor. *International Journal of Nonprofit and Voluntary Sector Marketing*, 14(3), 215–229. doi:10.1002/nvsm.356.

i (2019) Letters page. July 10.

Ingenhoff, D. & Fuhrer, T. (2010) Positioning and differentiation by using brand personality attributes. *Corporate Communications: An International Journal*, 15(1), 83–101. doi:10.1108/13563281011016859.

Isabelle, D., Horak, K., McKinnon, S. & Palumbo, C. (2020) Is Porter's Five Forces framework still relevant? A study of the capital/labour intensity continuum via mining and IT industries. *Technology Innovation Management Review*, 10(6), 28–41.

Jaffe, D.T., Tobe, G. & Tobe, G. (1993) *Organizational Vision, Values and Mission*. Course Technology Crisp.

Johnson, G., Whittington, R., Scholes, K., Angwin, D. & Regner, P. (2017) *Exploring Strategy: Text & Cases* (11th ed.). Harlow: Pearson Education.

Kantabutra, S. & Avery, G.C. (2010) The power of vision: Statements that resonate. *Journal of Business Strategy*, 31(1), 37–45. doi:10.1108/02756661011012769.

Kaplan, R.S. & Mikes, A. (2012) Managing risks: A new framework. *Harvard Business Review*. Retrieved February 22, 2024 from https://hbr.org/2012/06/managing-risks-a-new-framework.

Keller, E.W., Dato-on, C. & Shaw, D. (2010) NPO branding: Preliminary lessons from major players. *International Journal of Non-profit and Voluntary Sector Marketing*, 15(1),105–121. doi:10.1002/nvsm.361.

Kotter, J.P. (1996) *Leading Change*. Boston, MA: Harvard Business School Press.

Kotter, J.P. (2014) *Accelerate: Building Strategic Agility for a Faster-moving World*. Cambridge, MA: Harvard Business Publishing.

Kull, A.J., Mena, J.A. & Korschun, D. (2016) A resource-based view of stakeholder marketing. *Journal of Business Research*, 69, 5553–5560.

Le, D. & Phi, G. (2021) Strategic responses of the hotel sector to COVID-19: Toward a refined pandemic crisis management framework. *International Journal of Hospitality Management*, 94, April. https://doi.org/10.1016/j.ijhm.2020.102808.

Lewin, K. (1947) Frontiers in group dynamics: Concept, method and reality in social science; equilibrium and social change. *Human Relations*, 1(1), 5–41.

Liedtka, J.M. (1998) Strategic thinking: Can it be taught? *Long Range Planning*, February.

Maylor, H. (2010) *Project Management* (4th ed.). London: Pearson.

McGrath, R.G. (2013) *The End of Competitive Advantage: How to Keep Your Strategy Moving as Fast as Your Business*. Cambridge, MA: Harvard Business Review Press.

Meredith, J.R., Mantel, S.J. & Shafer, S.M. (2016) *Project Management – A Managerial Approach* (9th ed.). London: John Wiley & Sons.

Mirvis, P., Googins, B. & Kinnicutt, S. (2010) Vision, mission, values: Guideposts to sustainability. *Organizational Dynamics*, 39, 316–324. doi:10.1016/j.orgdyn.2010.07.006.

Nonaka, I. & Zhu, Z. (2012) *Pragmatic Strategy: Eastern Wisdom, Global Success*. Cambridge: Cambridge University Press.

Otubanjo, O. (2012) Embedding theory in corporate identity through the social construction lens. *International Journal of Business and Management*, 7(22), 62–75. doi:10.5539/ijbm.v7n22p62.

Otubanjo, B.O. & Melewar, T.C. (2007) Understanding the meaning of corporate identity: A conceptual and semiological approach. *Corporate Communications: An International Journal*, 12(4),414–432. doi:10.1108/13563280710832542.

Peters, T.J. & Waterman, R.H. (1982) *In Search of Excellence: Lessons from America's Best-run Companies*. New York: Harper and Row.

PMI (Project Management Institute) (2017) *A Guide to the Project Management Body of Knowledge (PMBOK Guide)* (6th ed.). PA: PMI.

Porter, M.E. (1985) *Competitive Advantage: Creating and Sustaining Superior Performance*. New York: Free Press.

Quigley, J.V. (1994) Vision: How leaders develop it, share it, and sustain it. *Business Horizons*, 37(5), 37–41. doi:10.1016/0007-6813(94)90017-5.

Rosen, D. (2023) It's all about culture: Mission, vision, values exercises in non-profits. *Board Leadership*, September/October. Wiley Periodicals.

Schelini, A.L.S., Martens, C.D.P. & Garcez, M.P. (2017) Project management as a competitive advantage for the internationalization of Brazilian companies. *Internext – Review of International Business*, 12(3), 1–15.

Slack, N. (2009) *Operations and Process Management: Principles and Practice for Strategic Impact* (2nd ed.). Harlow: Financial Times/Prentice Hall.

Smith, P.R. (1998) *Marketing Communications – An Integrated Approach* (2nd ed.). London: Kogan Page.

Sneyd, K.P. & Rowley, J. (2004) Linking strategic objectives and operational performance: An action research-based exploration. *Measuring Business Excellence*, 8(3), 42–51. https://doi.org/10.1108/13683040410555609.

Soosay, C., Fearne, A. & Dent, B. (2012) Sustainable value chain analysis – a case study of Oxford Landing from 'vine to dine'. *Supply Chain Management An International Journal*, January. doi: 10.1108/13598541211212212.

Spear, S. (2017) Impression management activity in vision, mission, and values statements: A comparison of commercial and charitable organizations. *International Studies of Management & Organization*, 47(2), 159–175, doi: 10.1080/00208825.2017.1256165.

Suvatjis, J.Y. & de Chernatony, L. (2005) Corporate identity modelling: A review and presentation of a new multidimensional model. *Journal of Marketing Management*, 21(7–8), 809–834. doi:10.1362/026725705774538480.

Turner, R. (2014) Projects and their management. In R. Turner (Ed.), *Gower Handbook of Project Management* (5th ed.). Farnham: Gower.

UK Parliament (2024) HS2: Update following Northern leg cancellation – Committees – UK Parliament. Retrieved November 27, 2024 from https://committees.parliament.uk/work/8581/hs2-update-following-northern-leg-cancellation/#:~:text=The%20Committee%E2%80%99s%20February%202024%20report%20found%20that%20the,oversight%20over%20spiraling%20costs%20after%20years%20of%20warnings.

Verma, H.V. (2009–2010) Mission statements: A study of intent and influence. *Journal of Services Research*, 9(2), 153–172.

Verschoor, C.C. (2005) Is there financial value in corporate values? *Strategic Finance*, 87(1), 17–18.

Weihrich, H. (1982) The TOWS matrix --A tool for situational analysis. *Long Range Planning*, 15(2), 54–66.

Whittington, R., Regnér, P., Angwin, D., Johnson, G. & Scholes, K. (2020) *Exploring Strategy, Text & Cases* (12th ed.). Harlow: Pearson Education.

Whittington, R., Angwin, D, Regner, P., Johnson, G. & Scholes, K. (2023) *Exploring Strategy* (13th ed.). Harlow: Pearson Education.

CHAPTER 3

The Strategic Thinker's Guide to Politics

Peter Wells

CHAPTER OUTLINE

This chapter explains the dominant themes in the relationship between business and politics, from self-interest and leader power to maximise self-interest, individualism, and economic profit, to the modern, arguably more mundane strategic management view where governments and politics are seen as outside influences which must be taken account of in a passive way.

This chapter challenges those themes and explains how the modern, complex environment requires strategic thinkers to think differently, both about their business or organisation and their relationship with politics and policy-making.

To aid the strategic thinker, this chapter shows how the current challenges facing business are grounded in a longer understanding of the relationship between business and policy-making and politics. It also supplies some models for understanding policy-making, including Factors for Policy Analysis and the Stages Model of Policy-making. By discussing these models, the strategic thinker is guided as to how they might get involved and change their relationship with politics and policy-makers to encourage economic, social, and environmental sustainability.

The chapter ends with key challenges for the strategic thinker – tips on what they might do to optimise their organisation's ability to tackle the political landscape.

DOI: 10.4324/9781003475545-3

KEY POINTS

- Strategy-making has always been entwined with politics, yet models of the relationship between strategy-making and politics either stress the self-interest and power of leaders' concept or the business as at the mercy of politics and policy-making.
- Strategic thinkers need to educate themselves as to the evolution of approaches to policy-making to understand their own role and influence.
- Strategic thinkers face a series of tensions in marshalling and building capabilities but also in navigating the tensions of how they work from outside a political system and how they can work within a political system.
- Lobbying and advocacy approaches are considered as tools to aid strategic thinkers to influence the political landscape.
- Strategic thinkers *can* shape responses to political, social, and economic levels at local to global levels and to polycrisis-type challenges.

CHALLENGING THE DOMINANT THEMES IN THE RELATIONSHIP BETWEEN BUSINESS AND POLITICS

Strategy has traditionally seen the political arena through two lenses: power and self-interest, and analytical paralysis.

Power and Self-interest

First is the recourse to the ideas of Machiavelli (1532; see 1988 translation): namely that the role of any leader whether in business or politics is to retain power and to use that power for their own ends. Leaders adopt the cunning of the fox and the power of the lion and apply these assiduously to all situations they face. The metaphor of the fox and the lion is powerful, it is easy to understand, and analogies can be easily drawn on to show leaders acting with cunning and power.

But the metaphor and especially subsequent analogies are dangerous: they reflect an economically liberal model where the business and political leader acts as though everyone is a rational economic actor or homo economicus (Macaulay & Lawton, 2003), meaning that leaders pursue first and foremost the maximisation of wealth as the preeminent form of the pursuit of self-interest (Tittenbrun, 2013). This economic idea can be traced from Adam Smith (1776) and John Stuart Mill (1874) and has held sway and influenced business and economic decision-making for the best part of two centuries. Now may be the time to challenge this idea.

Analytical Paralysis

Second, and more narrowly, modern management requires leaders to weigh different systematic risks and to respond accordingly. This is the basis for approaches such as PESTLE (Political, Economic, Social, Technological, Legal, and Environmental) as already discussed in Chapter 2. Political factors and their influence can be assessed through:

- **Government stability** (especially in terms of providing economic stability for businesses)
- **Rule of law** (including freedom of speech and extent of corruption)
- **Ideological bases** (including balance between regulation and liberalisation)
- **Economic policy** (including tax policy, trade controls, and interest rate setting)
- **Major risks** (including war, terrorism, and severe social and environmental change)
- **Elections** (including volatility in the approach to policy-making)
- **Institution building and development** (for instance, the idea that some institutions such as independent central banks support economic stability).

Each of these factors can provide a helpful guide to leaders and a framework for identifying and mitigating key risks. For instance, anticipating a regulatory change following an election and preparing a business response is likely to be vital for sustaining a business, regardless of sector.

However, there are also the risks that such frameworks lead to a paralysis of analysis or perhaps worse a tick-box exercise. What pervades each of these 'big P' political risks is essentially an emphasis that the role of government, beyond providing security, is to provide stability for businesses to maximise wealth and there is a sense that strategy-makers are in a one-way relationship with politics and policy-makers and at the mercy of their decisions. That too is a relationship that can now be challenged.

LIMITATIONS OF AND CHALLENGES TO THE DOMINANT THEMES

These approaches to strategy-making's relationship with politics have a series of limitations and challenges:

- **Misreading of history:** The application of philosophical metaphors and analogies from Aristotle, Niccolo Machiavelli, or Adam Smith is often simplistic at best and dangerous at worst. Aristotle, Machiavelli's or Smith's work is frequently poorly understood and consistently applied with little understanding of historical context or its location within a wider philosophical and social discourse. As was discussed in Chapter 1 when challenging the 'war metaphor' for strategy-making, these comparisons are likely unhelpful in contemporary strategy-making.
- **Level playing fields:** All businesses in some ways are affected by and engage with policy-making, even if it is just the process of paying taxes on profits, following planning rules, or the consistent reporting of business activities. In most developed economies a function of government has been to provide consistency or what can be understood as a level regulatory playing field. This is true of a local government applying planning policy, through to the European Union ensuring

consistency in the application of product standards. However, since the rise of transnational corporations and more recently of globalisation, business leaders have to varying extents been able to operate beyond the boundaries of individual states. This is not necessarily a new phenomenon but one which has accelerated since the 1980s (Gamble, 2019). The scope for politics, at least in the form of nation states, has become more limited. The political realm for business remains critical, but for businesses and business leaders able to operate across states there has come the opportunity to exert greater leverage of the decisions of individual states (Wilkinson, 2014).

- **Business agency:** The PESTLE approach is helpful as a starting point but is weak in terms of a deeper understanding of how businesses can, do, and perhaps should, engage with the policy-making process. PESTLE suggests that all businesses have no agency over their external operating environment. This is not the case. However, engagement of business in politics is a contested area.

  The position of the political and libertarian right is that the role of government is to ensure security at a national level (the protection of national borders) and to preserve the rights of businesses to maximise value for shareholders. A variant of this is that businesses should, like individual citizens, be seen as constituents of government. This is essentially a model of corporatist government where government is for the benefit of companies.

  Conversely, a social democratic and more left-leaning position would be that while government can preserve and enhance institutions that support markets, these markets are not unbridled. That is, markets, are an effective but not perfect means to deliver benefits to people and ensure other things, such as the preservation of nature or provision of welfare. These tensions have always existed in capitalism and have shaped how business leaders engage in political arenas. How strategic thinkers engage with politics reflects a need to move beyond narrow rationalist models of the firm and to think around the wider influences (positive and negative) that businesses have.

- **Broader business objectives:** Company law in the UK and USA but increasingly elsewhere has embedded the idea that the primary duty of the company is to its shareholders, and that this primary duty is to maximise shareholder value. In extremis this position can be taken as one over and above the long-term sustainability of the company. The interests of employees or the environment can be secondary to ensuring that shareholder value increases (Froud et al., 2000). These views are being increasingly challenged from local to global levels and by the emergence of commitments to a broader set of objectives and to the management of organisations for wider societal and environmental benefits. The work of Raworth (2017) exemplifies this approach and the call for businesses to work within existing planetary boundaries and to consider their impacts on their workers and other stakeholders. Similarly, legislation by the Welsh Government in the Well-being of Future Generations Act 2015 – while the focus of this Act is on public bodies in Wales – also means that any business engaging with public bodies in Wales is now expected to comply with the aims of the Act. Decision-making, whether through the lens of planetary boundaries or future generations, is about more than the maximisation of shareholder value (Jones et al., 2020). This challenges the traditional view of political and business leaders following blindly the maximisation of wealth.

WHAT DOES A STRATEGIC THINKER NEED TO KNOW?

- To aid the strategic thinker, the next section of this chapter explores the dominant themes of the last 100 years in the relationship between strategy-makers and politics and approaches to policy-making.
- The chapter then outlines how the forces shaping policy can be understood and the critical importance of understanding the stages of policy-making.
- The following sections then explore the practices of lobbying and advocacy in more detail.
- The chapter concludes with the political risks facing business and, more positively, how new models of strategic business thinking can respond to, and not exacerbate, the challenges of volatility and uncertainty.

CHANGING APPROACHES TO POLITICS AND PUBLIC POLICY-MAKING

Politics and public administration in the twenty-first century are undergoing dramatic change. The certainties which governments had in the mid-twentieth century are being undermined and challenged due to VUCA or the ongoing polycrisis in the face of the existential and related threats of climate change, poverty, migration, and war (Lawrence et al., 2024). Hindsight is always helpful for understanding the relative scale of past concerns and is sometimes useful in understanding the shaping of future crises.

At least for the first part of the twentieth century the key concerns facing policy-makers were around globalisation and the pluralisation of service provision: policy problems have come to be less simple, linear, and national and instead more complex, wicked, and global in nature. Policy-makers have sought to respond to and reorientate models of public policy to these challenges, while at the same time preserving the basic model of the nation state which has been the foundation of most Western democracies for over 150 years.

The basis of 'traditional' models of public administration in the nation state are that the following are in place:

- A separation between elected politicians and the administration, with independently appointed administrators
- Administration is continuous, predictable, and rule-governed
- Administrators are trained professionals who are appointed on merit
- There is a functional division of labour, and a hierarchy of tasks and people
- Resources belong to the organisation, not to the individuals who work in it
- Public servants serve the public rather than the private interest.

At the heart of this model is that there is a clear separation of powers between executives (the government), legislatures (the parliament), and the enforcement of laws (the judiciary). In this model the civil service is independent and services the elected government.

To understand how and why policy has changed it is useful to understand how different approaches sought to respond to different problems or questions; this has been explored in a report for the United Nations which explains how the questions or challenges governments have faced have changed over time (Global Centre for Global Public Service Excellence (GCPSE), 2015).

1. **How can we put government on an orderly and efficient footing?** Addressing this question was the founding basis for forming democratic government and then building its capacity to act.
2. **How can government get closer to the people?** From the nineteenth century democratic government was often portrayed as being aloof from the concerns of the people. Initially this was the impetus for the building of local government but throughout the twentieth century there has been a pressure to further decentralise power (to regions, localities, and to neighbourhoods).
3. **How can government be more affordable?** The post-World War Two expansion of the state in Western democracies was essential to sharing the benefits of economic prosperity of the post-war era. However, as economies struggled and governments were faced with growing pressures to provide welfare and social security, so the role of the state was challenged on the basis that it had reached too far into the lives of citizens. The rallying call since the late 1970s for many on the political right has been to cut the size of government and to make it more affordable to tax payers.
4. **How can government better deliver its objectives?** Allied to calls for smaller government were also calls for it to achieve the same objectives but with less. An approach called New Public Management emerged which sought to solve the problems of government by better leadership and management practices.
5. **How can government be more accountable?** From the 1990s but perhaps accelerated since the global financial crisis of 2008 has been calls by the public, by business, and by civil society organisations such as charities for government to be more accountable. This has occurred through stronger practices of scrutiny by parliaments of executives and a more consultative model of government.
6. **How can government be more responsive to citizens?** Since the 1990s there has been a rapid expansion of interest in forms of deliberative democracy – where citizens are given much greater direct control over decision-making. The most prominent examples are the rise of models of participatory budgeting (for instance, where a neighbourhood is given a proportion of the public budget to control) or citizens' assemblies where representative samples of a population are engaged in a process of deliberation of key political agendas (from reproductive rights to climate change to assisted dying).
7. **How can government respond to polycrisis problems?** This is the current most live issue facing all governments and one which is driving increasing division in international politics. For the United Nations and other intergovernmental mechanisms

of governing (such as the European Union or the World Bank), the solutions lie with far greater efforts to coordinate activities at a global or continental level. But there are other models, from greater isolationism and withdrawal from a 'world order' to states seeking to increase their regional power through economic and militaristic means.

The global (e.g. UN, World Bank and IMF) and regional (e.g. EU) were solutions and models essentially developed and led by Western democracies in the aftermath of World War Two. They sought to put an end to war and bring stability through coordinated economic (but also social and environmental) action. How they are remade in the twenty-first century and a simultaneous period of polycrisis but also (imbalanced) economic growth (in Asia, Africa, and South America) is a central challenge not just for policy-makers but also for business and other stakeholders.

Table 3.1 outlines how models of politics and approaches to public management have reflected a wider economic context. The dominant model of delivery was around New Public Management but there was growing interest in New Public Service and Open Public Services. In the latter there is no ideological bias towards who delivers the services, only that they meet pre-specified standards and are responsive to citizens. The global financial crisis and subsequent recession led to a period of public policy retrenchment and a politics of austerity. This period has been termed the 'Great Unsettlement'. The certainties of the previous period, the guarantee of a specified social security safety net, and a social contract between government and its citizens have come under extreme pressure (Brewis et al., 2021).

The Great Unsettlement in public policy has been a precursor to what has been termed an era of polycrisis (Lawrence et al., 2024) which includes the Covid-19 pandemic, climate change, wars in Ukraine and Gaza, and large-scale migration/displacement of populations. At the root of the polycrisis are seen to be the generation of fast-moving crises with international reach (e.g. war) meeting with deep-seated and slow-moving stresses already facing states (e.g. the ageing population). It is the combination of these forces (fast-moving crises and slow-moving stresses) which then push established orders out of equilibrium.

TABLE 3.1 Timeline of Economic and Public Management Change

	1950s–1970s	1970s–1980s	1990s–2008	2008 onwards	2015 onwards
Economic context	Cold War; Stable economic conditions in the West; Low unemployment	Crisis in world economic system; Structural economic change	Globalisation; 'Great Moderation'; Free trade; Opening of new markets	Crisis in world financial system; 'Great Unsettlement'; Austerity economics	Polycrisis; Breakdown of model of economic growth; Conflict
Approach to public management	Old Public Administration	New Public Management (NPM)		NPM and emergence of New Service Management and Open Public Services	

Management of these crises – by business, political, or civil society leaders – is extremely difficult. In part this is for reasons of extreme complexity with only sub-optimal outcomes seemingly apparent. Critically, democratically elected leaders have institutional constraints and are likely, without wider political and societal consensus, to focus on solving immediate problems, when longer term problems require coordinated and consensual decision-making. The complexity in the nature of the events, and their volatility, means that poor decisions or adverse situations can quickly escalate and lead to extreme outcomes. These forces place incredible pressures on the effective functioning of democratic government.

WHAT CAN A STRATEGIC THINKER DO? LEARNING FROM FACTORS FOR POLITICAL AND POLICY ANALYSIS AND THE STAGES MODEL OF POLICY-MAKING

If policy-making and politics is becoming increasingly complex, volatile, and contested, what are the starting points for strategic thinking in relation to politics? How can a strategic thinker unpick complexity to formulate and implement strategy?

This section introduces two main frameworks:

1. The factors which lie behind political analysis
2. The stages model of policy-making.

The section concludes with consideration of different strategies which may be taken by strategic thinkers.

Factors for Political and Policy Analysis

John (2013) reviews the following five factors which shape the policy-making process: *institutions; groups and networks; societal and economic values; individual interests;* and *ideas*. These factors have been at the heart of policy analysis. Each provides a different way to understand how policy is made.

Institutions

Political science has historically been rooted in the study of institutions: the executive, the legislature, and the judiciary. These have been seen as clearly defined bodies which evolve and change in predictable ways. In most functioning democratic nations they remain the key foci for attention. However, as March and Olsen (1989) recognise, there is an urgent need to recognise that 'social, political, and economic institutions have become larger, considerably more complex and resourceful, and prima facie more important to collective life' (p. 734). Lowndes (2017) takes this further and identifies areas in which policy-making needs to be understood (p. 59):

- Institutions should be less understood as bounded organisations and more as sets of rules
- Institutions should be seen less as formal bodies but more informally, for instance, with porous boundaries
- Institutions are dynamic and not static
- Values play a key role in the purpose and approach of institutions and shape decisions and outcomes
- Institutions should be seen in a disaggregated way
- Institutions should be seen as being embedded within wider social, political, and economic structures – they do not act independently.

Further insights into the role of institutions have been brought by the seminal work of North (1990) which highlighted the evolutionary nature of institutions. He invoked a more critical approach to institutions and their collective impact on outcomes (for North, on economic performance) and how these are often shaped by path-dependent and long-term factors.

The implication for the strategic thinker is to begin to see the policy-making process more critically, with a nuanced and changing understanding of rules, of decision-making, and critically of change being required.

Groups and Networks

Why do businesses form industry associations and civil society organisations form umbrella bodies? In part they are seeking to support their memberships. Part of this is to ensure that policy-makers are better informed about the needs of companies and civil society. Membership bodies do work alone, especially the largest, such as the Confederation of British Industry (CBI), but they also form networks: for instance, a network of environmental charities seeking to improve biodiversity regulation.

There is a long literature of how companies and civil society organisations come together to shape and influence policy. In the UK these have been termed policy networks and span loosely aligned 'issue networks' through to much more tightly formed policy communities (Lowndes & Roberts, 2013). In whatever form of policy network, the network reaches out beyond a narrow group of members to include policy officials, politicians, and other interested parties. In the USA these groups are termed policy advocacy coalitions. A key goal of policy networks is the influence of policy. From a value-neutral perspective such influencing activities can be seen as being benign and simply to ensure policy becomes more effective. From a more critical perspective, such influence, and the mobilisation of resources through networks, is malignant and enters the realm of corruption.

Network formation by organisations is largely seen as a means to share information and support strategic capacity. It improves information flows and reduces the risks to businesses of adverse shocks. For policy-makers, network formation has become a key part of the policy-making process and it is recognised that it should be bound by rules. The effectiveness of such endeavours is another matter and would largely be seen to reflect power and resources: larger, better resourced networks simply have more opportunities to form close-knit relations with key policy-makers. The strength of such networks is often seen as how resilient they are to political change: the most successful are able to operate effectively regardless of which mainstream party is in power.

The implication for the strategic thinker is to investigate groups and networks to which they could belong.

Societal and Economic Values

Approaches to policy-making vary between countries. In part this is due to differing constitutions and organisational arrangements. Two seminal studies have sought to understand this in more detail. The first is Esping-Anderson (1990) which argues that national differences are not shaped by autonomous market forces and trends towards post-industrialisation but by deeply institutionalised and socially constructed processes. His work holds that three broad groupings of democratic welfare states can be identified: an Anglo-American one (including the USA and UK but also Australia and New Zealand), a Scandinavian one (formed on high levels of redistribution and social solidarity), and a mainstream European one (formed around principles of social democracy). Hall and Soskice (2001), in their work on varieties of capitalism, take a similar line and find clear institutionalised and social differences between states. Unlike Esping-Anderson, the work of Hall and Soskice is less categorical in terms of defining specific state types. It is instead more relational, both in terms of how firms operate and the role, for example, of industrial relations; and how states regulate and institutionalise certain types of activity. Examples would include the role of finance in relation to the market (is it focused on a banking model or institutionalised in a stock market), and the levels of porosity of national economies (for instance, their exposure to international trade and capital movements).

Both approaches to understanding the role of societal and economic factors have been challenged, especially in the face of globalisation. It has been argued that rather than clear differences between national systems, what is more apparent is the rise of convergence around an Anglo-American model of capitalism. This trend held at least until the end of the great moderation and the global financial crisis (see Table 3.1). The period since can be seen less in terms of economic convergence through forces of increasingly integrated economies, and potentially greater national divergence and protectionism.

The implication for the strategic thinker is to understand how economies are shaped by a range of institutional factors. Some may lead to distinctly differing business models – for instance, greater call on bank finance in Germany compared to share equity in the UK which are critical for the success of the business.

Individual Interests

The archetypal model of politics and policy-making is often the one of Machiavelli and the metaphor of the fox and the lion: politicians act using cunning and power. They form coalitions and networks but these are often representations of their own self-interest. This is a vision of rational choice politics. Networks and institutions may exist, but what matters much more are the interests of politicians.

In this understanding of politics, the strategic thinker is, in theory, able to act completely rationally. They will pursue agendas which appear to bring benefits, typically

TABLE 3.2 Business Strategies and Political Responses

Regulatory pressure	Distributional effect	
	Costs>benefits	**Benefits>costs**
Low	Oppose	Abstain
High	Hedge	Support

Source: Adapted from Meckling (2015)

in the form of economic advantage, and they will not pursue agendas for which there is little gain. Meckling (2015) argued, in the context of environmental politics, that the regulatory policies have distributional consequences for firms (some will gain, others lose). Meckling combines this with the notion that policy-makers are able to exert different levels of regulatory pressure. This produces four sets of different responses as outlined in Table 3.2.

In this model two sets of distributional effects are modelled (where costs are greater than benefits, and vice versa) and two sets of regulatory pressure (low and high). These conditions will thus lead to four different behaviours:

- **Opposition**: where costs exceed benefits but where the firm perceives it is able to challenge and resist regulatory pressure. Such an example might be a water utility which can act with some impunity because the regulator has weak powers.
- **Abstention**: where the costs are lower than benefits and the firm is simply able to accept the (weak) regulatory environment (e.g. in the context of food standards which create a level playing field for the firm and benefit all participants).
- **Hedging**: where the firm needs to continue to hold different options before committing to action, which may include exit or resistance (e.g. a tobacco company in which regulation and tax policy will challenge its existence without seeking new market opportunities in lower regulatory regimes).
- **Supporting**: where the costs are less than benefits but where regulatory pressure is high. Again, there is a level playing field benefit to compliance but also access to lucrative markets, such as a pharmaceutical company gaining approval for a new product.

This however is not a model of policy-making where all actors or agents are equal. There are significant disparities in power between firms as there are between individuals. Firms or individual citizens may choose different strategies, partly on their perceived benefits to costs and partly on the barriers they face in remaining in or exiting a system. For Hirschman (1970), this is expressed in three ways:

- exit (to leave the system)
- voice (to seek to change the system)
- loyalty (to accept the prevailing rules of the game).

Hirschman's insights are at odds with rational models of policy-making. This is on two grounds: first, that rational models of decision-making are overly simplistic; and second, that there are negative consequences from decision-making. Individual interest models are an ideal type of policy-making but one in which the ideal is only truly accessible for a few firms.

The implication for the strategic thinker is that they are faced with different decision-making paths in terms of whether and how to engage with policy and politics. For the vast majority of businesses, the chosen route will probably be one of abstention (using Meckling's framework) or loyalty (following Hirschman). Larger, more complicated businesses are likely to choose other courses of engagement.

Ideas

What do institutions, networks, and individuals do? In modern democracies none make policy alone. They operate in tandem in the context of national societal and economic norms. And what they convert to policy often comes from ideas – the basis for policies whether ideological, technocratic, or simply expedient and contingent. Political parties need ideas to fuel their manifestos and campaigns to win elections. Ideas can mean everything (e.g. New Labour's the Third Way between state and market or the UK Coalition Government of the Conservative and Liberal Democrats' Big Society) and at the same time nothing (see also the Third Way and the Big Society). Ideas can help position political parties in terms of what they are not (e.g. a statist model of politics) as much as what they are for (e.g. delivery through markets).

At a more granular level policies are shaped by ideas, often in line with the meta narratives such as the Third Way or Big Society. Ideas can be infused with political values ranging from reactionary to conservative to progressive. Above all, ideas often work within a notion of the overriding model of capitalism or the welfare state which is being pursued.

Ideas used to be formed much more within a tripartite system of government, economic or business, and social partners. While this form of negotiation continues to some extent, idea development is increasingly outsourced to think tanks and advisory groups. Ideas therefore become the currency of policy transfer and knowledge exchange and, at least during the period of the Great Moderation, patterns of policy convergence can be seen. While ideas may be seen to have a value-neutral and technocratic basis, they can also be separated from any apparent evidence of success and represent reflections of supposed better times in the past.

Ideas matter for strategic thinking and strategy-making. They can help businesses align missions positively with wider state missions. An example would be the alignment of business strategy to the UN Sustainable Development Goals (SDGs). The SDGs (listed in Chapter 6) are a collection of ideas as to how sustainable development should be done; but they have political salience and in the medium term represent something with which businesses can align. At national and local levels, business strategy may align to agendas such as zero carbon. Such alignment signals an important direction of travel and potentially increases sales for business. Similarly, businesses operating locally may support specific campaigns and agendas; for instance, committing to a charter for good work and the provision of decent employment.

The implication for the strategic thinker is to understand and respond to current political ideas, although how they engage can be informed by the frameworks developed by Meckling or Hirshman.

Having considered the Factors for Political and Policy Analysis, another model to help strategic thinkers is the Stages Model of Policy-making.

The Stages Model of Policy-making

A common model for understanding policy-making is to break it down into stages. Most policies have some form of gestation or agenda setting and then a series of steps which lead through to legislation and/or funding decisions and implementation. In most cases whether formally or informally, policy-makers seek to learn from the policy development and seek to make improvements.

For the strategic thinker, the major opportunity to shape policy is clearly at the agenda-setting stage. This is when the big decisions are taken, and thought is given to how policies will be implemented. While change can happen in any of the subsequent stages it is this first step which matters for the direction of policy.

The discussion around institutions, groups and networks, societal and economic values, individuals and ideas in many respects matters most in this phase. How interests are mobilised and the opportunity for mobilisations depends on the interplay between all these different factors.

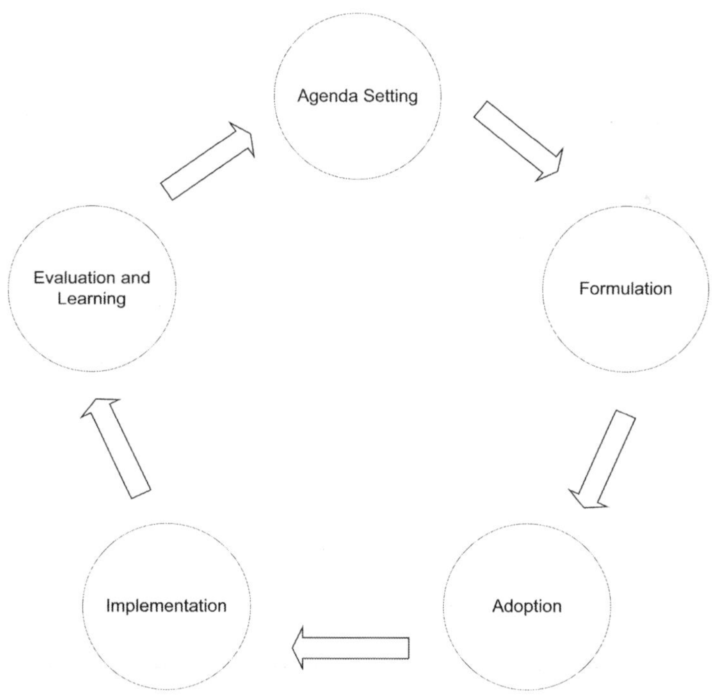

FIGURE 3.1 Policy-making in the Stages Model
Adapted from various outlines of policy stages but drawing most from John (2013)

One of the keynote studies into when and how policies change is contained in Kingdon's (1984) *Agendas, Alternatives and Public Policies*. The model outlined by Kingdon is still heavily cited and influential, as Cairney and Jones (2016) show. Kingdon's foremost contribution was to argue that policies change when there is a confluence of three different streams, what he calls the policy streams model. These three streams are as follows:

- *Problem stream:* policy-makers lack attention or rather they lack the capacity and capability to engage with multiple challenges. They prioritise, sometimes rationally, sometimes irrationally. But when a problem has attention, for instance, due to a crisis or opportunity, there is the *potential* for policy change.
- *Policy stream:* policies can form quickly or slowly. Some need to be formulated based on incomplete and changing information, such as the response to a pandemic. Other ideas take time to formulate and gain acceptance among publics and elites. But there is, as Kingdom describes, a 'policy primeval soup' from which institutions, networks, individuals, and ideas come together to form policies. Typically, and as Kingdom argues, policy entrepreneurs emerge, capable of formulating solutions to opportunities.
- *Politics stream*: finally, politicians need to meld policies to meet their wider agendas, national opinions, and interests of key groups and networks.

Understanding how agendas are formed within a policy streams model is important knowledge for the strategic thinker. It means that resources, networks, and ideas can be marshalled to inform and influence policies at critical junctures. There is no point marshalling resources six months after the agenda was set.

In conditions of volatility, growing complexity of policy problems, and increasing competing interests, it is arguable that policy-making processes, despite recourse to open government, have on the contrary become more curtailed and closed. Policy-makers are faced with much greater levels of 'noise'. This means that strategic business thinkers are likely to have relatively small windows of opportunity to inform or shape the major direction of policy. Outside of this window the opportunity for change is largely limited to informing implementation (for instance, inputting to local development plans) or in understanding the costs and benefits of the policy for the business.

WHAT CAN A STRATEGIC THINKER DO? LOBBYING AND ADVOCACY

Lobbying and advocacy are the most direct expression of how societal and economic interests act 'politically' to secure some form of policy change. This section explores what these terms have meant and what they mean now for strategic thinking and practice. Lobbying and advocacy have advanced considerably in the last century but three features shape both the influence of organisations in the early 1900s and the 2020s.

Structures

Businesses may wish to stimulate myriad changes to policy but ultimately they face choices as to which ones are most likely to succeed. The structures they face – variably discussed as political opportunity structures, policy windows, or punctured equilibria in the academic literature – shape the boundaries of the possible (see previous sections on institutions and networks). Faced with these structures, businesses tend to gravitate towards one of two major options: to influence the state (government policy, regulations, and resources) or the economy (the behaviours and actions of individuals, companies, and civil society organisations). However, this choice is not a simple binary one and more often is around shaping social attitudes which can have a significant bearing on changing policy.

Resources

Resources are more than simply a matter of financial scale – although finance is incredibly important. They are also to do with an organisation's networks (both formal and informal) and its information and knowledge (both codified in, for example, research reports or the insights and experience of staff and partner organisations).

Issues

There is a subject or focus to all lobbying and advocacy in terms of the issues which are raised with policy-makers. More recent research has stressed two features around such issues: first, the way in which they are communicated or 'framed' (for instance, either in terms of a dominant policy discourse or to directly challenge that discourse); and second, whether lobbying and advocacy takes place through an insider strategy (e.g. influence and shaping of policy-making directly) or through an outsider strategy (e.g. through influencing wider public opinion or building a coalition of organisations seeking a change).

There is a rich literature on policy change and policy learning dating back to the 1980s, and this section gives a short outline of some salient features rather than a comprehensive overview. The work of Kingdon (1984) and Sabatier (1988) provide launchpads for much subsequent thinking.

The notion of **advocacy coalitions** (Sabatier, 1988; Baumgartner & Jones, 1991) highlights that lobbying and advocacy are collective endeavours, taking place across organisations and institutions but with shifting priorities and alliances among participants. For Baumgartner and Jones, change occurs at the interface of policy image (*beliefs and values*) and policy venues (*institutions*). It thus involves applying the right rhetoric to the right institutions to make the case for change.

Allied to this work is Rein and Schön's emphasis (1996) on the importance of **framing** in terms of positioning a policy issue as a problem to be addressed, and Hajer's work (1995) on **discourse coalitions**, which again emphasises the importance of creating shared stories of change – but stories that are malleable enough to adapt to changing circumstances and political priorities. Discourse is a key element of 'the dynamics through which ... policy networks are formed, contested, and reconfigured' (Bulkeley, 2014). These themes were taken further by Lakoff's (2014) research examining how progressive agendas could (again) gain policy attention.

A related field of literature concerns **epistemic communities** (Haas, 1992), groups, or networks of experts who by virtue of their position as acknowledged experts are advantaged in framing problems and suggesting solutions. However, expertise can be a two-edged sword, carrying the risk of incorporation into communities of insiders who mutually reinforce received wisdom, defaulting to a 'respectable politics' that is no longer able to challenge the status quo (Gough & Shackley, 2001).

Much of the work on advocacy and epistemic communities suggests a gradual building of consensus to shift policy incrementally. However, Kingdon (1984) also suggests that '**policy windows**' occur where more significant changes are possible. Haughton and Allmendinger (2016) show how think tanks deliberately adopt radical, 'kite-flying' approaches to advocacy in the hope of exploiting policy windows and changing accepted narratives. Unlike the work of advocacy coalitions, this approach is intentionally disruptive and seeks to exploit the political need for new ideas to attract public attention.

While the literature on coalitions and networks focuses on the groups who seek to change or implement policy, there is also a body of literature focusing on the areas of policy or 'fields' in which policy change may occur. The focus is less on the actors and more on where and how the action takes place, although the concern with the field leads scholars to consider the attributes that enable actors to navigate and influence the field. The notion of **strategic action fields** (Fligstein & McAdam, 2011) is that any organisation operates within a field in which it has motivations and opportunities to act using what is termed 'social skill'.

Within policy fields, actors respond to disruption by reframing problems (Chen, 2018) and **sensemaking** in new ways. Sensemaking and **sensegiving** (Gioia & Chittipeddi, 1991) are important aspects of the advocacy process because they enable actors to develop a common language and rationale for their actions and respond to the unexpected without changing their fundamental beliefs. Sensemaking 'involves turning circumstances into a situation that is comprehended explicitly in words and that serves as a springboard for action' (Weick et al., 2005, p. 83).

However, sensemaking and sensegiving are not uncontested activities. There is a significant body of literature on change within organisations. Internal advocacy is often an important initial stage in building coalitions for change. The idea of **institutional entrepreneurship** (Seo & Creed, 2002; Battilana et al., 2009) highlights how change can be generated internally. Actors can exert agency leading to change within institutions, dependent on field characteristics and their social position. Seo and Creed describe this as 'the paradox of embedded agency'.

Here are three examples of how lobbying and advocacy works in practice and draws on lessons from across sectors.

CASE STUDY 3.1

International Development NGOs

Major Non-governmental Organisations (NGOs) are charitable organisations working across territories but they often seek to influence policy and resource decisions in either donor or funded countries, international governmental bodies, or other organisations. They may also be seeking to gain public support or funding from individuals (what are called 'outsider' strategies) rather than directly obtain state funding. The use of funding is also intended not just to have direct impacts on beneficiaries but often to demonstrate ways of working to others (either in the host or donor country).

Edwards' (1993) large-scale study of UK NGOs identified four main weaknesses in their approach to lobbying and advocacy: NGOs in the UK often did not have an overall and clear strategy for the advocacy work; they failed to build long-term and sustained alliances – action tended to focus on addressing the short-term issue and not the wider structural issue; there was insufficient attention to developing alternatives to dominant narratives of governments and corporations; and it was unclear how the relationship with donors was managed (was it a contractual one, a subservient one or a partnership one?).

Many NGOs have responded to the challenges Edwards posed over 30 years ago. This can be seen in coalitions that supported the Millennium Development Goals or more recently the UN Sustainable Development Goals, to the challenging of donors more critically, and the greater focus on mission and purpose in advocacy campaigns to ensure results (in terms of funding raised and beneficiary benefits realised).

CASE STUDY 3.2

Think Tanks

There has been a proliferation of think tanks across jurisdictions and seemingly in all policy areas. This growth alone does not mean they have become more influential, however. What is striking though is the ways in which they serve to communicate, transfer, and translate ideas into lessons for policy-makers.

Most think tanks seek a distinctive brand and political position and, usually operating as charitable organisations (in the UK at least), they also seek to act consistently with their stated charitable objects. But this distinction is not the same as independence. As Stone (2001, 2009) has shown, they are incredibly powerful conduits of ideas and lessons within and across political boundaries in their formation of epistemic communities. Two features of think tanks stand out: first, their skills in agenda setting through sophisticated operation within policy milieu and the marshalling of ideas to achieve broad goals; and second, their role as policy entrepreneurs, not necessarily the inventors of new ideas but the developers of ideas into coherent models for policy.

CASE STUDY 3.3

Small Businesses

There are approximately 6 million businesses in the UK employing fewer than 50 people with total employment of around 13 million people (as at the start of 2020). Unlike the advocacy for sectoral policies (e.g. support for steel or the regulation of the drinks industry), the sector is fragmented. Nonetheless, over the last 50 years two advocacy groups have grown in their prominence and arguably influence over UK public policy: the Federation of Small Businesses (FSB) and the Forum of Private Business. Jordan and Halpin (2003) chart the rise of the FSB from a weak issue-based lobbying organisation to a trusted partner in the formation of policy. Jordan and Halpin draw on Grant's (1978) distinction between insider groups that are seen as such 'trusted partners' and engaged on a regular basis and outsider groups that do not have recognition by policy-makers or who choose to sit outside the inner circles of policy-making and influence. They argue that the FSB has moved into the former group, albeit one which also tried to maintain connections with its members.

Much has changed in small business policy since the late 1990s which have seen attempts at coordination through the Small Business Service (through the 2000s) and then its subsequent dismantling (since 2010) (Curran & Storey, 2002). This case study reveals several key features though: the choice and strategy of small business representative bodies to move to a more 'insider relationship' with government, the risks in this in the short- and long-term, and the tension between whether issues are identified by the core executive or from the wider membership.

KEY CHALLENGES AND TIPS FOR THE STRATEGIC THINKER

These case studies highlight eight key challenges which organisations face in engaging with lobbying and advocacy and more broadly for their engagement in politics.

- **Setting the scene: overall goal of lobbying and advocacy:** some of the key challenges for organisations seem to be around identifying what their clear goal is and the alignment of this goal with the wider mission of the organisation.
- **Strategy versus initiative led:** businesses need to maintain a focus on strategy and mission and recognise the tensions that arise in responding to opportunities and initiatives.
- **Context and timing:** strategic thinkers need to be alive to changes in the operating environment and to political events. They may not be able to shape the wider narrative and outcome of policy (such as the impact of Brexit) but arguably they can inform the implementation of these key policy decisions.

- **Organisation**: lobbying and advocacy activities may be undertaken in house, by dedicated teams, as part of wider communications activities or as part of executive functions, or they may be fully or partly outsourced to a membership body or independent lobbying and communications agency. Strategic thinkers will have different opportunities here, as the case of small business lobbying reveals.
- **Key skills:** communications, public relations professionalism, and the compliance of professional standards have become of greater importance. In part building expertise in these areas matters but of more importance is the way the strategic thinker may inform the direction and utilisation of these capabilities. Skillsets often required are around the need for patience and diplomacy, the building of relationships and at times the need to jostle for position, and how to marshall evidence and stories to inform narratives which are framed with key agendas.
- **Networks:** network building was seen to be an absolutely crucial part of lobbying and advocacy. Network building is often seen as 'relentless work' which needs (professional) friends. This may be astute recruitment of individuals with networks to policy-makers at different levels (from agenda setting to implementation to research).
- **Global-national-local interplay and differences:** this will vary depending on the nature of the organisation and its ambition. A multinational corporation or NGO may seek links at global and national levels, whereas a medium-sized firm or charity may focus on national action but also work with communities around local operating sites.
- **Tensions and insider–outsider relationships:** most organisations will be working as outsiders, at least in terms of global and national relationships. But as policy-making has become more porous, larger organisations have often sought to establish trusted relationships with policy-makers, often helping to form and co-design policy.

CHAPTER SUMMARY

In conditions of volatility, growing complexity of policy problems and greater competing interests, it is arguable that policy-making processes have become more curtailed and closed. Policy-makers are faced with much greater levels of noise and of greater economic and social upheaval. The same is true for businesses. Short- to medium-term certainties of the Great Moderation have been undermined by the global financial crisis and the subsequent emergence of an era of polycrisis. Past certainties seem gone. Moreover, models of shareholder value maximisation and short-termism seem ever more part of the problem than the solution. And yet, markets and finance have the enormous power not simply to solve economic challenges but also social and environmental ones. The consensus for action, at least at a global level though, has not been as weak since before World War Two.

This chapter has challenged orthodoxies in liberal and neoclassical thought and how they have infused approaches of politics and policy-makers. More nuanced and plural accounts of policy-making have been advanced, in which the role of ideas, of networks, and an emphasis on service have been advanced. Solution forming, through coalition building or open innovation, are being embraced more albeit in the face of greater concentrations of economic power and structural imbalances in the world economy.

This all poses multiple challenges but also opportunities to the strategic thinker. It requires a breaking of some past certainties, not least around models of shareholder value maximisation, but *there is an important and urgent need for political imagination to think beyond existing approaches, to learn lessons assiduously, and to challenge models which have led places, countries, and the world to a position of severe and existential crisis.* A starting point, as Keynes saw both in 1918 at the signing of the Versailles Treaty, and in the establishment of the Bretton Woods economic order in 1944, is that peace and an end to conflict provide the true basis for human ingenuity and human potential to be realised. The threats of war, climate emergency, and extreme poverty are the most challenging pressures for strategic thinking and require new skills of political and policy-making craft.

RECOMMENDED READING

Lawrence, M., Homer-Dixon, T., Janzwood, S., Rockstöm, J., Renn, O. & Donges, J.F. (2024) Global polycrisis: The causal mechanisms of crisis entanglement. *Global Sustainability*, 7. doi:10.1017/sus.2024.1.

Peters, B.G. & Nagel, M.L. (2020) *Zombie Ideas: Why Failed Policy Ideas Persist.* Cambridge: Cambridge University Press.

REFERENCES

Battilana, J., Leca, B. & Boxenbaum, E. (2009). How actors change institutions: Towards a theory of institutional entrepreneurship. *The Academy of Management Annals*, 3(1), 65–107.

Baumgartner, F. & Jones, B. (1991) Agenda dynamics and policy subsystems. *Journal of Politics*, 53(4), 1044–1074.

Brewis, G., Paine, A.E., Hardill, I., Lindsey, R. & Macmillan, R. (2021) Challenging the moving frontier? In *Transformational Moments in Social Welfare* (pp. 141–156). Bristol: Policy Press.

Bulkeley, H. (2014) Revisiting … Discourse coalitions and the Australian climate change policy network. *Environment & Planning* C., 32, 957–962.

Cairney, P. & Jones, M.D. (2016) Kingdon's multiple streams approach: What is the empirical impact of this universal theory? *Policy Studies Journal*, 44(1), 37–58.

Chen, K. (2018) Interorganizational advocacy among nonprofit organizations in strategic action fields: Exogenous shocks and local responses. *Nonprofit and Voluntary Sector Quarterly*, 47(4_suppl),97S–118S.

Curran, J. & Storey, D.J. (2002) Small business policy in the United Kingdom: The inheritance of the small business service and implications for its future effectiveness. *Environment and Planning C: Government and Policy*, 20(2), 163–177. doi:10.1068/c0113.

Edwards, M. (1993) Does the doormat influence the boot? Critical thoughts on UK NGOs and international advocacy. *Development in Practice*, 3(3), 163–175. doi: 10.1080/096145249100077281.

Esping-Andersen, G. (1990) *The Three Worlds of Welfare Capitalism*. Englewood Cliffs, NJ: Princeton University Press.

Fligstein, N. & McAdam, D. (2011) Toward a general theory of strategic action fields. *Sociological Theory*, 29(1), 1–26.

Froud, J., Haslam, C., Johal, S. & Williams, K. (2000) Shareholder value and financialization: Consultancy promises, management moves. *Economy and Society*, 29(1), 80–110.

Gamble, A. (2019) *The Spectre at the Feast: Capitalist Crisis and the Politics of Recession*. London: Bloomsbury Publishing.

GCPSE (2015) *From Old Public Administration to New Public Service Delivery*. Retrieved July 4, 2024 from https://www.undp.org/sites/g/files/zskgke326/files/publications/PS-Reform_Summary.pdf.

Gioia, D.A. & Chittipeddi, K. (1991) Sensemaking and sensegiving in strategic change initiation. *Strategic Management Journal*, 12(6), 433–448.

Gough, C. & Shackley, S. (2001) The respectable politics of climate change: The epistemic communities and NGOs. *International Affairs*, 77(2), 329–346.

Grant, W. (1978) *Insider Groups, Outsider Groups and Interest Group Strategies in Britain*. University of Warwick, Department of Politics Working Paper, No 19.

Haas, PM. (1992). Introduction: Epistemic communities and international policy coordination. *International Organization*, 46(1), 1–35.

Hajer, M.A. (1995) *The Politics of Environmental Discourse: Ecological Modernization and the Policy Process*. Oxford: Oxford University Press.

Hall, P.A. & Soskice, D. (Eds.) (2001) *Varieties of Capitalism, The Institutional Foundations of Comparative Advantage*. Oxford: Oxford University Press.

Haughton, G. & Allmendinger, P. (2016) Think tanks and the pressures for planning reform in England. *Environment and Planning C: Government and Policy*, 34(8),1676–1692.

Hirschman, A.O. (1970) *Exit, Voice, and Loyalty: Responses to Decline in Firms, Organizations, and States*. Cambridge, MA: Harvard University Press.

John, P. (2013) *Analyzing Public Policy*. Abingdon, Oxon: Routledge.

Jones, R., Goodwin-Hawkins, B. & Woods, M. (2020) From territorial cohesion to regional spatial justice: The well-being of Future Generations Act in Wales. *International Journal of Urban and Regional Research*, 44(5), 894–912.

Jordan, G. & Halpin, D. (2003) Cultivating small business influence in the UK: The Federation of Small Businesses' journey from outsider to insider. *Journal of Public Affairs*, 3, 313–325. https://doi.org/10.1002/pa.160.

Kingdon, J.W. (1984) *Agendas, Alternatives and Public Policies*. New York: Harper Collins.

Lakoff, G. (2014) *The All New Don't Think of an Elephant! Know Your Values and Frame the Debate*. Vermont: Chelsea Green Publishing.

Lawrence, M., Homer-Dixon, T., Janzwood, S., Rockstöm, J., Renn, O. & Donges, J.F. (2024) Global polycrisis: The causal mechanisms of crisis entanglement. *Global Sustainability*, 7:e6. doi:10.1017/sus.2024.1.

Lowndes, V. (2017) Institutionalism. In V. Lowndes, D. Marsh & G. Stoker (Eds.), *Theory and Methods in Political Science* (pp 54–74). London: Bloomsbury Publishing.

Lowndes, V. & Roberts, M. (2013) *Why Institutions Matter: The New Institutionalism in Political Science*. London: Bloomsbury Publishing.

Lowndes, V., Marsh, D., & Stoker, G. (Eds.). (2017) *Theory and Methods in Political Science*. London: Bloomsbury Publishing.

Macaulay, M. & Lawton, A. (2003) Misunderstanding Machiavelli in management: Metaphor, analogy and historical method. *Philosophy of Management*, 3, 17–30.

Machiavelli, N. (1988) The Prince edition (trans. Quentin Skinner and Russell Price). Cambridge: Cambridge University Press.

March, J. & Olsen, J. (1989) *Rediscovering Institutions: The Organizational Basis of Politics*. New York: Free Press.

Meckling, J. (2015) Oppose, support, or hedge? Distributional effects, regulatory pressure, and business strategy in environmental politics. *Global Environmental Politics*, 15(2), 19–37. https://direct.mit.edu/glep/article-abstract/15/2/19/14822.

Mill, J.S. (1874) *Essays on Some Unsettled Questions of Political Economy* (2nd ed.). London: Longman.

North, D.C. (1990) *Institutions, Institutional Change and Economic Performance*. Cambridge: Cambridge University Press.

Raworth, K. (2017) *Doughnut Economics: Seven Ways to Think Like a 21st-century Economist*. London: Chelsea Green Publishing.

Rein, M. & Schön, D. (1996) Frame-critical policy analysis and frame-reflective policy practice. *Knowledge and Policy*, 9, 85–104. https://doi.org/10.1007/BF02832235.

Sabatier, P.A. (1988) An advocacy coalition framework of policy change and the role of policy oriented learning therein. *Policy Sciences*, 21, 129–168.Seo, M-G. & Creed, W.E.D. (2002) Institutional contradictions, praxis, and institutional change: A dialectical perspective. *Academy of Management Review*, 27(2), 222–247.

Smith, A. (1776) *The Wealth of Nations. Edition Consulted:* London: Wordsworth Editions, 2012.

Stone, D. (2004) Transfer agents and global networks in the 'transnationalization' of policy. *Journal of European Public Policy*, 11(3)–, 545–566. doi: 10.1080/13501760410001694291.

Stone, D. (2001) Think tanks, global lesson-drawing and networking social policy ideas. *Global Social Policy*, 1(3), 338–360.

Stone, D. (2009) Rapid knowledge: 'Bridging research and policy' at the Overseas Development Institute. *Public Administration and Development*, 29, 303–315.
Tittenbrun, J. (2013) The death of the economic man. *International Letters of Social and Humanistic Sciences*, 11, 10–34.
Weick, K.E., Sutcliffe, K.M. & Obstfeld, D. (2005) Organizing and the process of sensemaking. *Organization Science*, 16(4), 409–421.
Wilkinson, R. (2014) *What's Wrong with the WTO and How to Fix it*. New York: John Wiley & Sons.

CHAPTER 4

Engaging with the Plurality of Economics for Integrated Strategic Thinking

Nichola Williams and Drew Woodhouse

CHAPTER OUTLINE

Strategy-making can be influenced by insights from economics. Economics as a subject is plural, and this chapter identifies two economic perspectives: 'Neoclassical Economics' (the mainstream) and 'Institutional Theory'. Neoclassical economics' key concepts include individualism, instrumentalism, equilibrium, utility maximisation, rationality, marginalism, and profit maximisation. Conversely, institutional theory highlights the role of institutions (society's norms, rules, regulations, and cultural expectations) in shaping economic behaviour and organisational outcomes. Each offers something unique for the strategic thinker.

Strategy-making, when guided by neoclassical economics, focuses on resource management, production optimisation, operational efficiency, and competitiveness to result in profit maximisation. However, this short-term focus can lead to ethical dilemmas, environmental neglect, and a disregard for broader societal goals, necessitating the incorporation of more comprehensive considerations. Institutional theory broadens strategic decision-making contexts by emphasising the role of institutions in shaping organisational behaviour, helping businesses align with regulatory changes, cultural shifts, and societal expectations.

By integrating institutional theory, organisations become more adaptable, able to foster innovation and resilience in dynamic environments, and navigate long-term sustainability challenges. Aligning strategies with institutional expectations enhances organisational legitimacy, fostering trust and ensuring that businesses are more ethically and socially responsible.

DOI: 10.4324/9781003475545-4

In conclusion, integrating both neoclassical economics and institutional theory into strategy-making enhances both short-term performance and long-term sustainability. Strategic thinkers who leverage both frameworks can balance operational efficiency with ethical considerations, allowing for comprehensive and robust decision-making.

KEY POINTS

- Neoclassical economics rests upon several key foundational concepts: individualism, instrumentalism, equilibrium, utility maximisation, rationality, marginalism, and profit maximisation that shape its theoretical framework and analytical methods, offering several implications for strategy-making. Neoclassical models provide performance metrics.
- Institutional theory counters neoclassical assumptions of perfect information and rationality, emphasising the constraints of incomplete information and transaction costs in economic behaviour. Institutional theory helps anticipate social, cultural, and regulatory shifts.
- Varied institutional contexts, shaped by regulatory, cultural, and historical factors, significantly influence strategic decisions and economic outcomes, necessitating thorough institutional analysis for effective strategic thinking.
- Integrating neoclassical economics and institutional theory results in a strategy-making approach more aligned to the expectations of the strategic thinker, balancing profitability with long-term sustainability.

THE DEVELOPMENT AND KEY MEANINGS OF NEOCLASSICAL ECONOMICS

When we hear the word 'economics', we are really referring to a mainstream 'type' of economics called 'Neoclassical Economics'. Neoclassical economics arose from a response to the shortcomings of classical economics and the marginal (more of this below, in 'Marginalism') revolution of the nineteenth century (Neck, 2022). Neoclassical economics represented a shift in economic thinking towards a more rigorous and systematic analysis of individual behaviour, market interactions, and resource allocation that laid the groundwork for modern mainstream economics.

In the late twentieth century, a small group of self-identified neoclassical economists (namely George Stigler, Paul Samuelson, Milton Friedman, etc.) actively shaped the discipline (Morgan, 2015). Neoclassical economics rose to prominence by presenting itself as a scientific and objective discipline. Through the adoption of mathematical modelling and formal analysis, neoclassical economists established their work as the standard approach within the field of economics. This emphasis on rigour and precision lent credibility to their theories, allowing them to dominate both academic disclosure and policy discussions (Henry, 2012; Morgan, 2015; Neck, 2022). This is the 'core' of economics we know today.

It is important to note that neoclassical economics continues to evolve and there are diverse interpretations within the field. It has meant different things to different authors, including:

1. The subjective marginal utility theory of the 1870s onwards.
2. The economic theories of Alfred Marshall.
3. The works of the twentieth-century scholars, established by Marshall, Leon Walras, and others.
4. A combination of the above.
5. The Samuelsonian neoclassical synthesis, merging microeconomic price and resource allocation theory with Keynesian macroeconomics, among others (Henry, 2012; Neck, 2022).

The following section outlines the core principles of neoclassical economics to enable the strategic thinker to navigate its impact on society/life.

THE CORE PRINCIPLES OF NEOCLASSICAL ECONOMICS

Neoclassical economics rests upon several key foundational concepts that shape its theoretical framework and analytical methods. Understanding these concepts can offer a fuller understanding of how economics informs strategy-making.

Figure 4.1 demonstrates the fundamental pillars of Neoclassical Economics.

Individualism

Neoclassical economists base their explanations on the behaviour and decisions of individual agents, such as consumers and firms, as a basis for understanding economic phenomena (Gueldry, 2015). This school of thought asserts that individuals act rationally, seeking to maximise utility (for consumers) or profits (for firms), and that markets operate efficiently when left to the forces of supply and demand.

Margaret Thatcher (Prime Minister of the United Kingdom from 1979 to 1990) was a proponent of individualism and in 1987 she contended that:

> There is no such thing [as society]! There are individual men and women and there are families, and no government can do anything except through people and people look to themselves first.
>
> *(Thatcher, 1987)*

Moreover, both neoclassical economics and Thatcher's individualist ideology emphasise the central role of individual agents as the primary drivers of economic behaviour, while

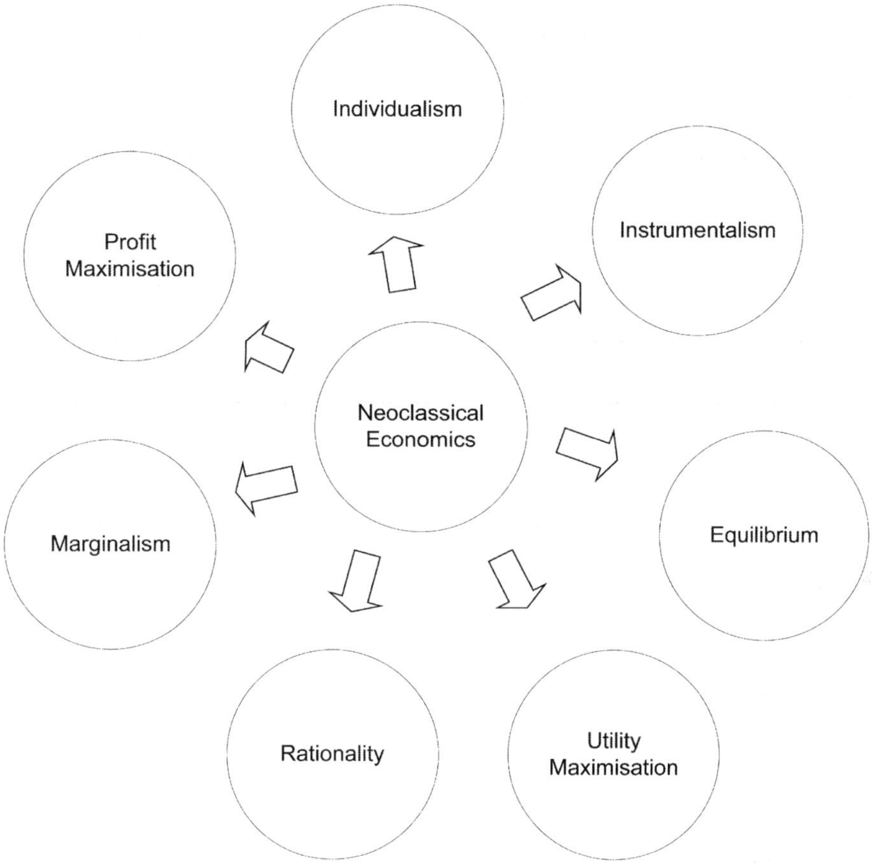

FIGURE 4.1 The Fundamental Pillars of Neoclassical Economics

minimising the role of collective action or government intervention in shaping economic outcomes (Klees, 2008).

Instrumentalism

Instrumentalism is also known as Preferentialism and Preference Theory. It assumes that all behaviour is preference-driven, or more precisely, it is understood as the means of maximising preference or satisfaction. Every action and utterance is instrumental to satisfaction to such an extent that there is no philosophical space left for questioning whether the agent will act on her preferences.

Neoclassical theory represents a narrow form of consequentialism (Holbrook, 1991; Tanyi and Bruder, 2014) in which the sole consequential concern is the degree to which a uniform index of preference satisfaction is maximised (Arnsperger & Varoufakis, 2006).

Equilibrium

First introduced by Cournot in 1983, 'equilibrium' is often referred to as the third axiom of neoclassical economics (Arnsperger & Varoufakis, 2006, 2008). The imposition of equilibrium is simple: 'it could not be otherwise!' In other words, neoclassicism cannot demonstrate that equilibrium would naturally arise from agents' instrumentally rational choices (Arnsperger & Varoufakis, 2006, 2008). If equilibrium cannot naturally arise, the second-best alternative for the neoclassical theorist is to assume that behaviour fluctuates around a theoretically determined equilibrium and then explore the likelihood that, once at equilibrium, the system will tend to remain there or drift away. This exploration is known as 'stability analysis' (Arnsperger & Varoufakis, 2006, 2008).

This idea can be traced back to the two success stories that emerged from neoclassical economics since World War Two: General Equilibrium Theory and Game Theory. In neither case does the equilibrium solution naturally arise from the assumptions of the models (Arnsperger & Varoufakis, 2006, 2008).

In General Equilibrium Theory, its leading practitioners assert that convergence to a general equilibrium can only be demonstrated in highly restrictive special cases. More broadly, it is not just challenging to prove that a theoretical system of markets will reach equilibrium in each market based on the rational actions of buyers and sellers; it is impossible (See Mantel, 1975; Sonnenschein, 1973, 1974).

Similarly, in Game Theory, the same outcome is observed: in the most intriguing socio-economic interactions (or games), the common knowledge that all players are instrumentally rational rarely leads to one of the interaction's Nash equilibria. Nash equilibrium refers to a scenario in a strategic game where no player can achieve a better outcome by independently altering their strategy provided that the strategies of the other players remain the same (Kreps, 1989; Holt & Roth, 2004). Moreover, something additional is needed to achieve equilibrium. This additional element manifests in the form of an axiom stating that the beliefs of all players are consistently aligned at every stage of every game (see Hargreaves-Heap & Varoufakis, 2004).

This assumption introduces another type of methodological balancing: by assuming that agents' beliefs are consistently aligned, we treat them as if they are already in Nash equilibrium. Once again, equilibrium is assumed from the start, even before analysing how stable the system is or how vulnerable it might be to disruptions. In this, Cournot's influence continues to shape economic thought (Arnsperger & Varoufakis, 2006).

Utility Maximisation

The concept of utility maximisation in economics is as old as the field of economics itself and is the source for the neoclassical theory of consumption (Gilad et al., 1987). Neoclassical economists argue that *homo economicus* (or a rational person) aims to maximise their utility or satisfaction, subject to their budget constraints (Gueldry, 2015; Maialeh, 2019). Consequently, neoclassical theory of utility maximisation assumes that irrational behaviour is unsystematic and, consequently, impossible to model (Gilad et al., 1987). The Utility Maximisation (choice) model is also called the individual choice model (Aleskerov et al., 2007).

Rationality

The neoclassical economist views humans as *homo economicus* (or a rational, self-interested individual who maximises their own utility or welfare) (Bernoulli, 1738).

Consequently, neoclassical economics assumes that individuals are rational beings who make decisions that maximise their utility. This forms the basis of consumer and producer behaviour models (Gueldry, 2015; Soukup et al., 2015; Neck, 2022). For neoclassical economists, the concept of rationality is associated with maximising net revenue or total gain (Soukup et al., 2015). However, a downside to the rational choice theory is that it is aimed solely at maximising utility which often neglects ethical considerations (Marckmann, 2009).

Marginalism

Neoclassical economics is referred to as 'marginalism' because it revolves around marginal concepts like marginal utility, marginal cost, and marginal revenue. Marginalism views the capitalist economy as fundamentally efficient, sees production as a cooperative effort between the contributions and sacrifices of suppliers of productive services, and considers income distribution to follow the principle of 'to each according to his/her contribution to social welfare'. While this principle may require adjustments, it is rarely deemed fundamentally unfair.

Marginalism argues that in a market economy, prices, quantities produced, and the distribution of the social product among wages, rents, and interest is determined by the interaction between supply and demand, which are functions of prices. This interaction, it is argued, causes the economy to gravitate towards a state of equilibrium, where supply and demand for all goods and services of production factors are balanced (Petri, 2021). Furthermore, marginalism refers to production inputs – labour, land, and capital – as 'factors of production'. It argues that, like produced goods, these factors also have supply and demand functions and a tendency towards equilibrium between supply and demand. Consequently, the marginal approach focuses on the analysis of marginal changes in economic variables in which the key concepts of marginal utility, marginal cost, marginal revenue, marginal productivity, profit maximisation, consumer equilibrium, marginal rate of substitution (MRS), marginal rate of technical substitution (MRTS), equilibrium, efficiency, and distribution of income were birthed.

By focusing on these marginal adjustments, the marginal approach offers a precise framework for understanding complex economic behaviours. It helps clarify how small changes at the margin influence broader resource allocation decisions, pricing strategies, and the interactions between consumers and producers in competitive markets. The approach also plays a key role in addressing how equilibrium is achieved and maintained, providing insight into both short-term adjustments and long-term market stability.

Furthermore, the marginal approach is essential for evaluating efficiency in an economy. It examines whether resources are being used to maximise output without wasting inputs and ensures that consumer preferences are being met as effectively as possible. As a result, this approach has wide applications across microeconomics, welfare economics, and policy-making, influencing discussions about income distribution and market dynamics (Royer, 2014; Petri, 2021).

Profit Maximisation

Profit maximisation is one of the core assumptions within economic theory and is seen as a necessary condition for achieving efficient market outcomes. It maximises the benefits for individual suppliers and buyers, as well as for society (Brueckner, 2013). As previously noted, economic theory assumes that humans pursue self-interest, maximising it through rational decision-making by economic agents striving to satisfy their unlimited needs and wants with limited resources (i.e. time, capital, labour). Firms are assumed to act in ways that maximise their profits. This occurs through decisions about the quantities of goods to sell at given prices. Suppliers aim to sell more goods at higher prices because selling quantities at higher prices increases revenue and maximises profits. Contrarily, the law of demand states that the higher the price of a good, the fewer buyers will demand it. The higher the price, the lower the quantity demanded. The interplay of demand and supply affects the price of goods supplied and demanded. When supply meets demand, the economy is said to be at equilibrium, achieving economic efficiency as the amount of goods supplied equals the amount of goods demanded (Brueckner, 2013; Keen & Standish, 2006).

IMPLICATIONS OF NEOCLASSICAL ECONOMICS FOR STRATEGY-MAKING

The approach of neoclassical economics has implications for strategy-making within organisations.

Limited Consideration of Non-economic Factors

- *Social*: Neoclassical economics often overlooks the impact of social norms, cultural values, and institutional frameworks on economic behaviour (Casson, 1997; Ntibagirirwa, 2009). However, strategic thinking should account for these factors to ensure that strategies are culturally sensitive, socially responsible, and that institutional frameworks, including formal regulations and informal societal norms, which shape organisational behaviour and influence business outcomes are integrated. Neoclassical economics assumes rational behaviour, but real-world decisions are influenced by cognitive biases and emotions (Reisch & Zhao, 2017; Abhyankar, 2019). Strategic thinking could incorporate insights from behavioural economics and consumer psychology to better understand and predict consumer behaviour. Furthermore, the focus on profit maximisation in neoclassical economics can lead to ethical dilemmas, such as exploitation, unfair labour practices, and neglect of corporate social responsibility (Robin & Reidenbach, 1988; Hosmer, 2007). Strategic thinking needs to incorporate ethical considerations to build trust and a positive image. Institutions play a key role in setting the rules and norms that influence ethical business behaviour, ensuring that corporations are held accountable to both societal and governmental standards (North, 1991).

Neoclassical economics fails to address the issues of income inequality and social welfare (Wade, 2011; Wade & Alaceyvich, 2018; Chibba & Luiz, 2019). However, strategic thinking considers the social impact of business decisions to foster inclusive growth and equity (Kaplan et al., 2019). Institutional structures, such as welfare systems, labour laws, and social safety nets, are critical in shaping equitable economic outcomes. Businesses that align their strategies with these institutional frameworks are more likely to contribute to inclusive and sustainable economic development. It is evident that neoclassical economics considers labour as a key factor of production; however, it often underestimates the importance of long-term human capital development (Sodirjonov, 2020). Strategic thinking should prioritise employee development, education, and well-being (Grigorescu & Chiper, 2016). Institutions, such as educational systems and vocational training programmes, play a crucial role in fostering this human capital development, and businesses that collaborate with these institutions can gain a competitive advantage through a more skilled and motivated workforce.

- *Environmental*: Traditional neoclassical models typically do not incorporate environmental externalities (Halkos & Psarianos, 2016). Strategic thinking should integrate environmental considerations to promote sustainability and comply with regulatory requirements (Gustafsson et al., 2019). Institutional frameworks, such as environmental regulations, international treaties, and societal expectations for corporate responsibility, are increasingly shaping how businesses must operate to remain sustainable. Companies that anticipate and align with these institutional demands can not only avoid legal risks but also build a reputation for environmental stewardship, enhancing their long-term viability and market position.
- *Change*: Finally, neoclassical models are often seen as static, thus assuming conditions of equilibrium. However, strategic thinking must be dynamic and adaptive, considering the rapid technological advancements and evolving market conditions (Mufudza, 2018) as already discussed in Chapter 1. Institutions provide stability through rules and norms, but they must also evolve to keep pace with changing environments. Strategic thinkers who understand the institutional landscape can better anticipate regulatory changes and societal shifts, enabling organisations to adapt proactively and remain competitive.

Focus on Profit Maximisation

Neoclassical economics assumes that the aim of a firm is to maximise profits by optimising production and minimising costs. The more traditional vocabulary around strategy-making does aim to maximise profits, prioritising initiatives that improve operational efficiency, manage resource allocation to optimise efficiency, and reduce waste (Mazzarol et al., 2009) and traditionally, strategies have been evaluated based on their potential to enhance profitability and competitive positioning (Harrison & Kennedy,

1997; Mazzarol et al., 2009). Consequently, the traditional concept of strategy-making represented by **strategic management** and neoclassical economics' core concept of profit maximisation are closely related because both are seen as fundamental to the successful management and growth of a firm.

Strategic management establishes long-term goals and short-term objectives that guide the organisation's effort, and profit maximisation is often a prerequisite within this framework (Steiner, 2010). Moreover, strategic management provides integration by ensuring that all strategic initiatives are aligned with the goal of increasing profitability, thus making profit maximisation a central tenet of strategic plans (Monye & Ibegbulem, 2018).

Strategic management involves analysing market conditions, competitor strategies, and customer needs to position the company effectively in the market. By understanding these factors, companies can better position themselves effectively in the market, which enhances profitability. Furthermore, profit maximisation is achieved by gaining a competitive advantage, which strategic management facilitates through targeted strategies that enhance market position and profitability (Monye & Ibegbulem, 2018).

Strategic management also involves a culture of innovation and growth to remain competitive and meet evolving consumer needs results. Innovation, in turn, leads to new products, services, and processes that promote the growth in revenues and reduce costs, thus directly impacting profitability (AlQershi, 2021).

Strategic management also encourages continuous monitoring of the external environment and internal performance, allowing for agile adjustments to strategies. Profit maximisation requires flexibility to adapt to market changes, competitive pressures, and emerging opportunities, which strategic management facilitates (Ghobadian et al.,2008).

However, as has been discussed previously, the focus on profit maximisation, or competitive advantage or relative value is insufficient to meet the wider expectations of sustainability (where it is not just about growth) and wider stakeholder expectations.

Assumption of Rationality

There are benefits to rationality in strategy-making and these have already been reflected on in chapters 1 and 2, with the recognition of the importance of strategic management activities, and the use of planning tools as a foundation for systematic analysis. Rationality ensures that decisions are based on comprehensive analysis and objective data, potentially enhancing strategic initiatives. Rationality involves careful cost-benefit analysis to optimise resource allocation and minimise waste (Celik, 2019).

Rationality involves using predictive models and data analysis to foresee and manage risks effectively. Rationality uses scientific data and models to create effective environmental regulations and policies (Celik, 2019; Alhosseiny, 2023). In terms of long-term sustainability, rationality ensures that sustainability initiatives are economically viable and based on solid evidence (Celik, 2019). Rationality should contribute to a more efficient market where resources are optimally allocated. It should also foster an environment that is conducive to innovation and economic growth. Rationality serves to enhance a firm's competitiveness and provide frameworks for effectively responding to economic crises (Celik, 2019; Alhosseiny, 2023).

In other words, the integration of rationality can lead to more informed, efficient, and effective decision-making, thereby driving success and resilience in businesses, although when considered alone, rationality is surely insufficient, given its potential inability to consider human behaviour.

Marginalism

Neoclassical economics relies on marginal analysis to guide decision-making, focusing on small, incremental changes. In economics, marginal analysis serves as a decision-making tool that assesses the additional benefits and costs of a small (or marginal) change in the production of goods or services. This process helps businesses and individuals evaluate whether the added cost of a specific action or decision is outweighed by the additional benefit, ensuring that resources are allocated efficiently and decisions are economically sound (Palmer et al., 1999).

In contrast, strategic thinking provides the vision and innovation, i.e. a comprehensive framework for decision-making that incorporates various tools and analysis, including marginal analysis (Kehbila, 2021). In other words, strategic thinking provides the overall direction, and marginal analysis helps optimise specific decisions with that strategy (Lowder, 2009). Or strategic management (planning) focuses on assessing each strategic decision based on its incremental benefits, costs, and optimisations. This approach focuses on reducing marginal costs and increasing marginal revenue, rather than transformative or disruptive innovations (Barney, 2000).

Consequently, strategic planning employs insights from marginal analysis to ensure optimal allocation of resources or the allocation of resources where they will have the most significant impact, thus ensuring that strategic initiatives are both efficient and effective (Bağdigen & Avci, 2013; Flach & Mendes, 2013). Strategic planning ensures that firms operate in an optimal and efficient manner by incorporating marginal analysis to ensure that strategies are designed to maximise efficiency and effectiveness, thereby achieving the best possible outcomes (Swicegood, 1987). Moreover, strategic planning also employs marginal analysis to refine strategies, focusing on initiatives that offer the highest incremental returns relative to their costs.

In terms of managing organisation risks, strategic planning uses marginal analysis to refine management strategies, thus ensuring that the additional risks taken are justified by the incremental benefits gained.

One of the primary goals of strategic planning is to foster innovation and growth by identifying opportunities that align with the organisation's long-term vision and goals. This process requires a careful balance of creativity and analysis, as organisations seek to pursue new initiatives and improvements while ensuring the efficient allocation of resources (Nadikattu, 2020; Gutterman, 2023). Consequently, strategic planning incorporates marginal analysis as an essential tool to assess and rank innovations based on their potential to deliver the greatest incremental growth compared to their associated costs (López & Oliver, 2023).

Effectively, marginal analysis and strategic planning are linked because marginal analysis offers detailed, incremental insights that help optimise resource allocation and optimise value. On the other hand, strategic planning provides the broader framework for making these decisions. Therefore, by integrating marginal analysis into strategic planning, firms can carefully evaluate each step for its incremental impact, resulting in more efficient, effective, and adaptable strategies. It is this combination of broad vision and detailed analysis that enables firms to achieve their long-term objectives while maintaining optimal operational efficiency.

It would be fair to say at this stage that the discipline of neoclassical economics is more suited to the concept of strategic management/planning with its foundations in rational thought and approaches. There are overlaps and complements between neoclassical economics and certain intentions of businesses and organisations; however, the core principles of neoclassical economics are also out of touch with the sustainable strategic thinking argued for in Chapter 1. Hence, we turn to alternative ways of thinking.

PLURALITY: AN ALTERNATIVE APPROACH TO NEOCLASSICAL ECONOMICS – INSTITUTIONAL THEORY

While neoclassical economics remains the dominant school of thought in the field, providing foundational theories on supply, demand, and market equilibrium, we argue that there are valuable insights to be gained from perspectives that extend beyond this framework. Neoclassical thought focuses primarily on individual rationality, utility maximisation, and equilibrium states, often overlooking the complexities of human behaviour, social institutions, and the impact of historical and cultural contexts on economic outcomes.

In this chapter, we explore diversity and plurality within the broader field of economics. This section investigates the concept, scope, and definitions of 'institutions' as discussed in the competing school of thought known as Institutional Theory. The goal is to enhance our understanding of 'institutions' and to examine their role in economic actions while contrasting this viewpoint with the mainstream perspective of neoclassical economics. Different institutional approaches offer unique theoretical frameworks for understanding the institutional environment and evaluating their potential impact on strategic decision-making. This chapter will delve into these institutional approaches and their implications for strategic thinking.

The Development and Key Meanings of Institutional Theory

Without a shared understanding of how others will respond and the effectiveness of sanctions in addressing potential opportunistic behaviour, interpersonal and business interaction becomes impossible (North, 1987, 1991). Economic entities like firms engage in transactions based primarily on trust and the assurance that their expectations will be met. The nature of exchanges between entities, which are often repetitive and frequent, requires predictability, smoothness, and security. This demand for reliability in exchanges embodies what is termed 'transactional trust'. Consequently, human interactions, whether economic or non-economic, rely on various forms of confidence established by rules and regulations that guard against unpredictable and opportunistic conduct. These rules and regulations, fundamental to institutional theory, are collectively referred to as 'institutions'. The idea of the need for trust in exchanges is discussed further in Chapter 8 as the basis for ethical behaviour in business.

Institutional theory has become a significant field within the social sciences, offering new analytical perspectives that have enriched various disciplines, including business management, economics, sociology, and political science. The theory aims primarily to explore and explain the impact of the broader economic, social, and cultural environments on behavioural and economic outcomes, as noted by scholars such as Scott (2008), Kenworthy (2006), Jackson and Deeg (2008), and Hodgson (1998, 2001). Institutional theory challenges traditional paradigms like neoclassical economics and strategic management, which often view equilibrium as a persistent state. Authors such as North (1991) and Hodgson (2001) have critiqued these established views, advocating for a broader understanding that incorporates the complexity and dynamism of the economy. This approach has progressively shifted how social sciences understand and study various phenomena, moving away from static models to embrace more fluid and evolving interpretations. For this reason, institutional theory provides valuable insights into strategic thinking and the broader study of organisations.

This shift towards institutional theory aligns us with the transition from traditional strategic management, which is supported by neoclassic economics, towards more flexible, iterative forms of strategic thinking. Institutional theory offers valuable insights into this evolving landscape by emphasising the importance of rules, norms, and structures that guide organisational and economic behaviour. Unlike neoclassical economics, which focuses on equilibrium and optimal outcomes, institutional theory recognises that organisations operate within complex, evolving environments, where change is constant, and outcomes are not easily predictable.

In this context, the term 'institutions' takes on a variety of meanings, often shaped by the disciplinary lens through which it is viewed. As Jackson and Deeg (2019) and Redding (2005) highlight, the lack of a universally accepted definition of 'institutions' can lead to ambiguity in its application. Despite this, the dual role of institutions – as both enablers and constraints on the actions of firms, individuals, and states – is a consistent theme across the literature. Institutions not only set up the frameworks that shape incentives but also influence decision-making processes and drive change within and between businesses. This capacity to influence behaviour underscores the importance of understanding institutional dynamics in the context of strategic thinking, as they have the potential to underpin critical decisions in business, economics, and beyond.

Although definitions of institutions vary widely (Woodhouse, 2024), they consistently highlight the role of institutions in both enabling and constraining the actions of entities such as firms, individuals, or nation states. Institutions set up overarching frameworks that influence incentives, thereby shaping business, economic, social, and political interactions across various spheres and levels. By establishing these frameworks, institutions not only dictate certain behaviours but also act as drivers of change within and between businesses. These have the potential to underpin decisions of businesses.

What Does Institutional Theory Offer Differently to Conventional Economics?

Institutional theory can be divided into three distinct approaches: new institutional economics, new organisational institutionalism, and comparative institutionalism (Woodhouse & Johnston, 2023; Woodhouse, 2024) (see Figure 4.2). Institutional approaches differ extensively by way of their conceptualisation of institutions, their level of analysis, and subsequently their explanation of how institutions matter for strategic thinking (see Table 4.1 for a summarised discussion). We introduce each approach in turn, then extend the discussion to the overall implications for strategic thinking.

New Institutional Economics

By challenging the conventional neoclassical economics assumptions of perfect information, unbounded rationality, and immediate market transactions, institutional economics provides a significant departure from mainstream economic analysis of economic systems and actors, such as firms. This perspective asserts that individuals operate under constraints of incomplete information and limited cognitive capacity, relying on the 'bounded' information available to them. Consequently, market participants face uncertainty about future outcomes, leading to the occurrence of 'transaction costs' to gather information. To mitigate these risks and expenses individuals establish institutions, which include formal entities like regulations, laws, and contracts, as well as informal elements such as belief patterns, thought habits, and cultural norms. Institutions play a crucial role in determining economic performance and define the decisions made by firms. This integration of institutional analysis into economic thought has led to the

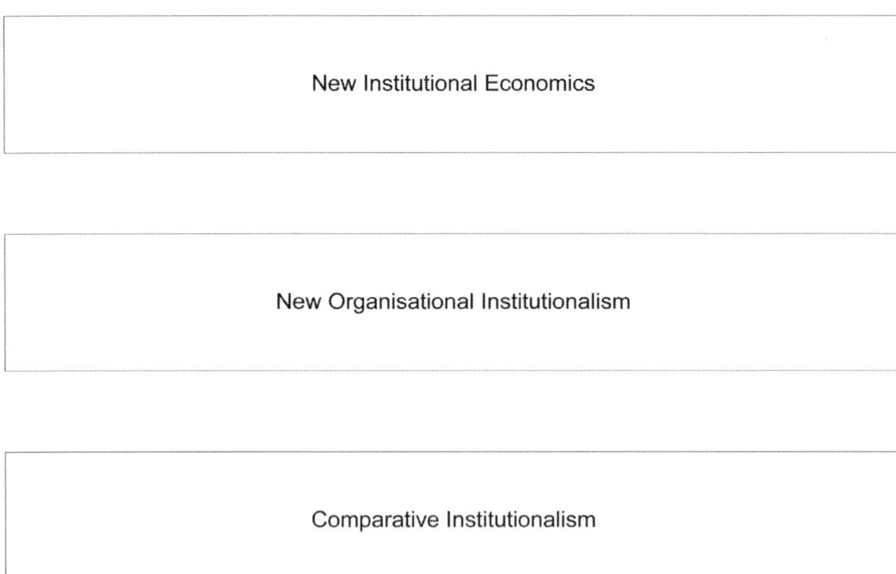

FIGURE 4.2 Three Approaches to Institutional Theory

TABLE 4.1 The Three Approaches to Institutional Theory

Institutional theory and its three approaches			
Institutional approach	**New Institutional Economics (NIE)**	**New Organisational Institutionalism**	**Comparative Institutionalism**
Focus	Formal and informal institutions that mitigate the costs of transacting in a market setting, focusing on property rights, governance structures, and contract enforcement.	Analysing the dissemination and adoption of organisational patterns and explaining variations in organisational practices through isomorphism and legitimacy.	Comparative analysis of institutional configurations, their complementarities, and how they shape the diversity of capitalist systems and economic performance.
Theoretical perspectives	Rooted in economic theory, NIE emphasises transaction cost economics, bounded rationality, and the role of institutions in reducing uncertainty and enabling cooperation between economic agents.	Social constructivist approach, focusing on how organisations conform to cultural norms, rules, and structures to gain legitimacy and how institutional logics shape organisational behaviour.	Focuses on varieties of capitalism, institutional complementarities, and the interplay of political, social, and economic institutions that explain different capitalist outcomes.
Key concepts	Transaction costs, property rights, bounded rationality, opportunism, and agency theory. Institutions are seen as the rules of the game that reduce uncertainty and facilitate market transactions.	Institutional isomorphism (coercive, mimetic, normative), legitimacy, decoupling, and institutional logics. Emphasises how organisations adapt to their environments to gain legitimacy and survive.	Institutional complementarity, path dependency, comparative advantage, and varieties of capitalism. Analyses how different institutional frameworks (e.g. labour market, financial systems) interact to shape the performance of national economies.

(Continued)

TABLE 4.1 Continued

Institutional theory and its three approaches			
Institutional approach	**New Institutional Economics (NIE)**	**New Organisational Institutionalism**	**Comparative Institutionalism**
Implications for strategy-making	NIE informs strategies focused on reducing transaction costs, designing efficient governance structures, and ensuring property rights and contract enforcement. Strategy-making is viewed through the lens of optimizing firm performance by aligning internal governance with external institutional frameworks.	Organisations must navigate institutional environments by adhering to social norms, rules, and expectations to gain legitimacy. Strategy-making involves balancing efficiency with conformity to institutional expectations, often leading to practices of decoupling or ceremonial adoption of formal structures.	Comparative institutionalism suggests that firms' strategies must align with the specific institutional configurations of their home country or region. This approach emphasises that 'one-size-fits-all' strategies do not work, as different institutional contexts lead to different forms of competitive advantage.
Examples of application	Analysing how firms in emerging markets navigate weak institutional frameworks to reduce transaction costs and improve market efficiency. Examining the impact of legal reforms on property rights and investment.	Explaining how multinational corporations (MNCs) adopt local organisational practices to gain legitimacy in foreign markets. Analysing how firms engage in isomorphism to resemble successful competitors.	Understanding why firms in coordinated market economies (e.g. Germany) pursue different strategies than those in liberal market economies (e.g. the U.S.). Investigating how institutional complementarities support specific industries in different capitalist systems.
Key literature	North (1987, 1991); Williamson (1975); Coase (1937 1998)	DiMaggio & Powell (1983); Scott (2008); Meyer & Rowan (1977)	Hall & Soskice (2001); Whitley (1999); Amable (2003); Woodhouse & Johnston (2023)

development of new methodological approaches within economics, now known as 'New Institutional Economics' (NIE).

To provide a more nuanced approach, NIE focuses on the concept of transaction costs. These costs create frictions in economic exchanges, which are crucial in shaping production, transactions, and economic outcomes (Coase, 1937; North, 1991). The focus on the frictions inherent in economic and business exchanges, central to NIE, has shed light on the concept of asset specificities in transactions. Asset specificities refer to the unique characteristics and qualities of assets that make them particularly valuable in specific transactions or contexts, but less so in others. In the context of NIE, asset specificities create frictions in economic exchanges by increasing transaction costs. These specificities can arise from various factors, including physical attributes, human skills, or investments made for a particular transaction, which limit the asset's value in alternative uses or transactions. As a result, when asset specificities are high, firms may opt for non-market transactions or hierarchical exchanges to mitigate risks and reduce transaction costs. This focus on asset specificities helps explain why firms exist and expand, as they manage and optimise specialised assets in a way that enhances efficiency and economic outcomes.

NIE examines the role of institutions and their interactions with organisational structures. In this analysis, institutions are seen as both formal and informal norms, rules, and constraints established by humans to manage uncertainty and exert control over their environments (Menard & Shirley, 2005). These institutions are often referred to as the 'rules of the game in a society' (North, 1991, p. 3), which coordinate and influence societal actions.

NIE argues that the dynamics of market exchanges and related frictions are shaped by the institutional context, also known as the 'institutional framework', 'institutional regime', or 'institutional environment'. This includes specific sub-institutions that govern economic behaviours and the strategic alignment of organisations. It encompasses both informal conventions and routines as well as formal regulatory mechanisms that guide and restrict socioeconomic behaviours. Crucially, factors like the efficacy of property rights and contract enforcement within this framework significantly impact transaction costs (Coase, 1937;Williamson, 1975;). According to North (1991, p. 110), the institutional context 'dictates the margins at which organisations operate', providing a critical lens through which the behaviour of economic agents, especially businesses, can be understood. This perspective views the institutional environment as a foundational framework that underpins all economic exchange and production activities.

In the field of NIE, institutions are recognised to include both formal and informal components (North, 1991):

- **Formal** institutions comprise constitutions, laws, regulations, and contracts.
- **Informal** institutions consist of societal norms, values, and customs that are often shaped by longstanding cultural and religious influences.

While NIE acknowledges the importance of both types of institutions, its practical application has focused on formal aspects. This emphasis has led to a substantial interest in studying how various rules and regulations influence the selection and effectiveness of governance structures used to manage economic activities.

Institutions in a country shape the viability of engaging in certain economic activities, like foreign direct investment, by affecting the costs associated with transactions and production (Coase, 1998). 'Effective' institutional regimes are crucial because they help reduce transaction costs by eliminating the need for upfront expenditures, particularly when there is a lack of 'transactional trust'. High transaction costs can negatively impact economic productivity and subsequently inhibit economic growth (North, 1991). Therefore, the study of transaction costs underscores the fundamental role of institutions in minimising these costs. Viewing transaction costs as the 'cost of running the economic system' (Williamson, 1975), this analysis provides a unique perspective on how institutions influence the behaviour and decisions of economic agents, endorsing a pragmatic 'best way' approach (Rodrik, 2008).

As such, and for strategic thinking, understanding the interplay between institutions and transaction costs is vital for both policy-makers and businesses. By analysing how institutional frameworks can be optimised to minimise transaction costs, stakeholders can create an environment conducive to economic activity, attracting foreign direct investment and fostering entrepreneurship. Policy-makers must recognise that enhancing institutional quality – such as improving legal frameworks, enforcing contracts, and fostering transparency – can significantly lower the barriers to entry for new businesses and stimulate existing ones. Similarly, businesses can leverage this understanding to strategise their market entry and operational decisions, ensuring that they align with the institutional context to minimise costs and maximise efficiency. This insight is particularly relevant in a globalised economy, where the competitive landscape often hinges on the ability to navigate diverse institutional environments effectively. Thus, the relationship between institutions and transaction costs shapes economic outcomes and guides strategic decision-making, emphasising the necessity for adaptive approaches in both public and private sectors.

New Organisational Institutionalism

Grounded in sociology and organisational theory, organisational institutionalism views institutions as intra-organisational forms, practices, and activities shaped by coercive, mimetic, and normative mechanisms (DiMaggio & Powell, 1983; Scott, 2008). Unlike NIE, which focuses primarily on national-level institutions, organisational institutionalism provides a more granular, organisation-level analysis by emphasising how institutional pressures influence organisational structures and behaviours. This framework has proven especially useful for examining the diffusion of organisational patterns and the similarities and differences in practices across organisations.

Organisational institutionalism has sparked a rich body of literature focused on the internal and external legitimacies of firms (e.g. Kostova & Zaheer, 1999). The distinction between 'old' and 'new' organisational institutionalism further clarifies its evolution. Early institutionalists such as Selznick (1953) and Clark (1968) are regarded as the pioneers of old organisational institutionalism, which highlighted how organisations develop unique practices and competencies through institutionalisation. Selznick (1996) argued that institutionalisation results from the interplay between an organisation's internal dynamics and external environment, which shapes the 'character' of the organisation. This process creates enduring patterns of behaviour, allowing organisations to resist external pressures for change and maintain internal legitimacy.

In contrast, new organisational institutionalism, led by scholars like DiMaggio and Powell (1983) and Scott (1995), shifts the focus to understanding how organisations conform to external institutional pressures. These pressures drive isomorphism – where organisations become to resemble each other – as they seek legitimacy in their broader environments. While old organisational institutionalism emphasised institutionalisation as an adaptive process for internal stability and legitimacy, the new approach focuses on how organisations respond to institutional pressures for external legitimacy, offering a more dynamic view of organisational change and conformity.

Comparative Institutionalism

In contrast to other branches of institutional theory, the core idea behind comparative institutionalism is that diverse socioeconomic models are not simply variations of a singular 'market capitalist economy' nor a random assembly of economic institutions. This perspective challenges the dominant belief that there is one universally optimal growth model for maximising economic performance, as often pursued by contemporary governments. It also rejects the notion that structural reforms should aim for uniform liberalisation and deregulation across economies. Instead, comparative institutionalism views capitalism as a political economy characterised by institutionally diverse production regimes, where different institutional configurations and forms lead to distinct economic outcomes. Replicating identical institutional frameworks, such as sub-spheres or domains, across political economies does not guarantee similar growth trajectories, as each system is shaped by unique path dependencies and institutional complementarities (Amable, 2016).

A key tenet of comparative institutionalism is that societal institutions fundamentally shape the organisation of economic activities, which in turn affects organisational, business, and country-level outcomes (Hall & Soskice, 2001; Jackson & Deeg, 2008; Woodhouse, 2024). Unlike NIE and New Organisational Institutionalism, which often emphasise convergence towards similar institutional forms or practices, comparative institutionalism highlights divergence and diversity as essential features of institutional development (Woodhouse & Johnston, 2023). This divergence is crucial to understanding the variety of capitalist systems and the distinct pathways economies take based on their institutional arrangements.

Within this framework, national political economies are understood to follow specific 'logics' of economic agency, developed through distinct typologies of institutional configurations. Comparative institutionalism suggests that the character and interests of economic actors are shaped by these arrangements, which in turn condition the development of their resources, strategies, and capabilities. Thus, institutions do not just set the rules of the game; they actively shape the 'supply side' of the economy by determining how key inputs – land, labour, capital, and products – are organised and accessed by businesses (Hancke, 2009). This perspective underscores the role of institutional complementarity, where different institutional elements interact in ways that reinforce and enhance each other, contributing to the unique outcomes observed in various capitalist economies.

Comparative institutionalism also emphasises that institutional configurations are deeply embedded in historical and social contexts, resulting in path dependency – the tendency for economic and institutional development to follow historical trajectories, making radical shifts or transformations difficult. This helps explain why attempts to impose identical institutional reforms in different contexts often fail – different political economies have distinct institutional histories and interdependencies that shape their present and future trajectories. Therefore, instead of striving for convergence towards a uniform model of liberal capitalism, comparative institutionalism argues for the recognition of institutional variety and the importance of tailoring economic reforms to the specific institutional contexts of each country.

This perspective has significant implications for policy-making, as it cautions against one-size-fits-all approaches to economic reform. Comparative institutionalism suggests that successful growth and development depend not on replicating a single ideal model but on recognising and working within the unique institutional configurations of each political economy. This diversity in institutional structures and practices creates the varied forms of capitalism observed across different countries, each with its own strengths, weaknesses, and growth potential.

The three approaches to institutional theory are summarised in Table 4.1.

INSTITUTIONAL THEORY AND INSIGHTS FOR STRATEGIC THINKING

Institutional theory offers significant insights for strategic thinking and decision-making in several ways. At a top level, by incorporating insight from institutional theory into strategic thinking and decision-making, organisations can effectively navigate their complex business and economic environments, making choices that are strategically sound and institutionally informed. This enhances their ability to achieve long-term sustainability and success. There are four key ways in which institutional theory can offer insights for strategic thinking.

Understanding of Institutional Context

Understanding the broader institutional contexts in which organisations operate is a fundamental aspect of strategic thinking and decision-making (Woodhouse & Johnston, 2023). This scopes how various norms, regulations, and cultural expectations collectively shape the business environments, offering insights that can be pivotal for organisational strategy.

The core idea behind (comparative) institutional perspectives is that diverse economies do not represent nearly identical versions of the same 'market capitalist economy' nor a random assembly of institutions. Capitalism, in this view, is perceived as consisting of institutionally varied production regimes, adopting diverse institutional configurations and forms. Therefore, replicating identical institutional areas (such as institutional sub-spheres or domains) across different political economies would not result in identical growth trajectories, especially considering path dependencies and institutional complementarities (Amable et al., 2011). In business, strategic decisions such as expansion and defining subsidiary roles may not yield the same results in two countries, even if both countries appear similar. The work of Woodhouse and Johnston (2023), for example, finds a variety of country clusters. In this view, Germany is as different to the United Kingdom as is the UK to Mexico. Preconceptions of country similarity can be dangerous, and more recognised insights of the formal and informal institutions that define countries are required.

Moreover, the nuances of institutional contexts extend beyond superficial categorisations like 'Western and capitalist'. Even within supposedly similar regions, such as Europe or North America, significant variations exist in terms of regulatory frameworks, cultural norms, and historical legacies. For example, while both France and the United States may be considered Western capitalist economies, their institutional landscapes differ vastly due to factors such as legal traditions, labour market regulations, and attitudes towards foreign investment.

These institutional differences can impact the success of strategic decisions. For instance, a strategy that proved effective in one country may falter in another due to contrasting regulatory environments or divergent cultural expectations. Ignoring these institutional nuances can lead to costly missteps and missed opportunities for organisations seeking to expand internationally. To navigate this complexity, organisations must conduct thorough institutional analysis before making strategic decisions. This involves examining not only formal institutions like laws and regulations but also informal institutions such as social norms, trust networks, and cultural practices. By understanding how these institutions interact and shape behaviour within a given context, organisations can develop strategies that are better aligned with the realities of their operating environments.

Furthermore, institutional analysis enables organisations to identify potential synergies and conflicts between different institutional spheres. A strategy that aligns with regulatory requirements in one area may clash with cultural norms in another, highlighting the need for consideration and adaptation of the strategy.

In conclusion, understanding the different environments where organisations operate is key to making smart strategic decisions. By including institutional analysis in their planning, organisations can reduce risks, seize opportunities, and improve their chances of success in a complex global market.

Ability to Understand and Adapt to Institutional Change

Understanding the broader institutional contexts in which organisations operate is fundamental, but this offers a static perspective. It is a snapshot in time. Institutions of economies are dynamic. While national institutions typically change at a slow rate, research has shown that institutional change does occur (Gingrich, 2015). Institutional change reflects political and business coalitions that emerge and provides a critical mass of actioned change. Chapter 3 includes insight on a strategic thinker's role in politics and policy-making.

Managing institutional change is a critical aspect of strategic decision-making, especially in environments characterised by rapid regulatory changes or cultural shifts. Organisations must be prepared to adapt their strategies in response to these evolving institutional landscapes to remain competitive and resilient.

One key aspect of managing institutional change is anticipating shifts in the institutional environment. By closely monitoring political developments, regulatory trends, and societal movements, leaders can identify emerging changes and proactively adjust their strategies accordingly. This proactive approach allows organisations to stay ahead of the curve and capitalise on new opportunities while mitigating potential risks associated with evolving institutional dynamics.

Additionally, organisations must be agile and responsive in their strategic decision-making processes to effectively navigate institutional change. This requires a willingness to embrace innovation and experimentation, as well as the ability to quickly pivot strategies in response to shifting institutional pressures. By fostering a culture of adaptability and change readiness, organisations can position themselves to thrive in dynamic institutional environments.

Furthermore, managing institutional change requires effective communication and stakeholder engagement. Leaders must communicate the rationale behind strategic shifts and involve stakeholders in the decision-making process to garner support and facilitate buy-in. Engaging with key stakeholders, including government agencies, industry associations, and community groups, can also help organisations navigate regulatory changes and build collaborative partnerships that enhance their resilience to institutional change. Stakeholders are discussed further in Chapter 6.

Institutional theory offers unique insights into the potential trajectory of institutional change. It suggests that institutional changes may be predictable, allowing insight into how much economies/institutions can change. The business environment is made up of several institutions (referred to as institutional sub-spheres) that define an economy's (1) labour markets, (2) the financial system, and (3) education system, for example. These institutions are non-random and compatible with each other. They are jigsaw pieces that fit together. More formally, the business environment has the presence of 'institutional complementarities' (Amable, 2016).

The notion of 'institutional complementarity' is widely used in comparative institutional analysis to express the idea that certain institutional forms, when jointly combined, continue to reinforce each other, and contribute to improving the functioning, stability, and coherence of specific institutional configurations or 'models of capitalism' (Amable, 2016). The existence of institutional complementarities explains how differentiated economies may exist based on complements between institutional forms. For example, flexible labour markets (regulations that make it easy to 'hire and fire') complement a financial system that permits short-term capital provision, allowing organisations

TABLE 4.2 The Types of Interactions/Complementarities between Institutional Sub-spheres

Institutional sub-sphere	Key features	Complementarities and interactions
Product markets	• Structured to encourage competition and innovation. • Regulation to control monopolistic behaviour.	• Connected to financial system through capital needs for innovation. • Requires skilled labour from labour markets.
Education system	• Quality-based competition for skill development. • Focus on long-term skill formation. • Strong vocational training.	• Links to labour markets through skill development. • Supports financial systems by providing skilled human capital.
Financial system	• Focus on long-term capital investment. • Encourages innovation and stability.	• Requires employment stability from labour markets. • Supports product markets by providing capital for innovation.
Labour markets	• Employment protection enhances workforce stability. • Strong emphasis on specific skills development.	• Linked to education system through skill formation. • Stability supports long-term investments from financial system. • Influences demand in product markets.

to control costs more easily and yield profits. This 'combination' is typical of liberal economies like the UK and USA (Hall & Gingerich, 2009; Woodhouse & Johnston, 2023). The consensus on institutional complementarities on market/liberal economies (e.g. UK, USA, Canada) and coordinated based economies (e.g. Germany, Netherlands, Sweden, etc.) is set out in the work of Amable (2016). We provide a simplified schematic of the types of interactions/complementarities between institutional sub-spheres in Table 4.2.

Institutional complementarity provides important insight into institutional change. Change, triggered by political will, aimed at altering the composition of given institution(s) may cause incoherence or disequilibria that weaken the stability of the overall institutional system. For example, the impact of the European Union 'Lisbon Agenda' has been called into question about its impact on the coherence of non-liberal capitalist models (Amable, 2016). In this view, complete change of all institutions is impossible, and any institutional change is likely to reinforce the status quo of the institutional context. Simply, the UK economy will never be like the German economy (a more coordinated economy), even if there was political and business will in the UK to be so. Any longer-term change is likely to be predictable.

Enhancing Organisational Legitimacy

Strategic decisions frequently extend beyond economic ramifications and encompass considerations of organisational legitimacy. According to institutional theory, legitimacy holds paramount significance for the success of organisations. Strategies that align with the expectations of institutional stakeholders, including governmental bodies, trade associations, and cultural communities, stand a greater chance of garnering support and recognition.

Organisations operate within a broader institutional environment that dictates norms, regulations, and cultural expectations. Conforming to these institutional norms bolsters an organisation's legitimacy, enhancing its standing within the societal framework. Conversely, strategies that diverge from institutional expectations risk facing resistance and scrutiny, undermining the organisation's credibility and long-term viability.

Therefore, strategic decision-makers must evaluate the institutional context in which their organisation operates. By aligning strategic initiatives with institutional expectations, organisations can cultivate trust and goodwill among key stakeholders, fostering a supportive environment conducive to growth and sustainability. This emphasis on organisational legitimacy underscores the interconnectedness between strategic decision-making and the broader institutional landscape, highlighting the need for strategic alignment with institutional norms and values.

Let us consider a multinational corporation planning to expand its operations into a new market. Before entering the market, the corporation conducts thorough research on the local regulatory environment, cultural norms, and societal expectations. It identifies that the government in the target market has stringent environmental regulations and a strong emphasis on sustainability practices. Additionally, there is a prevalent cultural sentiment favouring businesses that demonstrate a commitment to environmental stewardship.

Considering these institutional factors, the organisation devises a strategic plan that not only focuses on profitability but also emphasises environmental sustainability. It invests in green technologies, implements eco-friendly manufacturing processes, and initiates community outreach programmes to support environmental causes. By aligning its strategy with the institutional expectations of the government and the local community, the organisation not only enhances its legitimacy but also gains the support and trust of key stakeholders.

Influence on Organisational Behaviour

Institutional theory offers valuable insights into how institutions shape organisational behaviours and processes (North, 1991). By examining these influences, organisations can understand the underlying reasons behind their (and others') strategic decisions. For instance, consider a retail company operating in the United Kingdom's fashion industry.

In this example, institutional theory reveals how the company's strategic choices are influenced by various external factors. The company must comply with regulatory standards set by government agencies, such as those pertaining to labour laws, consumer rights, and environmental regulations. These regulations not only dictate the company's operational practices but also influence its strategic decisions, such as sourcing materials from ethical suppliers and implementing sustainable business practices to mitigate environmental impact.

Furthermore, institutional theory highlights the importance of adhering to cultural norms within the fashion industry. In the UK, there is a growing awareness and demand for sustainable and ethically sourced fashion products. Therefore, the company's strategic decisions, such as investing in eco-friendly manufacturing processes and promoting ethical fashion initiatives, are influenced by societal expectations and industry standards.

Additionally, institutional pressures from industry peers, trade associations, and consumer advocacy groups can influence the company's behaviour and strategic choices. For example, the company may face pressure to align with industry-wide initiatives aimed at promoting diversity and inclusion in the workforce or reducing carbon emissions throughout the supply chain.

By recognising these institutional pressures and influences, the company can make informed strategic decisions that not only ensure compliance with regulatory standards but also enhance its reputation, brand image, and long-term sustainability. Institutional theory helps explain how external factors influence organisational behaviour, enabling companies to adapt to their environments effectively. This understanding is at the heart of strategic thinking.

A summary of implications for strategic thinking is given in Table 4.3.

CASE STUDY 4.1

Strategic Decision-making at Marks & Spencer (M&S)

Introduction

Marks & Spencer (M&S), a renowned British multinational retailer, faces the challenge of expanding its operations into new international markets while maintaining its position as a leader in the retail industry. Incorporating insights from institutional theory into its strategic decision-making processes can provide valuable guidance for navigating the complex institutional contexts of various countries.

1. Understanding of Institutional Context

M&S recognises the importance of understanding the diverse institutional contexts in which it operates. The company conducts thorough analyses of the regulatory frameworks, cultural norms, and historical legacies of potential new markets before making strategic decisions. For example, when considering expansion into European markets, M&S acknowledges the significant variations in institutional landscapes among countries, such as differences in legal traditions and labour market regulations.

Example: M&S conducted extensive research before entering the French market, recognising that despite being a Western capitalist economy like the UK, France has distinct institutional differences, particularly in terms of labour laws and consumer preferences. By understanding these institutional nuances, M&S tailored its market entry strategy to align with French regulatory requirements and cultural expectations, thereby mitigating risks and enhancing its chances of success.

2. Ability to Understand and Adapt to Institutional Change

M&S acknowledges that institutional environments are dynamic and subject to change over time. The company actively monitors political developments, regulatory trends, and societal movements to anticipate shifts in institutional landscapes. By embracing innovation and fostering a culture of adaptability, M&S remains responsive to evolving institutional pressures, ensuring its continued competitiveness and resilience.

Example: In response to growing consumer demand for sustainable and ethically sourced products, M&S underwent a strategic shift to incorporate eco-friendly manufacturing processes and promote ethical fashion initiatives. By aligning its strategy with evolving institutional expectations regarding environmental sustainability, M&S not only enhanced its legitimacy but also gained the support and trust of key stakeholders, including consumers and advocacy groups.

3. Enhancing Organisational Legitimacy

M&S recognises the importance of aligning its strategic decisions with institutional expectations to enhance its legitimacy within the broader societal framework. By conforming to regulatory requirements and cultural norms, M&S cultivates trust and goodwill among key stakeholders, fostering a supportive environment conducive to growth and sustainability.

Example: When expanding into markets with stringent environmental regulations and a strong emphasis on sustainability, such as Scandinavia, M&S proactively adjusted its strategy to prioritise environmental stewardship. By investing in green technologies and community outreach programmes, M&S not only complied with institutional expectations but also bolstered its legitimacy and garnered support from governmental bodies and local communities.

4. Influence on Organisational Behaviour

Institutional theory sheds light on how external institutional factors influence M&S's strategic decisions and organisational behaviour. By recognising these influences, M&S can make informed decisions that ensure compliance with regulatory standards, enhance its reputation, and promote long-term sustainability.

Example: In response to institutional pressures to promote diversity and inclusion in the workforce, M&S implemented initiatives aimed at fostering a more inclusive workplace environment. By aligning its behaviour with industry-wide standards and societal expectations, M&S not only enhanced its brand image but also strengthened its position as a socially responsible retailer.

Conclusion

By incorporating insights from institutional theory into its strategic decision-making processes, Marks & Spencer effectively navigates the complex institutional contexts of international markets, ensuring its long-term sustainability and success in an ever-changing business landscape.

TABLE 4.3 A Summary of Implications for Strategic Thinking

Insight from institutional theory	Description	Implications for strategic thinking
1. Understanding of institutional context	• Organisations must comprehend their broader institutional environments, including norms, regulations, and cultural expectations, to navigate strategic decisions effectively (Woodhouse & Johnston, 2023). • Different institutional configurations influence economic outcomes, meaning that similar strategies may yield different results across countries. • Organisations should conduct thorough institutional analyses to identify nuances that may affect their strategies and success.	• Develop context-specific strategies by conducting comprehensive institutional analyses. • Avoid assumptions of similarity across markets and tailor strategies to local conditions.
2. Ability to understand and adapt to institutional change	• Institutions are dynamic, changing over time; organisations must manage these changes effectively to remain competitive (Gingrich, 2015). • Organisations should monitor political and regulatory developments to anticipate changes and adapt strategies accordingly. • A culture of adaptability and effective stakeholder engagement is crucial for managing institutional change and building resilience.	• Foster a culture of adaptability within the organisation to respond swiftly to institutional changes. • Implement continuous monitoring of the political and regulatory landscape.
3. Enhancing organisational legitimacy	• Legitimacy is vital for organisational success; aligning strategies with institutional expectations fosters support and trust among stakeholders. • Organisations that conform to norms and regulations can enhance their credibility and long-term viability. • For example, multinational corporations must consider local regulatory and cultural factors when entering new markets to build legitimacy.	• Prioritise stakeholder engagement to build trust and enhance legitimacy. • Align strategic initiatives with institutional expectations to secure support.
4. Influence on organisational behaviour	• Institutional theory explains how external factors influence organisational behaviour and strategic decisions (North, 1991). • Compliance with regulations and adherence to cultural norms shape operational practices and strategic choices, such as ethical sourcing and sustainable practices in the fashion industry. • Understanding these influences allows organisations to adapt their strategies effectively.	• Recognise and analyse external pressures influencing organisational behaviour. • Adapt strategies to meet regulatory requirements and societal expectations.

CHAPTER SUMMARY

What Can a Strategic Thinker Do?

The integration of neoclassical economics and institutional theory into strategy-making offers a comprehensive approach to navigating the complexities of modern business environments. We summarise the pros and cons of each theoretical approach, with their implications for strategic thinking, in Table 4.4. By combining these frameworks, organisations can develop robust, ethical, and sustainable strategic plans that are well aligned with both economic objectives and institutional contexts.

1. **Balancing short-term and long-term goals:** Neoclassical economics emphasises short-term profit maximisation and operational efficiency, while institutional theory encourages a long-term focus on sustainability, social responsibility, and regulatory adaptation. Strategic thinkers can harness this duality, creating a balance between optimising short-term profitability and ensuring long-term viability. This approach allows firms to remain competitive while also addressing evolving societal and institutional demands, such as environmental sustainability and corporate ethics.
2. **Adaptive strategy in dynamic markets:** Neoclassical models provide tools for responding to market fluctuations and making data-driven decisions. However, institutional theory adds a layer of adaptability by equipping businesses with insights into how institutions and regulatory environments change over time. Strategic thinkers can leverage this to create flexible strategies that not only respond to immediate market conditions but also anticipate institutional shifts and evolving social expectations.
3. **Organisational resilience:** By integrating institutional insights, organisations can build resilience against external shocks, such as regulatory changes, societal pressure, or cultural shifts. Strategic thinkers who incorporate institutional theory into their planning can anticipate changes and develop proactive measures, such as improving stakeholder relations or aligning business practices with emerging social norms. This leads to stronger, adaptable organisations capable of thriving in unpredictable environments.

4. **Ethical and inclusive decision-making:** Neoclassical economics tends to focus on profit maximisation, often sidelining ethical considerations, while institutional theory promotes a deeper engagement with social norms, ethical issues, and stakeholder expectations. Strategic thinkers can use this combined perspective to craft strategies that are not only financially sound but also socially responsible. This ethical dimension enhances corporate reputation, stakeholder trust, and long-term sustainability.
5. **Leveraging quantitative and qualitative insights:** Neoclassical economics offers powerful quantitative tools for evaluating performance, costs, and market dynamics, while institutional theory brings a qualitative understanding of how culture, values, and institutions influence behaviour. A strategic thinker who draws on both frameworks can apply quantitative analysis to measure business performance while using qualitative insights to ensure that strategies are aligned with broader social and institutional contexts.
6. **Innovation and collaboration:** Institutional theory emphasises the importance of collaboration, networks, and partnerships, encouraging organisations to work with stakeholders and external institutions. By fostering such collaborations, businesses can drive innovation, share knowledge, and stay ahead of industry trends. Neoclassical insights, meanwhile, provide the analytical framework to ensure that these collaborations remain efficient and value-driven.

This integrated approach not only enhances organisational success but also contributes to the broader goal of creating more inclusive, equitable, and sustainable economic systems. Strategic thinkers who understand that economics extends beyond mainstream neoclassical thought are better equipped to generate novel insights and devise strategies that are multidimensional. By incorporating both individualistic and institutional perspectives, businesses can remain competitive while also contributing to a more sustainable and equitable global economy.

TABLE 4.4 The Pros and Cons of Neoclassical Economics and Institutional Theory

The plurality of economics and the implications for strategic thinking			
Neoclassical economics		**Institutional theory**	
The good (pros)	**The not so good (cons)**	**The good (pros)**	**The not so good (cons)**
Individualism focus: It prioritises individual decision-making and personal responsibility, aligning with liberal democratic principles. Moreover, this framework assumes that individuals, acting in their self-interest, make rational decisions that contribute to overall economic efficiency. Consequently, by focusing on personal responsibility, individuals are expected to bear the outcome of their decisions, whether positive or negative.	**Overlooks social institutions**: It overlooks the importance of social institutional, and collective dynamics that shape economic behaviour and outcomes. This is because it focuses primarily on individual decision-making and assumes that each person acts independently to maximise personal utility or profit. Economic actions are deeply influenced by factors such as social norms, cultural values, institutions, and historical contexts, all of which guide how individuals behave in markets.	**Recognising the role of institutions**: Institutional theory emphasises how institutions (formal and informal rules, norms, and practices) shape economic behaviour and organisational outcomes. This understanding helps organisations navigate complex environments influenced by societal expectations and cultural norms.	**Analysing operational efficiency**: Institutional theory tends to focus more on the social and cultural contexts that shape behaviour rather than on the specific mechanisms that drive operational efficiency. It may not provide the quantitative tools or models needed to evaluate performance metrics effectively. It emphasises longer-term issues over short-term ones.
Rationality assumption: Neoclassical economics assumes individuals behave rationally, seeking to maximise utility or profit, which ensures that scarce resources are allocated to their most valuable uses. This rational behaviour assumption provides a clear and structured framework for understanding and predicting economic decision-making. Furthermore, it assumes that all economic agents – whether individuals, firms, or governments – have access to perfect information, allowing them to weigh the costs and benefits of every decision they make.	**Irrational nature of humans**: The assumption that individuals always act rationally in neoclassical economics is often criticised as overly simplistic. People frequently make decisions that are not purely logical or self-serving. Instead, individuals often act irrationally, driven by a variety of factors such as emotions, cognitive biases, or incomplete information, all of which can impact on strategic decision-making in organisations.	**Understanding organisational behaviour**: It provides insights into how organisations adapt to their institutional contexts. By analysing the pressures and expectations from various stakeholders, organisations can better align their strategies with the realities of their environments that extend beyond markets.	**Quantitative evaluation of initiatives**: While institutional theory emphasises qualitative aspects of decision-making influenced by institutional norms and values, it often lacks rigorous quantitative analysis. This can make it challenging for organisations to evaluate the financial impact of specific strategic initiatives systematically.

(*Continued*)

TABLE 4.4 Continued

The plurality of economics and the implications for strategic thinking			
Neoclassical economics		**Institutional theory**	
The good (pros)	**The not so good (cons)**	**The good (pros)**	**The not so good (cons)**
Focusing on profit maximisation: By focusing on profit maximisation, firms can contribute to overall economic efficiency by ensuring that scarce resources are allocated to their most valuable uses. This can lead to an increase in both producer and consumer surplus within competitive markets. Moreover, profit maximisation also fosters investment and economic growth, as successful firms reinvest profits into expanding operations, creating jobs and improving productivity.	**Ignores border societal goals:** Profit maximisation ignores broader societal goals, such as equitable wealth distribution and environmental sustainability, which often requires sacrificing immediate profit for the greater good. As such, it often leads to short-term thinking by prioritising immediate profit over long-term sustainability or ethical considerations. This approach can also lead to the prioritisation of profit at the expense of employee well-being and corporate ethics.	**Navigating regulatory changes:** Institutional theory equips organisations with frameworks to understand and adapt to regulatory changes effectively. It emphasises compliance and the role of regulations in shaping business practices, helping organisations avoid legal pitfalls and align with government expectations.	**Focusing on profitability:** Institutional theory can sometimes prioritise social and ethical considerations at the expense of profitability. While this perspective is crucial for sustainable practices, it may lead to suboptimal financial outcomes for organisations that need to balance profit with social responsibility.
Marginalism: Uses marginal analysis to guide decisions, focusing on incremental changes that maximise utility or profit, which is useful in business and resource allocation. This approach assumes that individuals and businesses make rational decisions by comparing the marginal cost (the cost of producing one additional unit of a good or service) with the marginal benefit (the additional satisfaction a person or business gains from consuming or producing one more unit of a good or service).	**Overlooks systemic issues**: Marginalism often overlooks larger systemic issues, focusing more on short-term or small-scale optimisation while ignoring broader social impacts. This narrow focus also means that marginalism may not be well equipped to deal with long-term systemic challenges such as climate change, inequality, or financial crises.	**Facilitating change management**: By understanding institutional pressures, organisations can develop strategies for managing change more effectively. Institutional theory helps identify the forces driving change and the resistance that may arise, allowing for more informed and strategic responses.	**Adaptability in dynamic markets:** Although institutional theory recognises the importance of institutions in shaping behaviour, it may struggle to keep pace with rapid changes in market conditions. Organisations might find it challenging to adapt quickly to new trends or disruptions when relying heavily on institutional frameworks.

(Continued)

TABLE 4.4 Continued

The plurality of economics and the implications for strategic thinking			
Neoclassical economics		**Institutional theory**	
The good (pros)	**The not so good (cons)**	**The good (pros)**	**The not so good (cons)**
Focus on equilibrium: Neoclassical economics provides insight in how economies move towards equilibrium, a state where supply and demand in the market naturally balance each other. This equilibrium is achieved through market forces: when there is excess supply (a surplus), prices tend to fall, and when there is excess demand (a shortage), prices rise. These adjustments help guide the market back to a balance state.	**Market equilibrium – a rare condition**: The assumption of equilibrium is often criticised because real-world markets are highly dynamic and rarely, if ever, reach a state of perfect equilibrium as described in traditional neoclassical economic models. In practice, markets are constantly evolving and influenced by various factors that lead to fluctuation, imbalances, and inefficiencies.	**Enhancing collaboration and networks:** Institutional theory highlights the importance of collaboration and relationships among organisations, stakeholders, and institutions. This perspective encourages companies to build networks and partnerships that can enhance innovation and knowledge sharing.	**Adaptability in dynamic markets:** Although institutional theory recognises the importance of institutions in shaping behaviour, it may struggle to keep pace with rapid changes in market conditions. Organisations might find it challenging to adapt quickly to new trends or disruptions when relying heavily on institutional frameworks. It promotes longer-term strategic thinking over short-term decision-making.
Short-term focus: Neoclassical economics is well suited for guiding firms and markets in short-term optimisation. It prioritises immediate resource allocation, enhancing operational efficiency and competitive positioning. It focuses on maximising short-term profits, minimising cost, systematically evaluates the incremental benefits and costs of strategic initiatives, and ensures that every strategic decision is evaluated for its potential to enhance profitability, thereby supporting the organisation's long-term success.	**Lack of long-term focus**: Neoclassical economics often overlooks long-term strategies like innovation, sustainability, and investment in research and development, which are crucial for future growth and resilience. As a result, it tends to neglect non-economic factors, such as ethical considerations, dynamic market conditions, social inequality, and environmental impacts. This focus can lead to myopic behaviour, where firms prioritise short-run profit gains at the expense of long-term viability. Moreover, by emphasising competition and profit maximisation, Neoclassical economics relies heavily on simplistic assumptions.	**Fostering long-term strategic thinking:** Institutional theory promotes a long-term view of strategy by encouraging organisations to consider the impact of their actions on institutions and society. This perspective helps businesses make more informed decisions that align with long-term goals, ensuring sustainability and resilience in changing environments.	**Underestimating competitive forces:** Institutional theory can sometimes underplay the role of competition and market forces. While it acknowledges the impact of institutions, it may not adequately address how competitive dynamics can influence organisational behaviour and strategic decision-making. It involves itself more with 'meta' market issues.

RECOMMENDED READING

Harvey, J. (2015) *Contending Perspectives in Economics: A Guide to Contemporary Schools of Thought* (1st ed.). London: Edward Elgar.
(For exploring further the plurality of economics)
Woodhouse, D. & Johnston, A. (2023) Comparative capitalism and the empirical taxonomy of context: Enhancing the institutionalist blueprint. *Critical Perspectives on International Business*, 19(5), 661–698.
(*On institutional theory*)

REFERENCES

Abhyankar, A. (2019) Behavioural economics towards better decision making. *Journal of Global Economy*, 16(2), 2278–1277.

Aleskerov, F., Bouyssou, D. & Monjardet, B. (2007) *Utility Maximisation, Choice and Preference* (Vol. 16). London: Springer Science & Business Media.

Alhosseiny, H.M. (2023) The impact of strategic planning, strategic thinking, and strategic agility on competitive advantage: Literature review. *Academy of Strategic Management Journal*, 22, 1–14.

AlQershi, N. (2021) Strategic thinking, strategic planning, strategic innovation and the performance of SMEs: The mediating role of human capital. *Management Science Letters*, 11(3),1003–1012.

Amable, B. (2003) *The Diversity of Modern Capitalism*. Oxford: Oxford University Press.

Amable, B. (2016) Institutional complementarities in the dynamic comparative analysis of capitalism. *Journal of Institutional Economics*, 12(1), 79–103.

Amable, B., Ledezma, I. & Robin, S. (2016) Product market regulation, innovation, and productivity. *Research Policy*, 45(10), 2087–2104.

Arnsperger, C. & Varoufakis, Y. (2006) What Is neoclassical economics? The three axioms responsible for its theoretical oeuvre, practical irrelevance and, thus, discursive power. *Panoeconomicus*, 53(1), 5–18.

Arnsperger, C. & Varoufakis, Y. (2008) Neoclassical economics. Three identifying features. *Pluralist economics*, 13–25.

Bağdigen, M. & Avcı, M. (2013) An empirical analysis of the strategic plan implementation in public administrations, 1306–2174. https://www.academia.edu/111930639/An_Empirical_Analysis_of_the_Strategic_Plan_Implementation_in_Public_Administrations.

Barney, J.B. (2000) Firm resources and sustained competitive advantage. In J.A.C. Baum & F. Dobbin (Eds.) *Economics Meets Sociology in Strategic Management* (pp. 203–227). Emerald Group Publishing.

Brueckner, M. (2013) 'Profit maximisation.' In *Encyclopedia of Corporate Social Responsibility* 2. doi: 10.1007/978-3-642-28036-8_129.

Casson, M. (1997) *Culture, social norms and economics*. London: Edward Elgar.

Celik, T.S. (2019) The rational vs. behavioral approaches to strategy thinking. *International Journal of Contemporary Economics and Administrative Sciences*, 9(1), 184–204.

Chibba, M. & Luiz, J.M. (2019) Inequality: Concepts, data, perspectives and solutions. *World Economics*, 20(1), 1–54.

Clark, T.N. (1968) Institutionalization of innovations in higher education: Four models. *Administrative Science Quarterly*, 1–25.

Coase, R. (1937) The nature of the firm. *Economica*, 4(16), 386–405.

Coase, R. (1998) The New Institutional Economics. *The American Economic Review*, 88(2), 72–74.

DiMaggio, P. & Powell, W. (1983) The iron cage revisited: Institutional isomorphism and collective rationality in organisational fields. *American Sociological Review*, 48(2), 147–160.

Flach, B. & Mendes, C.R. (2013) Strategic project planning: Optimal contracting and resource allocation. *IFAC Proceedings Volumes*, 46(24), 438–442.

Ghobadian, A., O'regan, N., Thomas, H. & Liu, J. (2008) Formal strategic planning, operating environment, size, sector and performance: Evidence from the UK's manufacturing SMEs. *Journal of General Management*, 34(2), 1–20.

Gilad, B., Kaish, S. & Loeb, P.D. (1987) Cognitive dissonance and utility maximisation: A general framework. *Journal of Economic Behavior & Organisation*, 8(1), 61–73.

Gingrich, J. (2015) Varying costs to change? Institutional change in the public sector. *Governance*, 28(1), 41–60.

Grigorescu, A. & Chiper, A. (2016) The importance of human capital in the strategic development of an organisation. *Studies and Scientific Researches. Economics Edition*. https://www.academia.edu/60039031/The_Importance_of_Human_Capital_in_the_Strategic_Development_of_an_Organization.

Gueldry, M. (2015) The double discipline of neoclassical economics: When the map both hides and reveals the territory. *Real-world economics review*, 72, 27–57.

Gustafsson, S., Hermelin, B. & Smas, L. (2019) Integrating environmental sustainability into strategic spatial planning: The importance of management. *Journal of Environmental Planning and Management*, 62(8), 1321–1338.

Gutterman, A.S. (2023) Introduction to strategic planning. Available at SSRN 4407351.

Halkos, G. & Psarianos, I. (2016) Exploring the effect of including the environment in the neoclassical growth model. *Environmental Economics and Policy Studies*, 18, 339–358.

Hall, P.A. & Gingerich, D.W. (2009) Varieties of capitalism and institutional complementarities in the political economy: An empirical analysis. *British Journal of Political Science*, 39(3), 449–482.

Hall, P. & Soskice, D. (2001) *Varieties of Capitalism: The Institutional Foundations of Comparative Advantage*. Oxford: Oxford University Press.

Hancke, B. (2009) Debating varieties of capitalism: Introduction. In B. Hancke (Ed.), *Debating Varieties of Capitalism: A Reader*. Oxford: Oxford University Press, pp. 1–20.

Hargreaves-Heap, S. & Varoufakis, Y.(2004) *Game Theory: A Critical Introduction*. Abingdon, Oxon: Routledge.

Harrison, R. & Kennedy, P. (1997) A neoclassical economic and strategic management approach to evaluating global agribusiness competitiveness. *Competitiveness Review: An International Business Journal*, 7(1), 14–25.

Henry, J.F. (2012) *The Making of Neoclassical Economics (Routledge Revivals)*. Abingdon, Oxon: Routledge.

Hodgson, G. (1998) The approach of institutional economics. *Journal of Economic Literature*, 36(1), 166–192.

Hodgson, G. (2001) Frontiers of institutional economics. *New Political Economy*, 6(2), 245–253.

Holbrook, D. (1991) Consequentialism: The philosophical dog that does not bark? *Utilitas*, 3(1), 107–112.

Holt, C.A. & Roth, A.E. (2004) The Nash equilibrium: A perspective. *Proceedings of the National Academy of Sciences*, 101(12), 3999-4002.

Hosmer, L.T. (1994) Strategic planning as if ethics mattered. *Strategic Management Journal*, 15(S2), 17–34.

Jackson, G. & Deeg, R. (2008) Comparing capitalisms: Understanding institutional diversity and its implications for international business. *Journal of International Business Studies*, 39(4), 540–561.

Jackson, G. & Deeg, R. (2019) Comparing capitalisms and taking institutional context seriously. *Journal of International Business Studies*, 50(1), 4–19.

Kaplan, R.S., Serafeim, G. & Tugendhat, E. (2019) Intelligent design of inclusive growth strategies. *Harvard Business School Accounting & Management Unit Working Paper* (20-050).

Keen, S. & Standish, R. (2006) Profit maximisation, industry structure, and competition: A critique of neoclassical theory. *Physica A: Statistical Mechanics and its Applications*, 370(1), 81–85.

Kehbila, A.G. (2021) The entrepreneur's go-to-market innovation strategy: Towards a decision-analytic framework and a road mapping process to create radically successful businesses driving spectacular growth and profitability. *Journal of Small Business & Entrepreneurship*, 33(6), 689–716.

Kenworthy, L. (2006) Institutional coherence and macroeconomic performance. *Socio-Economic Review*, 4(1), 69–91.

Klees, S.J. (2008) A quarter century of neoliberal thinking in education: Misleading analyses and failed policies. *Globalisation, Societies and Education*, 6(4), 311–348.

Kostova, T. & Zaheer, S. (1999) Organisational legitimacy under conditions of complexity: The case of the multinational enterprise. *The Academy of Management Review*, 24(1), 64–81.

Kreps, D.M. (1989) Nash equilibrium. In J. Eatwell, M. Milgate & P. Newman (Eds.), *Game Theory* (pp. 167–177). London: Palgrave Macmillan UK.

López, D. & Oliver, M. (2023) Integrating innovation into business strategy: Perspectives from innovation managers. *Sustainability*, 15(8), 6503.

Lowder, B.T. (2009) Strategic thinking and strategic planning: Two pieces of the same puzzle. Available at SSRN 1418793.

Maia, I.R.D. & Chaves, G.M. (2016) Integration of risk management into strategic planning: A new comprehensive approach. *Society of Actuaries and Casualty Actuarial Society*.

Maialeh, R. (2019) Generalization of results and neoclassical rationality: Unresolved controversies of behavioural economics methodology. *Quality & Quantity*, 53, 1743–1761.

Mantel, R.R. (1975) General equilibrium and optimal taxes. *Journal of Mathematical Economics*, 2(2), 187–200.

Marckmann, G. (2009) Utility maximisation with fairness constraints: Perspectives of an ethically justifiable cost-utility analysis. *Das Gesundheitswesen*, 71(S 01), S2–S8.

Mazzarol, T., Reboud, S. & Soutar, G.N. (2009) Strategic planning in growth oriented small firms. *International Journal of Entrepreneurial Behavior & Research*, 15(4), 320–345.

Menard, C. & Shirley, M. (2005) *Handbook of New Institutional Economics*. New York: Springer.

Meyer, J. & Rowan, B. (1977) Institutionalised organisations: Formal structure as myth and ceremony. *American Journal of Sociology*, 83(2), 340–363.

Monye, M.C. & Ibegbulem, A.B. (2018) Effect of strategic planning on organizational performance and profitability. *International Journal of Business & Law Research*, 6(2), 31–40.

Morgan, J. (2015) *What is Neoclassical Economics?* Abingdon, Oxon: Taylor & Francis.

Mufudza, T. (2018) Dynamic strategy in a turbulent business environment. *Strategic Management – a Dynamic View*, 7(2), 21–36.

Nadikattu, R.R. (2020) Effective innovation management in strategic planning. *International Journal of Engineering*, 9(5), 106–116.

Neck, R. (2022) Neoclassical economics: Origins, evolution, and critique. In *The Palgrave Handbook of the History of Human Sciences* (pp. 1501–1540). Singapore: Springer Nature Singapore.

North, D. (1987) Institutions, transaction costs and economic growth. *Economic Inquiry*, 25(3), 419–428.

North, D. (1991) Institutions. *Journal of Economic Perspectives*, 5(1), 97–112.

Ntibagirirwa, S. (2009) Cultural values, economic growth and development. *Journal of Business Ethics*, 84, 297–311.

Palmer, S., Byford, S. & Raftery, J. (1999) Types of economic evaluation. *British Medical Journal*, 318(7194), 1349.

Petri, F. (2021) Microeconomics for the critical mind: Mainstream and heterodox analyses. London: Springer.

Redding, G. (2005) The thick description and comparison of societal systems of capitalism. *Journal of International Business Studies*, 36(2), 123–155.

Reisch, L.A. & Zhao, M. (2017) Behavioural economics, consumer behaviour and consumer policy: State of the art. *Behavioural Public Policy*, 1(2), 190–206.

Robin, D.P. & Reidenbach, R.E. (1988) Integrating social responsibility and ethics into the strategic planning process. *Business & Professional Ethics Journal*, 29–46.

Rodrik, D. (2008) Second-best institutions. *American Economic Review*, 98(2), 100–104.

Royer, J.S. (2014) The neoclassical theory of cooperatives: Part I. *Journal of Cooperatives*, 28, 1–19.

Scott, W. (2008) *Institutions and Organisations: Ideas and Interests*. London: Sage.

Sodirjonov, M.M. (2020) Education as the most important factor of human capital development. *Theoretical & Applied Science*, 4, 901–905.

Sonnenschein, H. (1973) Do Walras' identity and continuity characterize the class of community excess demand functions? *Journal of Economic Theory*, 6(4), 345–354.

Sonnenschein, H. (1974) An axiomatic characterization of the price mechanism. *Econometrica: Journal of the Econometric Society*, 425–433.

Soukup, A., Maitah, M. & Svoboda, R. (2015) The concept of rationality in neoclassical and behavioural economic theory. *Modern Applied Science*, 9(3), 1.

Steiner, G.A. (2010) *Strategic Planning*. London: Simon & Schuster.

Swicegood, S. (1987) Strategic facilities planning. *Property Management*, 5(3), 245–247.

Tanyi, A. & Bruder, M. (2014) Consequentialism and its demands: A representative study. *The Journal of Value Inquiry*, 48, 293–314.

Wade, R. (2011) Global trends in income inequality: What is happening, and should we worry? *Challenge*, 54(5), 54–75.

Wade, R.H. & Alacevich, M. (2018) Why has income inequality been neglected in economics and public policy? *Inequality: Trends, Causes, Consequences, Relevant Policies*, 323–365.

Whitley, R. (1999) *Divergent Capitalisms: The Social Structuring and Change of Business Systems*. Oxford: Oxford University Press.

Williamson, O. (1975) *Markets and Hierarchies: Analysis and Antitrust Implications*. New York: Free Press.

Woodhouse, D. (2024) *Institutional Theory. Reference Module in Social Sciences*. Elsevier. https://doi.org/10.1016/B978-0-443-13701-3.00150-X.

Woodhouse, D. & Johnston, A. (2023) Comparative capitalism and the empirical taxonomy of context: Enhancing the institutionalist blueprint. *Critical Perspectives on International Business*, 19(5), 661–698.

CHAPTER 5

Re-examining Economic Responsibility

Olivia Ramsbottom and Anne Wylie

CHAPTER OUTLINE

This chapter outlines how thinking differently about the purpose and/or value of a business or organisation and balancing the economic, social, and environmental goals can result in success.

The chapter introduces a spectrum to look at alternative approaches to business, considering those that emphasise economic value but also have societal impact on one end of the spectrum to those that emphasise societal value but also incorporate economic success at the other end of the spectrum.

The chapter considers approaches such as 'Bottom of the Pyramid', Frugal Innovation, Coopetition, Disruptive Innovation, and Social Enterprise and explains what these are, opening new avenues of how to think about how we operate.

KEY POINTS

- It is possible to achieve economic success while also achieving environmental and social responsibility. In fact, giving environmental and social responsibilities precedence can achieve economic success.
- Strategic thinkers can shift the focus to people (social responsibility) and environment (environmental responsibility) and to enhanced stakeholder relationships away from a focus on competitors to achieve value. Current ideas to consider include

DOI: 10.4324/9781003475545-5

Bottom of the Pyramid approaches, frugal innovation, disruption, coopetition, and social enterprise.

THINKING DIFFERENTLY: ECONOMIC RESPONSIBILITY AS ONE FACET OF SUSTAINABILITY

There can be some scepticism about whether an organisation can thrive if it concentrates on environmental or social responsibility more than, or on an equal basis to, economic responsibility. However, there *are* examples of a more balanced (triple-bottom-line) approach where this focus has led to success.

Critically, this 'thinking differently' requires a different framework or perspective for strategic thinking. First, we need to *accept* that something needs to be done to tackle the environmental and social challenges that the world is faced with, and then we can make decisions in line with this, *or* we recognise that there are economic benefits that can be achieved through solving environmental and social challenges. This is a different way of seeing the business/organisational world compared to the traditional economic perspective which is driven by profit-making.

Here we give examples of this different perspective, using a spectrum that shows approaches from the more economic focus/societal impact approach (where the economic perspective comes first, but there is a societal aspect) to the more societal focus/economic impact approach (where the drive to solve social challenges is paramount, but economic targets are also achieved).

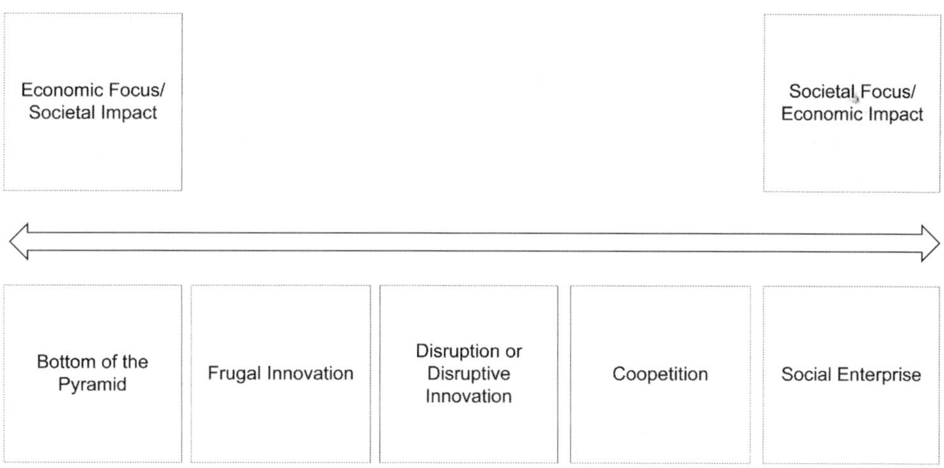

FIGURE 5.1 From Economic Focus/Societal Impact to Societal Focus/Economic Impact Decision-making

Bottom of the Pyramid (BoP) Approaches

In BoP approaches organisations concentrate explicitly economically on those at 'the bottom of the pyramid' (Prahalad, 2004); these are the 'more than 4 billion people who individually earn less than $1,500 per year' (Simanis & Duke, 2014, p 88) who 'represent $5 trillion worth of purchasing power' (Karamchandani et al., 2011, p. 108).

Concentrating on these people is an economic sustainability perspective, with profit-making in mind. However, within this perspective lies the assumption that making money is the way to improve life more generally (a Friedmanite perspective (Friedman, 1970)), as that money should trickle down into the surrounding community (but only if the product or service's profits stay locally, of course). Whether or not you agree with this *primary* focus, the point is that serving the bottom of the pyramid and making profit is possible using actions appropriate to this market, and there may be a corresponding beneficial social impact of concentrating on this market.

Actions to make BoP approaches a success include:

- Changing consumers' behaviour and dependence on certain accepted products and services with education about *new* or *untried* products
- Taking the *long-term* view, working *locally* and *collaboratively* and over long periods
- *Rethinking* the way products are made (*specialise* and *standardise*)
- *Rethinking* distribution and delivery (consider *direct sales, bundle* products and services, provide in *smaller* amounts, consider pay-per-use, payment in *instalments*)
- Finding appropriate *partners* to improve distribution networks.

Karamchandani et al. (2011); Simanis & Duke (2014)

If the profit-making approach does not work or does not garner big returns, it may be that profit-making companies can 'reconstitute their (BoP) ventures as break-even social investments that are destined to remain small' (Simanis & Duke, 2014, p. 88). While Simanis and Duke (2024) would *favour* the profit-making approach, any action that improves the lives of those who are less fortunate is surely a good thing and these social investments can sit alongside more economically successful ventures. Successes include:

- Lafarge, the world's largest cement manufacturer, created a dedicated affordable housing team based at its Paris headquarters
- Godrej Appliances launched the Chotukool, a revolutionary portable refrigerator for the rural Indian market
- BRAC created large-scale microfinance programmes and trained women as community health entrepreneurs.

However, there are criticisms of these BoP approaches as exploiting the poor. This criticism extends to what is seen as a similar approach, that of frugal innovation.

Frugal Innovation

BoP approaches have similarities with frugal innovation, where the latter is product or service innovation taking its lead from the needs of the poorest in societies rather than the more 'technology push' approach of technological research and development which caters for the needs and requirements of those at the higher levels of society (Whittington et al., 2023, p. 338). There is an interesting debate about frugal innovation in academic literature and here we will provide a definition and a summary of the benefits and issues. In short, some see frugal innovation as a natural way to achieve the balance of the economic, social, and environmental responsibilities of sustainability. Others see it as a way for large multinational companies to 'greenwash' or 'carewash' (Chatzidakis & Littler, 2022) building their reputations as responsible organisations, while in reality exploiting the poor.

As well as a similarity between BoP and frugal innovation, you will also see other overlaps as the discussion continues, between BoP, frugal innovation, and disruption or disruptive innovation in terms of 'sufficient' solutions, *and* the extension of a theme of collaboration and cooperation from frugal innovation into the discussion about coopetition and social enterprise.

Definition of Frugal Innovation

Frugal innovations are new solutions, generated through a creative, rethought improvisation and innovation process that minimises the use of resources (raw materials, production resources, energy, fuel, water, waste, financial resources) and this reduction is passed on in terms of lower prices to customers, making them more affordable. The concentration on reduction of the use of resources necessitates a focus on sufficiency or something that is 'good enough' in terms of the service or value provided and the provision of core functionalities (or vice versa in that the development may concentrate on core functionalities which necessitates the stripping back of resources). Importantly, quality of provision will not be compromised, in fact more will be done with less (Peng, 2001; Rogers, 2003; Zeschky et al., 2011; Radjou & Prabhu, 2014; Tiwari et al., 2016; Weyrauch & Herstatt, 2016a, 2016b; Albert, 2019; Ananthram & Chan, 2021).

Examples include a fridge made entirely of clay that uses no electricity and can keep fruits and vegetables fresh for many days; in Africa, if your cell phone battery runs low on power, you can often find resourceful entrepreneurs who will recharge it with their bicycle; in Peru, a giant advertising billboard that absorbs humid air and converts it into purified water (Radjou, 2017).

Benefits of Frugal Innovation

- Frugal innovations not only provide value to lower socioeconomic groups who might otherwise be priced out of a market (social justice) but also use fewer resources (environmental responsibility). If a company is also making profit from them, then economic responsibility is also achieved. This would suggest that frugal innovations are truly sustainable (they achieve the 'triple bottom line').

- Anyone can do it. Initiators can range from big multinational corporations to individuals and grassroots entrepreneurs (Albert, 2019).
- Frugal innovation can create first-mover advantage for an organisation: an innovation that achieves a high market share before others copy and follow.
- While not necessarily an essential in the definition, it tends to be the case that frugal innovations help address pressing social and environmental problems (Hossain et al., 2022).

Issues with Frugal Innovation

- Frugal innovations do not solve the bigger problem of the fact that so many poor people exist in the world. Tesfaye and Fougère (2022) are concerned that frugal innovation maintains the status quo of economies and powers, presumably when innovations are driven by larger companies and away from needs-driven or justice-driven innovations and instead motivated by the exploitation of poorer bands of customers (as with the criticism of BoP approaches) (Knorringa et al., 2016 ; Hossain, 2021).
- Frugal innovation is targeted at 'poor, resource-constrained, cost-conscious, price-sensitive, and middleclass consumers, respectively low-income and rising middle income segments ... on emerging countries as target markets' (Albert, 2019, p. 4), whereas one might hope for the development of frugality and simplicity *across* the socioeconomic groups to minimise impact on environmental systems (this would be a more philosophical approach, overriding the established form of consumerism which links the high price of goods with status).
- It is argued that frugal innovation is only possible using underhand means and bypassing rules and regulations, which also have a negative impact on the environment (Albert, 2019; Ananthram & Chan, 2021).
- Frugal innovation may otherwise be called hybrid strategy or value innovation but can only be socially responsible *if* value is interpreted in this instance as value to the consumer or absolute value rather than just value to the shareholder. Cutting back on resources (otherwise called cost leadership) to optimise profit does not necessarily lead to good, or value to the consumer. For example, products that cost little to produce, with production being managed at low cost by outsourced suppliers and where working conditions may be poor, may yet demand high prices from customers and offer high shareholder value. When less use of resources is applied to *human* resources, the results may not be socially responsible.

Disruption

The above ideas flow into a discussion of disruption or disruptive innovation, or at least the original meaning of it from Christensen (1997) (there has been some discussion about the tendency since the original development of the idea to apply it to everything that is new, but that is not how the original idea was framed). Disruptive innovation is that which targets the 'overlooked segments' much as frugal innovation does, as opposed to concentrating on the 'higher profitability in more-demanding segments' that incumbent organisations focus on (Christensen et al., 2015). Much like frugal innovations, disruptive innovations tend to be 'good-enough', which in turn can be traced back to the appropriate technology movement in the 1970s (Schumacher, 1973; Kaplinsky, 2011; Tesfaye & Fougère, 2022).

Disruption occurs when organisations successfully move their product or service from the overlooked segments into the mainstream. This is counter to the standard 'S curve' of technology adoption (from higher socioeconomic first adopters to the mainstream). Disruptive innovations take incumbent organisations by surprise and usurp their hold on the market. Even more interesting is the idea that companies who focus on sustainability (environmental and social sustainability as well as economic sustainability) are more open to developing disruptive innovations (Wang et al., 2022). This suggests that putting the environment and society on an equal footing with economic responsibility can have favourable results from a competitive advantage/profit-making perspective.

Coopetition

In Chapter 1 we discussed and challenged the idea of competitive advantage, suggesting that organisations should aim for absolute rather than relative value, not trying to 'beat' the competition necessarily but concentrating on what the customer might value. An interesting example of where this approach was followed, contrary to more traditional business practice, is detailed in the idea of a 'pure' form of coopetition to achieve absolute value which can be seen in actions taken during the COVID-19 pandemic by those who would traditionally have been competitors:

- British supermarkets shared resources and capabilities to manage a national response to panic-buying. They shared data and employees and coordinated closure times.
- Pharmaceutical companies and medical equipment manufacturers shared scientific data, knowledge, and equipment to develop a vaccine for COVID-19 and produce medical supplies.
- Technological businesses joined forces to combat the cybersecurity threats associated with the pandemic.
- UK charities worked together on joint fundraising, borrowing equipment, and sharing staff and volunteers.

(Crick & Crick, 2020)

By 'a pure form of coopetition', we are suggesting that pure coopetition established a relationship to meet consumer needs (absolute value) as a *guiding* factor. The Covid response was a strong example of working together for the common good, for customer and societal value but with benefits for the partners, as opposed to having a *principal* consideration for the individual firms' success. However, a business decision made in response to Covid could stand as an outlier in the whole discussion – this was businesses working together in the face of a significant external threat. In 'normal' circumstances, what is coopetition?

'Coopetition is a strategic and dynamic process in which economic actors jointly create value through cooperative interaction, while they simultaneously compete to capture part of that value' (Bouncken et al., 2015, p. 591). Kim explains that coopetition (an extension of joint ventures and strategic alliances) is a 'way of acquiring resources such as new technical skills, capabilities, and knowledge (and) firms can effectively acquire new capabilities when they already have a similar competence base' (Kim, 2020, p. 2). So it is the similarity between businesses operating in the same industry (competitors) that can enable each to offer the other strength in areas where they are less strong. This is contrary to the idea that a competitor's weaknesses should be exploited to gain superiority. The idea of coopetition is not particularly new. 'Raymond Noorda, CEO of Novell, coined the term "coopetition" to capture the complex phenomenon of simultaneous cooperation and competition among firms' (Kim, 2020, p. 1) in the early 1990s. The book *Coopetition* by Brandenburger and Nalebuff was published in 1996 – recognising that business could not always be about war and that there was space for cooperation as well as competition.

The various literature provides us with many positions on coopetition and they can be organised on a 'protectionist' to 'free' spectrum:

1. Towards the more protectionist end of the spectrum, competitors work together to increase the size of the market (the pie) and then individual competitors work to appropriate as much of the market (or the pie) as possible. There can be negative effects of this working together; cooperation on pricing, for example, can leave consumers feeling at the mercy of what feels like a monopoly when we were promised at least an oligopoly, for example, where a few companies appear to act in concert (e.g. energy companies in the UK). The need to win or compete while cooperating can jar in its paradoxical nature and negatively lead to opportunism and misunderstandings.
2. As we move across the spectrum into a more open relationship, coopetition can be a mutually beneficial relationship of sharing resources and capabilities.
3. Across the spectrum again, we can achieve a network approach of learning and sharing which can improve business processes, procedures, and business models as competitors learn from each other.
4. More to the right of the spectrum again, we look outside of the firms and to the wider market, industry, consumer base, and society, and cooperation between firms results in technological development, price decreases, and social value to society.

(Bengtsson & Kock, 2014; Bouncken et al., 2015; Velu, 2016; Corbo et al., 2022; Nyuur et al., 2023)

Coopetition builds on the more recent developments in business in an increasingly open (due to technology), disintermediated, and global world. Coopetition is also seen as an important response to the complex VUCA environment (Bengtsson and Kock, 2014; Bouncken et al., 2015) where the more traditional, simple ways of doing things just don't work anymore.

Examples of working together have been Toyota and General Motors who worked on fuel cell-powered cars. Coca-Cola, Pepsi Co., Red Bull, Unilever worked on 'Refrigerants

Naturally', sustainable refrigeration techniques. Note how businesses have been working together to tackle the challenge of environmental responsibility through coopetition.

Social Enterprise

Next to consider in the spectrum, after coopetition, is social enterprise. The related terms of social enterprises and social entrepreneurship are often used interchangeably and there are challenges in capturing the complex nature of social enterprises and conceptualising social entrepreneurship. In this section we navigate the subject area with you and will define various terms and present a range of vocabulary before agreeing the use of 'Social Enterprise' as a catch-all term.

Social Enterprises

Social enterprises carry out revenue-generating activities to achieve social value creation, using most of any profit to further a social mission (Zahra et al., 2009; Goyal & Sergi, 2015; Social Enterprise UK, 2024). Thus, social enterprises focus on adding value in terms of the traditional 'bottom line' of profit, as well as creating value for social good: the 'double bottom line'. There does not have to be a trade-off between profit and social value creation (Rae, 2010); there can be a duality of mission. Indeed, to be sustainable, social enterprises need to generate a surplus to enable them to grow and to avoid becoming reliant on grants for operational costs. However, instead of being measured by profit, social enterprises are assessed by how they achieve their social goals and have social and environmental impact (Ridley-Duff & Bull, 2016).

Social enterprises can also be associated with the 'triple bottom line', creating social, economic, and environmental/ecological value (McCulloch & Ridley-Duff, 2019): distributing profit, addressing economic inequality, improving social justice, and contributing to environmental sustainability (Social Enterprise UK, 2024).

CASE STUDY 5.1

How Economic Success, Social Innovation, Social Purpose, and Environmental Aims are Integrated

The Eden Project

The Eden Project ('the mothership') in Cornwall, UK, is an educational charity and social enterprise funded by Lottery funding, EU and Southwest Regional Development Agency, commercial funds, and funds generated from the project itself. Since opening in 2001 it has generated over £2 billion for the regional economy (Eden Project, 2024b).

The Eden Project is now developing UK and international projects: 'New Edens', based on meeting local needs in response to the planetary emergency (Eden Project, 2024a).

For more information, go to https://www.edenproject.com.

Community Wood Recycling

Community Wood Recycling launched in Brighton and Hove, UK, in 1998 and was the country's first community wood recycling social enterprise that uses volunteering as a pathway back to work and self-confidence. It specifically targets disadvantaged people. Receiving the National Social Enterprise of the Year Award in 2003 stimulated interest in the project and with funding from WRAP and the Esmee Fairburn Foundation the founder launched the National Community Wood Recycling Project (NCWRP) franchising the model nationwide (Community Wood Recycling, 2024). There are currently 29 social enterprises collectively forming Community Wood Recycling that collect around 20,000 tonnes of wood each year.

For more information, go to https://communitywoodrecycling.org.uk.

While the nature of the activities undertaken by social enterprises is diverse, a common denominator is a focus on local needs, as in the examples of The Eden Project and Community Wood Recycling. Also, as with Community Wood Recycling, one of the intentions of many social enterprises is to reach marginalised groups in society, including refugees, asylum seekers, neuro-diverse individuals, people with disabilities, long-term unemployed, and ex-offenders. Many such individuals experience difficulties in seeking paid employment and social integration through social enterprises can help.

This local 'embeddedness' helps generate local knowledge and builds relationships with the beneficiaries of the social enterprise activity. Note the similarity here between social enterprises and BoP approaches, which recommended collaboration and building relationships as best practice.

CASE STUDY 5.2

Local Action with Marginalised Groups

Upbeat Clean

In 2023, 67,337 applications for asylum were made in the UK, which related to 84,425 individuals (more than one applicant can be included in a single application) (Sturge, 2024). For those successful in having their application accepted they often face challenges in social integration and obtaining employment.

Upbeat Clean is a social enterprise that provides employment opportunities and generates revenue to fund the charitable aims of Upbeat Communities, a Derby-based charity that exists to help refugees and asylum seekers settle and rebuild their lives in the UK, empowering them to thrive. Established in 2021, Upbeat Clean is an award-winning commercial cleaning company partnering with over 25 organisations across Derby. The organisation's five-year goal is that every refugee woman in Derby can find training and employment to help them rebuild their lives, support their families, and contribute to society (Upbeat Clean, 2024).

Beneficiaries

The social mission is to create employment particularly for refugee women and asylum seekers, especially mums, who often face the biggest challenges to find their first job due to multiple barriers such as language, confidence, and childcare commitments. Out of the 52 cleaners employed since 2021, 39 have a refugee background and at least 32 are women. While employment provides financial and mental health benefits, working alongside British nationals helps refugees with societal integration and reduces segregation and feelings of isolation.

Balancing economic, social, and environmental demands

While Upbeat Clean's main focus is on creating employment, it is just and fair in terms of its commitment to the environment by choosing environmentally friendly cleaning supplies and by paying its employees the real living wage that is considered enough for them to support themselves and their families and paying holiday, sick pay, and pension contributions, something which not all cleaning companies honour. Prices are increased annually in line with the percentage increase in the real living wage to ensure economic viability. The social enterprise is transparent to its customers that its aim is to transform lives and, although by paying a real living wage Upbeat Clean is more expensive than some of its competitors, it does not aim to compete on price but does want to make a profit to reinvest and be sustainable. Treating employees ethically and being just and fair is paramount and pays dividends to Upbeat Clean. Behaving ethically has increased staff retention, reduced recruitment efforts, and reduced management time, and word of mouth ensures a ready supply of willing recruits and Upbeat Clean is the employer of choice for cleaners.

Upbeat Clean emphasises its social mission through the strapline: 'Partnering with companies to transform lives through cleaning' and differentiating itself from the competition not on price but on social impact and quality.

Ensuring that the business is sustainable

Scaling up and generating a surplus is important for building a sustainable business and enables Upbeat Clean to pay a competitive wage to management and attract talent. Grants are used for growth, such as website development and idea generation and not to pay running costs. The revenue stream covers running costs.

Attracting sufficient finance is a major challenge for social enterprises.

> Almost half of social enterprises report an insufficient amount of suitable finance available, with over a third saying the available forms of finance are unsuitable for their business and a third lacking the skills to obtain external finance or investment.
>
> *(Social Enterprise UK, 2024)*

This is not the case for Upbeat Clean, which operates on a financially sound business model in which it does not compete on price.

Main challenges

Social enterprises are hard businesses to run as in general they have a low profit margin and often cannot afford to pay a competitive wage. There are individuals who are willing to trade off their corporate salary for job fulfilment but there is a danger in paying too low that the right talent is not attracted to the social enterprise.

> If you pay too low you attract people who don't have the experience or the skills, and then it's a self-fulfilling spiral because you just end up having lower performance and then you end up paying less.
>
> *(Head of Enterprise, Upbeat Clean)*

Business acumen and strategic thinking is often lacking in social entrepreneurs, restricting their ability to scale up. Social entrepreneurs are often people who are kind and compassionate who want to act out that compassion in a sustainable way, but often rely too heavily on grant funding. Upbeat Clean recognises this danger and that as a low profit margin business it is always vulnerable to economic risks and uncertainty. The organisation aims to insulate itself from the financial misfortunes of its clients by having a diversified pool of clients from different sectors and avoiding overreliance on one main client.

So what does the future hold for Upbeat Clean?

Upbeat Clean has beaten the average life expectancy of a social enterprise. While start-up rates for social enterprises are high, longevity is an issue with only one in three social enterprises operating for more than three years (Social Enterprise UK, 2024). Through scaling impact by packing the business model into a 'freemium model', Upbeat Clean intends to continue focusing on its mission of 'transforming lives through cleaning' and supporting others in replicating its success.

For more information, go to https://www.upbeatclean.co.uk/.

The perspectives of social enterprises may be different:

- Those that align themselves with pursuing the social mission or innovation of an individual social entrepreneur – philanthropic entities with a unidirectional relationship between managers and workers, trustees and beneficiaries (Dees, 1998; Martin & Osberg, 2007; Scofield, 2011; Ridley-Duff & Bull, 2016).
- Those focused on developing mutual relationships with members and wider communities that structure themselves as cooperatives and mutuals – a bi-directional or network relationship – a socialisation perspective emphasising collective action and mutual principles (Borzaga & Defourny, 2001; Sahakian & Dunand, 2014) to educate members for participation in the social economy (Moreau & Mertens, 2013, in Ridley-Duff & Bull, 2016). In the Mondragon Co-operative Corporation (MCC)

(https://www.mondragon-corporation.com/en/about-us/), for example, the bigger the decision the greater the number of worker and consumer members involved.
- Social enterprises tend to use socially responsible production and distribution methods (Borzaga & Defourny, 2001; Defourny & Nyssens, 2010) and they may also bring about social transformation through a wider concentration on education, widening their scope and influence.

Social Entrepreneurs

Social entrepreneurship is broad and encompasses those introducing social initiatives in profit-seeking businesses as well as those operating in social enterprises, and those encouraging entrepreneurial trends in non-profit organisations and in the public sector (Mair & Marti, 2006; Becchetti & Borzaga, 2010), so social entrepreneurship does not need to be restricted to those working in social enterprises.

Social entrepreneurs are viewed as change agents that use their enterprising mindset in pursuit of their social mission to make a difference using visionary or innovative approaches (Dees, 1998; Catherall & Richardson, 2017).

As change agents, social entrepreneurs are involved in:

- Adopting a mission to create and sustain social value (not just private value)
- Recognising and relentlessly pursuing new opportunities to serve that mission
- Engaging in a process of continuous innovation, adaptation, and learning
- Acting boldly without being limited by resources currently in hand
- Exhibiting a heightened sense of accountability to the constituencies served for the outcomes created.

(Dees, 1998, p. 4)

As with social enterprises, social impact, social value creation (Nicholls, 2006; Martin & Osberg, 2007; Dacin et al., 2010), and social mission (Nicholls, 2006; Weerwardena & Mort, 2006; Martin & Osberg, 2007) are terms all associated with social entrepreneurship. Social entrepreneurs will come up with social innovations (Austin et al., 2006; Perrini, 2006) or social inventions (Bradley & Gelb, 1980; Ellerman, 1982; Thomas & Logan, 1982, in Ridley-Duff and Bull, 2016, p. 5) where people rather than money are the fundamental unit of concern. Note here the similarity between social entrepreneurship and frugal innovation.

CASE STUDY 5.3

A Nobel Peace Prize-winning Social Entrepreneur

The Grameen Bank and Mohammed Yunus

Mohammed Yunus, internationally known as 'The Banker to the Poor', is well known for founding the Grameen Bank in 1976 with just $27 from his own pocket. The

Grameen Bank and Yunus were jointly awarded the Nobel Peace Prize in 2006. The Grameen Bank is a financial institution providing small loans, particularly to women in Bangladesh with no collateral. Yunus and the bank pioneered the concepts of micro-credit and microfinance. In providing small loans to women to start their own micro businesses, within 30 years the bank had 6.6 million borrowers, of which 97 per cent were women (BBC, 2006). The Grameen Bank was instrumental in helping women escape poverty in a society where women traditionally were home-makers and banks traditionally lent to people who already had money and collateral. This case is an example of a social enterprise empowering individuals to create their own business, enabling them to be independent and building capacity in an economy.

Yunus spoke of the need for reform:

> The current economic system exacerbates environmental and unemployment problems and accelerates the concentration of wealth. We aim to reverse this trend and create a world that achieves the three zeros: zero poverty, zero unemployment, and zero net carbon emissions. The new economic system will be based on sharing, caring and helping each other.
>
> *(Yunus Centre, 2024)*

Social Enterprise

Bearing the above terms and discussions in mind, it seems fair to use the term 'Social Enterprise' to encapsulate all, using it to explain an entity, the behaviour of being socially enterprising, and social entrepreneurship as a more general, driving behaviour, and the behaviour of those who run social enterprises. All terms are used to try to capture a movement that, overwhelmingly, focuses on social value primarily or jointly (when compared to the economic).

Based on research by Social Enterprise World Forum and other Global Alliance members, the World Economic Forum (2024) lists the following five common characteristics in the definitions of social enterprise:

- Purpose: Exists to solve a social and/or environmental problem
- Operations: Prioritises purpose, people, and planet over profit in operational and strategic decisions
- Revenue: Has a self-sustaining revenue model
- Use of surplus: Reinvests most of any surplus towards its purpose
- Structure: Chooses legal structures and financing that protect and lock in purpose long-term.

Common recurring themes when defining social enterprise all reflect areas we have previously spoken about when discussing social enterprises and social entrepreneurs:

- Social change (Leadbeater, 1997)
- Social benefits (Fowler, 2000) with a specific focus on the marginalised and poor (Leadbeater, 1997)
- The creation of sustainable financial, organisational, social, and environmental solutions (Thake & Zadek, 1997)
- Driving social value through innovation (Ashoka Foundation, 2012)
- Creating social value by stimulating social change or meeting social needs (Mair & Marti, 2006)
- Addressing market failure (Thompson et al., 2000; Said School, 2005)
- The promotion of social justice (Thake & Zadek, 1997)
- Ethical behaviour (Bornstein, 1998).

Differentiating Social Enterprise

Having recognised the variety of terms used to define activity in social enterprise, let us go deeper into understanding its difference to conventional or economic entrepreneurship (Chell et al., 2016) and charities and other forms of organisation.

FOR PROFIT TO NOT FOR PROFIT

One strand on this continuum is from 'for profit' to 'not for profit' with economic enterprises classified as 'for profit' and social enterprises often associated with 'not for profit' (Dees, 1998; Chell, 2007). Social enterprises are also associated with the 'third' sector, the 'social economy', and the 'non-profit' sector, where the third sector is seen as organisations that do not fit into either the public or 'for-profit' sectors, and where the mission of members of the social organisation aims to benefit its members or wider community (Becchetti & Borzaga, 2010). However, the positioning of social enterprise in the 'not-for profit' end of the continuum is *erroneous*. There is a common misunderstanding that social enterprises are 'non-profit'. On the contrary, social enterprises do make profit; it is the extent to which they *focus* on profit and the way they distribute it which makes them different from economic enterprises (Becchetti & Borzaga, 2010; McCulloch & Ridley-Duff, 2019). Also, the focus on 'profit' or 'not-for profit' leads to underreporting of the social and economic value of charitable trading activities (in voluntary associations), cooperative and mutual enterprises, and socially responsible businesses, and does not recognise the contribution of social enterprises (Ridley-Duff & Bull, 2016, 2019). Charities and non-profit organisations may have a social mission but do not necessarily have a commitment to democratic ownership and control (see Low, 2006; Ridley-Duff & Southcombe, 2012) which may be a feature of social enterprise, as previously discussed.

PRIVATE TO PUBLIC

Another simplistic binary classification is based on private compared to public enterprises. This distinction is also inadequate, as there are privately owned enterprises that pursue public objectives. Many privately owned for-profit enterprises combine a corporate social responsibility agenda or some social entrepreneurship behaviours with the generation of profit (Borzaga & Tortia, 2010; Defourny & Nyssens, 2017; Addae & Ellenwood, 2021). However, there is a distinction between those organisations which operate through democratic governance and mutuality as opposed to private organisations which exercise control through private property rights (Ellerman,1990; Ellerman, 1997, in McCulloch & Ridley-Duff, 2019, p. 6). Worker co-ops and employee-owned businesses are innovative in terms of ownership and control but do not have a social mission beyond their members/workers (Restakis, 2010).

FINANCIAL TO SOCIAL

Borzaga and Tortia's (2010) conceptual framework distinguishes between entities based on their main objective with financial objectives at one end of a continuum and social objectives at the other, or economic at one end and social or non-financial at the other. Enterprises can be placed along the continuum depending on their orientation. At one end there are 'for-profit' organisations seeking to maximise economic outcomes constrained by the satisfaction of needs, and at the other, social enterprises seeking to satisfy needs constrained by economic and financial equilibrium; enterprises can be found at different positions along the continuum depending on whether they pursue the benefits of their members or pursue wider community benefits. The increasing convergence between economic entrepreneurship and social entrepreneurship, creating new insights into the potential for 'responsible entrepreneurship' (Rae, 2010, p. 603), is reinforced by a shift in attitude towards those who do not have a social agenda being classified as an outlier, while those with a social agenda are considered 'the entrepreneurs of the 21st century' (Catherall & Richardson, 2017, p. 5). 'As boundaries between the business and social sectors dissolve, social entrepreneurship has emerged as a phenomenon that bridges two worlds previously divided' (Addae & Ellenwood, 2021, p. 1).

NOT FOR PURPOSE TO FOR PURPOSE

Another challenge to the conventional classification of profit/not for profit (Becchetti & Borzaga, 2010; McCulloch & Ridley-Duff, 2019) is that it inappropriately focuses on what something is not – 'not for profit' – rather than in terms of what they do, namely their purpose (McCulloch & Ridley-Duff, 2019). McCulloch and Ridley-Duff (2019) use the terms 'for purpose' and 'not for purpose', arguing that it helps make a clearer differentiation between for-purpose enterprises (primarily social) and not-for-purpose enterprises (primarily financial). Social enterprises can then be positioned as social wealth creators compared to what is seen to be the social wealth destruction of private enterprises locked into the pursuit of profit (McCulloch & Ridley-Duff, 2019).

UNETHICAL TO ETHICAL

Another binary distinction to tackle is unethical to ethical.

You will have noted the use of the criterion of ethical behaviour (Bornstein, 1998) when trying to summarise social enterprise, but ethical behaviour has not yet been discussed in any depth (although it will be discussed further in Chapter 8).

Ethical practice can be described as doing what is right, just, and fair. Social enterprises are concerned with 'doing business by doing good' with a focus on a social and/or environmental mission. Social entrepreneurs 'adopt a mission to create and sustain social value' (Dees, 1998, p. 4). Therefore it is implied that a social enterprise will make decisions ethically because it makes its decisions for the benefit of its target beneficiaries, and those target beneficiaries tend to be a wider group of the community than those who benefit from private business. In some cases, there are legal regulations linked to certain social enterprises, those who elect to be Community Interest Companies (CICs): 'A company satisfies the community interest test if a reasonable person might consider that its activities are being carried on for the benefit of the community' (Department for Business, Energy & Industrial Strategy, 2016, p. 7). Unlike other companies, CICs are subject to an 'asset lock' that locks in the assets for the benefit of the community it was set up to serve and to prevent any demutualisation and windfall profits from being paid out to its members and directors. CICs are required to produce a community interest company report detailing, among other things, how the company's activities have benefited the community. The majority of CICs are private companies limited by guarantee. 'A community interest company (CIC) limited by guarantee is a 'not-for-profit' company, this means that it does not operate for private profit. Any profit generated is used to grow and develop its business which is benefiting an identified community, or goes directly to benefit that community' (Department for Business, Energy & Industrial Strategy, 2016, p. 14).

Ethical decision-making is linked to social responsibility and the ability to make caring and constructive decisions based on ethical considerations as well as social norms. It is more likely that social enterprises and social entrepreneurs will make ethical decisions because their very existence is predicated on an external perspective that looks to society's needs. We cannot say that private or for-profit organisations are unethical, but it may be true to say that a social outlook tends to lead to ethical behaviour as opposed to a private outlook.

The Emergence of Social Enterprise

There are many reasons for the emergence of social enterprise:

- **To address the inadequacies in state and private provision of goods and services.** For example, the United Kingdom in the 1980s saw a growth in social enterprise as a result of the Thatcher era of privatisation and increase in marketisation of public services (Burton, 1987; Martin & Parker, 1995; Becchetti & Borzaga, 2010) that meant that many goods and services designed for the public good were instead now led by profit motives. This led to a decrease in the provision of non-profitable goods and services. Also in the United Kingdom, since 2010, government funding has been cut. The scope of the state has shrunk locally with the most deprived areas, where local governments were most reliant on grants and where social care spending represents a higher percentage of local authority budgets, experiencing the deepest grant cuts (Atkins & Hoddinott, 2022). Social enterprise tries to fill the gaps left. Although social enterprises have a relatively small presence in relation to FTSE 100 companies, they are increasingly an indispensable tool for creating sustainable communities using innovative business solutions in the UK. This is particularly true in areas with the highest levels of deprivation where the share of government funding fell from 69 per cent in the first round of funding to 57 per cent in the second round of funding (BBC, 2023). 'Social enterprises in the UK's most deprived communities reinvested more than £270m profit – equivalent to more than a fifth of the amount invested through Phase Two of the Government's Levelling Up Fund' (Social Enterprise UK, 2024).

- **As a result of wider cultural movements.** The emergence of increased advocacy movements, more socially responsible consumers, community-driven enterprises, and the increase in for-profit enterprises embracing corporate social responsibility agendas all serve to drive the growth of social responsibility and social entrepreneurship (Becchetti & Borzaga, 2010).
- **Financial crisis**. The global financial crisis of 2008 (Catherall & Richardson, 2017) sparked a recession lasting over a year from quarter two in 2008 to quarter two in 2009. The Covid crisis from 2019 caused an economic slump and resultant inflationary increases that in turn caused global cost-of-living crises. The increased emergence of social enterprises during a crisis can be viewed as a response to redundancy, an alternative to unemployment, or as a response to the reduction in public sector provision.
- **Climate crisis.** The climate emergency coupled with the cost-of-living crisis contributes to the 'perfect storm' facing social enterprises 'both in the challenges of running the business itself and the increasing urgency of the mission it serves' (Social Enterprise UK, 2024).
- **Individual motivation.** Non-self-seeking individuals driving change as demonstrations of their increased social responsibility and in response to discontent with public policy led by neoliberal economic paradigms. Capitalist economic growth theory (Rae, 2010) believes that market forces, the 'invisible hand', will create value and allocate resources, and the state will address the deficiencies. In many cases these deficiencies have become extreme, prompting the emergence of social enterprises to reconcile economic imperatives with social and environmental sustainability entrepreneurship. Despite often paying less than economic enterprises, social enterprises can attract employees through relational and non-monetary incentives (Borzaga & Tortia, 2010). Millennials and Generation Z seek out employers with aligned values to their own; over the period 2019 to 2021, 44 per cent of millennials and

49 per cent of Gen Zs surveyed said their personal ethics have influenced their choice of work and employer (Deloitte, 2021). Company values and making a positive contribution to society are factors influencing choice of employer (PWC, 2021). While self-selection is evident for all entrepreneurial typologies, it is more prevalent in social enterprises; 'people motivated by intrinsic, relational, and other-regarding preferences will tend to choose organisations that have social objectives' (Borzaga & Tortia, 2010, p. 28).

- **Individual motivation.** Wanting to make a difference and solve a social problem emanating from a personal interest or problem. For social entrepreneur Richard Mehmed, founder of Community Wood Recycling, his idea originated by chance:

> 'Founder Richard Mehmed first realised the potential of waste wood in 1998 when building a playhouse for his daughter. He spotted some plywood outside a local factory, and when he asked if he could take a couple of them for his playhouse he was shocked to find the pile was just a fraction of the perfectly reusable wood waiting to be landfilled. Saddened by the waste, Richard came up with a plan to divert wood out of the waste stream, and the social enterprise Brighton and Hove Wood Recycling Project was born.
>
> *(Community Wood Recycling, 2024)*

- **Individual motivation**. Wanting to solve a wider social problem. For Head of Enterprise Michael Caldwell at Upbeat Clean, the origins of the social enterprise were explicitly based on the identification of the biggest social issue, namely the employability of refugee women. This was driven by the mission of the parent charity Upbeat Communities.

> We have two social enterprises that provide employment opportunities as well as generate income for us to be able to carry out our charitable aims. These include Upbeat Clean, a cleaning business set up in 2021 to provide work for refugees, and Derby Language School, set up to provide language learning for local people and organisations.
>
> *(Upbeat Communities, 2024)*

- **Individual motivation**. In Case Study 5.4, Ola Fagbohun was motivated by a gap in support for a particular demographic.

CASE STUDY 5.4

A Gap in Support

Zest OF: You

Founded in October 2000 by social entrepreneur Ola Fagbohun, Zest OF: You focuses on health behaviour change and gender health equity.

The impetus behind this social enterprise was the observation of the marginalisation of midlife women and the lack of positive imagery of midlife women in the media. Taking a holistic approach to tackling health inequality issues around women's health, creativity, including dance, collage boards, and creative writing, are used during workshops to explore hopes and fears around the menopause and emotional mental well-being. Breaking down language barriers and using alternative mediums of expression, the workshops ensure accessibility for all women irrespective of their ethnicity.

Beneficiaries

The current focus is on 'supporting midlife women ... to achieve their health and wellness goals, so they can live a more purposeful, peaceful and pleasurable life as they age' with a key aim of changing attitudes in the wellness industry towards midlife women by empowering women who want to age well and have fun at the same time.

Balancing economic, social, and environmental demands

Running a social enterprise and balancing the social mission with the bottom line has proven to be challenging. Community groups operating on limited budgets often have the misconception that social enterprise services are free, but this is not feasible for the survival of the enterprise. Zest OF: You, while acknowledging the financial constraints of such groups, offers a social tariff under which those that can pay, pay. This allows charging of subsidised rates to cash-strapped not-for-profit community groups, while ensuring that business expenses are covered.

Ensuring that the business is sustainable

The need to generate a surplus is key to being sustainable. As the founder Ola highlighted from lessons learned from others, relying solely on funding is a dangerous place for a social enterprise.

> Whether they were social enterprises or charities that relied 100% on funding, the lessons I learned from those organisations was, is that if you are flavour of the month, you will get the funding, once you're no longer flavour of the month, your funding will dry up no matter how impactable, impactful and wonderful your business.

Working with a business coach and exploring different business models was key to deciding on the most appropriate way of doing business. Securing long-term contracts that pay up front for services and costing out services accurately to reflect preparation, delivery, and debriefing helps ensure financial sustainability.

Main challenges

For Zest OF: You, an initial challenge was building the client base while ensuring that operational costs were covered and running the social enterprise as a business and not a charity. The latter might be possible during the early life of the social enterprise when building up a client base but is not sustainable long-term. Time is a valuable commodity and must be included in pricing. Due to the personalised nature of the service offered, scaling up is challenging; one person cannot do everything; the challenge is how to scale up without losing personalisation.

So what does the future hold for Zest OF: You?

Not unlike many social enterprises, Zest FOR: You is happy to remain small. Rather than scaling up in the conventional sense, the vision is for the business to develop through digitalisation and to become a thought leader in the women's health and well-being space.

For more information, go to https://zestofyou.com/.

The Growth of Social Enterprises

The growth of social enterprises is clearly gaining momentum. In 2018 there were 100,000 social enterprises contributing £60 billion to the UK in the UK employing two million people, representing 5 per cent of the working population (Social Enterprise UK, 2018). This has risen to 131,000 in 2023, contributing £78 billion (equivalent to 3.4 per cent of GDP), employing 2.3 million people and generating over £1.2 billion in profits, of which £1 billion was reinvested in social and environmental missions (Social Enterprise UK, 2024). Based on estimates of 5.5 million UK businesses in operation (GOV.UK, 2022), one in 42 UK businesses is a social enterprise (Social Enterprise Knowledge Centre, 2023).

The World Economic Forum (WEF) provides a comprehensive global dataset to estimate the size and scope of social enterprise worldwide. The research covers over 80 countries, making up 83 per cent of the global population and includes social enterprises operating across all sectors, including, for example, agriculture to fashion and financial services all contributing to the Sustainable Development Goals (SDGs), particularly those directed towards health and education, climate and jobs, and the reduction of poverty and inequality. India, China, and the United States respectively have an estimated 2 million, 1.75 million, and 1.3 million social enterprises (WEF, 2024).

While acknowledging that there are gaps in the data, the WEF (2024) research reveals the headline data in Table 5.1 to provide an 'informative overview' of the state of global social enterprise.

The contribution of social enterprises worldwide of $2 trillion equates to around 2 per cent of global Gross Domestic Product (WEF, 2024) and 3.4 per cent of UK GDP (Social Enterprise UK, 2024).

However, despite the increase in social entrepreneurship and enlargement of their range of activities contributing to making social enterprises the leading social sector in

TABLE 5.1 The State of Social Enterprise

10 million social enterprises	There are around 10 million social enterprises globally, united by the principle of putting purpose before profit, representing around 3 per cent of businesses.
$2 trillion annual revenue	Social enterprises are generating around $2 trillion in revenue each year while creating a positive impact.
200 million jobs	Social enterprises are creating 200 million jobs across various sectors, from agriculture to financial services.
Financing need $1.1 trillion	Social enterprises are seeking around $1.1 trillion in external financing (beyond personal savings).
1 in 2 led by women	One in two social enterprises around the world are led by women, compared to one in five conventional enterprises.
2x larger than advertising	The sector is larger than the $1.79 trillion apparel industry and twice the size of the $1.01 trillion advertising.

WEF (2024)

the economy of social responsibility (Becchetti & Borzaga, 2010), the move towards 'for purpose' or 'mission-driven' enterprises only represents a small percentage of all economic activity (Social Enterprise UK, 2018, 2023) in comparison to for-profit-driven enterprises. In 2022, although social enterprises generated more than £1.2 billion in profits, this is significantly overshadowed by the level of FTSE 100-generated net profit of £168 billion (AJBell, 2023). Furthermore, despite having a long history, social enterprises have largely been overlooked in policy circles due to a lack of impact awareness (Bridge, 2015).

CHAPTER SUMMARY

Call to Action

This chapter has collected examples of how we can think differently about the economic responsibility of a business and organisation and has supplied many examples of people doing just that.

Strategic thinkers can shift the focus to people (social responsibility) and environment (environmental responsibility) and to enhanced stakeholder relationships away from a focus on competitors to achieve value.

Current ideas to consider include Bottom of the Pyramid approaches, frugal innovation, disruption, coopetition, and social enterprise. A refocusing can increase the likelihood of responsible, sustainable strategic thinking.

RECOMMENDED READING

Albert, M. (2019) Sustainable frugal innovation – The connection between frugal innovation and sustainability. *Journal of Cleaner Production*, 237. https://doi.org/10.1016/j.jclepro.2019.117747.

Bouncken, R.B., Gast, J., Kraus, S. & Bogers, M. (2015) Coopetition: A systematic review, synthesis, and future research directions. *Rev Manag Sci*, 9, 577–601. doi:10.1007/s11846-015-0168-6,

These are systematic literature reviews; therefore they select, evaluate, and summarise relevant literature on frugal innovation and coopetition respectively, revealing the history of a subject debate as well as the alternative views that exist up to the time of writing.

REFERENCES

Addae, A.E. & Ellenwood, C. (2021) Integrating social entrepreneurship literature through teaching. *Entrepreneurship Education and Pedagogy*, 5(2). https://doi.org/10.1177/25151274211021999.

AJBell (2023) *Dividend Dashboard, December 2023*. Retrieved February 19, 2024, from https://www.ajbell.co.uk/sites/default/files/AJB_Q4-2023_Dividend_dashboard.pdf.

Albert, M. (2019) Sustainable frugal innovation – The connection between frugal innovation and sustainability. *Journal of Cleaner Production*, 237. https://doi.org/10.1016/j.jclepro.2019.117747.

Ananthram, S. & Chan, C. (2021) Institutions and frugal innovation: The case of Jugaad. *Asia Pacific Journal of Management*, 38, 1031–1060. https://doi.org/10.1007/s10490-019-09700-1.

Ashoka Foundation (2012) Social entrepreneurship. Retrieved November 27, 2024, from https://www.ashoka.org/en-gb/focus/social-entrepreneurship-0.

Atkins, G. & Hoddinott, S. (2022) Neighbourhood services under strain: How a decade of cuts and rising demand for social care affected local services. Retrieved March 3, 2024, from https://www.instituteforgovernment.org.uk/sites/default/files/publications/neighbourhood-services-under-strain.pdf.

Austin, J., Stephenson, H. & Wei-Skillen, J. (2006) Social and commercial entrepreneurship: Same, different, or both? *Entrepreneurship Theory and Practice*, 30(1), 1–22.

BBC (2006) Nobel for anti-poverty pioneers. Retrieved May 4, 2024, from http://news.bbc.co.uk/1/hi/world/europe/6047020.stm.

BBC (2023) What is levelling up and who is it helping? Retrieved March 3, 2024, from https://www.bbc.co.uk/news/56238260.

Becchetti, L. & Borzaga, C. (2010) *The Economics of Social Responsibility*. Abingdon, Oxon: Routledge.

Bengtsson, M. & Kock, S. (2014) Coopetition – Quo vadis? Past accomplishments and future challenges. *Industrial Marketing Management*, 43, 180–188.

Bornstein, D. (1998) The price of a dream: The story of the Grameen Bank and the idea that is helping the poor to change their lives. In R. Ridley-Duff & M. Bull (Eds) (2016) *Understanding Social Enterprise*, 2nd edition. London: Sage.

Borzaga, C. & Defourny, J. (2001) *The Emergence of Social Enterprises*. London: Routledge.

Borzaga, C. & Tortia, E. (2010) The economics of social enterprises, an interpretative framework. In L. Becchetti & C. Borzaga (Eds) *The Economics of Social Responsibility* (pp. 15–33). Abingdon, Oxon: Routledge.

Bouncken, R.B., Gast, J., Kraus, S. & Bogers, M. (2015) Coopetition: A systematic review, synthesis, and future research directions. *Rev Manag Sci*, 9, 577–601.doi:10.1007/s11846-015-0168-6.

Bradley, K. & Gelb, A. (1980) Motivation and control in the Mondragon experiment. *British Journal of Industrial Relations*, 19(2), 211–231.

Brandenburger, A. & Nalebuff, B.J. (1996) *Coopetition*. New York: Currency Doubleday.

Bridge, S. (2015) Is enterprise education relevant to social enterprise? *Education and Training*, 57(8/9), 1009–1019.

Burton, J. (1987). Privatization: The Thatcher case. *Managerial and Decision Economics*, 8(1), 21–29.

Catherall, R. and Richardson, M. (2017) *Social Entrepreneurship in Education, Empowering the Next Generation to Address Society's Needs*. (Report British Council). Retrieved May 1, 2021, from https://www.britishcouncil.org/sites/default/files/british_council_social_entrepreneurship_in_education_web_final.pdf.

Chatzidakis, A. & Littler, J. (2022) An anatomy of carewashing: Corporate branding and the commodification of care during Covid-19. *International Journal of Cultural Studies*, 25(3–4), 268–286. doi:10.1177/13678779211065474. PMID: 37519850; PMCID: PMC9127538.

Chell, E. (2007) Social enterprise and entrepreneurship: Towards a convergent theory of the entrepreneurial process. *International Small Business Journal*, 25(1), 3–19.

Chell, E., Spence, L., Perrni, F. & Harris, J.D. (2016) Social entrepreneurship and business ethics: Does social equal ethical? *Journal of Business Ethics*, 133, 619–625.

Christensen, C.M. (1997) *The Innovator's Dilemma: When New Technologies Cause Great Firms to Fail*. Boston, MA: Harvard Business Review Press.

Christensen, C.M., Raynor, M. & McDonald, R. (2015) What is disruptive innovation? Twenty years after the introduction of the theory, we revisit what it does – and doesn't – explain. *Harvard Business Review*, 93(12), 44. Boston, MA: Harvard Business School Press.

Community Wood Recycling (2024) *Our Story*. Retrieved May 4, 2024, from https://communitywoodrecycling.org.uk/our-story/.

Corbo, L., Kraus, S., Vlacic, B., Dabic, M., Caputo, A. & Pellegrini, M. (2022) Coopetition and innovation: A review and research agenda. *Technovation*, 122. doi:10.1016/j.technovation.2022.102624.

Crick, J.M. & Crick, D. (2020) Coopetition and COVID-19: Collaborative business-to-business marketing strategies in a pandemic crisis. *Industrial Marketing Management*, 88, 206–213.

Dacin, P.A., Dacin, M.T. & Matear, M. (2010) Social entrepreneurship: Why we don't need a new theory and how we move forward from here. *Academy of Management Perspectives*, 24(3), 37–57.

Dees, J.G. (1998) The meaning of social entrepreneurship. Stanford University: Kauffman Center for Entrepreneurial Leadership. Retrieved June 28, 2021, from https://centers.fuqua.duke.edu/case/wp-content/uploads/sites/7/2015/03/Article_Dees_MeaningofSocialEntrepreneurship_2001.pdf.

Defourny, J. & Nyssens, M. (2010) Conceptions of social enterprise and social entrepreneurship in Europe and the United States: Convergences and divergences. *Journal of Social Entrepreneurship*, 1(1), 32–53.

Defourny, J. & Nyssens, M. (2017) Fundamental for an international typology of social enterprise model. *Voluntas*, 28(6), 2469–2497.

Deloitte (2021) A call for accountability and action. THE DELOITTE GLOBAL 2021 MILLENNIAL AND GENZ SURVEY. Retrieved June 25, 2021, from https://www2.deloitte.com/content/dam/Deloitte/global/Documents/2021-deloitte-global-millennial-survey-report.pdf.

Department for Business, Energy & Industrial Strategy (2016) *Office of the Regulator of Community Interest Companies: Leaflets. Frequently Asked Questions for Funding Organisations*. Retrieved May 4, 2024, from https://assets.publishing.service.gov.uk/media/5a81c8abed915d74e34000a0/13-782-community-interest-companies-frequently-asked-questions-for-funding-organisations.pdf.

Eden Project (2024a) *New Edens*. Retrieved May 4, 2024, from https://www.edenproject.com/new-edens.

Eden Project (2024b) *About us*. Retrieved May 4, 2024, from https://www.edenproject.com/about-us.

Ellerman, D. (1982) Entrepreneurship in the Mondragon Cooperatives. *Review of Social Economy*, 42(3), 272–294.

Ellerman, D. (1990) *The Democratic Worker-owned Firm: A New Model for East and West*. Boston, MA: Unwin.

Ellerman, D. (1997) *The Democratic Firm*. Beijing: Xingua Publishing House. Retrieved May 14, 2015, from www.ellerman.org/the-democratic-worker-owned-firm/.

Fowler, A. (2000) NGDOs as a moment in history: Beyond aid social entrepreneurship or civic innovation. *Third World Quarterly*, 21(4), 637–654.

Friedman, M. (1970) The social responsibility of business is to increase its profits. *New York Times Magazine*, September 13, 1970, 122–126.

GOV.UK (2022) Business population estimates for the UK and regions 2022:Statistical release. Retrieved March 3, 2024, from https://www.gov.uk/government/statistics/business-population-estimates-2022/business-population-estimates-for-the-uk-and-regions-2022-statistical-release-html.

Goyal, S. & Sergi, B.S. (2015) Social entrepreneurship and sustainability – Understanding the context and key characteristics. *Journal of Security and Sustainability Issues*, 4(3), 269–278. doi:10.9770/ jssi.2015.4.3(7).

Hossain, M. (2021) Frugal innovation: Unveiling the uncomfortable reality. *Technology in Society*, 67, 101759. https://doi.org/10.1016/j.techsoc.2021.101759.

Hossain, M., Agarwal, N., Bhatti, Y. & Levanen, J. (2022) Frugal innovation: Antecedents, mediator, and consequences. *Creativity and Innovation Management*, 31(3), 521–540. https://doi.org/10.1111/caim.12511.

Kaplinsky, R. (2011) Schumacher meets Schumpeter: Appropriate technology below the radar. *Research Policy*, 40, 193–203.

Karamchandani, A., Kubzansky, M. & Lalwan, N. (2011) Is the Bottom of the Pyramid really for you? *Harvard Business Review*, March 2011.

Kim, K-H. (2020) Coopetition: Complexity of cooperation and competition in dyadic and triadic relationships. *Organisational Dynamics*, 49, 16.

Knorringa, P., Peša, I., Leliveld, A. & Van Beers, C. (2016) Frugal innovation and development: Aides or adversaries? *The European Journal of Development Research*, 28, 143–153. https://doi.org/10.1057/ejdr.

Leadbeater, C. (1997) *The Rise of the Social Entrepreneur*. London: Demos.

Low, C. (2006) A framework for governance of social enterprises. *International Journal of Social Economics*, 33(5/6), 376–385.

Mair, J. & Marti, I. (2006) Social entrepreneurship research: A source of explanation, prediction and delight. *Journal of World Business*, 41, 32–44.

Martin, R. & Osberg, S. (2007) *Social Entrepreneurship: The Case for Definition. Stanford Social Innovation Review*. https://ssir.org/articles/entry/social_entrepreneurship_the_case_for_definition.

Martin, S. & Parker, D. (1995) Privatization and economic performance Throughout the UK business cycle. *Managerial and Decision Economics*, 16 (3), 225–237.

McCulloch, M. & Ridley-Duff, R. (2019) To profit or not to profit? That is the wrong question. *Sustainable Development Through Social Enterprise, Cooperative and Voluntary Action EMES Selected Conference Papers*. Sheffield Hallam University, June 24–27 June.

Moreau, C. & Mertens, S. (2013) Managers' competence in social enterprises: Which specificities. *Social Enterprise Journal*, 9(2), 164–183.

Nicholls, A. (2006) *Social Entrepreneurship: New Models of Sustainable Social Change*. Oxford: Oxford University Press.

Nyuur, R.B., Donbesuur, F., Owusu-Yirekyi, F., Ampong, G.O.A. & Tantawy, A.A. (2023) Owner-managers failure experience and business model innovations in B2B firms: The roles of coopetition, managerial persistence, and financial resource slack. *Industrial Marketing Management*, 113, 128–137.

Peng, M.W. (2001) How entrepreneurs create wealth in transition economies. *Academy of Management Executive*, 15(1), 95–108.

Perrini, F. (2006) *The New Social Entrepreneurship: What Awaits Social Entrepreneurship Ventures*. Northampton, MA: Elgar.

Prahalad, C.K. (2004) *The Fortune at the Bottom of the Pyramid: Eradicating Poverty through Profits*. Upper Saddle River, New York: Pearson Education.

PWC (2021) Hopes and fears 2021. Retrieved June 30, 2021, from https://www.pwc.com/gx/en/issues/upskilling/hopes-and-fears.html.

Radjou, N. (2017) The genius of frugal innovation, March 21, 2017. Retrieved November 8, 2024, from https://ideas.ted.com/the-genius-of-frugal-innovation/.

Radjou, N. & Prabhu, J. (2014) *Frugal Innovation: How to Do More with Less*. London: Profile Books.
Rae, D. (2010) Universities and enterprise education: Responding to the challenges of the new era. *Journal of Small Business and Enterprise Development*, 17(4), 591–606.
Restakis, J. (2010) *Humanizing the Economy: Cooperatives in the Age of Capital*. Gabriola Island, BC: New Society Publishers.
Ridley-Duff, R. & Bull, M. (2016) *Understanding Social Enterprise* (2nd ed.). London: Sage.
Ridley-Duff, R. & Bull, M. (2019) *Understanding Social Enterprise: Theory and Practice* (3rd ed.). London: Sage.
Ridley-Duff, R. & Southcombe, C. (2012) The Enterprise Mark: A critical review of its conceptual dimensions. *Social Enterprise Journal*, 8(3), 178–200.
Rogers, E.M. (2003) *Diffusion of Innovations*. New York: Free Press.
Sahakian, M. & Dunand, C. (2014) The social and solidarity economy towards greater 'sustainability': Learning across contexts and cultures, from Geneva to Manilla. *Community Development Journal*.
Said School (2005) The Skoll Centre. Retrieved October 9, 2024, from https://www.sbs.ox.ac.uk/research/centres-and-initiatives/skoll-centre-social-entrepreneurship,
Schumacher, E.F. (1973) *Small is Beautiful: Economics as if People Mattered*. New York: Harper and Row.
Scofield, R. (2011) *The Social Entrepreneur Handbook*. New York: McGraw-Hill.
Simanis, E. & Duke, D. (2014) Profits at the Bottom of the Pyramid. *Harvard Business Review*, October.
Social Enterprise Knowledge Centre (2023) *Mission Critical, State of Social Enterprise Survey 2023*. Retrieved February 19, 2024, from https://www.socialenterprise.org.uk/seuk-report/mission-critical-state-of-social-enterprise-survey-2023/.
Social Enterprise UK (2018) The Hidden Revolution, size and scale of social enterprise in the UK. Retrieved June 26, 2021, from https://www.socialenterprise.org.uk/wp-content/uploads/2019/05/The_Hidden_Revolution_-_FINAL-1.pdf.
Social Enterprise UK (2024) *All About Social Enterprise*. Retrieved March 9, 2024, from https://www.socialenterprise.org.uk/all-about-social-enterprise/.
Sturge, G. (2024) *Asylum Statistics*, House of Commons Library. Retrieved May 4, 2024, from https://commonslibrary.parliament.uk/research-briefings/sn01403/.
Tesfaye, L.A. & Fougère, M. (2022) Frugal innovation hijacked: The co-optive power of co-creation. *Journal of Business Ethics*, 180, 439–454. https://doi.org/10.1007/s10551-021-04883-4.
Thake, S. & Zadek, S. (1997) *Practical People, Noble Causes. How to Support Community Based Social Entrepreneurs*. New Economic Foundation.
Thomas, H. & Logan, C. (1982) *Mondragon: An Economic Analysis*. New York: Harper Collins.
Thompson, J.L., Alvy, G. & Lees, A. (2000) Social entrepreneurship: A new look at the people and the potential. *Management Decision*, 38(5), 328–338.
Tiwari, R., Fischer, L. & Kalogerakis, K. (2016) Frugal innovation in scholarly and social discourse: An assessment of trends and potential societal implications. In: Working Paper, part of the project 'Potenziale, Herausforderungen und gesellschaftliche

Relevanz frugaler Innovationen in Deutschland im Kontext des globalen Innovationswettbewerbs.'

Upbeat Clean (2024) Upbeat Clean. Retrieved May 1, 2024, from https://www.upbeatclean.co.uk/.

Upbeat Communities (2024) Welcoming refugees. Empowering individuals and families to thrive as they rebuild their lives. Retrieved May 1, 2024, from https://www.upbeatcommunities.org,

Velu, C. (2016) Evolutionary or revolutionary business model innovation through coopetition? The role of dominance in network markets. *Industrial Marketing Management*, 53, 124–135.

Wang, C., Qureshi, I., Guo, F. & Zhang, Q. (2022) Corporate social responsibility and disruptive innovation: The moderating effects of environmental turbulence. *Journal of Business Research*, 139, 1435–1450. https://doi.org/10.1016/j.jbusres.2021.10.046.

Weerwardena, J. & Mort, G.S. (2006) Investigating social entrepreneurship: A multidimensional model. *Journal of World Business*, 41, 21–35.

Weyrauch, T. & Herstatt, C. (2016a) What is frugal innovation? Three defining criteria. *Journal of Frugal Innovation*, 2 (1), 1–17.

Weyrauch, T. & Herstatt, C. (2016b) Frugal innovation – what is it? Criteria for frugal innovation. In *R & D Management Conference 'From Science to Society: Innovation and Value Creation'*, July 3–6 2016, Cambridge, UK.

Whittington, R., Angwin, D., Regner, P., Johnson, G. & Scholes, K. (2023) *Exploring Strategy: Text & Cases* (13th ed.). Harlow: Pearson Education.

WEF (World Economic Forum) (2024) The state of social enterprise 2024. Retrieved March 9, 2024, from https://initiatives.weforum.org/global-alliance-for-social-entrepreneurship/state-of-the-sector.

Yunus Centre – Global Hub for Social Business (2024) Grameen Bank Founder Yunus: 'Everyone of world's 8 billion people is an entrepreneur'. Retrieved May 4. 2024, from https://www.muhammadyunus.org/.

Zahra, S.A., Gedajlovic, E., Neubaum, D.O. & Shulman, J.M. (2009) A typology of social entrepreneurs: Motives, search processes and ethical challenges. *Journal of Business Venturing*, 24(5), 519–532. doi:10.1016/j.jbusvent.2008.04.007.

Zeschky, M.B., Widenmayer, B. & Gassmann, O. (2011) Frugal innovation in emerging markets. *Research and Technology Management*, 54(4), 38–45.

CHAPTER 6

Strategic Thinking's Relationship with Society

Marc Duffy, Jules O'dor, and Jo Watts

CHAPTER OUTLINE

Society plays a pivotal role in shaping the landscape within which businesses and organisations operate. Yet the role of society and its members, or 'stakeholders', have often been overlooked, as traditional strategy-making prioritised competitive advantage and profit maximisation for shareholders. The relationship between society and strategy-making was recognised in Chapter 1 of this book with the systems thinking approach to strategy-making recommended, with the strategic thinker at the centre of a bigger picture of which 'Society/Life' is the outer layer. In Table 1.1, the impact of societal change on the workplace situation and consequently management styles was presented. This chapter expands on this relationship between society and strategic thinking.

Expectations from society and its actors are constantly evolving over time, and complexities arise from such varied and changing societal contexts which demand nuanced strategic thinking. Businesses and organisations need to navigate differences adeptly. In the history of the relationship between strategic leadership and management and wider society, we learn how the Quakers' strong personal, religious, and cultural concern with the societies they were part of informed their paternalistic employment practice from the nineteenth century. As time has moved on and those who hold power have changed, neoliberal societies have increasingly moved towards independent societies responsible for solving their own problems. Alongside embedded austerity in the face of public service cuts, societies have seen the emergence of complex problems: an unequal society, globally and locally, and stakeholders who are eager for change. Increasingly, the current context for strategic thinking frames the challenging issues strategic thinkers are grappling with.

DOI: 10.4324/9781003475545-6

When we talk about 'Society' we are talking about people, or business and organisational stakeholders. The chapter considers stakeholders and their influence on strategy-making, unpacking how effective strategic thinkers can navigate societal currents, leverage emerging opportunities, and mitigate challenges through visionary and adaptable approaches in a dynamic, complex environment as they harness the strengths of diverse perspectives to inform strategic initiatives.

Our focus also turns to the future, looking at the challenges and complexities of current society and foregrounding Generation Z and subsequent younger generations as significant stakeholders in society in the context of workers and consumers. The consequences of their values and expectations are explored as a contributor to strategic change initiatives. We debate the issues and opportunities that strategic thinkers will need to connect with in future as part of the dynamic web of societal expectation (Nonaka & Zhu, 2012).

Throughout this chapter, readers will gain actionable insights into how strategic thinkers can leverage societal trends and dynamics to cultivate a more responsive and forward-thinking approach to strategy-making. By understanding the intricate relationship between society and strategic thinking, professionals and leaders will be better equipped to anticipate shifts, embrace innovation, and foster sustainable strategies that resonate with evolving societal needs.

KEY POINTS

- Taking responsibility for people and society in business is nothing new, can be mirrored, and there is an emergence (or re-emergence) of thinking that incorporates society into strategic thinking.
- Stakeholders have always been a part of strategy-making but the understanding of their role has changed in the development from classical to contemporary strategy-making. New stakeholder relationships are trust-based, collaborative, and integrate multiple perspectives.
- Society is complex and there are contemporary challenges presented by loneliness, consumption, internationalisation, and Generation Z.
- A strategic thinker can adopt the traits of a systems view of strategy-making to navigate the dynamic complexity of society.

A BRIEF HISTORY OF THE RELATIONSHIP BETWEEN STRATEGY-MAKING AND SOCIETY

Historically, some organisations have taken a wider view of business growth, beyond a short-term focus on wealth creation (Cunningham, 1897). In the nineteenth and twentieth centuries, for example, the Quakers dominated the business domain in areas such as banking, brewing, and chocolate-making (Isichei,1970) but their religious beliefs were reflected in a concern for the well-being of their employees, wider families, and communities. They recognised obligations towards society and the commons (shared public and community resources) as part of a philanthropic heritage (Burton & Hope, 2017). Attributed to their religious orientation, strong social and professional networks emerged nationally and internationally among Quakers who were excluded in society and in universities because of their reluctance to swear allegiance to the Crown. Their strategic approach was framed by their experience, relationships, and belief systems. Strategic thinking involved wider investment with wealth distributed for societal good. Effectively, the Quakers' strategic thinking straddled economic, political, and social action (Parker, 2014).

Strands of the Rowntree family, for example, used their financial legacies to give access to learning and education by opening libraries, seeking to address poor education as a root cause of poverty. Based on his research, Joseph Rowntree, prominent in the Quaker movement, regulated and limited the working day for employees, provided decent affordable housing as well as access to a works canteen, dentists, and social facilities such as swimming pools and theatre. For some Quakers, such provision was purely altruistic, though grafted with a sense of duty associated with religion. Nevertheless, this also provided a reliable and regular source of reinvestment as employees' earnings were ploughed back into the housing and welfare resources provided (Burton & Hope, 2017) and ensured a healthy, local workforce to support productivity.

Strategic thinking in this context not only improved working conditions for employees but also created pressure on governments to influence policy in ways that benefited workers throughout the UK. This spanned policy in prison reform and social care contexts. Hence the Quakers' involvement in policy domains shaped societal values as well as economic interests and values, blurring the lines between business philanthropy and politics and reconciling economics with justice (Briggs, 1926). This supports the discussion in Chapter 3 about the power of business to impact on politics and policy-making, rather than supporting the view of business as 'done to' by government.

Although the Rowntrees sold the company to Nestlé in 1988, up to the present day the Joseph Rowntree Foundation continues to deliver on the legacy of the Quaker movement, focusing on global politics and injustice (Maclean et al., 2022).

However, there is an argument that these enlightened employment practices paid scant attention to issues of wider accountability (Parker, 2014). It is argued that this management was not simply altruistic but rather paternalistic, driven to limit industrial action and nurture compliant workers. Further critique questioning the scope of the Quakers' societal concern highlights the propensity of policy-shaping to omit issues such as child and slave labour. Some factory owners maintained long working days that meant limited sleep and poor conditions for children in factories. Equally, the paternalistic approaches that were a feature at a national level were not afforded to those involved in cocoa farming overseas who were treated as slaves and engaged in forced labour (Rowlinson & Hassard, 1993; Rowlinson, 2015).

From the industrial revolution, capitalism experienced a meteoric rise across Europe, North America, and Japan, facilitating thriving business and economic wealth.

Strategy-making in this context was defined by rivalry and intense competition with the drive to conquer and colonise. Historically, as part of the slave trade, for example, humans were objectified, exchanged for manufactured goods such as cloth and copper. The British East India Company colonised Bangladesh and Pakistan, and controlled societies across the world, doing what they saw as acceptable in their strategic pursuit of profit (Maslin, 2021).

The slave trade was abolished, and over time in the UK, the rise of Fabianism and, more widely, associated post-war consensus gave rise to a focus on the voice of workers alongside the drive for equity across society. At a governmental level in the UK, for example, this led to widespread consensus across society with far-reaching policy change underpinned by the Beveridge report, to alleviate poverty and improve access to health and education (Coule & Bennett, 2018).

Thus, we see the seesaw of strategy-making's relationship with society, at times with profit maximisation and corresponding societal diminution in ascendance, and then at other times we see the rise of the people and their accommodation in business.

By 2008 the assumptions of neoliberalism were firmly entrenched in society and popular culture. Now we expect people to be responsible for their own lives and livelihoods. This has had societal implications which can be felt acutely today in wicked problems marked by challenges in understanding causes or solutions (Rittel & Webber, 1973; Haslam & Shenoy, 2018; Grewatsch et al., 2023), such as poverty, homelessness, addiction, climate change, and access to education. Since the post-war period, the divide in access to wealth and resources remains unequal. Notably, the Western world is responsible for most consumption, with the Eastern hemisphere suffering the consequences (e.g. in terms of climate change). Alongside the rise of capitalism, the growth of the population has been exponential. As the population has risen, so has consumption of consumer goods and energy related to the way we live and work (Ritchie & Roser, 2024).

Now, countries across the world are taking stock of the need to limit global warming to 1.5 degrees through the Conference of the Parties (COP) with (unequal) business growth to blame and businesses under pressure to act responsibly. The picture is not optimistic, particularly for the poorest parts of the world such as South Sudan where combating climate change is crucial for peace and stability (Sax et al., 2023). Certainly, the world is divided in terms of wealth, the poorest parts of the world increasingly affected by climate change arguably imposed by the richest, and with resulting ever greater disparities between the rich and poor.

To consider responsibility towards society as equal to that of economic success, the focus needs to shift away from profit maximisation for a small group of shareholders and towards a wider view of the system that businesses and organisations are part of and the needs, lacks, and wants therein. Hence, strategic thinking needs to take into consideration societal perspectives from employees, partners, and suppliers, and the communities they operate in and are part of – the wider spectrum of **stakeholders** and not just shareholders (see also Chapter 4 for a critique of Neoclassical Economics with its focus on profit maximisation).

THE DEVELOPMENT OF STAKEHOLDER ENGAGEMENT

The stakeholder concept first surfaced as an important consideration for strategic thinking in a memo from the Stanford Research Institute in 1963 (cited in Freeman, 1984) and it referred to stakeholders as 'those groups without whose support the organisation would cease to exist'. Since its inception, stakeholder theory has explicitly positioned itself as an alternative to economic theorising (Freeman et al., 2010), placing stakeholders at the heart of strategic thinking and as a truly important element of the systems approach to strategy-making.

Stakeholders Defined

Following Freeman's (1984) seminal work on stakeholders, they can be defined as individuals or groups who could affect the performance of an organisation through their decisions and actions or who may be affected by a firm's decisions and actions (Freeman, 1984).

The importance and role of stakeholders is discussed at some length in the bulk of popular strategy textbooks (Sachs & Rühli, 2011; Clegg et al., 2022; Whittington et al., 2023; Laasch, 2024) with presentations that span both old and new world strategy-making practices (Laasch, 2024). While definitions vary slightly, the key elements presented by Freeman (1984) remain consistent. There is also a general acceptance that the purpose of an organisation will be affected by stakeholder expectations, and that this may also shape the corporate governance structures of the organisation.

Freeman suggests two contrasting conceptions of stakeholders: a classical, narrow view where a stakeholder is any group or individual who is vital to the survival and success of the corporation (1983), and the broad or contemporary view of a stakeholder as 'any group or individual who can affect or be affected by the corporation' (Freeman, 1984, p. 46).

The following section explains the difference between the classical and contemporary views of stakeholder engagement.

Classical and Contemporary Views of Stakeholders

Classical

- **Responsibility**: The management of stakeholders within the classical view was embodied in the view of managers and leaders to social responsibility more generally, aligned with Friedman's view that 'there is one and only one social responsibility of business – to use its resources and engage in activities designed to increase its profits so long as it stays within the rules of the game, which is to say, engages in open and free competition without deception fraud' (Friedman, 1970). This approach to social responsibility was echoed in the approach to stakeholders through to the 1990s and beyond, with a clear focus on the importance of shareholder rather than stakeholder value. This further explains the rather functionalist approach to stakeholders and stakeholder mapping presented in many strategy textbooks to this day.

- **Accountability**: Under the classical view, this was related to the contractual arrangements of the organisation, arguing that where accountability is not a contractual or legal requirement there is no accountability (Swift, 2001).
- **Value creation**: From a classical 'narrow' perspective of stakeholders (Freeman,1983), business model concepts tend to conceptualise value creation as a simple exchange process. The central aim being the creation of value for customers for reciprocal economic value for the organisation (Freudenreich et al., 2020).
- **Management and leadership:** The narrow view sees stakeholders as parts of the macro- or micro-environment of the organisation that needs to be monitored and managed in some way. The first step in this process is stakeholder identification. The next step is stakeholder prioritisation, in which managers determine the nature of the relationship that the organisation should adopt with its various stakeholders. The aim is to categorise and develop responses to the potential actions or reactions of those stakeholders to the organisation's strategic actions and intentions. To facilitate this mapping of stakeholders the often-cited power/interest (Mendelow, 1991), power/attention (Newcombe, 2003, adapted in Whittington et al., 2023, or attitude/influence (Grundy, 1997) matrices are used to facilitate stakeholder mapping, as a prelude to risk response and the mitigation of potential damage to organisational reputation.

Contemporary

- **Responsibility**: In the 1990s we began to see a move away from paying attention primarily to 'shareholders' and towards the more inclusive approach to 'stakeholders' as strategic thinkers began to include considerations of ethics (Mitchell et al., 1997; Wicks & Freeman, 1998) alongside issues of responsibility and sustainability (Laasch, 2024). This more relational view of stakeholders has led organisations to focus on how they can build close and trusting relationships with a range of stakeholders (Jones et al., 2018; Swift, 2001). Interestingly and in parallel to these developments in thinking, we see the notions of coopetition (Hamel et al., 1989) and complementors (Nalebuff & Brandenburger, 1996, 1997) emerging in the strategic management literature and serving to develop a deeper understanding of and sensitivity to the role of stakeholders in strategic thinking. Building on this, and going beyond bilateral collaboration or supply chain relationships, the emergence of the business ecosystem has begun to further shape the approaches that organisations take to stakeholders. The ecosystem of the organisation refers to the 'community of organisations, institutions, and individuals that impact the enterprise and the enterprise's customers and suppliers' (Zahra & Nambisan, 2011, p. 6) and therefore concerns the management of stakeholder relationships. The positioning of the organisation within an ecosystem suggests that 'each member of a business ecosystem ultimately shares the fate of the network as a whole, regardless of that member's apparent strength' (Iansiti & Levien, 2004) and suggests that strategic thinking needs to incorporate a sophisticated and interconnected understanding of stakeholder relationships. Bringing these strands together and when discussing new-world management thinking, Laasch (2024) presents the strategy-making process as one of collaboration and coopetition (Nalebuff & Brandenburger, 1997) working together to achieve corporate and societal value.

In considering these multiple factors in strategic thinking concerning stakeholders, some obvious challenges present themselves in terms of classical strategic management approaches. For example, when thinking about the organisation as an ecosystem rather than as a business, this tends to blur industry boundaries, creating problems with the established competitive environmental analysis models (Porter, 1991). The blurring of industry boundaries was also discussed in Chapter 1 in relation to the advance of technology, and thus we can see that combined changes in society have the result of creating a complex environment in which strategic thinkers operate. Innovation is now very often between rather than within companies, suggesting problems with the notion of portfolio management and ownership. Finally, we can also observe competitors collaborating and competing simultaneously, further challenging strategic thinking concerning the positioning of stakeholders. Coopetition is considered further in Chapter 5.

As organisations have begun to address broader conceptualisations of stakeholder interests, one approach that has emerged that suggests such an integration of ethics and strategy is that of responsible leadership (Maak & Pless, 2006). Some argue that this approach to leadership is most closely associated with pluralist strategic thinking (Agarwal & Bhal, 2020), though the discourse is still emerging. Responsible leadership is presented as a values-based and ethically centred relationship between leaders and stakeholders, that through shared purpose drives joint commitment to the achievement of sustainably created value and social change (Pless, 2007). The sustainability focus that is central to the notion of responsible leadership is clearly grounded in the global challenges facing organisations and their stakeholders, placing them at the heart of strategic thinking for the organisation (Muff et al., 2022).

- **Value creation**: Contemporary, broad views (Freeman, 1983) present value creation as a collaborative exchange process that should benefit both the organisation and all its stakeholders (Freeman et al., 2010). This type of multi-directional exchange of value suggests strategic thinking that includes complex analysis of what types of value each relationship creates and for whom that value is created (Freudenreich et al., 2020). Further, this suggests a process of joint value creation in which all stakeholders have intrinsic value, and no sets of interests are assumed to be dominant (Donaldson & Preston, 1995).
- **Accountability:** Only through engagement is it possible for leaders and managers to truly understand their stakeholders' expectations. The notion of accountability therefore needs to focus on addressing wider considerations for ethics, responsibility, and sustainability. Laasch goes further and positions stakeholder accountability as the goal of the organisational accounting process, suggesting that the aim of this process is to 'give an explanation and justification of the organisation's intentions, judgements, acts and omissions' (Laasch, 2024, p. 769).
- **Management and leadership:** While mapping and prioritisation of stakeholders remains a feature of stakeholder engagement in the contemporary environment,

stakeholder engagement in contemporary thought extends beyond monitoring, risk control, and mitigation. Stakeholder communication is employed to facilitate activities through which managers and stakeholders collaborate to create shared value. In terms of the practice of stakeholder engagement, AccountAbility (2015, p. 22) suggests ten possible levels of stakeholder engagement, ranging from the least to the most engaged.

1. **Remain passive** – No active communication
2. **Monitor** – One-way communication: stakeholder to organisation
3. **Advocate** – One-way communication: organisation to stakeholder
4. **Inform** – One-way communication: organisation to stakeholder, there is no invitation to reply
5. **Transact** – Limited two-way engagement: setting and monitoring performance according to terms of contract
6. **Consult** – Limited two-way engagement: organisation asks questions, stakeholders answer
7. **Negotiate** – Limited two-way engagement: discuss a specific issue or range of issues with the objective of reaching consensus
8. **Involve** – Two-way or multi-way engagement: learning on all sides but stakeholders and organisation act independently
9. **Collaborate** – Two-way or multi-way engagement: joint learning, decision-making, and actions
10. **Empower** – New forms of accountability; decisions delegated to stakeholders; stakeholders play a role in shaping organisational agendas.

(AccountAbility, 2015)

As we move from the classical, narrow view of stakeholders to the more contemporary, broad, and inclusive view, the latter levels of AccountAbility's communication list seem more appropriate.

The possible levels of stakeholder engagement envisaged by AccountAbility could perhaps be summarised in four modes:

- **Information**: Through a process of presentation and promotion via leaflets, media, video, etc.
- **Consultation**: Through processes of communication such as surveys and feedback mechanisms.
- **Deciding together**: Through processes of consensus building and planning for strategic choices.
- **Acting together**: Through a process of community development via advice, support, and funding.

(AccountAbility, 2015)

The Roles and Skills needed by Strategic Thinkers in Stakeholder Engagement

Certain abilities and approaches will be required for successful strategy-making bearing in mind the developments in stakeholder engagement noted above:

- Ability and willingness to manage high-quality relationships with stakeholders (AccountAbility, 2015; Freudenreich et al., 2020).
- Ability and willingness to make ethical decisions (Laasch et al., 2023; Laasch, 2024).
- Ethical, values-based behaviour and action (Pless, 2007; GRLI, 2009; Laasch, 2024).
- Acting with emotional/social intelligence (Goleman, 2007, 2020; Ahsan, 2023).

Laasch (2024) goes on to argue that to begin to practice effective stakeholder engagement there are certain organisational and attitudinal prerequisites, with strategic leaders needing to:

- have a clear vision, an identified audience, and a shared language
- have realistic options and an ability/willingness to deal with responses
- have a readiness to accept new ideas and follow through on them
- have a willingness to learn new ways of working
- have a commitment to continue support.

Finally, strategic thinking to reflect stakeholders' needs demands:

- diverse perspectives and co-production (Mintzberg, 1994; Liedtka, 1998)
- exploration (Hamel & Prahalad, 1994)
- decisions made framed by the implications for all (McGrath, 2013; Haslam & Shenoy, 2018)
- cultural consideration (Nasi, 1991; Liedtka, 1998)
- collaboration and dialogue (Liedtka, 1998).

Stakeholder Engagement Standards

A Competency Assessment for Responsible Leadership (CARL) tool exists to assess stakeholder engagement, leadership development, and corporate sustainable development transformation (Muff et al., 2020). (See https://carl2030.org/ for more on the Competency Assessment for Responsible Leadership).

The United Nations Global Compact (https://unglobalcompact.org/) along with the 17 Sustainable Development Goals (SDGs) (https://sdgs.un.org/goals) provides an international framework for stakeholder engagement. Although voluntary in nature, the Compact and SDGs set out the interconnected and complex challenges to strategic thinking. Going beyond the classic commercial interests to consider broader global responsibilities, including ethical behaviour, the environment, and communities and human rights.

The 17 SDGs are:

1. No Poverty
2. Zero Hunger
3. Good Health and Well-being
4. Quality Education
5. Gender Equality
6. Clean Water and Sanitation
7. Affordable and Clean Energy
8. Decent Work and Economic Growth
9. Industry, Innovation, and Infrastructure
10. Reduced Inequalities
11. Sustainable Cities and Communities
12. Responsible Consumption and Production
13. Climate Action
14. Life below Water
15. Life on Land
16. Peace, Justice, and Strong Institutions
17. Partnerships for the Goals.

(United Nations, 2024b)

Coupled with this call to action, the growing importance of stakeholder engagement among the leaders of organisations and state actors has led to the activity being codified in standards such as the AccountAbility AA1000 Stakeholder Engagement Standard mentioned earlier (AccountAbility, 2015). The AA1000 Standard provides an open-source practice framework for organisations to assess, design, implement, and communicate the quality of their stakeholder engagement. The architects of the Standard suggest that the organisation should integrate stakeholder engagement into its governance structure, decision-making processes, policies and/or processes for strategy development as well as operational management and measurement systems. In undertaking this level of integration, it is argued that the organisation might reach objectives that cannot be reached by a single organisation acting alone (AccountAbility, 2015). It is further argued that following such an integration, leaders and managers will be better able to understand their complex macro- and competitive environments (Porter, 1991), including market developments and cultural dynamics. Further, that this organisational learning from stakeholders will result in product and process improvements, alongside driving product and process innovation. The ultimate goal, however, is to develop and leverage trust-based and transparent stakeholder relationships (Swift, 2001) that deliver a sustainable, positive impact on the organisation and on society (Laasch, 2024).

CASE STUDY 6.1

The Importance of Consulting Stakeholders

Adam Parsons is Consultant from a Big Four Consultancy with a focus on the energy and natural resources sector. As such, he advises a wide range of clients on navigating the strategic opportunities and challenges associated with the energy transition and the move towards a net zero society. In the following case study he explains the importance of consulting stakeholders.

'I've seen things not work well where a small strategy team comes up with some brilliant ideas but has made no effort to socialise them across the business, made no effort to gather perspectives from lots of different teams. I work with people that have a diverse range of backgrounds: policy and regulatory experts; people from a commercial perspective that are focused more on the quantitative side of things; technical experts, engineers that have a very different perspective on a certain challenge; consumers and communities. All are part of the overall ecosystem of stakeholders. I don't think it's possible to develop an effective strategy without bringing together the perspectives of lots of different stakeholders. And the challenge there is making sure that strategy is being distilled effectively into something which is coherent and clear and can be built on.'

THE CURRENT SOCIETAL CHALLENGES FOR STRATEGIC THINKING

Having established where we have come from, and the changing view of stakeholders' role in strategic thinking, what next for strategy-making and society, and how do we best cater for our stakeholders in this new world? This section explains some of the challenges a strategic thinker will need to be aware of.

Individualism and Loneliness

Under the neoliberal agenda, we expect greater societal independence in that people are responsible for their own lives and livelihood. In this context governments have stepped back, and humans are increasingly expected to self-regulate and meet their own needs. This has been coined as a self-service society (Bennett et al., 2019: Eriksson, 2012). For some organisations it has led to a greater expectation that stakeholders will serve themselves. This includes the use of self-service checkouts and ordering kiosks in shops and restaurants, online chatbots for answering FAQs and troubleshooting, as well as apps for banking, ordering, and booking appointments.

However, some organisations are beginning to shift away from self-service models. In 2024, Sainsbury's Supermarket reported a growing trend of consumers preferring in-store shopping (BBC, 2024). This suggests a movement towards personal interactions and away from virtual experiences in food retail. Such a trend raises important questions about strategy-making in a society increasingly affected by loneliness, impacting stakeholders from remote workers (Bartel & Rockmann, 2022) to users of self-checkouts (Gamman et al., 2023). It also prompts a reconsideration of how businesses might redefine relationships with stakeholders to inform strategic decision-making, as well as the short-, medium-, and long-term implications of these decisions.

Consumption, Population Growth, and Climate Change and Inequality

The impact of consumption has and is having real consequences. As highlighted in Chapter 9, the poorest in society contribute just 10 per cent of the carbon in the atmosphere while the richest 10 per cent in society cause more than 40 times the poorest 10 per cent (Butler & Begum, 2023). The societal implications of this are detailed in Chapter 9, but suffice it to say here that the societal reach of the impact of climate change forms part of the complexities and challenges in strategic thinking highlighted by international agendas such as the UN Global Compact and associated Sustainable Development Goals (United Nations, 2024) as previously discussed. Our global population is rapidly growing, impacting climate change, and is responsible for carbon emissions that are rising four times faster than in the previous 100 years (IPCC, 2023).

International Responsibilities in a Globalised Economy

In more recent times, the lack of consideration for international contexts has proved problematic for societal stakeholders. As well as environmental impact, The Rana Plaza factory disaster of 2013, where over 1,134 people lost their lives and another 2,000 were injured (Butler & Begum, 2023), exemplifies societal imbalance and the human impacts of demand in a complex system. Similarly, oil companies have faced criticism for the role they have played in human rights violations and land degradation in Nigeria in relation to the oil spills, imprisonment, and the execution of activists such as Ken Saro Wiwa (Wettstein, 2020). Although incidents like this can catalyse change, societal responses and strategic thinking can fall short of remedying responses (Butler & Begum, 2023).

Generation Z as Influencers of Strategic Design

The newest generation of adults, Generation Z, will be key stakeholders in strategy-making and their expectations are different than those of previous generations.

Friedman famously claimed that the *'only responsibility of business was business'* and *'business'* should only be concerned with making a profit, so long as they *'stayed within the rules of the game'* (Friedman, 1970). While Friedman's comments have been far-reaching and impactful in terms of our attitudes towards business, Generation Z have been exposed to a much-changed environment to the one Friedman enjoyed in 1950s America, particularly in terms of their opportunities in employment.

While those on the political right have commented negatively on Generation Z and their overall work ethic, and prominent media personalities have enjoyed taunting the youngest generation for enjoying staples such as takeaway coffee or avocados, the reality for young people is that they face uncertainty in employment, a lack of stability from society, and are increasingly unlikely to be in a position to purchase property and start families. The emerging Generation Z adult looks longingly at the opportunities that were available to their recent ancestors.

Generation Z look to their parents and grandparents who had significantly better opportunities and experiences from society. Their grandparents likely enjoyed lifelong employment, generous final salary pensions, and benefited from large, fully paid property (purchased for a fraction of its current value). Their parents likely enjoyed similar but less generous opportunities and are likely to have benefited similarly, while not enjoying the full Friedman experience. Since then, however, society has changed, and particularly the role and benefits available from employment in society. Becker (1960) went so far as to argue in the mid-twentieth century that any 'man' who changed employment too often would be seen as erratic: 'we can expect that men ordinarily settle down to a career in a limited field and do not change jobs and careers with the alacrity of the proverbial economic man under changing market conditions' (Becker, 1960).

While there is much to unpack in Becker's arguments, not least the reference to *'men'* and omission of women entirely, it does offer an insight into society at that time. It is clear that the society experienced by Becker no longer exists for Generation Z. Becker (1960) went so far as to claim that a *'man'* who changed his work too often would be seen as 'untrustworthy and erratic'. Ninety-one per cent of millennials (born between 1977 and 1997) expect to stay in a job for less than three years, and the average worker today remains in each of his or her jobs for 4.4 years (Forbes, 2012), and while this has often been presented as a benefit, and enriching their experience, more often it is due to necessity on the part of the worker. On these projections, it would lead to a typical millennial or Generation Z worker having between 15 and 20 jobs over a lifetime. Further hidden costs are masked in this data, including the cost of recruitment and unpaid labour in multiple application processes, gaps in employers, gaps in pension contributions, multiple pension pots, and the various costs in relocation for new employment.

Generation Z have been born into a society where a job for life is not offered, nor is it sought in most cases (Skidelsky, 2017). Generation Z's experience of work has been their watching parents face constant job uncertainty, economic recessions, and pessimism from employers. Further, between 2007 and 2016 they have seen that high-income earners have increased their wealth by 1,425 per cent more than the low-income group and four times the middle-income cohort – and the gap is widening (Deloitte, 2021). The environment of Becker's *'job for life'* would be a more suitable topic for a history lesson or documentary from their perspective. In fact, they are contending with a student debt crisis, staggering racial wealth inequities, and lack of certainty about their future. They have been kneecapped by the Great Recession and the average millennial in 2016 was earning about 20 per-cent less than baby boomers did at the same stage of life. The wage gap casts a long shadow over what millennials can save and invest for their future (*New York Times*, 2022). In the media, they are taunted by older generations for wasting money on discretionary spending.

Generation Z have inherited a drastically different society to the one their parents and grandparents experienced. Earlier generations have relied on linear television and the printed press to inform their knowledge and opinions. This has been beneficial for governments who have a level of control over the media, particularly in the United Kingdom and for media outlets who are sympathetic to the political right and advocates for capitalism. Generation Z rely on social media for their views and are much more likely to see multiple perspectives and varied and global news and perspectives on any given topic. Instagram, TikTok, and YouTube are now the top three most-used sources for news for British teens, according to the broadcasting regulatory authority Ofcom (Ofcom, 2022). Young people cannot turn away from the discourse, so it is no wonder that many digital native Gen-Zers are spurred to act on their societal grievances. They are mobilising out of fear and necessity (BBC, 2022).

This brings a significant shift in the paradigm for business responsibility from the perspective of Generation Z, notably what they will accept from employment and society. This is important and relevant because Generation Z are expected to make up 25 per cent of workers by 2030. Generation Z do not have the loyalty to their employers as offered by earlier generations, largely because they have never been offered it in return. Generation Z have had the confidence to call out employers for bad practice, prioritise their own mental health, and expose inequality. Generation Z do care about their salary; however, Deloitte (2021) found that this was the least important factor, behind work–life balance, the environment, and their experiences at work. Their counterparts in mid-career have offered little support, citing their inexperience and lack of understanding for how work should 'work' when perhaps in reality they have a degree of jealousy or admiration for their confidence.

Deloitte (2024) argued that entire industries and businesses will rise and fall in the wake of Generation Z and alerted organisations to prepare themselves for the change that is due.

> They prefer digital communication to avoid face-to-face interaction, they're harder to reach because of their short, 'eight second' attention span and they're focused on authenticity in a brand. Yet companies and organizations would be wise not to fall for the myths and stereotypes: Whether you're talking about gender and ethnicity or modes of learning, Gen Z refuses to fit into neat little boxes.
>
> *(Deloitte, 2024)*

Generation Z will not accept greenwashing or carewashing from organisations; they are value-driven and expect organisations to practice what they preach. They are fast to call out organisations who make environmental or well-being claims. The Cone Study (Cone, 2008, 2019) found that Generation Z perceive the environment to be the number one issue facing society, above health, poverty, and human rights. The Cone Study (Cone, 2019, p. 5) argues that '94 percent [of Generation Z] believe we need to come together to make progress on important issues'.

Sustainability can be considered as one of the great challenges facing humanity today and addressing the concept of sustainability includes not only engaging with environmental issues but also making decisions to improve social and economic issues in society (Guinot et. al., 2022).

This brings significant change to the workplace and radically different expectations from its future workers. Employers must be ready for the change in the demographic of their average employee; several employers are seeing this change already from this value-driven generation. Indeed, in some cases entire industries are experiencing a mass exodus of workers and suffering from a lack of entry-level recruitment. *Climate quitting* is becoming an emerging reality for fossil fuel companies whose employees are leaving en masse, often offering public resignations on social media (Ware, 2024).

In line with Deloitte's (2021) arguments that salary alone is not enough to attract and retain Generation Z employees, *The Wall Street Journal* (2023) found that high salaries in the fossil fuel industry are no longer enough to retain talent. Managers setting strategic directions for organisations and creating values for their employees to follow would be well served in remembering these expectations from Generation Z, and universities are some of the first to experience these value-laden expectations

Ware (2024) found that Generation Z workers are struggling to disconnect between personal values and values of their employer:

> 'On a Friday afternoon travelling home, I would feel physically uncomfortable. And I was wondering: why am I feeling physically uncomfortable? I had a good week; I've done good work. And then you realise that you may have done good work, but the goal that you're working towards is evil in a way; does not align with your moral compass.'

While Generation Z have been fast to call for change from organisations, there is evidence to suggest that their own actions do not always match their expectations from business. In Case Study 6.2., the evidence suggests that Generation Z's actions do not always perfectly follow their expectations from business. The case study explores the example of 'fast fashion' and the challenges associated with carbon emissions and single-use nature of fast fashion products. The study explores the case of students and their actions versus intentions, leading the authors to question whether there is an 'attitude–behaviour gap' present in behaviour.

CASE STUDY 6.2

Wearing your Ethics: The Sustainability Gap between Purchasing Intentions and Actions

The global fashion industry is expected to reach $360 billion by 2025 (Deslandes, 2020). This demand for production and consumer consumption is causing significant environmental implications, including pollution, waste accumulation, and excessive water consumption (Anguelov, 2015). Niinimäki et al. (2020) argue that every year the fashion industry accumulates 92 million tons of waste, consumes 79 trillion litres of water, and contributes to 10 per cent of worldwide global carbon dioxide emissions.

There are deeper and growing concerns around social implications of the global fashion industry, including exploitation of workers, child labour, and inhumane working conditions (Brownbridge et al., 2018; Khan, 2019; Heinze, 2020). According to the International Justice Mission (2020), there are over 40 million slaves in the world, more than at any other point in human history, with many working in fashion supply chains (IJM, 2020).

Organisations are increasingly aware of and engaged in this issue, with 93 per cent of CEOs viewing sustainability as a business issue (KPMG, 2017) and 53 per cent expecting to spend more on sustainability (Laasch & Conaway, 2015). Fashion companies such as Nike and Adidas are increasingly reporting their sustainability commitments, dedicating significant portions of their annual reports and corporate websites to sustainability initiatives.

The Cone (2019) study identified that 69 per cent of millennials wished to work for organisations with sustainable and responsible strategies. It's time to 'take this generation seriously' who are 'tired of how negative our country has become' and 'stand ready to take action' (Cone, 2019, p. 2). Generation Z (1997–2012) have been described as the 'most ethnically and culturally diverse generation to-date' with 94 per cent believing we 'need to come together to make progress' (Cone, 2019, p. 3). Generation Z brings new expectations and values, and this underpins the need for businesses to account for the future workforce, younger activists, employees and consumers, society, and their wider stakeholders.

Consumers are waking up to the facts of sustainability and responsibility in business and the United Nations' 'Sustainable Development Goals' focus strongly on responsible and sustainable consumption (United Nations, 2024b). Societal change is clearly essential. Siegel and Jorgensen (2011) and the United Nations argue that sustainable fashion is fundamental to protecting the world we live in. Consumers are said to be showing greater concern for the need for sustainable fashion; however, industry experts have begun to question the reality of consumer action, finding that attitudes do not translate into buying behaviours. This phenomenon is called the 'attitude–behaviour gap' (Terlau & Hirsch, 2015).

The disparities between attitudes and purchasing behaviours are still not adequately understood (Terlau & Hirsh, 2015). In addition, there is a clear lack of literature devoted to the attitude–behaviour gap, specifically in sustainable fashion. This case study focuses upon sustainable fashion. The urgent need for greater sustainable consumption emphasises the importance and relevance of this research, and only once the perceived barriers to sustainable consumption are truly understood can this 'gap' be closed. The purpose of this research is to investigate the attitudes and behaviours of Generation Z relative to purchasing behaviours and fashion.

To assess the expectations and purchasing behaviours of Generation Z, a questionnaire was issued to a cohort of final-year Generation Z students in a large UK university. In total, 75 responses were received, representing an 80 per cent response rate from the sample.

Seventy-five per cent of respondents stated that they buy new clothing monthly, 18 per cent weekly, and 7 per cent yearly. Other data identified that 17 per cent of participants shopped at a fast fashion retailer on a weekly basis, 62 per cent monthly, 11 per cent yearly, and 10 per cent claiming that they had never purchased from a fast fashion retailer. Price and quality were the two biggest factors participants considered when purchasing new clothing. Just under half of the participants (43 per cent) stated that they consider where and how their clothes are made pre-purchase.

Twelve per cent of participants stated that they 'bin' their unwanted clothing, while the remainder disposed of them in a sustainable manner. Respondents were asked to specify 'how' if the option of 'other' was selected; the common recurring theme was the concept of 'reuse'. One participant wrote: 'I use my sewing machine to make them into something new to wear.' Another added: "I reuse denim for textile projects at university.'

Sixty-three per cent agreed overall that they are concerned about the social implications of the fast fashion industry and 48 per cent agreed that they were concerned about the environmental implications. Only 3 per cent of participants stated that they were not concerned at all about either social or environmental implications.

Attitudes were positive towards the need for sustainable fashion; however, the extent of concern differed between male and female participants. Females expressed greater concern; however, they lacked translation of this into their purchasing behaviours. One of the more significant findings to emerge from this study is that even though males lacked positive attitudes towards wanting to consume sustainable clothing they were the ones to behave in a more sustainable manner. However, this relationship was not purposeful but down to factors benefiting the self (Niinimäki, 2010).

The barriers and justification from Generation Z students as to why they did not act more sustainably fell into two categories of internal and external logic. Externally, concern for environmental and social welfare, including understanding of sustainable fashion, understanding of fast fashion, and attitudes towards sustainable brands. Internally related to purchasing behaviours, the appeal to shop at a particular brand, post-purchase outcomes (in terms of recycling and disposal), and perceived barriers to easy sustainable consumption, including price, lack of knowledge, lack of choice, lack of aesthetic, scepticism over business transparency, and social desirability. Several respondents admitted that barriers could easily become justifications to continue their normal behaviours.

Overall, the extent and type of 'gap' varies between genders, however collectively, Generation Z students show a clear gap between pro-sustainable attitudes and consumption behaviours. The findings around barriers to sustainable consumption contribute to a greater understanding of why the gap occurs.

Adapted from Calver et al., 2022

CHAPTER SUMMARY

What We Have Learned

- Societal influence on strategy-making and vice versa is not a new idea.
- Strategy-making has had a mixed relationship with society. We've seen good and bad times in terms of either side's involvement and support for the other. The Quakers came up with some good ideas for worker support, but their strategy-making fell short given their lack of focus on wider, domestic, or international issues: those who may be distant or powerless and disadvantaged. Importantly, in the twentieth century, thinkers were not faced with the importance of environmental change impacting on their stakeholders.
- Stakeholder involvement has moved from the classical perspective of management and control to the contemporary view of collaboration.
- Unfortunately, we currently have a general state of inequality, complexity, and challenge that requires a new approach.
- The stakeholders of the future are Generation Z, which have grown up in a vastly different environment compared to previous generations, facing significant challenges such as job instability, student debt, and widening income inequality. They are less loyal to employers and prioritise work–life balance, environmental sustainability, and authenticity in employment. Generation Z are highly critical of greenwashing and demand genuine corporate responsibility, often mobilising through social media to call out corporate malpractices and advocate for societal change. Generation Z value ethical alignment with employers and reject the notion that high salaries alone can retain talent, particularly in industries like fossil fuels. Activist movements led by Generation Z, such as the boycott of fossil fuel companies, reflect this generation's commitment to environmental issues. However, there is evidence of a gap between Generation Z's expectations and their personal actions, as seen in the fast fashion industry's popularity despite its environmental impact.

What We Can Do

Practise strategic systems thinking for society: Adopt a holistic perspective that values not only the internal operations of organisations but also the broader societal structures, individuals, and natural resources of which they are a part. Adopt systems thinking to recognise the interconnectedness of organisations and complex and 'wicked' societal challenges (Haslam & Shenoy, 2018). Systems thinking presents a method of capturing wide-scale problems (Grewatsch et al., 2023), and 'broadens the problem space and expands the choice for solutions' (McKenna et al., 2014, p. 190). By emphasising the wider ecosystem and connected nature of organisations, the intertwined relationship between different ways of thinking and culture and society can emerge. Systems thinking can consider how to set new societal expectations around consumption, and how in a complex world stewardship might generate agility and facilitate transformation.

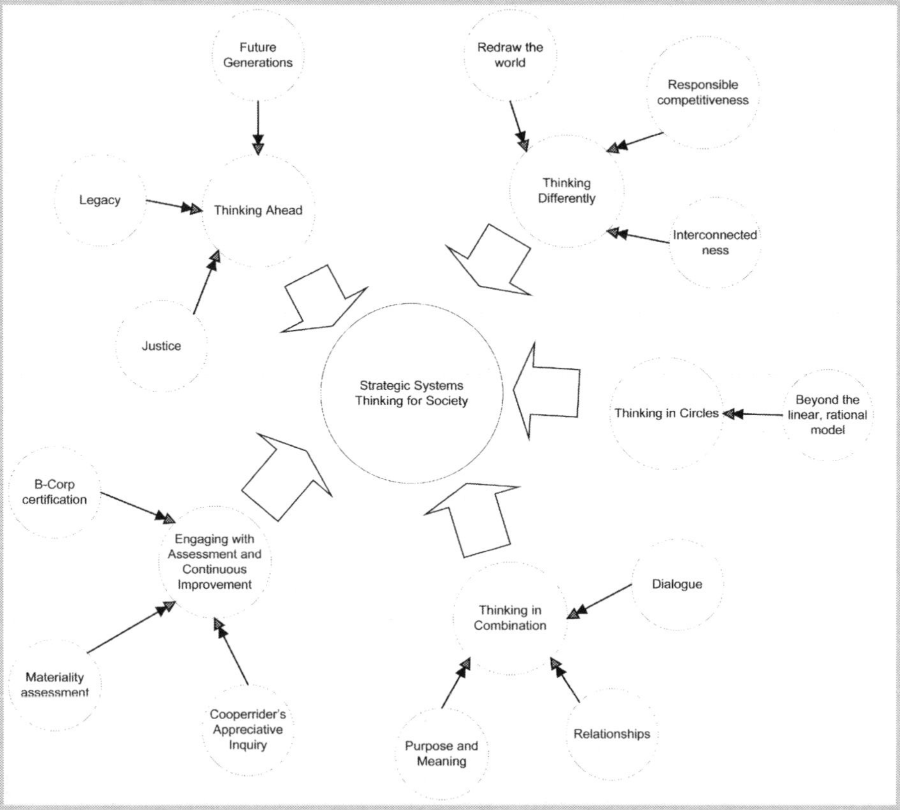

FIGURE 6.1 Strategic Systems Thinking for Society

Strategic Systems Thinking for Society includes

- **Thinking ahead**: Integrate thought and action to address the short-, medium-, and long-term impacts on future generations, for now Generation Z, and legacy. Rawls (1971) foregrounds the idea of justice. This underscores deep thinking about social inequalities to benefit those most disadvantaged in society (Moroni, 2023). Strategic thinking requires a systemic perspective across society, encompassing organisations, community custodians, and carers to diminish power imbalance and generate equitable allocation of resources. Rawls' (1971) ethical approach seeks to privilege those who are disadvantaged and who can be overlooked in strategic thinking.
- **Thinking differently:** Laasch (2024) highlights the overlapping boundaries of competition, collaboration, responsible competitiveness, and irresponsible competitiveness. Embrace responsible competitiveness by creating value for stakeholders beyond mere competition, avoiding exploitation or harm to those involved in your operations. Raworth's focus on twenty-first-century thinking in *Doughnut*

Economics'(2017) adopts the metaphor of the economist using a pencil to 'redraw the world'. The metaphor moves away from a purely economic paradigm that privileges wealth creation above the needs of society and the planet. Think differently about what success, purpose, and value looks like.

- **Thinking in circles:** Move beyond traditional strategic management, which often relies on linear rational models of planning and control (Taylor, 1911; Fayol, 1949). The increasingly complex and wicked problems we face, where each attempt to create a solution changes our understanding of the problem, require a different approach to thinking. Thinking in circles rather than straight lines becomes necessary as these complex problems cannot be solved in a traditional linear fashion, because the problem definition evolves as new possible solutions are considered and/or implemented (Rittel & Webber,1973).
- **Thinking in combination**: Merge strategic management with leadership to foster dynamic strategic thinking that includes intuition, dialogue, co-production, and idea generation. Engage a diverse array of stakeholders – from community groups to second-tier suppliers to future customers – and consider coopetition, where organisations collaborate on certain goals while maintaining their independence. For example, Tesla shares its technological expertise in electric vehicle development, illustrating how resource sharing can benefit multiple stakeholders while addressing external challenges (Musk, 2014). Empower societal stakeholders by involving them in decision-making processes, such as having environmental custodians on boards or enhancing staff voting power. Deep engagement with stakeholders can challenge assumptions, redistribute power, remove hierarchies, and foster resource sharing and education (Dalal & Carberry, 2018; Dalal et al., 2019). The Doughnut Economics Action Lab (2022) purports deep thinking and strategy-making around the interconnected criteria of purpose, networks, governance, ownership, and finance (discussed further in Chapter 9). Each of these themes relies on dialogue and relationships to influence business design and strategic action. There is a need in society and strategic thinking to innovate and explore the deeper purpose and meaning of business (Laasch, 2024). This approach promotes inclusive problem-solving as systems thinking involves engaging multiple perspectives and fostering collaboration and dialogue (Liedtka, 1998; Nonaka & Zhu, 2012). As argued by Grewatsch et al. (2023), strategy-making as an inclusive process that focuses on the dynamic exchange of stakeholders rather than the static model of planning supports processual insights by identifying tipping points and the scope for transformational change. A learning-based organisation can involve stakeholders in the presentation and debate of problems, opportunities, and issues. Participative approaches such as Appreciative Inquiry can be adopted by organisations facilitating dynamic strategic thinking and process that combines multiple stakeholders in iterative thinking and planning and action.
- **Engaging with assessment and continuous improvement**: *B-Corp certification* was founded in 2006 with a goal of identifying and certifying companies based on their social and environmental impact. Certification is awarded every three years and demands ongoing improvement. *Materiality assessment* is

a systematic approach for evaluating the extent to which business and stakeholders are prioritising the issues that matter most. Materiality assessment draws on traditions of accounting and outcomes and therefore considers the context around decisions that are made based on qualitative and quantitative information relevant to the recipient stakeholder. These are financial impacts and risk, legal, regulatory, and policy drivers, peer-based norms, stakeholder concerns/societal trends, and opportunities for innovation (Laasch, 2024). Lego, for example, focuses specifically on customers, employees, partners and suppliers and the environment to identify and prioritise the most important issues they should address. The implications of decisions are then shifted to set out the cost implication of the strategy-making process, thereby adding legitimacy to the process, and helping create a sense of the financial benefits of actioning longer-term initiatives. Through such interventions, strategic thinking, debating the challenges and opportunities facing organisations, can be addressed in a co-evolutionary, dynamic process where issues are reviewed, revisited, and reiterated and actions debated. Concepts of double materiality look externally as well as internally, addressing business impact on society and the environment in which business operates. This invites thinking and discussion about both short-term needs but, notably, considers long-term issues that focus on responses to entrenched societal challenges (Grewatsch et al., 2023). Whitney and Cooperrider's *Appreciative Inquiry* (2011), used by organisations such as BP, provides an asset-based organisational development approach to mobilise systems and the individuals within them through meaningful questions that provoke thinking, meaning, and construct action across large systems.

RECOMMENDED READING

BBC (2022) Gen Z: How young people are changing activism. Retrieved November 27, 2024, from https://www.bbc.com/worklife/article/20220803-gen-z-how-young-people-are-changing-activism.

Laasch, O. (2024) *Principles of Business & Management: Practising Ethics, Responsibility, Sustainability*. London: Sage.

Whitney, D. & Cooperrider, D. (2011) *Appreciative Inquiry: A Positive Revolution in Change*. Berrett-Koehler Publishers.

REFERENCES

AcountAbility (2015) AA 1000 Stakeholder Engagement Standard. Retrieved November 27, 2024, from https://www.accountability.org/static/940dc017198458fed647f73ad5d47a95/aa1000ses_2015.pdf.

Agarwal, S. & Bhal, K.T. (2020) A multidimensional measure of responsible leadership: Integrating strategy and ethics. *Group & Organization Management*, 45(5), 637–673.

Ahsan, M.J. (2023) The role of emotional intelligence in effective corporate social responsibility leadership. *International Journal of Organizational Analysis*, 31(8), 75–91.

Anguelov, N. (2015) *The dirty Side of the Garment Industry: Fast Fashion and its Negative Impact on Environment and Society*. Boca Raton, FL: CRC Press.

Bartel, C.A. & Rockmann, K.W. (2022) Organizational attention towards relationships: A dynamic model of loneliness and resilience. In *Academy of Management Proceedings*, 1, 15508). Briarcliff Manor, NY: Academy of Management.

BBC (2022) Gen Z: How young people are changing activism. Retrieved November 27, 2024, from https://www.bbc.com/worklife/article/20220803-gen-z-how-young-people-are-changing-activism.

BBC (2024) Sainsburys says almost everyone now shops instore. Retrieved November 27, 2024, from https://www.bbc.co.uk/news/business-68895280#:~:text=Sainsbury's%20says%20shoppers%20are%20returning,now%20back%20to%20about%2013%25.

Becker, H.S. (1960) Notes on the concept of commitment. *American Journal of Sociology*, *66*(1), 32–40.

Bennett, E., Coule, T., Damm, C., Dayson, C., Dean, J. & Macmillan, R. (2019) Civil society strategy: A policy review. *Voluntary Sector Review*, 10(2), 213–223.

Briggs, M. (1926). *Economic History of England*. London: University Tutorial Press.

Brownbridge, K., Gill, S., Grogan, S., Kilgariff, S. & Whalley, A. (2018) Fashion misfit: Women's dissatisfaction and its implications. *Journal of Fashion Marketing and Management: An International Journal*, *22*(3), 438–452.

Burton, N. & Hope, A. (2017) *Responsible Business? What Can We Learn from the Quakers*. Public Lecture, July 3. Westminster Quaker Meeting House.

Butler, S. & Begum, T. (2023) Abuses 'still rife': 10 years on from Bangladesh's Rana Plaza disaster. *The Guardian*.

Calver, J., Littlewood, G., Duffy, M. & Watts, J. (2022) Wearing your ethics: The sustainability gap between purchasing intentions versus actions. The case of generation z students. https://pure.ulster.ac.uk/en/publications/wearing-your-ethics-the-sustainability-gap-between-purchasing-int.

Clegg, S.R., Whittle, A., Schweitzer, J. & Pitelis, C. (2022). *Strategy: Theory and Practice*. London: Sage.

Cone (2008) The 2006 Cone Millennial Case Study. https://www.conecomm.com/research-blog/2006-millennial-cause-study#download-research.

Cone (2019) Undivided. London. https://static1.squarespace.com/static/56b4a7472b8dde3df5b7013f/t/5da883bc77e66471a09a6240/1571324862662/2019+GenZ+Report+Layout+TO+PRINT+-+SinglePages.pdf.

Coule, T.M. & Bennett, E. (2018) State–voluntary relations in contemporary welfare systems: New politics or voluntary action as usual? *Nonprofit and Voluntary Sector Quarterly*, 47(4_suppl), 139S–158S.

Cunningham, J. (1897) *The Quakers, from Their Origin Till the Present Time: An International History*. Friends' Tract Association.

Dalal, M. & Carberry, A. (2018) Work in progress: Changing ways of thinking of interdisciplinary collaborators. *2018 ASEE Annual Conference & Exposition*

Proceedings. https://www.academia.edu/90998520/Work_in_Progress_Ways_of_Thinking_of_Interdisciplinary_Collaborators.

Dalal, M., Carberry, A. & Archambault, L. (2019) Work in progress: Exploring Ways of thinking of interdisciplinary collaborators. *2019 ASEE Annual Conference & Exposition Proceedings*. https://www.academia.edu/90998499/Work_in_Progress_Exploring_Ways_of_Thinking_of_Interdisciplinary_Collaborators

DEAL (The Doughnut Economics Action Lab) (2024) https://doughnuteconomics.org/.

Deloitte (2021) The great retail bifurcation, March 2018. https://www2. deloitte.com/content/dam/insights/us/articles/4365_The-great-retailbifurcation/DI_The-great-retail-bifurcation.pdf.

Deloitte (2024) Understanding Generation X in the workplace. Retrieved November 27, 2024, from https://www2.deloitte.com/us/en/pages/consumer-business/articles/understanding-generation-z-in-the-workplace.html.

Deslandes, P.R. (2020) Selling, consuming and becoming the beautiful man in Britain: The 1930s and 1940s. In *Consuming Behaviours* (pp. 53–70). London: Routledge.

Donaldson, T. & Preston, L.E. (1995) The stakeholder theory of the corporation: Concepts, evidence, and implications. *Academy of Management Review*, 20(1), 65–91.

Eriksson, K. (2012) Self-service society: Participative politics and new forms of governance. *Public Administration*, 90(3), 685–698.

Fayol, H. (1949) *General and Industrial Management*. London: Pitman.

Forbes (2012) *The Future of Work Job Hopping is the New Normal for Millennials*. Retrieved November 27, 2024, from https://www.forbes.com/sites/jeannemeister/2012/08/14/the-future-of-work-job-hopping-is-the-new-normal-for-millennials/?sh=7db8a79813b8.

Freeman, R.E. (1983) A stakeholder theory of the modern corporation. In T. Beauchamp and N. Bowie (Eds) *Ethical Theory and Business* (7th ed.). London: Prentice Hall.

Freeman, R.E. (1984) *Strategic Management: A Stakeholder Approach*. Boston, MA: Pitman.

Freeman, R.E., Harrison, J.S., Wicks, A.C., Parmar, B.L. & De Colle, S. (2010) *Stakeholder Theory: The State of the Art*. New York: Cambridge University Press.

Freudenreich, B., Lüdeke-Freund, F. & Schaltegger, S. (2020) A stakeholder theory perspective on business models: Value creation for sustainability. *Journal of Business Ethics*, 166(1), 3–18.

Friedman, M. (1970) The social responsibility of business is to increase Its profits. *New York Times Magazine*, September 13, 122–126.

Gamman, L., Doruff, J., Allen, A. & Ekblom, P. (2023) Rehumanising the self-checkout experience. Retrieved November 27, 2024, from https://www.ecrloss.com/research/rehumanising-the-self-checkoutexperience?from=/research.

Goleman, D. (2007) *Social Intelligence: The New Science of Human Relationships*. London: Arrow Books.

Goleman, D. (2020) *Emotional Intelligence: Why It Can Matter More Than IQ*. London: Bloomsbury Publishing.

Grewatsch, S., Kennedy, S. & Bansal, P. (2023) Tackling wicked problems in strategic management with systems thinking. *Strategic Organization*, 21(3), 721–732.

GRLI (2009) The Globally Responsible Leader: A call for action. https://grli.org/resources/the-globally-responsible-leader/.

Grundy, T. (1997) Accelerating strategic change: The internal stakeholder dimension. *Strategic Change*, 6(1).

Guinot, J., Barghouti, Z. & Chiva, R. (2022) Understanding green innovation: A conceptual framework. *Sustainability*, 14(10), 5787.

Hamel, G., Doz, Y.L. & Prahalad, C.K. (1989) Collaborate with your competitors and win. *Harvard Business Review*, 67(1), 133–139.

Hamel, G. & Prahalad, C.K. (1994) *Competing for the Future*. Boston, MA: Harvard School Press.

Haslam, S. & Shenoy, B. (2018) *Strategic Decision Making: A Discovery-led Approach to Critical Choices in Turbulent Times*. London: Kogan Page.

Heinze, L. (2020) Fashion with heart: Sustainable fashion entrepreneurs, emotional labour and implications for a sustainable fashion system. *Sustainable Development*, 28(6), 1554–1563.

Iansiti, M. & Levien, R. (2004) Creating value in your business ecosystem. *Harvard Business Review*, 3(1), 68–78.

IPCC (International Panel on Climate Change) (2023) Climate Change 2023 Synthesis Report. https://www.ipcc.ch/report/ar6/syr/downloads/report/IPCC_AR6_SYR_LongerReport.pdf.

IJM (International Justice Mission) (2020) https://www.ijm.org/.

Isichei, E. (1970) *Victorian Quakers*. Oxford: Oxford University Press

Jones, T.M., Harrison, J.S. & Felps, W. (2018) How applying instrumental stakeholder theory can provide sustainable competitive advantage. *Academy of Management Review*, 43(3), 371–391.

Khan, R. (2019) 'Be creative' in Bangladesh? Mobility, empowerment and precarity in ethical fashion enterprise. *Cultural Studies*, 33(6), 1029–1049.

KPMG (2017) *The KPMG Survey of Corporate Responsibility Reporting 2017*.

Laasch, O. (2024) *Principles of Business & Management: Practising Ethics, Responsibility, Sustainability*. London: Sage.

Laasch, O. & Conaway, R. (2015) *Principles of Responsible Management*. New York: Cengage Learning.

Laasch, O., Moosmayer, D.C. & Antonacopoulou, E.P. (2023) The interdisciplinary responsible management competence framework: An integrative review of ethics, responsibility, and sustainability competences. *Journal of Business Ethics*, 187(4), 733–757.

Liedtka, J.M. (1998) Linking strategic thinking with strategic planning. *Strategy & Leadership*, 4.

Maak, T. & Pless, N.M. (2006) Responsible leadership in a stakeholder society – a relational perspective. *Journal of Business Ethics*, 66, 99–115.

Maclean, M., Shaw, G. & Harvey, C. (2022) Business as service? Human relations and the British interwar management movement. *Human Relations*, 75(8), 1585–1614.

McGrath, R.G. (2013) *The End of Competitive Advantage: How to Keep Your Strategy Moving as Fast as Your Business*. Cambridge, MA: Harvard Business Review Press.

McKenna, A.F., Johri, A. & Olds, B.M. (2014) Adaptive expertise and knowledge fluency in design and innovation. *Cambridge Handbook of Engineering Education Research,* 227–242.

Maslin, M.A. (2021) *How to Save Our Planet: The Facts.* Harmondsworth: Penguin UK

Mendelow, A.L. (1991) *Environmental Scanning: The Impact of the Stakeholder Concept.* Proceedings from the Second International Conference on Information Systems, 407–418. Cambridge, MA.

Mintzberg, H. (1994) The fall and rise of strategic planning. *Harvard Business Review,* 72(1), 107–114.

Mitchell, R.K., Agle, B.R. & Wood, D.J. (1997) Toward a theory of stakeholder identification and salience: Defining the principle of who and what really counts. *Academy of Management Review, 22*(4), 853–886.

Moroni, S. (2023) Distinguishing 'planning' from the 'plan'. Institutional and professional implications of taking urban complexity seriously. *European Planning Studies,* 31(11), 2327–2341.

Muff, K., Liechti, A. & Dyllick, T. (2020). How to apply responsible leadership theory in practice: A competency tool to collaborate on the sustainable development goals. *Corporate Social Responsibility and Environmental Management,* 27(5), 2254–2274

Muff, K., Delacoste, C. & Dyllick, T. (2022) Responsible leadership competencies in leaders around the world: Assessing stakeholder engagement, ethics and values, systems thinking and innovation competencies in leaders around the world. *Corporate Social Responsibility and Environmental Management,* 29(1), 273–292.

Musk, E. (2014) All our patents belong to you. Retrieved March 5, 2024, from https://www.tesla.com/blog/all-our-patent-are-belong-you.

Nalebuff, B. & Brandenburger, A. (1996) *Co-opetition.* New York: Doubleday.

Nalebuff, B. & Brandenburger, A. (1997) Co-opetition: Competitive and cooperative business strategies for the digital economy. *Strategy & Leadership,* 25(6), 28–35.

Nasi, J. (Ed.) (1991) Arenas of strategic thinking. *Foundation for Economic Education,* Helsinki, Finland.

Newcombe, R. (2003) From client to project stakeholders: A stakeholder mapping approach. *Construction Management and Economics,* 21(8), 841–848.

New York Times (2022) The world's a mess. So they've stopped saving for tomorrow. Retrieved October 8, 2024, from https://www.nytimes.com/2022/05/13/style/saving-less-money.html.

Niinimäki, K. (2010) Eco-clothing, consumer identity and ideology. *Sustainable Development,* 18(3), 150–162.

Niinimäki, K., Peters, G., Dahlbo, H., Perry, P., Rissanen, T. & Gwilt, A. (2020) The environmental price of fast fashion. *Nature Reviews Earth & Environment,* 1(4), 189–200.

Nonaka, I. & Zhu, Z. (2012) *Pragmatic Strategy: Eastern Wisdom, Global Success.* Cambridge: Cambridge University Press.

Ofcom (2022) News consumption in the UK: 2022. Retrieved November 27, 2024, from https://www.ofcom.org.uk/__data/assets/pdf_file/0027/241947/News-Consumption-in-the-UK-2022-report.pdf.

Parker, L.D. (2014) Corporate social accountability through action: Contemporary insights from British industrial pioneers. *Accounting, Organizations and Society*, 39(8), 632–659.

Pless, N.M. (2007) Understanding responsible leadership: Role identity and motivational drivers: The case of Dame Anita Roddick, founder of the Body Shop. *Journal of Business Ethics*, 74, 437–456.

Porter, M.E. (1991) *The Competitive Advantage of Nations: Creating and Sustaining Superior Performance*. New York: First Free Press.

Raworth, K. (2017) *Doughnut Economics: Seven Ways to Think Like a 21st Century Economist*. London: Random House Business Books.

Rawls, J. (1971) *Theory of Justice*. Cambridge, MA: Belknap Press of Harvard University Press.

Ritchie, H. & Roser, M. (2024) How much of the world's land would we need in order to feed the global population with the average diet of a given country? *Our World in Data*. Retrieved November 27, 2024, from https://ourworldindata.org/global-land-for-agriculture.

Rittel, H.W. & Webber, M.M. (1973) Dilemmas in a general theory of planning. *Policy Sciences*, 4(2), 155–169.

Rowlinson, M. (2015) Revisiting the historic turn: A personal reflection. In *The Routledge Companion to Management and Organizational History* (pp. 70–80). Abingdon, Oxon: Routledge.

Rowlinson, M. & Hassard, J. (1993) The invention of corporate culture: A history of the histories of Cadbury. *Human Relations*, 46(3), 299–326.

Sachs, S. & Rühli, R. (2011) *Stakeholders Matter: A New Paradigm for Strategy in Society*. Cambridge: Cambridge University Press. ProQuest Ebook Central, https://ebookcentral.proquest.com/lib/shu/detail.action?docID=807135.

Sax, N., Hassan, G.M., Abdi, A.N., Madurga-Lopez, I., Carneiro, B., Liebig, T., Läderach, P. & Pacillo, G. (2023) How does climate exacerbate root causes of conflict in Sudan? *Climate Security Pathway Analysis*. FACTSHEET 2023/2. Rome, Italy: CGIAR Focus Climate Security.

Siegel, P.B. & Jorgensen, S. (2011) No-regrets approach to increased resilience and climate change justice: Toward a risk-adjusted social protection floor. Institute for Development Studies, Brighton. https://www.ids.ac.uk/download.php?file=files/dmfile/SiegelJorgensen2011RiskAdjustedSocialProtectionFloor02CSPconferencedraft.pdf.

Skidelsky (2017) Is Western civilization in terminal decline? *The Guardian*. Retrieved November 27, 2024, from https://www.theguardian.com/business/2015/nov/17/is-western-civilisation-in-terminal-decline.

Swift, T. (2001) Trust, reputation and corporate accountability to stakeholders. *Business Ethics: A European Review*, 10(1), 16–26.

Taylor, F.W. (1911) Principles and methods of scientific management. *Journal of Accountancy*, 12(3), 3.

Terlau, W. & Hirsch, D. (2015) Sustainable consumption and the attitude–behaviour-gap phenomenon – causes and measurements towards a sustainable development. *Proceedings in Food System Dynamics*, 199–214.

United Nations (2024a) The United Nations Global Compact. https://unglobalcompact.org/.

United Nations (2024b) The 17 Sustainable Development Goals. https://sdgs.un.org/goals.

Wall Street Journal (2023) Big Oil's talent crisis: High salaries are no longer enough. Retrieved November 27, 2024, from https://www.wsj.com/articles/big-oils-talent-crisis-high-salaries-are-no-longer-enough-194545be.

Ware, G. (2024) Climate quitting: The people leaving their fossil fuel jobs because of climate change. Retrieved November 27, 2024, from https://theconversation.com/climate-quitting-the-people-leaving-their-fossil-fuel-jobs-because-of-climate-change-226246.

Wettstein, F. (2020) The history of business and human rights and its relationship with corporate social responsibility. In *Research Handbook on Human Rights and Business*.

Whitney, D. & Cooperrider, D. (2011) *Appreciative Inquiry: A Positive Revolution in Change*. Berrett-Koehler Publishers.

Whittington, R., Regnér, P., Angwin, D., Johnson, G. & Scholes, K. (2023) *Exploring Strategy*. Harlow: Pearson Education.

Wicks, A.C. & Freeman, R.E. (1998) Organization studies the new pragmatism: Positivism, anti-positivism and the search for ethics. *Organization Science*, 9: 123–140.

Zahra, S.A. & Nambisan, S. (2011) Entrepreneurship in global innovation ecosystems. *AMS Review*, 1, 4–17.

CHAPTER 7

Technology's Influence on Strategic Thinking

Nick Lawrence and Helen Pollard

CHAPTER OUTLINE

In a rapidly evolving business world shaped by technology, strategic thinking faces both unique opportunities and significant challenges. Today's international business environment presents organisations with a diverse set of challenges. They must navigate fierce competition while achieving sustainable growth. At the same time, they are pressured by society to prioritise their circular economy practices, workplace well-being, and their impact on the planet. By exploring the intricate interplay between technology and strategic thinking, this chapter looks to discuss these complex challenges aiming for a balanced and adaptable strategic approach. This chapter examines technology's transformative potential while remaining sensitive to its ethical and human dimensions, ensuring that progress aligns with broader societal and environmental goals.

This chapter examines how technology empowers leaders to:

- Obtain unparalleled access to strategic intelligence and receive real-time analysis using AI algorithms, resulting in actionable insights and a more informed strategic direction.
- Leverage technology to advance ecosystems by constructing digital ecosystems, facilitate collaboration, enhance hyper connectivity, and improve value exchange.
- Harness the power of technology and AI to develop advanced business models that enhance value and provide a competitive advantage.
- Gather and interpret sophisticated market intelligence, empowering strategic choices by providing deep insights into trends, competitor actions, and customer preferences.

DOI: 10.4324/9781003475545-7

- Exploit AI-powered forecasting and scenario planning to anticipate market shifts and identify strategic opportunities.

However, the chapter also recognises the crucial need to address technology's inherent challenges:

- Managing cybersecurity risks and vulnerabilities, requiring robust strategies to protect critical data and ensure business continuity.
- Adapting to continuous innovation and disruptive changes, demanding dynamic and flexible strategic thinking to navigate unforeseen challenges and seize emerging opportunities.
- Balancing personalised customer engagement with data privacy and ethical considerations, necessitating a strategic approach that builds trust and safeguards user information.
- Addressing potential biases in AI-driven decision-making and ensuring that ethical considerations are factored into strategy-making.
- The rapid rise of autonomous systems and the need for human oversight in strategic decision-making.

KEY POINTS

- Technology and particularly AI offer great opportunities but at the same time risks that must be managed by the strategic thinker.
- A strategic thinker must be aware of the key challenges in technology evolution: Cybersecurity Threats, the Constant Evolution of Technology, the Negative Ethical Impact Personalisation has on an Individual's Well-being, Autonomy, and Privacy, the Bias in AI.
- A strategic thinker can take certain steps to manage these challenges: proactively adapt security measures to stay current with emerging threats; embrace change and disruption with proactive and adaptive strategic thinking; be transparent and open, diverse, empower user autonomy, follow the principles of fairness by design, and incorporate human judgement in its application.
- This proactive and strategic thinking can maintain an ethical and sustainable approach: optimising stakeholder confidence and trust and cultivating meaningful relationships with stakeholders while achieving economic success.

OPPORTUNITIES OF TECHNOLOGY IN STRATEGIC THINKING

In a world driven by technology, businesses and society are undergoing a revolution in how they operate and develop. This section explores how technology is enabling opportunities and solutions. It discusses:

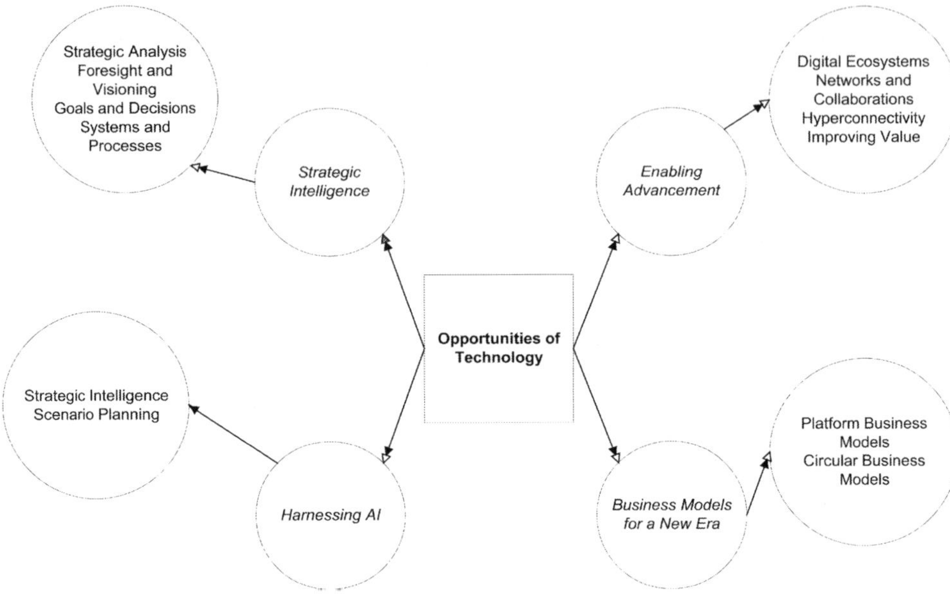

FIGURE 7.1 The Opportunities of Technology in Strategic Thinking

- The use of data science for strategic intelligence
- The ability to enable advancement through, for example, facilitating ecosystem development
- The relationship between technology and business models, uncovering novel approaches to value creation
- The use of AI to obtain market insights and carry out complex scenario planning.

From Big Data to Strategic Success: Harnessing Data Science for Strategic Intelligence

Leaders use data to conduct strategic analysis, inform strategic choices, implement actions, and evaluate performance. Shaping future strategies, policies, and plans requires strategic intelligence based on reliable and relevant data. Data science is essentially the extraction of insights from messy data (Grus, 2019). As noted by Van der Aalst (2016), data is everywhere and companies need to adapt, and introducing data science processes is the only way to survive in the technology revolution. The use of data science is critical for effective strategic intelligence, notably strategic analysis, foresight and visioning, goals and decisions, and systems and processes.

Strategic Analysis

In strategic analysis, a diverse range of data sources is utilised, including industry and market research, economic data, labour statistics, competitor information, and internal data. Data science provides a holistic approach to strategic analysis by gathering, organising, examining, analysing, and modelling relevant data to the strategic context. Adopting the principles of data science means the data is organised, synthesised, and leveraged to optimise strategy. Data science is of the utmost importance, as it can offer real-time data to tackle immediate problems faced by organisations. Big data consists of vast and intricate datasets, which can hold valuable information, patterns, insights, and understanding that can benefit various strategic aspects such as market expansion, portfolio development, and resourcing. Leveraging big data to derive valuable insights offers the opportunity to gain a competitive edge and drive sustainable outcomes.

Foresight and Visioning

Traditionally, data was used to analyse current and past performance. Advancements in data science methods, particularly predictive analytics, mean that data science is a driving force for understanding, predicting, and visioning the future. It is being used across all industries in areas such as product predictions, scenario planning, demand forecasting, predictive maintenance, and future visioning. The combination of data, machine learning, and algorithms in predictive analytics tools allows organisations to foresee and respond to market changes before they happen. Utilising predictive data can lead to a competitive advantage and staying ahead of the competition. The unpredictable future of work and the impact of industry revolutions like 5.0 and 6.0 pose significant challenges for organisations. Leveraging data science enables organisations to gain strategic insights and align their strategies for success in an uncertain future.

Over the past few years, organisations and industries have been using big data to anticipate and drive innovation. Innovation can be advanced using data science-based predictive strategic intelligence. This is apparent in fields like healthcare and computing, where big data is used to analyse emerging technologies, trends, and market gaps for innovation strategies. Understanding problems and finding solutions can be facilitated through data capture and analysis.

Goals and Decisions

Historically, data science was confined to its application in situation analysis for strategic planning. Nowadays it has the potential to be used in formulating plans and hypotheses. Data science allows organisations to analyse data collected and transform this into usable knowledge for setting goals and objectives. Strategy-making is increasingly adopting a scientific approach, relying on data analysis for decision-making, and the prominence of data-driven decision-making is becoming more evident in the field.

Systems and Processes

The process of strategic planning entails coordinating and focusing organisational efforts through the alignment and resourcing of systems and processes. In this context, there are numerous advantages to utilising data science. It aids in optimising internal processes, allocating resources effectively, automating repetitive tasks, cutting costs, and boosting productivity. The rise of digital data has transformed data analytics methods, shifting from 'cognitive and methodological procedures' (Hair & Sarstedt, 2021) to utilising scientific algorithms for predicting and optimising processes. The way organisations operate and execute strategies has been fundamentally changed by the digital revolution. There is a continuous effort to discover fresh strategies to utilise the data they generate for improved operational efficiency, streamlined processes, and valuable insights that drive profits and growth.

Technology and Ecosystems: Enabling Advancement

Considering the significance of ecosystems in today's world, strategic thinking demands attention to and contemplation of ecosystems. The business strategist James Moore (1996) was the first to define the term 'business ecosystem' in his book *The Death of Competition: Leadership and Strategy in the Age of Business*. He described it as 'An economic community supported by a foundation of interacting organisations and individuals – the organisms of the business world'. Ecosystems have become a vital aspect of organisational strategic direction. Platform business models, accelerating innovation, value-added collaboration, and driving transformational growth are just some of the benefits offered by ecosystems. The impact of technology on ecosystems includes the rise of digital ecosystems, enabling strong networks and collaborations, hyperconnectivity, and improving value.

Digital Ecosystems

Panetta (2016) defines a digital ecosystem as 'an interdependent group of enterprises, people and/or things that share standardised digital platforms for a mutually beneficial purpose, such as commercial gain, innovation or common interest, growth and shareholder returns'. A digital ecosystem is made up of interconnected technologies, digital infrastructure, platforms, and services that work together to generate value. It consists of software, hardware, data, and people, all collaborating to enable valuable digital transactions. A thriving digital ecosystem is characterised by synergistic relationships, customer centricity, data focus, scalability, and adaptability. Strategy-making is increasingly recognising the value of incorporating the digital ecosystem. It is important for leaders and strategists to contemplate ways in which they can foster the growth of essential components in the digital ecosystem, allowing technologies, people, and infrastructure to interact and evolve and thus create value.

Networks and Collaborations

Strong networks, collaborations, and partnerships are essential for implementing a successful strategy. Adner (2017) defines a business ecosystem as 'the alignment structure of the multilateral set of partners that need to interact in order for a focal value proposition to materialize'. Technology enables members in an ecosystem to network, communicate, collaborate, and share data. Digital platforms, data analytics, cloud computing, project management software, and communication tools enable powerful, mutual, and real-time interactions and information flow. Building and managing collaborative networks and balancing stakeholder interests are essential tasks for leaders. The role becomes even more intricate in ecosystems where there are more stakeholders, complex connections, and diverse needs.

Hyperconnectivity

Quan-Haase and Wellman (2005) introduced the concept of hyperconnection. They discussed it in relation to community in high-tech organisations and referred to it as 'hyperconnectivity', defining it as the constant availability of communication with people. In ecosystems, hyperconnectivity refers to the interconnectedness of individuals, devices, and systems within an ecosystem, enabling seamless information sharing and value creation. In strategy, hyperconnectivity offers opportunities for responsive, real-time stakeholder engagement, new business models, innovation, collaboration, and global engagement. The importance of hyperconnectivity in strategy-making will become more notable as we navigate the fifth industrial revolution which is described as when 'humans and machines dance together, metaphorically' (Noble et al., 2022) and a place where humans collaborate harmoniously with machines.

Improving Value

As noted by Moore (1996), the economic community produces goods and services of value to customers, who are themselves members of the ecosystem (Moore, 1996, p. 297). The ecosystem is 'A conceptual framework for identifying how a company creates, delivers, and extracts value. It typically includes a whole set of integrated components, all of which can be looked on as opportunities for innovation and competitive advantage' (Skarzynski & Gibson, 2008, p. 112). Value within an ecosystem is generated through collaboration, shared services, shared networks, data sharing, and the promotion of innovation. Partners and collaborators also benefit from shared risk, shared learning, and protection from competitors and the external environment. Value co-creation is an important strategy in ecosystems and platforms. It is a collaborative process between a company and its customers to create, find, or improve the value of a product or service.

Towards Tech-powered Business Models: Emerging Business Models for a New Era

A primary focus for leaders in strategic thinking is developing business and strategic operational models that are both sustainable and future proof. Technology is disrupting business models. The impact of data and digital technologies goes beyond just new business models and extends to the innovation of existing ones as well. Itami and Nishino (2010) argue that a business model is composed of two elements, a business system and a profit model, hence the term 'business model'. 'A business model defines how firms create, deliver and capture value in a market' (Teece, 2010, p. 173). Business model innovation is the process of changing the way a business operates, and it is a major factor in driving growth and competitiveness. It is no longer sufficient to focus on product or process innovation, as increasing competitive pressure, globalisation, and competitors erode formerly prominent positions. Empirical research has shown that business model innovation carries a greater potential for success than product or process innovation. A company's fate increasingly depends on its ability to apply the appropriate innovative business model that differentiates it from its competitors. The business models that will thrive in the future are those that combine data and digital infrastructure to foster collaboration, innovation, and a focus on purpose, sustainability, and inclusivity. Platform businesses and circular business models are two emerging business models that fulfil the criteria of innovation, sustainability, and future proofing.

Platform Business Models

A platform business model adopts an infrastructure that facilitates interactions among users. A platform-centred perspective helps us to see and understand ecosystems as the communities of buyers, sellers, and support providers who connect in multiple ways through a single platform (Ford, 2021). Amazon is an example of a platform ecosystem, and its ecosystem is vast and complex. It consists of retail, transportation, business-to-business (B2B) distribution, payments, entertainment, cloud computing, and other segments. Airbnb is another example of a platform-centred business ecosystem. Digital native companies such as Netflix, Google, and Uber dominate the platform business landscape. The trend will persist, leading to the growth and significance of digital native companies. As the global economy rapidly digitalises, an estimated 70per cent of new value created over the coming decade will be based on digitally enabled platform business models (WEF, 2024). Platform businesses heavily depend on technology for various purposes. Technology provides the structure for developing new products and services, streamlines operations, handles data, integrates systems, and enables sophisticated engagement.

Circular Business Models

The circular economy is a sustainable growth model for production and consumption. It is about creating business models that deliver value to the economy without waste, pollution, or adversely impacting the environment. In contrast to the 'take-make-waste' linear model, a circular economy is regenerative by design and aims to gradually decouple growth from the consumption of finite resources. According to the Ellen MacArthur Foundation (2022), the circular economy is based on three principles, driven by design: eliminate waste and pollution, circulate products and materials (at their highest value), **and** regenerate nature. The United Nations Conference on Trade and Development (UNCTAD) (UNCTAD, 2022) depicts the core elements of the circular economy (reduce, reuse, recycle, and remanufacture) along with the key benefits. A circular business model articulates the logic of how an organisation creates, offers, and delivers value to the broader range of stakeholders while minimising ecological and social costs (Board of Innovation, 2024). Common types of circular business models include circular supply, resource recovery, product life extension models, sharing models, and product service system models. The vast potential of digital technologies can be harnessed to advance environmental sustainability and promote a circular economy. Technology plays a crucial role in implementing circular business models by enabling the redesign of organisational structures and the creation of ecosystems that foster circular goals. It can support innovation, advance processes and systems, and create a framework for scalability and growth.

Harnessing AI

Strategic Intelligence

Market landscapes are becoming more complex. They are data rich, hyperconnected, multichannel led, unpredictable, tech powered and more competitive. In today's marketplace only the excellent strategic thinkers will survive as businesses seek new ways to improve performance (Kotler et al., 2016). Data science and AI are integral to all aspects of the marketing planning process. In marketing planning, data science plays a vital role in conducting situation analysis and monitoring and evaluation phases. The most significant impact of AI is seen in strategy, promotion, and customer relationship management and control. The efficiencies of data science and AI can optimise the marketing planning process and alleviate budget pressures by eliminating the need for human analysts. Significant time and effort are needed for market analysis and strategy development. In today's industry, the job is demanding and requires specialised knowledge in technology, data science, and AI. There is currently a skills gap in this field, making it expensive and difficult to recruit for this type of role. Certain aspects of marketing can be fulfilled by AI, avoiding the need for extensive recruitment, training, or labour costs.

Historically, data science was limited to being used in market research and increasing storage capacity (Saura, 2021). In recent times, marketers are utilising advanced analytics to acquire valuable marketing intelligence and make data-driven marketing decisions. The use of advanced analytic methods like deep learning, complex data mining, pattern matching, language processing, and cluster analysis in marketing has increased, allowing for the discovery of deeper insights from data and the creation of data-driven intelligent applications. Data science is particularly useful in statistical analysis, extracting patterns and formulating marketing hypotheses (Borges et al., 2021). It is instrumental in automating marketing analysis and control and allows for the analysis of unstructured data. Data science provides more precise outputs than business analysis and the data is often real-time. Market research datasets don't always align and make sense on their own, which is where data science comes in. Data science has applications beyond market research and situation analysis, such as segmentation, targeting, and positioning, as well as improving distribution systems and optimising warehouse inventory budgeting and pricing.

AI is revolutionising the marketing industry and market planning by imitating human intelligence and analysing big data patterns. The advent of AI has transformed data science, amplifying marketing possibilities. AI is applied in marketing to turn data science insights into actionable strategies, which encompass market forecasting, setting SMART targets, creating marketing plans, aligning strategies with market trends, and generating KPIs for monitoring and evaluation. Marketing greatly benefits from AI's capacity to carry out tasks that typically necessitate human-like intelligence, including developing promotional strategies and managing customer relationships. AI can create personalised content, specific to each user in real-time, pushing customers along the purchase funnel (Shah & Murthi, 2021).

From surveys to complex data analysis, AI automates various tasks in market research, resulting in valuable insights. In the past, market research required a lot of time and money, but AI automation now saves time, reduces costs, offers faster data, often in real-time, and minimises human mistakes. AI algorithms analyse data, forecasting trends and customer behaviour. It can rapidly and accurately analyse large volumes of data, uncovering patterns and trends that human analysts might miss. By using this, businesses can develop a more comprehensive understanding of consumer behaviour and market dynamics.

The process of sentiment analysis, also referred to as opinion mining, uses natural language processing and computational linguistics to analyse the emotional tone of text. It is not practical or efficient to manually analyse extensive text data using traditional methods. AI tools can rapidly analyse massive amounts of text-based market data, including social media posts, customer reviews, and FAQs, to assess sentiment towards brands and products. The algorithms categorise sentiment as positive, neutral, or negative, offering valuable insights into customer opinions on products and services. This real-time feedback is extremely valuable for making well-informed marketing decisions and effectively tracking and assessing the marketing effort.

Beyond the Crystal Ball: AI-driven Scenario Planning

Theorists (Mintzberg & Waters, 1985; Wolf & Floyd, 2017) suggest that strategies can either be planned or emergent, or a combination of both. By incorporating elements of both planned and emergent strategy-making approaches, scenario planning aids in predicting future possibilities. In the past, scenario planning has faced obstacles due to lack of data and slow or non-real-time data processing. AI is transforming scenario planning by assisting with tasks like modelling complex scenarios, managing risks, conducting stress tests, making predictive analyses, and cultivating innovation and creating new business models. Through harnessing these capabilities, AI empowers organisations to enhance their agility and readiness for future challenges.

AI is capable of simulating complex strategic scenarios, including market expansion, new product development, resource allocation, mergers and acquisitions, crisis management, and digital transformation. AI can consider various factors and their interconnections to simulate the implementation of strategic scenarios. It empowers the evaluation of diverse strategic scenarios and the potential impacts they could yield. The involvement of AI in scenario planning and modelling significantly improves the depth and accuracy of outcome analysis.

Organisations face a variety of risks that can affect their strategy, operations, and financial health. Strategic risks emerge from shifts in the external environment, including climate change, technological advances, economic downturn, and market shifts. AI can anticipate and analyse potential risks and vulnerabilities. By identifying patterns and anomalies it helps organisations anticipate and prepare for unfavourable situations.

Organisations benefit from AI's capacity to quickly stress test strategies, aiding in preparation for uncertain scenarios. AI algorithms, specifically machine learning, can predict system behaviour during stressful conditions by analysing historical and real-time data. The recognition of prior failure patterns and the ability to predict future scenarios enable AI to enhance stress testing. Additionally, AI can assist in reverse stress testing by detecting and evaluating potential scenarios that may result in the failure of a strategic decision. The process entails working backwards from failed events to grasp their impact.

Scenario planning is used to analyse the external environment to identify potential strategy influencers or driving forces. It can analyse and evaluate external factors like political, economic, social, technological, environmental, and legal influences. External analysis can be improved through AI's automation of data collection, accuracy enhancement, and provision of deeper insights. For instance, AI can predict future economic conditions by analysing GDP growth, unemployment, and inflation rates. It enables organisations to anticipate economic shifts and strategise accordingly.

AI can conduct predictive analysis by leveraging advanced machine-learning techniques and algorithms, such as linear regression and neural networks, to analyse historical data and forecast future results. It helps organisations make strategic decisions and plan for various future scenarios. Predictions become more reliable with the aid of AI and machine learning. The integration of predictive models allows organisations to predict issues and discover areas that can be optimised.

Using AI-powered scenario planning is an effective way to promote innovation and create new business models, particularly in uncertain and rapidly changing contexts. Its impact lies in its ability to enhance efficiency, drive innovation, and create new value propositions, revolutionising how organisations develop new products and business models. AI facilitates innovation by boosting creativity, generating ideas, providing data-driven insights, and enabling adaptive systems. The creative process is being transformed by GenAI, leading to alternative forms of innovation in product development. Organisations use scenario planning to explore new business models, like cloud-based enterprise applications and platform solutions, before making a significant investment. AI is changing how organisations do this by providing complex analysis with multiple variables and scenarios to predict outcomes before they decide to invest. AI is highly valuable for developing and testing new business models, enabling the exploration of innovative ways to create and deliver value. The role of AI-driven scenario planning will become more prominent in industry revolutions 5.0 and 6.0, as we get ready for future advancements and possibilities.

CHALLENGES OF TECHNOLOGY IN STRATEGIC THINKING AND WHAT A STRATEGIC THINKER CAN DO

The previous section explored how organisations can capitalise on the opportunities technology can provide to benefit their strategic thinking. However, it is equally important to understand the challenges technology presents. This section examines these complex challenges, emphasising the need for strategic approaches that are adaptable, ethically sound, and aligned with broader societal and environmental objectives.

TABLE 7.1 The Actions Strategic Thinkers Can Take to Deal with the Challenges of Technology

The challenges	What a strategic thinker can do	The impact for strategy-making
Cybersecurity threats	Proactively adapt security measures to stay current with emerging threats	Stakeholder confidence and trust
Continuous evolution of technology	Embrace change and disruption with proactive and adaptive strategic thinking	Survive and be more sustainable in the ever-changing world
The negative ethical impact personalisation has on an individual's well-being, autonomy, and privacy	Be transparent and open, diverse, empower user autonomy	Cultivate meaningful relationships with stakeholders
The bias in AI	Follow the principles of fairness by design and incorporate human judgement in its application	Ensure ethical and socially beneficial use of AI

Cybersecurity Threats and Cyber Defence: Safeguarding Data and Ensuring Business Continuity

Cybersecurity is the defensive method organisations employ to safeguard their internal systems, networks, and information from external attacks and unauthorised access (Craigen et al., 2014). Guarding against cyber-attacks is not just an IT issue; it is the responsibility of senior leaders and a strategic imperative across private, public, and third-sector organisations (Epstein, 2014).

The Shifting Cybersecurity Terrain: A Moving Target for All

In the ever-evolving technological landscape of international business, it is essential that organisations ensure they maintain the confidentiality, integrity, and availability of their data to preserve stakeholder confidence (Von Solms & van Niekerk, 2013). With cyber-criminals continuously developing new strategies to exploit system vulnerabilities, such as ransomware attacks, all sectors must evolve accordingly. Proactively adapting security measures to stay current with emerging threats is essential for mitigating risk. However, the advantages of the digital world come with inherent risks. The value of data to modern organisations is undeniable, it is seen as their lifeblood by many, and cyber-attacks against their systems can have dire consequences. It is imperative that strategic thinking across all sectors prioritises data security to safeguard personally identifiable information, intellectual assets, and sensitive information against cyber-crime and ensure organisational resilience (Boone, 2017).

Industry-specific Challenges: Navigating Sector-specific Cybersecurity Landscape

By capitalising on the cyber domain, organisations gain the flexibility to operate beyond conventional time and geographical constraints, enabling the development of unique business models. Paradoxically, a significant consequence of this reliance is an increased vulnerability to cyber threats (Sallos et al., 2019), and each sector has its own unique set of considerations, as illustrated in the examples below.

Private Sector

- **Intellectual property theft and data breaches:** Private organisations often have trade secrets and own valuable intellectual property that cyber-criminals often target. For instance, in 2024, millions of AT&T customers discovered their data had been leaked on the dark web (Seddon, 2024).
- **Financial gain and ransomware:** The private sector faces a significant threat from cyber-attacks motivated by financial gain, including ransomware attacks and various forms of cyber fraud. A prime example is the 2021 attack on Colonial Pipeline, a major American oil pipeline company (Kerner, 2022). The DarkSide cyber-criminal group held Colonial Pipeline's operational systems hostage with ransomware, disrupting operations and causing widespread fuel shortages. Colonial Pipeline reportedly paid the group a ransom of 64 bitcoin, valued at approximately $2.4 million at the time.

Public Sector

- **Data protection:** Public entities hold vast amounts of personally identifiable information, making them prime targets for cyber-criminals. Data breaches can erode public trust in essential services and expose stakeholders to a range of cyber threats, including identity theft and financial fraud. The May 2024 data breach compromising the personal information of serving British military personnel serves as a stark reminder of the potential consequences for individuals (Forsyth, 2024).
- **Critical infrastructure:** Cyber-attacks targeting public services like electricity, gas, water, and transportation systems pose a significant national security threat should cyber-criminals target them (Herzog, 2011). Such attacks have the potential to disrupt essential services, causing widespread chaos and jeopardising public safety. Organisations' strategy-making should prioritise the development of robust security measures to safeguard this critical infrastructure.

Third Sector

- **Trust and donor confidence:** Non-profit and Non-governmental Organisations rely on public trust to operate effectively (Gaskin, 1999). They handle sensitive information about donors, beneficiaries, and their operations, including potentially sensitive financial data or personal details. Cyber-attacks and data breaches pose a significant strategic threat as they can erode donor confidence and disrupt critical operations.

Effective cybersecurity is vital for them to maintain trust, secure funding, and continue their crucial work (Taylor et al., 2024).

The above examples demonstrate the risk of such attacks and highlight the importance for organisations across all sectors to incorporate strategic thinking into their cybersecurity initiatives to mitigate these threats and maintain customer confidence in their ability to protect their personal information. Developing and implementing robust strategies to mitigate these threats is essential not only for maintaining stakeholder confidence in their ability to protect personal information but also for ensuring long-term organisational resilience and sustainability.

Continuous Evolution: Embracing Disruption for Strategic Agility

Technology in strategic thinking is not static; it is dynamic and fluid, with innovation continually evolving, reshaping, and redefining strategic paradigms across all sectors. Technology's continual evolution highlights the need for organisations whether private, public, or non-profit to not only adapt but also actively embrace disruption as a catalyst for positive change. This section explores the concept of embracing disruptive technology to enable responsible, sustainable, and mission-centric strategic thinking.

The Nature of Disruption

Disruption, by definition, is substantial changes that shift conventional industries, products/services, or practices (Christensen, 1997). Technological advancements, such as AI, blockchain, and the Internet of Things (IoT), are examples of primary drivers of disruption. Imagine an organisation methodically developing a strategic plan, precisely outlining their path to success, but within a year, a new and innovative technological development effectively renders their meticulously crafted strategic plan obsolete. While this scenario is unfortunate, it is a situation we are seeing more frequently. Disruption, once viewed as a rare and negative force, is now recognised as an inevitable and normal aspect of modern business.

These technological evolutions present novel ideas on how organisations can improve efficiency and develop new business models that challenge established strategic thinking approaches transforming industries seemingly overnight. The internet itself is a primary example of how disruptive technology revolutionised how organisations communicate and access information. The rise of social media has forced organisations to adapt and become more transparent and accountable for their actions. Mobile devices have provided a ubiquitous connection to stakeholders reshaping how organisations interact with them. However, with this continual connection via technology come some fundamental concerns. Including high-profile incidents such as data breaches (discussed above), the spread of fake news (Gao et al., 2020), and the impact on our mental well-being (O'Keeffe & Clarke-Pearson, 2011). These concerns have led to increased scrutiny and calls for regulation (O'Keeffe & Clarke-Pearson, 2011).

Embracing Disruption: A Strategic Imperative

In the technologically dynamic landscape organisations operate in today, a reactive approach to change is no longer enough. Continuous development, an ongoing practice of adaptation and innovation, enables organisations to navigate change effectively.

Agile Thinking for Strategy

This requires an approach that sees disruption as an opportunity, not as a threat. This method requires the organisation to continuously reinvent and reposition themselves to understand the disruptive potential of technology and to become more responsive.

Strategic thinking must be dynamic and versatile, enabling organisations to adapt and adjust their direction as the disruptive technological landscape evolves. Inflexible, long-term plans can become liabilities in a world of continual change. Strategic agility, the ability to adapt and respond quickly to these changing technological environments, allows the organisation to respond rapidly and decisively to capitalise on emerging opportunities and mitigate threats. By continuously looking for innovative ways to improve strategic thinking through utilising technology, organisations can stay ahead of the curve and develop a forward-thinking culture.

Forward Thinking: Proactively Adapting to Change

Organisations should not passively wait for disruptive technologies to emerge but instead actively invest in new ideas and approaches to anticipate potential changes and threats to their operations. This proactive perspective should encourage an openness to experimentation with innovative ideas and technologies, from trialling new marketing channels to exploring the potential of AI. In the hyperdynamic environment using data-driven insights to continuously adapt their strategic thinking becomes indispensable and allows them to adapt their strategies and make informed decisions that meet their stakeholder needs. This forward-thinking approach provides organisations with the ability to not only survive but be more sustainable in the ever-changing world of technological advancements.

Empowering Data-driven Approaches for Continuous Evolution in Decision-making

For organisations to succeed in the ever-changing technological-driven business environment, they must foster a culture of continuous learning and innovation. Achieving this requires a multi-faceted approach:

- **Employee training and development:** Organisations need to invest in their employees' training and development to ensure that they are appropriately equipped with the skills and knowledge they need to navigate the continuously evolving technological landscape to adopt new and developing technologies.
- **Innovative thinking and proactive risk engagement:** It also means developing a safe environment that supports calculated risk-taking, where employees feel empowered

to experiment with novel ideas and approaches without fear of facing consequences for failure.

- **The power of collaboration drives creative strategic thinking:** Inspiring a culture of teamwork fosters the exchange of creative thinking and leads to new perspectives and innovative solutions.
- **Empowering data-driven approaches for continuous evolution in decision-making:** Employing a data-driven approach to strategic thinking enables organisations to continuously adapt and refine their strategies, thereby strengthening trust and confidence among stakeholders in their future.

Technology is not a static force, but rather a dynamic catalyst for change. The key to success in this ever-evolving landscape lies in embracing continuous evolution and developing strategic thinking that is agile, proactive, and data-driven. By understanding the disruptive potential of technology and fostering a culture of innovation, organisations can leverage long-term sustainability and ability to thrive in a constantly evolving world.

Beyond Personalisation: Ethical Considerations in Stakeholder Engagement

In the contemporary landscape of society and business, the idea of personalisation has developed as a basis for stakeholder engagement. Organisations use advanced data-analysis tools to collect data that enables them to tailor their communication to individual needs and preferences. Personalisation has become synonymous with improving stakeholder interaction and driving positive business outcomes. However, as technology continues to evolve and organisations push their exploration of data analytics and AI further, there is a need for responsible strategic thinking and ethical consideration in the use of big data and stakeholder engagement. This section explores the ethical considerations organisations need to pay attention to when dealing with the use of big data and stakeholder engagement, such as transparency, data privacy, and long-term value creation for a sustainable future.

Breaking Free of Filter Bubbles and the Creation of Echo Chambers

Personalisation, when implemented responsibly, can definitely offer significant benefit to individual users' experiences. By using data insights, organisations can offer targeted services and content that align with the unique preferences and requirements of the user, thereby creating stronger relationships. However, there remains the question of the ethical impact personalisation has on the individual's well-being, autonomy, and privacy.

Algorithms designed to provide us with a personalised online experience can unintentionally create 'filter bubbles', a world where we only see material that matches our own perspectives. This phenomenon can lead to the creation of 'echo chambers' limiting exposure to new ideas, contrasting perspectives, and open and constructive discussions, thereby fostering a sense of intellectual isolation.

To mitigate these challenges organisations can be proactive in their actions to promote a more diverse, inclusive, and engaged stakeholder base:

- **Transparency:** Encourage social media platforms and search engines to be more transparent about how their algorithms work and what factors influence the content you see.
- **Diversity:** Platforms can design algorithms to intentionally introduce diverse viewpoints and reduce the over-personalisation of content.
- **Empower user autonomy:** Organisations should foster an environment where users have the agency and resources to manage their own digital experiences.
- **Open communication:** The foundation of ethical stakeholder engagement.

As previously discussed in Chapter 6, a fundamental consideration for long-term success between an organisation and its stakeholders is the trust built between them. When it comes to technology, this trust centres around the transparency of the organisation's data-collection purpose, methods, use, and associated risks. Stakeholders have a right to know how their data is being used and for what purposes. Organisations therefore need to clearly communicate their data-handling policies, stating how they ensure data privacy and security. Engaging with stakeholders in open and transparent discussions on the ethical implications of data collection and addressing any fears promotes an environment of collaboration and trust.

However, the pursuit of hyper-personalisation, which uses real-time data and AI for highly individualised stakeholder engagement, can erode trust and damage the authenticity of the relationship. When users feel that their dealings with an organisation are only driven by data analytics and algorithms rather than personal human engagement, they could feel manipulated or alienated. Transparency and authenticity are crucial in cultivating meaningful relationships with stakeholders, and organisations should provide a balance between using technology for personalisation and maintaining human-centric values.

Ethical Considerations and Specific Stakeholder Groups

Customers/service users:

- **Data privacy:** Personalisation is often built on extensive data collection. Organisations should ensure that they comply with relevant data privacy regulations like General Data Protection Regulation (GDPR), the California Consumer Privacy Act (CCPA), and Health Insurance Portability and Accountability Act (HIPAA). They should also clearly communicate their data-retention policies and provide users with options to control their data.
- **Algorithmic bias:** Personalisation algorithms can inadvertently amplify biases, leading to discriminatory practices. Organisations should actively monitor and mitigate algorithmic bias to ensure fair treatment of all users.

Employees:

- **Data monitoring:** Some organisations use data to monitor employee activity. Ethical considerations require maintaining a balance between employee privacy and workplace monitoring. Organisations need to clearly define acceptable data-collection practices and maintain a transparent communication channel with employees regarding data monitoring.
- **Up-skilling and re-skilling:** As technology evolves, so too do skill requirements. Responsible organisations should invest in employee training to ensure they have the skills needed to operate in a data-driven environment.

Communities:

- **Community needs assessment:** Organisations need to actively engage with communities in identifying local needs and co-creating solutions. Engaging with local stakeholders allows organisations to use their resources to address current challenges and contribute to the community's well-being.
- **Technology access and inclusivity:** Not everyone has equal access to technology. Responsible organisations need to consider how their technology and data practices can be used to bridge the digital divide and promote inclusivity within their communities.

Fairness by Design: Addressing Bias in AI Decision-making

In the continuously evolving technological landscape, AI continues to pervade various facets of society and business. Ensuring that equality and impartiality are maintained throughout the strategic decision-making process has emerged as a critical imperative. As discussed previously, while AI algorithms are powerful tools for analysing data, they can reflect and amplify human biases that are embedded in the data they learn from. Their very strength can also be their Achilles' heel, as they have the potential to perpetuate existing societal inequalities leading to discrimination and disadvantaging certain groups. The idea of fairness by design requires organisations to develop proactive strategies and techniques used to identify, reduce, and prevent biases within AI (Mehrabi et al., 2022). Responsible strategic thinking requires practical approaches to promote development towards a more equitable future.

Understanding Bias in AI

Bias in AI can develop in various ways:

- **Data bias:** The datasets used to teach AI algorithms mirrors present societal perspectives leading to a perpetuation of any inherent biases. For example, an AI system trained on medical images primarily from fair-skinned people might be less accurate in identifying conditions in brown or dark-skinned people, leading to inequalities in healthcare outcomes (Goyal et al., 2020).

- **Algorithmic bias:** Choices made during the development and design of the process can lead to bias. For instance, if an algorithm designed for assessing loan applications prioritises maximising profits, it may unconsciously discriminate against applicants from lower socioeconomic backgrounds (Ntoutsi et al., 2020).
- **Human bias:** Human judgement can introduce bias at various stages, from selecting the data for training to interpreting the algorithm's outputs (Pessach & Shmueli, 2023).

The effects of biased AI decision-making can be wide-ranging. It can lead to unfair recruitment practices (Chen, 2023), inequitable loan rejections (Sachan et al., 2019), and algorithmic profiling that reinforces social disparities (Bornstein, 2018). This not only erodes trust in AI but can also have significant legal and ethical implications.

Principles of Fairness by Design

To address the concerns of potential bias in AI development and to ensure it is an ethical and socially beneficial application, the following principles will help guide responsible strategic thinking in mitigating bias throughout the development lifecycle of AI:

- **Building an inclusive design team:** This unlocks a wider range of perspectives and supports innovation. By actively recruiting people with diverse experiences and backgrounds, a team is created that can better understand the needs of a diverse user base, thereby leading to the design of AI platforms that are more user-friendly and inclusive.
- **Data diversity:** Developers should ensure that they use a diverse range of data-collection methods to train AI platforms. Moreover, when collecting data it should be representative of a wide range of experiences, backgrounds, and demographics. This can include data from different international locations, cultures, industries, and public datasets.
- **User-centric design:** Incorporating user perspectives and feedback in its design can improve fairness. Understanding how different stakeholder groups may be impacted by the decisions made by AI will enable developers to create systems that reduce inequalities.
- **Awareness and transparency:** Developers should be conscious of potential biases and transparent about the decision-making processes, algorithms, and data sources used in developing AI platforms. Transparency encourages accountability, allows for external scrutiny, and empowers stakeholders while cultivating trust.
- **Human oversight, continuous monitoring, and improvement:** Ensuring fairness in AI platforms goes beyond deployment; continuous monitoring is crucial to identify and mitigate emerging biases quickly. Human oversight plays a fundamental role in establishing robust review mechanisms to assess algorithmic outputs for fairness and facilitate prompt interventions when necessary. Moreover, fairness is not a one-time achievement; it is an iterative process that requires regular monitoring and continual refinement throughout the development lifecycle.

In summary, the journey towards fairness in AI is ongoing and multi-faceted, requiring collaborative efforts across disciplines and industries. By embedding fairness by design principles into the fabric of AI development, we can harness the transformative potential of AI while upholding fundamental principles of justice and equality in a rapidly changing technological landscape.

CASE STUDY 7.1

The United Kingdom's (UK) National Health Service (NHS) and the Use of Technology

The UK's NHS stands as one of the largest public healthcare organisations globally, serving a population of over 67 million people (Vankar, 2024). Recent years have seen a strategic growth in the NHS's use of technology, notably artificial intelligence (AI), aimed at improving operational efficiency, diagnosis, and ultimately the overall healthcare of service users. However, this strategic shift towards AI integration raises concerns about the security of patient data and the potential for cyber-attacks, particularly ransomware, which can cripple healthcare delivery (Ghafur et al., 2019).

NHS 2.0: The Role of AI in Modern Healthcare

The NHS has implemented AI systems across its services, recognising them as key drivers for improving patient health and service delivery (Bloomfield et al., 2021). Some areas where AI is having the most impact are as follows:

- **Medical analysis imaging:** The NHS uses AI to analyse medical images such as MRI, X-Ray and CT scans, allowing for a faster and more accurate identification of conditions and potential diseases such as heart disease, neurological disorders, or cancer. For instance, AI analytical support tools increase diagnostic detection performance of breast cancer in mammograms with a higher level of accuracy than human radiologists, leading to potentially improved patient outcomes (Kim et al., 2020).
- **Predictive healthcare and personalised treatment plans:** The NHS data encompasses a vast amount of information on over 65 million people, making it one of the most comprehensive datasets of medical records in the world. This data includes information on patients' previous illnesses and operations, current and historical medications, test results, vaccinations, allergies, genetic information, and lifestyle factors. The sheer volume and detailed nature of the data make it highly valuable. Analysing this information enables predictive modelling to identify those most at risk of developing conditions such as diabetes or heart disease, allowing for preventative measures and the development of personalised treatment plans.

The Data Dilemma: Treasure Trove or Achilles' Heel?

Although the integration of AI by the NHS provides countless benefits, it is not without its risks. Medical data is particularly sensitive, containing personal identification information, medical histories, and financial details. The value of this data creates security risks such as data breaches (the theft of personal data) and ransomware attacks (encryption of personal data). For instance, during 2023 and 2024 the NHS fell victim to several cyber-attacks, the most notable being the following:

- **The 2024 Synnovis ransomware attack:** In June 2024 Synnovis, a London-based provider of pathology services, was the victim of a ransomware attack, believed to have been carried out by the Russian cyber-criminal group known as Qilin. The attack, on June 3, 2024, resulted in the cancellation of thousands of operations and hundreds of appointments at several London Hospitals in the UK (Humphreys, 2024).
- **The 2023 Trauma Audit and Research Network (TARN) data breach:** In June 2023, the University of Manchester confirmed a cyber-attack on an NHS database held by TARN compromising records of more than one million patients. The network holds sensitive and personally identifiable information on patients across the UK and Ireland. While the full extent of the breach and who posted the data online remain unclear, the incident exposed millions of patients' diagnoses, treatment details, and possibly even demographic data. The scope of the data breach and the identity of the attackers are still under investigation, but the attack undeniably compromised sensitive patient information, potentially including diagnoses, treatment details, and even demographics, for millions of individuals (Scroxton, 2024).

These attacks demonstrate the NHS' vulnerability to cyber threats or indeed organisations handling sensitive healthcare information and the critical need for robust cybersecurity measures and training. To help mitigate these risks, organisations could implement several measures:

- **Enhanced cyber defence strategies:** Organisations should prioritise investments in advanced cybersecurity technologies like intrusion detection systems, firewalls, and encryption, while also conducting regular security audits and vulnerability assessments.
- **Staff training:** Organisations should provide comprehensive cybersecurity training programs on strong passwords, phishing awareness, data protection policies, and cybersecurity best practices.
- **Collaborative initiatives:** Organisations should strengthen their cybersecurity defences by collaborating with government agencies, cybersecurity experts, and technology providers to share knowledge and best practices.
- **Regulatory compliance:** Organisations should adhere to data protection regulations, including GDPR, to maintain strict standards for personal identification information data security and privacy.

Conclusion

As can be seen, AI and other digital technologies hold huge potential in the advancement of healthcare delivery in the NHS, providing operational efficiencies, improved diagnostics, and personalised treatment. However, this digital revolution also comes with significant risks predominantly related to ransomware attacks and data breaches. It is therefore imperative that these changes be supported by robust cybersecurity measures. Through strategic thinking and decision-making, and by fostering collaboration, staff training, and strong governance protocols, the NHS can mitigate these risks and ensure that technological innovations contribute to sustainable and secure healthcare delivery.

Beyond Automation: The Need for Human Judgement in Strategic Decisions

As we move towards fairness in AI, it is equally important to acknowledge the requirement of maintaining human judgement, especially when it comes to making strategic decisions in a world increasingly relying on automation.

Automation and AI are transforming industry and society, introducing a new way we do business. While automation provides organisations with significant benefits in cost reduction, process optimisation, efficiency, predictive modelling, and data analysis (Tschang & Almirall, 2021), a fundamental question arises: Does the use of AI in automation supersede human judgment in strategic decision-making? The answer, fortunately, is a resounding *no*: it is evident that human judgement remains irreplaceable (Huq, 2020). This section explores why human judgement is fundamental in strategic thinking, despite the evolution in AI and automation.

The Benefits and Challenges of Automation in Strategic Thinking

AI learning algorithms can rapidly analyse large quantities of data to identify trends and emerging patterns. Excelling at these data-intensive and repetitive tasks, AI does require defined parameters and clearly defined rules and objectives (Wang, 2019). However, strategic decision-making often requires the navigation of uncertain, multi-faceted, and complex situations that surpasses automated AI's abilities (Thiel et al., 2012).

Let us explore some ways the judgement of humans remains fundamental in strategic decision-making:

1. **Contextual understanding**: Humans possess unique qualities required for strategic decision-making, such as the ability to comprehend the broader context of a given situation. Aspects such as organisational culture, stakeholder relationships, societal considerations, external factors, and industry-specific challenges can all significantly impact strategic decisions. Human knowledge and experience of contextual situations relevant to their particular organisation and sector provide important perspectives, allowing them to make informed decisions that align with the organisation's values and long-term goals. This is something that AI, at present, cannot replicate.
2. **Creative and innovative thinking:** An essential aspect of strategic decision-making is the ability to visualise novel possibilities that foster inventive solutions beyond the boundaries of rule-based algorithms. Fundamentally, creativity is a human characteristic, and draws upon diverse experiences, intuition, and the ability to think outside the

box. These skills are crucial for navigating unexpected challenges and capitalising on unique opportunities that challenge the status quo and drive innovation. AI automation can aid in the innovation process by providing operational efficiency and data-driven insights, but it cannot replicate the lightbulb moment that leads to breakthrough ideas.

3. **Ethical considerations:** Algorithms for AI automation are primarily designed to achieve specific objectives; however, they lack the inbuilt moral compass of humans. Strategic decisions frequently comprise ethical dilemmas that necessitate careful consideration of all the possible consequences. AI, while becoming increasingly sophisticated, lacks the ability for moral reasoning. Decisions that impact the welfare of stakeholders, such as environmental sustainability initiatives or downsizing, require a human touch to balance the ethical responsibilities towards people and the planet with motives of profit (Elkington, 1999). Human leaders, guided by empathy, moral frameworks, and an appreciation of societal responsibility, can navigate these complexities.
4. **Leadership and long-term vision:** It is evident that AI surpasses human efficiency in automation. However, strategic thinking and decision-making extend beyond analysing historical data and making short-term predictions. It involves inspiring the people within an organisation to work towards a shared vision, and long-term goals, while considering potential future disruptors, trends, and changing stakeholder needs. These characteristics are inherently human and fundamental for sustainable success.

Human–AI Collaboration: The Optimal Approach

The ideal scenario is not a competition between AI and humans, but instead a harmonious collaboration. Human intuition and strategic thinking can be improved by the analytical power of AI. By utilising the strengths of both, organisations can accomplish a balanced approach to strategic decision-making. Automation would be used to complete data-driven tasks, providing insights, and improving operational efficiency, while human leaders interpret these insights, apply contextual knowledge, and make decisions that consider the broader implications for the organisation and society. This synergy ensures that strategic decisions are not only data-informed but also value-driven and aligned with the human elements that define successful leadership.

CHAPTER SUMMARY

Technology has granted strategic thinkers unprecedented power to shape the future. AI offers a wealth of intelligence and real-time insights, enabling leaders to make informed, data-driven decisions. By constructing digital ecosystems, strategic thinkers can foster collaboration, enhance connectivity, and drive innovation within their business ecosystems. AI-powered tools can revolutionise business models, predict market trends, and identify strategic opportunities. However, this technological advancement comes with its own set of challenges. Cybersecurity risks, the need for agility, and ethical considerations, such as data privacy and bias in AI, must be carefully addressed. Ultimately, the human–AI collaboration is key, with humans providing strategic direction and oversight while AI empowers decision-making and execution.

RECOMMENDED READING

Ris, K. & Puvača, M. (2023) *Digital Transformation Handbook* (1st ed.). Boca Raton, FL: CRC Press.

Turban, E., Pollard, C. & Wood, G. (2021) *Information Technology for Management: Driving Digital Transformation to Increase Local and Global Performance, Growth and Sustainability.* (12th ed.). Hoboken, Belgium: Wiley.

REFERENCES

Adner, R. (2017) *The Wide Lens: A New Strategy for Innovation*. Cambridge, MA: Harvard Business Review Press.

Bloomfield, P., Clutton-Brock, P., Pencheon, E., Magnusson, J. & Karpathakis, K. (2021) Artificial Intelligence in the NHS: Climate and emissions. *The Journal of Climate Change and Health*, 4, 1–8. https://doi.org/10.1016/j.joclim.2021.100056.

Board of Innovation (2024) Circular Economy business models explained. https://www.boardofinnovation.com/circular-economy-business-models-explained/.

Boone, A. (2017) Cyber-security must be a C-Suite priority. *Computer Fraud & Security, 2017*(2), 13–15. https://doi.org/10.1016/S1361-3723(17)30015-5.

Borges, A., Silva, M., & Santos, F. (2021). Innovative approaches to sustainable business models in the digital economy. *Journal of Business Innovation, 12*(3), 45-67. https://doi.org/10.xxxx/jbi.2021.0305

Bornstein, S. (2018) Antidiscriminatory algorithms. *Alabama Law Review,* 70(2), 519–572.

Chen, Z. (2023) Ethics and discrimination in Artificial Intelligence-enabled recruitment practices. *Humanities and Social Sciences Communications,* 10(1), 567. https://doi.org/10.1057/s41599-023-02079-x.

Christensen, C.M. (1997) *The Innovator's Dilemma: When New Technologies Cause Great Firms to Fail.* Cambridge, MA: Harvard Business School Press.

Craigen, D., Diakun-Thibault, N. & Purse, R. (2014) Defining cybersecurity. *Technology Innovation Management Review,* 4(10), 13–21.

Elkington, J. (1999) *Cannibals with Forks : The Triple Bottom Line of 21st Century Business.* Vermont: Capstone.

Ellen MacArthur Foundation (2022) What is a circular economy? https://www.ellenmacarthurfoundation.org/topics/circular-economy-introduction/overview.

Epstein, A.J. (2014) Thinking strategically about cyber risk. *NACD Directorship,* 32–35.

Ford, C.J. (2021) *Business Ecosystems: A Guide.* ICAEW. https://www.icaew.com/-/media/corporate/files/technical/business-and-financial-management/strategy-risk-and-innovation/strategy/reports/business-ecosystems-a-guide.ashx.

Forsyth, A. (2024) MoD data breach: UK armed forces' personal details accessed in hack. *BBC News,* May 6. https://www.bbc.co.uk/news/uk-68966497.

Gao, J., Zheng, P., Jia, Y., Chen, H., Mao, Y., Chen, S., Wang, Y., Fu, H. & Dai, J. (2020) Mental health problems and social media exposure during COVID-19 outbreak. *PLOS ONE,* 15(4), e0231924. https://doi.org/10.1371/journal.pone.0231924.

Gaskin, K. (1999) Blurred vision: Public trust in charities. *International Journal of Nonprofit and Voluntary Sector Marketing*, 4(2), 163–178. https://doi.org/10.1002/nvsm.66.

Ghafur, S., Grass, E., Jennings, N.R. & Darzi, A. (2019) The challenges of cybersecurity in health care: The UK National Health Service as a case study. *The Lancet. Digital Health*, 1(1), e10–e12. https://doi.org/10.1016/S2589-7500(19)30005-6.

Goyal, M., Knackstedt, T., Yan, S. & Hassanpour, S. (2020) Artificial intelligence-based image classification methods for diagnosis of skin cancer: Challenges and opportunities. *Computers in Biology and Medicine*, 127, 104065. https://doi.org/10.1016/j.compbiomed.2020.104065.

Grus, J. (2019). *Data Science from Scratch: First Principles with Python* (2nd ed.). O'Reilly Media.

Hair, J.F. & Sarstedt, M. (2021) *A Primer on Partial Least Squares Structural Equation Modeling (PLS-SEM)* (2nd ed.). Thousand Oaks, CA: Sage..

Herzog, S. (2011) Revisiting the Estonian cyber attacks: Digital threats and multinational responses. *Journal of Strategic Security*, 4(2), 49–60. https://doi.org/10.5038/1944-0472.4.2.3.

Humphreys, J. (2024) London hospitals declare critical incident over cyber attack. *Security Journal United Kingdom*, June 4. https://securityjournaluk.com/london-hospitals-declare-critical-incident/.

Huq, A.Z. (2020) A right to a human decision. *Virginia Law Review*, 106(3), 611–688. https://www.jstor.org/stable/27074704.

Itami, H. & Nishino, K. (2010) The dynamics of sustained innovation: Strategic business models. *Long Range Planning*, 43(2–3), 1–14. https://doi.org/10.1016/j.lrp.2010.01.005.

Kerner, S.M. (2022) Colonial Pipeline hack explained: Everything you need to know. *TechTarget*, April 26. https://www.techtarget.com/whatis/feature/Colonial-Pipeline-hack-explained-Everything-you-need-to-know.

Kim, H-E., Kim, H. H., Han, B-K., Kim, K.H., Han, K., Nam, H., Lee, E.H. & Kim, E-K. (2020) Changes in cancer detection and false-positive recall in mammography using Artificial Intelligence. *The Lancet Digital Health*, 2(3), e138–e148. https://doi.org/10.1016/S2589-7500(20)30003-0.

Kotler, P., Armstrong, G., Cunningham, P. & Turnbull, P. (2016) *Principles of Marketing* (16th ed.). Harlow: Pearson Education.

Mehrabi, N., Morstatter, F., Saxena, N., Lerman, K. & Galstyan, A. (2022) A survey on bias and fairness in machine learning. *ACM Computing Surveys*, 54(6), 1–35. https://doi.org/10.1145/3457607.

Mintzberg, H. & Waters, J.A. (1985) Of strategies, deliberate and emergent. *Strategic Management Journal*, 6(3), 257–272. https://doi.org/10.1002/smj.4250060306.

Moore, J.F. (1996) *The Death of Competition: Leadership and Strategy in the Age of Business*. London: Harper Business.

Noble, S.M., Mende, M., Grewal, D. & Parasuraman, A. (2022) The fifth industrial revolution: How harmonious human–machine collaboration is triggering a retail and service [r]evolution. *Journal of Retailing*, 98(2), 199–208. https://doi.org/10.1016/j.jretai.2022.04.003.

Ntoutsi, E., Fafalios, P., Gadiraju, U., Iosifidis, V., Nejdl, W., Vidal, M., Ruggieri, S., Turini, F., Papadopoulos, S., Krasanakis, E., Kompatsiaris, I., Kinder-Kurlanda, K., Wagner, C., Karimi, F., Fernandez, M., Alani, H., Berendt, B., Kruegel, T., Heinze, C., … Staab, S. (2020) Bias in data-driven Artificial Intelligence systems: An introductory survey. *WIREs Data Mining and Knowledge Discovery,* 10(3). https://doi.org/10.1002/widm.1356.

O'Keeffe, G.S. & Clarke-Pearson, K. (2011) The impact of social media on children, adolescents, and families. *Pediatrics,* 127(4), 800–804. https://doi.org/10.1542/peds.2011-0054.

Panetta, D. (2016) *Top Strategic Technology Trends for 2016.* Gartner, Inc. https://www.gartner.com.

Pessach, D. & Shmueli, E. (2023) A review on fairness in machine learning. *ACM Computing Surveys,* 55(3), 1–44. https://doi.org/10.1145/3494672.

Quan-Haase, A. & Wellman, B. (2005) Hyperconnected network: Computer mediated community in a high-tech organization. In C. Heckscher & P. Adler (Eds.), *Collaborative Community in Business and Society.* New York: Oxford University Press, 281–333. https://doi.org/10.1093/oso/9780199286034.003.0008.

Sachan, S., Yang, J-B., Xu, D-L., Benavides, D.E. & Li, Y. (2019) An explainable AI decision-support-system to automate loan underwriting. *Expert Systems with Applications,* 144, 113100. https://doi.org/10.1016/j.eswa.2019.113100.

Sallos, M.P., Garcia-Perez, A., Bedford, D. & Orlando, B. (2019) Strategy and organisational cybersecurity: A knowledge-problem perspective. *Journal of Intellectual Capital,* 20(4), 581–597. https://doi.org/10.1108/JIC-03-2019-0041.

Saura, J.R. (2021) Social media analytics and marketing: The role of big data in digital transformation. *Journal of Business Research,* 134, 508–517. https://doi.org/10.1016/j.jbusres.2021.04.047.

Scroxton, A. (2024) NHS experts raise warning over patient data breach risk in registries project. *Computer Weekly,* June 25. https://www.computerweekly.com/news/366589530/NHS-experts-raise-warning-over-patient-data-breach-risk-in-registries-project.

Seddon, S. (2024) AT&T data breach: Millions of customers caught up in major dark web leak. BBC, March 30.

Shah, D. & Murthi, B. (2021) Consumer behavior and digital marketing: A comprehensive review of the literature. *Journal of Marketing Research,* 58(3), 453–469. https://doi.org/10.1177/00222437211011121.

Sharma, R. (2024) *The Blueprint for AI Success: Creating AI Strategy Framework.* Markovate, January 8 . https://markovate.com/blog/ai-strategy-framework/.

Skarzynski, P. & Gibson, R. (2008) *Innovation to the Core: A Blueprint for Transforming the Way Your Company Innovates.* Cambridge, MA: Harvard Business Press.

Taylor, J., Henriksen-Bulmer, J. & Yucel, C. (2024) Privacy essentials. *Electronics,* 13(12), 2263. https://doi.org/10.3390/electronics13122263.

Teece, D.J. (2010) Business models, business strategy and innovation. *Long Range Planning,* 43(2–3), 172–194. https://doi.org/10.1016/j.lrp.2009.07.003.

Thiel, C.E., Bagdasarov, Z., Harkrider, L., Johnson, J.F. & Mumford, M.D. (2012) Leader ethical decision-making in organisations: Strategies for sensemaking. *Journal of Business Ethics*, 107(1), 49–64. https://doi.org/10.1007/s10551-012-1299-1.

Tschang, F.T. & Almirall, E. (2021) Artificial Intelligence as augmenting automation: Implications for employment. *Academy of Management Perspectives*, 35(4), 642–659. https://doi.org/10.5465/amp.2019.0062.

UNCTAD (2022) *Circular Economy: The New Normal*. https://unctad.org/publication/circular-economy-new-normal.

Van der Aalst, W.M.P. (2016) *Process Mining: Data Science in Action* (1st ed.). New York: Springer.

Vankar, P. (2024) *National Health Service (NHS) UK – Statistics & Facts*. https://www.statista.com/topics/3128/national-health-service-nhs-uk/#topicOverview.

Von Solms, R. & van Niekerk, J. (2013) From information security to cyber security. *Computers & Security*, 38, 97–102. https://doi.org/10.1016/j.cose.2013.04.004.

Wang, P. (2019) On defining Artificial Intelligence. *Journal of Artificial General Intelligence*, 10(2), 1–37. https://doi.org/10.2478/jagi-2019-0002.

WEF (World Economic Forum) (2024) *Digital Transformation for SMEs: A Strategic Framework*. https://www3.weforum.org/docs/WEF_Digital_Transformation_for_SMEs_2024.pdf.

Wolf, J. & Floyd, S.W. (2017) Strategic leadership and the management of strategic change. *Strategic Management Journal*, 38(1), 13–41. https://doi.org/10.1002/smj.2599.

CHAPTER 8

Legal Responsibilities

Olivia Ramsbottom, Marc Duffy, Jules O'dor, and Jo Watts

CHAPTER OUTLINE

The legal issues in a PESTLE are often quite difficult to distinguish, as they overlap with other areas (political, as that is the environment in which legal responsibilities are developed and economic as it is the economic system that sets the expectations for how we do business) but here we present a selection of legal responsibilities of which the responsible strategic thinker needs to be aware. A strategic thinker has the benefit of being able to call on expertise in this area (a lawyer, accountant, and a myriad of local and national and international governmental bodies) and it would be wise to take advice if required, but when thinking about strategy it is a good idea to have an overview of the constraints and enablers related to legal issues by which a strategy will be shaped.

To give some structure to this chapter, we have used the balanced sustainability approach to categorise legal responsibilities: some issues are more to do with **economic** as they cover trade, costs, prices, and impact on profit maximisation. Then there are those that affect the **social** (the organisation's stakeholders) and the **environmental**.

What emerges from this discussion of legal responsibilities is that there is a potential gap between legal responsibilities and responsible strategic thinking, for many reasons. Legal responsibilities are framed, and therefore confused, by different political and legal contexts, so a universal approach should be sought; laws are broken; and laws do not cover social and environmental responsibilities adequately. This chapter uses Carroll's (1991) Corporate Responsibility pyramid to discuss the potential absorption of legal responsibilities into ethical responsibilities as a way to optimise the likelihood of sustainable strategic thinking, and draws on Visser's (2011) Ages and Stages of CSR to contrast Carroll's theory, before concluding with a new process model for responsible strategic thinking.

DOI: 10.4324/9781003475545-8

KEY POINTS

- A strategic thinker will always have to operate with the constraints and enablers of legal expectations in their countries of origin and operation.
- A strategic thinker can scan developments in trading, company set-up, tax, and competition to get an idea of economic impacts.
- A strategic thinker can scan developments in employment law, health and safety, and consumer law to get an idea of social issues.
- A strategic thinker should be aware of the increasing prevalence of environmental legal actions challenging organisations in the light of the climate change crisis.
- While legal responsibilities are important, an emphasis on acting ethically and sustainably would, by its very nature, encompass the required legal requirements. A restriction to thinking to legal requirements may in fact prevent responsible and sustainable practice. Indeed, organisations can fall foul of legal systems where responsible and ethical practice has been overlooked or ignored, as highlighted later in the chapter.
- Ethical and responsible thinking is intrinsically linked with responsible leadership and relationships with stakeholders, as discussed in Chapter 6.

LEGAL RESPONSIBILITIES

All strategic thinkers must operate within the legal framework of which they are a part. Legal responsibilities represent the rules and norms their society considers to be important to the smooth functioning of their society. Of course, those rules and norms will be different depending on where the organisation is based, and that is one of the difficulties organisations are facing now, in the increasingly globalised and therefore complex environment of which we are a part.

The legal issues to be addressed when strategy-making are many and varied, and examples are as follows (not an exhaustive list). There is a danger for the strategic thinker here in getting waylaid by detail while trying to formulate something that is meaningful and long-term, but we do have to be aware of two things. First, as Chapter 2 explained, all strategy must be implemented, and awareness of the potential pitfalls will be key to formulating something applicable and worthwhile. Second, legal responsibilities remind us of the wider impact of our strategic decisions and could therefore lead us to more responsible strategy-making, to be discussed later in this chapter.

Economic

The following impact on an organisation's ability and capacity to make a profit.

Tariff Policies and Trade Agreements

Who can you do business with and what are the constraints on that business? Brexit changed the rules and regulations under which British companies could operate in the

European Union. For example, events companies found there were restrictions on their ability to travel and work within the European Union and their ability to move equipment and workers. Donald Trump, as of the time of writing, has become President-Elect of the USA and has promised a tariff on imports to protect the US automotive industry, launching a 'trade war' between the USA and China.

Company Setup and Governance

When a business/organisation begins, there are decisions to make about how it is set up and therefore the legal rules by which it will operate. Sole proprietors, partnerships, limited companies, social enterprises, community interest companies, corporations (not an exhaustive list and there are different terms used in different countries) are all options for set-up and this will govern the checks and balances which are incorporated into the organisation's practice. Different organisations, led by industry-specific compliance standards, will also have unique needs in terms of accreditation, qualifications, and liability insurance. For example, an organisation operating with volatile substances or issues, from gas to people (!), will be expected to be qualified in certain areas and recognised by the trade bodies or professional standards in that area. The choice of organisation set-up will balance risk, liability, and formality and of course consider the purpose/value of the organisation as discussed in Chapter 1.

Company Taxation

Companies will pay tax on their earnings. There may also be (depending on country of origin) national insurance to pay, VAT, sales tax, and local and national taxes. The change in government from a more liberal tax regime to a stricter one often leads to companies threatening to move their operations to other, more lenient locations. A strategic thinker may want to consider whether this movement would compromise their social responsibilities.

Competition Laws

Open and free competition is a fundamental pillar of the capitalist economy, and so, in societies operating within this philosophy, one could expect to comply with laws that are designed not to stifle competition or to create monopolies. Linked to this is the issue of protection of an organisation's intellectual property, and the trademarks, patents and copyrights, logos, domain names, business names, symbols, or specific illustrations that ensure that an organisation's unique selling point or competitive advantage are maintained.

Our increasingly globalised, open, and technology-led world is challenging both concepts (of open and free competition and protection of intellectual property) that have previously been fundamentals in strategic management. Examples of this challenge are as follows:

- In chapters 5 and 6 it was discussed how 'coopetition' (two or more competitors working together to complement each other's resources and capabilities) is an alternative way of doing business and potentially counter to the traditional idea of competitive rivalry in business.

- Another feature of our globalised and open technology world is the ease with which organisations can access and copy ideas and products, and the difficulty in cross-border legislation to deal with this. For example, Chinese-made replicas of products are big business.
- Finally, another aspect is the unstoppable domination of certain (technology-based) companies. Recently, US regulators accused Amazon of being a monopoly (Clayton & Espiner, 2023). The critical point about competition laws is that they are intended to prevent prices from being driven up for consumers, but one might argue that Amazon's success is based on quite the opposite: Amazon have created a level of competition by driving costs and prices down.

Are existing competition laws capable of dealing with a VUCA (Bennett & Lemoine, 2014) environment?

Social

All the following impact on an organisation's ability and capacity to make a profit while maintaining their commitment to their stakeholders.

Employees: Employment Laws/Protection and Minimum Wage

Around the world, there are different laws regarding how people are employed, what their conditions should be, and how much they should be paid.

This is a complex issue. All strategic thinkers will be aware of the resources their organisation has or can access and will be aware of the cost of those and sometimes the need to cut the cost of those resources to stay in business. One of those resources is human resources, and despite laws being in place, these are often bypassed to the detriment of workers.

For example, outsourcing of production can be a way to cut human resource costs and move production to a cheaper country. Workers there will take work that contributes to their family income, and companies can still operate within the law while paying what a (normally Western) consumer would not consider to be a minimum or living wage. In fact, while child labour laws exist in many countries, they do not in others, and children are expected and needed in poorer countries to contribute to household incomes. This is not illegal, but it may be unethical. Global attention was drawn to worker exploitation in 2013 after the collapse of the Rana Plaza garment factory in Bangladesh killed over 1,100 workers (Ferguson, 2020). Exploitation is not reserved to poorer countries, with exploitation exposed in Leicestershire in the UK in 2018. Modern slavery has become a focus of many, with some motivated to deal with the fallout from that (a Derby-based company called Just Ice (https://www.just-ice.org/) has made it their mission to employ people who have escaped modern slavery and draw attention to its prevalence).

Other examples of operating within the law but unethically regarding employment practice are fire and rehire (where mass dismissals are enacted to bring in terms and conditions more favourable to the business or organisation), and the gig economy where workers are self-employed and offered work with no job security.

Other employment laws/protection include attitudes towards and support for maternity and paternity leave, prevention of discrimination on grounds of sex, race, sexual orientation, promotion of quality, dismissal, and redundancy and will be different according to country.

Health and Safety

While health and safety regulations are different, and differently applied the world over, one could assume an interest in maintaining a safe place to work. Safety training, protective gear, maintenance of machinery, temperature controls, breaks, and hygiene facilities will all contribute to this, and in many jurisdictions there are regular safety checks.

Other Stakeholders: Consumers/Customers and Suppliers

Our stakeholders – customers, suppliers, and those we do business with – should be able to expect certain services from us. We must stipulate carefully what we will and will not do, and the price for that product or service. Attention to weights, measures, contracts, terms and conditions, and credit agreements must be clear, and our customers have the right to reliable and quality services (or at least the quality that was promised). There are watchdogs and regulators in key fields that keep an eye on transactions and relationships in this area. There is also law regarding our collection and use and storage of data as the result of our interactions with our stakeholders. This has received increased attention in our new world which relies so much on technology and where data is power. We are still to a certain extent figuring out how to ethically deal with data. In 2018, this issue came to prominence in the Cambridge Analytica scandal where data collected for academic purposes was used for other purposes. In certain jurisdictions, organisations can face significant fines for inadequate data protection. For example, Facebook's owner, Meta, was fined €1.2 billion (£1 billion) for people's data when transferring it between Europe and the United States (McCallum, 2023).

Environmental

Chapter 9 concentrates on environmental responsibility. Suffice to say that there are often rules on waste management, emissions, and resource usage that affect businesses and organisations. But the most pressing issue here is the wider climate change challenge, and Chapter 9 looks at some of the movements, from COP conferences to the Global Compact to encourage business and organisational positive performance in reducing emissions and resource usage. One of the crucial issues currently is often the voluntary nature of these movements, and the lack of commitment from certain governments to act and move a 'nice to have' into law. However, there are areas of action; for example, 'The High Seas Treaty' provides a framework for setting up marine protected areas, to protect 30 per cent of the world's oceans by 2030 (BBC, 2023) and the European Commission has brought in a Regulation on Deforestation-free Products (EC, 2024). There are also examples of where organisations are being challenged, and strategic thinkers need to be aware of these issues as part of their environmental scan and in their efforts to move towards more responsible strategic thinking. For example, Bateman (2021) drew attention to 'a snowballing of court rulings in favour of environmentalists around the world' and in 2023 noted that Danone (with brands such as Evian, Activia and Volvic) and PepsiCo (maker of Pepsi, Doritos) were being challenged regarding plastic pollution (BBC, 2023).

THE ISSUE WITH RESTRICTING OUR ATTENTION TO LEGAL RESPONSIBILITIES

One of the key problems with discussing legal responsibilities is that all of us know of situations where businesses and organisations have either broken the law in the pursuit of economic success or found ways in which to circumvent the law in a way that does not seem to honour the intention of the law. Some examples have been given above, and then there are the international scandals such as Enron, WorldCom, Tyco International, Arthur Andersen, Qwest, Global Crossing, Parmalat, Barings Bank, Systembolaget, Skandia, and Lehman (and see the case study in Box 8.1).

This is why we should now look at the relationship between the legal and ethical in relation to strategic thinking and consider a novel approach to responsible strategic thinking that subsumes the legal within the 'higher' ethical approach.

Here we use Carroll's Corporate Social Responsibility Pyramid (1991), represented in Figure 8.1 as a framework for this discussion. This is a well-established tool for considering an organisation's actions, and its constituent parts. The pyramid takes us from Friedman's perspective at the bottom of the pyramid, 'economic responsibilities'

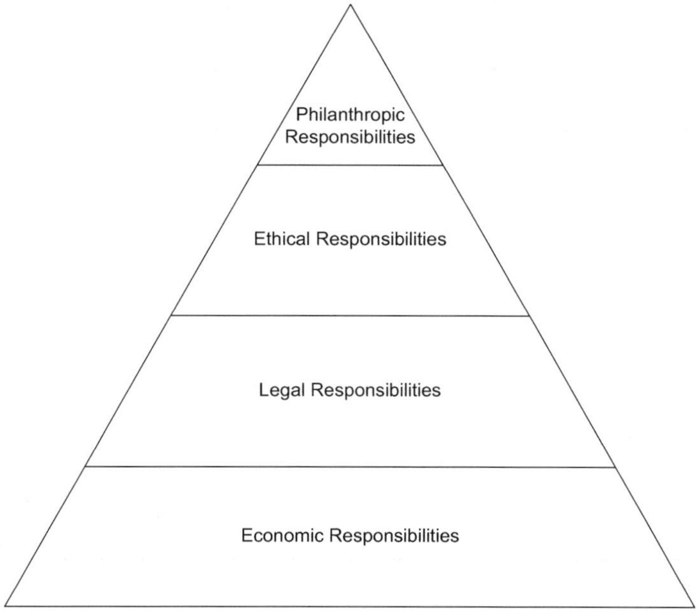

FIGURE 8.1 The Corporate Social Responsibility Pyramid
Simplified from Carroll (1991)

through legal responsibilities and ethical responsibilities to the 'pinnacle' of corporate citizenship and philanthropic responsibility. Carroll expected an interrelation of the components and that for a company to be considered socially responsive it must meet all four components (Henry, 2021). Discussing each of the layers will help examine the ideas, and then we can re-set those ideas in the light of what has been discussed so far.

Economic Responsibilities

Economic responsibilities are to gain and sustain competitive advantage, and Friedman (1970) said that a business' economic responsibilities were to use its resources and engage in activities designed to increase its profits so long as it stays within the rules of the game, which is to say, engages in open and free competition without deception fraud. Thus, Friedman referred to the first two layers of Carroll's pyramid: economic and legal responsibilities. Friedman also said that a business' economic responsibilities were its social responsibilities (Friedman, 1970) given his belief that successful businesses had beneficial effects on all of those around them.

Legal Responsibilities

Some, but not all, ethical responsibilities are covered by law as laws are manifestations of the ethical expectations of the society in which they are based and in which businesses and organisations operate. However, laws can never be fully comprehensive (Schnebel & Bienert, 2004) not least because we are operating in an increasingly globalised business and economic environment, managed by many different legal systems, and if we rely on laws to dictate our responsibilities we cannot guarantee a coherent approach when the laws in one area in which we operate might be different from another. Neither can laws be fully up to date (Schnebel & Bienert, 2004), as the complex environment in which we are operating is dynamic and political and legal responses are notoriously lagging.

Add to this discussion the many examples of illegal behaviours in businesses and organisations in order to make money (or gain competitive advantage) and which have resulted in many negative economic and societal impacts (personal, business and job losses, expensive and time-consuming court battles, reputation and brand equity loss, lack of confidence for governments, shareholders and therefore society also) and this suggests that supposed legal responsibilities are insufficient to promote good and effective practice. We therefore look to ethical responsibilities, the next layer of the pyramid, to see if acting ethically would guide us to better practice and encompass the legal responsibilities we have discussed.

CASE STUDY 8.1

The Law and Stakeholders: Oil Refineries and Ogoni Land

In the 1950s, oil was discovered in commercial quantities in Nigeria. In the west of the country, the Niger Delta region became a site of significant exploration. The area was largely dominated by the Ogoni People, who live in a homeland they call Ogoniland. The Ogoni 'wealth' was, and continues to be, supported by farming and fishing the area – one of the largest mangrove ecosystems in the world (UNEP, 2017). Shell discovered the site's rich oil resources in 1958. Over time, the Niger Delta accounted for a large proportion of national exports and in the 1980s and 1990s formed some 80 per cent of government revenue (Kline, 2010).

The prosperity of the oil companies and the Nigerian government came at a cost to the Ogoni People. In the early 1990s, protracted social injustice and environmental degradation led to public unrest in the area. Revenue for the oil industry mostly benefited the government and multinational oil corporations, notably Shell. Little of the wealth trickled down to the Ogoni People. Activists, including Ken Saro-Wiwa, a playwright and poet, challenged oil companies about the impact drilling was having on the livelihoods of farmers. As well as economic implications, concerns mounted about the destruction to the environment rendering it wasteland. They accused Shell and the Nigerian government of 'economic genocide', arguing that the environmental devastation was tantamount to a systematic marginalisation of the Ogoni People (Lauwo et al., 2023),

Prior to this period, Shell was selective in its dealings with stakeholders in the area, concentrating efforts on leaders in the community who were compliant with Shell's position, ignoring activists, the Movement for the Survival of The Ogoni People (MOSOP) led by Ken Saro-Wiwa (Wheeler et al., 2002). Over time, the movement gained recognition by key groups such as Amnesty International and Greenpeace, The United Nations as well as organisations sensitive to the plight of the Ogoni People including high street retailer The Body Shop. Despite gaining international legitimacy, Saro-Wiwa, along with nine other key representatives of MOSP, was imprisoned and subsequently executed by the Nigerian government. This led to global condemnation and highlighted the issue of oil interests and profiteering at the expense of human rights. Operations were suspended and have since remained largely dormant because of public unrest.

In 2009, Shell faced legal ramifications associated with a failure to recognise MOSOP as a legitimate civil society organisation, key stakeholders in the area, as bystanders who failed to intervene in government exploitation of MOSOP members, ignoring the concerns of the group. Consequently, Shell was forced to pay a €10 million out-of-court settlement to the families of Sara-Wiwa and other executed activists (Crane et al., 2014). The challenges of law, ethics, human rights, and environmental degradation continued. A further landmark case positioned Shell as complicit in human rights abuses, including torture and killings perpetrated by the Nigerian military.

The historical, legal case of the Ogoni continues to rumble for Shell. In 2023, the High Court in London ruled that farmers and fishers from the areas could bring claims against Shell for 'alleged breaches of the environment' (*The Guardian*, 2023). It was argued that pollution continues to undermine the Ogoni's human right to a clean environment. Although Shell is preparing to divest operations from the area, the case may continue. In February 2024, a report published by the Center for Research on Multinational Corporations claimed that Shell was avoiding responsibility to clean up the area given the company's historical profiteering, falling short of Nigerian law (SOMO, 2024).

For organisational leaders, the case highlights the implications of violating 'soft' law in the context of human rights and the environment. The case demonstrates the short- and long-term impact, devastation, and consequences where strategic thinking fails to take account of civil society stakeholders.

Ethical Responsibilities

We need to understand what ethics is and what acting ethically entails. Carroll (1991) describes ethical practice as doing what is right, just, and fair. This assumes that we are being right, just, and fair to people, to stakeholders, to members of our society. Businesses and organisations are inextricably linked to the people and their associations that make up society, from using those people as resources to produce outputs and impacts to expecting people to use and purchase what they have to offer. If you want to have such impact or influence (and impact and influence are assumed with the business or organisation's existence as part of society), then Demartino says that you necessarily take on ethical obligations (Demartino, cited in Raworth, 2017, p. 161).

This relationship between businesses, organisations, and people is a social contract or psychological contract (Rousseau, 1995), where a stakeholder is willing to enter a mutually beneficial relationship with a business or organisation on the basis that certain standards will be respected, and a stakeholder does not expect to be treated badly or put in a subordinate position: 'ethics necessarily requires the preservation and increase of legitimate options available to others as well as to oneself. Legitimate options are those that do not reduce the options available to others' (Ackoff, 1996). Good and ethical behaviour contributes to collective benefit and establishes a win-win relationship.

Ethical behaviour also supports the economic responsibilities of an organisation. It saves on costs (a straightforward relationship of trust is less time-consuming and involves less effort in terms of contracts and agreements or breaking those contracts and agreements). Also, if we do not act ethically, our very structure of capitalism will be broken. Schnebel and Bienert (2004) argue that unethical and illegal behaviour undermines capitalist society, making it no longer fit for purpose.

But how do we design ethical strategic thinkers and ethical organisations? We could expect strategic thinkers to employ Rawls' (1971) concept of the 'veil of ignorance which posits that only a person ignorant of his or her own identity is capable of a truly ethical decision' (Rawls, cited in Banaji et al., 2003, p. 181). This means making a conscious effort to be aware of one's own unconscious bias and to be objective in one's approach. This ties in with personal mastery and establishing objective mental models (Senge, 1997; Higgins, 2015) which assumes a self-awareness and a desire and ability to understand external realities objectively, and to try to abandon the individualistic, selfish, and egotistical approach of the ordinary human being who is seen as prey to short-term thinking and consumerism, the latter supporting and funding the emphasis on economic success over societal and environmental issues.

Organisations should also, in their strategy-making process, establish the values that strategic ideas need to be filtered through (see Chapter 2) with a set of key questions about what they want to achieve and why, and what their ethical and social responsibilities are. These questions are returned to in Chapter 10 with a model of how managers can best place themselves to think in a responsible, strategic way. However, this setting of values could still miss what is ethical, depending on the culture and leadership of an organisation. Thus, each strategic thinker would need to engage the veil of ignorance and it will be extremely important to engage multiple perspectives in standard-setting, as discussed throughout this book and largely, an open, honest approach to raising issues will encourage more of an open and honest organisation (an integrity-based ethics approach as opposed to a compliance-based ethics approach) (Dess et al., 2019) as governance controls curb bad behaviour.

When we talk about ethics, these are the moral principles guiding us and our decisions. There are obvious signs that we are not acting ethically, and these signs fit within the legal expectations (i.e. we should not commit fraud for our own gain), but it is where those legal commitments end that there may be 'grey' areas and where we may start to favour ourselves and those who we know rather than thinking about the wider impacts of what we do. This is where the guiding principle of thinking ethically returns. We should not intend to impact on the choices of others and the generations that follow, only to increase the quality of our lives today.

Transparency (Flynn & Asquer, 2024, p. 134) is a good control mechanism for ensuring moral behaviour. 'Transparency', which is commonly understood as 'the ability to look clearly through the windows of an institution' (den Boer, 1998; Meijer, 2013), is surely a good check. If someone were to see what we were doing, would we be proud, or would we want to hide it away? 'The very prospect that others are informed of one's conduct can induce individuals to self-discipline themselves to high standards of integrity, which makes employees adhere to ethical principles and values of honesty, impartiality, and selflessness' (Flynn & Asquer, 2024, p. 134). The only problem with this is if we have personally questionable morals, and another check is the Rawls veil of ignorance and the ability to step outside of one's own mind and think in terms of society's expectations (Svensson & Wood, 2008). Additionally, in Chapter 6 we discussed the role of stakeholders as an accountability mechanism, where, following Laasch (2024), the aim is to publicly and transparently explain and justify the organisation's strategic actions, judgements, and omissions.

Of course, this transparency only works if society's expectations are sound! And often we see paradoxes in society. While in Chapter 5 we recognised the growth of social enterprise, in response to a growing sense of social responsibility, society is, it seems, willing to put up with quite a lot. There are indeed scandals from time to time, and it can take time for certain issues to be exposed, but there is certainly no universal protest at how certain issues are dealt with, even if they seem unjust or unfair. There is a certain amount of defeatism, of 'what can **I** do?' about issues of the day.

An ethical perspective of what is right, just, and fair would create better businesses and organisations than a narrow focus on what is legal. Ethical behaviour should encompass legal responsibilities, ensuring fairness even if the legal structures of any country or society are inadequate in protecting all of its citizens.

Philanthropic Responsibilities

Finally in the Corporate Social Responsibility pyramid is a layer called 'philanthropic responsibilities'. Included in this discussion regarding ethical issues encompassing legal issues should be a discussion of whether philanthropy should be required in its current form. It is seen as doing good, and many wealthy people have been admired for being philanthropists in the past, whereas some have been accused of greenwashing or care-washing, especially when their often-excessive profits have been built on questionable business practice or on anti-environmental activities (such as the Sackler family's connection with the US opioid crisis). Dean (2020) retells a revealing story about Donald Trump who 'always wanted people to believe he is generous; he spent years constructing an image as a philanthropist by appearing at charity events and making very public, even nationally televised promises to give his own money away, which he never did' (Farenthold, 2016).

We might ask whether philanthropy or charity should be required in the modern world. This sort of action is a sign of failure, by the state certainly, but we would argue by the economy also. If organisations are not employing people, if they are not paying enough for people to live, and if they are not creating value for their communities and societies, then they are not necessarily fulfilling their responsibilities. One might argue that if the system worked properly, philanthropy and charity would not be necessary.

So the 'pinnacle' of the pyramid is not the nice to have; it should be what has variously been called corporate social responsibility, social purpose, conscious capitalism, adherence to the triple or quadruple bottom line and most recently environmental, societal, and governance (ESG) responsibilities, or, given all our discussions, we can replace all these terms with 'sustainability' if we recognise, as detailed throughout this book, that sustainability implies an organisation's commitment to environmental, economic, and societal responsibilities.

A sustainable approach naturally encompasses a philanthropic approach defined as giving, benevolence, welfare, altruism, prosocial behaviour, and 'doing good' (*Journal of Philanthropy and Marketing*, 2023) because a sustainable approach would make these activities part of a business or organisation's natural behaviour. A sustainable approach, given our definition of sustainability as 'intra- and intergenerational justice as well as ecological limitations' (WCED, 1987, cited in Neugebauer et al., 2015) and considering 'the needs of the present without compromising the ability of future generations to meet their own needs' (WCED, 1991, cited in Higgins, 2015, p. 2) encompasses an ethical approach: 'the preservation and increase of legitimate options available to others as well as to oneself. Legitimate options are those that do not reduce the options available to others' (Ackoff, 1996).

Philanthropy has the tone of being altruistic and an additional 'nice to have' rather than an essential. If we replace this with 'sustainable' and assume its importance alongside 'ethical' we have economic success as arising from ethical and sustainable actions.

TABLE 8.1 The Ages and Stages of CSR

Business age	Stage of CSR	Modus operandi	Key enabler
Greed	Defensive	Ad hoc	Investments
Philanthropy	Charitable	Donations	Projects
Marketing	Promotional	Public relations	Media
Management	Strategic	Systems	Codes
Responsibility	Systemic	Models	Products

Visser (2011)

If you cannot act ethically and sustainably, then the reward (given that we are assuming a wider, system impact than just maintaining a profitably sustainable business) will not be yours.

Now let us complement our discussion of Carroll (1991), with Visser's (2011) theory of an organisation's age and stage of Corporate Social Responsibility (CSR), charting the organisation's attitude and approach to social responsibility (Table 8.1).

Greed

In the first business age, organisations are greedy, defensive, and engage with responsibility on an ad-hoc basis, the key barrier to progress is investments, and the culture in the organisation is reactive to change. Sustainability efforts are unlikely to be implemented unless in way of defence to some external threat. The business environment of 1950s America is often cited as an example of this stage.

Philanthropy

In the second business stage, organisations are said to be philanthropic and charitable, willing to provide donations to local charity for the purpose of virtue signalling. Organisations might make donations for local projects, while doing nothing to change themselves. Consider an organisation which pollutes the river as normal business, and continues to pollute the river, but then donates to the local children's hospital.

Marketing

In stage 3, organisations wake up to the possibility of corporate social responsibility becoming a marketing strategy, one that enables them to create promotional materials and good public relations. The media are a key enabler of success in this phase, in the same way that stage 1 was discussed as being similar to the 1950s business environment in America, perhaps stage 3 is more representative of the late 1990s or early 2000s in terms of how a business might respond to public pressure for sustainability initiatives. Examples of this approach during that time might have included obtaining solar panels or recycling waste. Initiatives that were impressive at the time, but perhaps not particularly revelatory in terms of organisational development and attitudes towards corporate social responsibility.

Management

In stage 4, the organisation begins to change meaningfully for the first time, and the management begin to make strategic decisions in relation to how the organisation operates, and how it might change. Stage 4 includes the organisation creating new systems, new codes of practise, and new policies. Perhaps in this case it could include procurement policies for work–life balance, strategies for meaningfully changing elements of the business to influence stakeholders. Examples of this approach to CSR include organisations which meaningfully engage with their employees, assess a genuine improvement in their HE policies, and change something genuinely about the business.

In reality, whether it is accepted or not, most organisations sit in stage 4, there are some attempts to change, some new policies, and some evidence of change. In a meaningful way, the organisation operates in exactly the same way; however, senior managers can quickly pull out examples of strategic initiatives the organisation has undertaken to become more sustainable. For sustainability experts, they can quickly see past the shallow efforts and are often frustrated by the lack of meaningful change in progress as evidenced by the final stage of this theory.

Responsibility

In the fifth and final stage, organisations begin to take responsibility and there is systemic change in their business. The modus operandi of the business begins to change, products might be cannibalised, discontinued, and new products created in their place. In reality, very few organisations have ever reached stage 5, as it involves creating meaningful lasting and permanent change in business structure, product development, and in some cases even de-growth of the business.

The theory as presented by Visser (2011) is relatively straightforward to understand, but meaningful in impact. Organisations can easily and quickly assess where they are in their age and stage of CSR, and while organisations will be quick to place themselves further down in their stage, the most critical and forward-thinking organisations may admit that they are still philanthropists or marketeers.

Having considered these theories, we suggest a change in the shape of this discussion. One must act ethically, legally, and sustainably to enjoy economic performance.

Ethical Actions

- Follow all laws of the country and the business/organisational sphere of which you are a part, but go further.
- Be objective.
- Be right, just, and fair in one's practices.
- Preserve and increase the legitimate options available to others.

Sustainable Actions

- Understand the impact of decisions on society and environment while pursuing economic success.
- Collaborate and cooperate to understand others' perspectives.

Economic Performance

- Thrive.
- Reinvest.

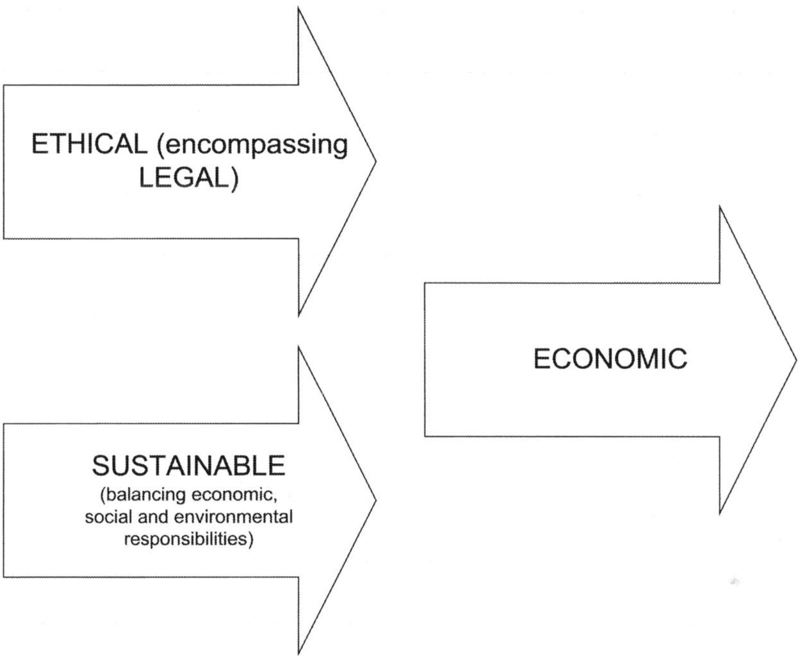

FIGURE 8.2 Responsible Strategic Thinking

A CALL TO ACTION

But is this 'ethical and sustainable-first' approach realistic?

There is support. Compare Friedman's view in the 1970s with research done in 2014: 'The tone of organisational purpose (as the combination of its intention and motives) has itself shifted.' Jennifer Sindberg in *Director* magazine (Scott, 2014) reports a survey by Deloitte that asked a sample of millennials whether they agreed with US economist Milton Friedman's statement that the only responsibility of business is to increase its profits. 'Of the sample, 92 per cent said no, as did 93 per cent of the 300 directors (Scott, 2014)' (Haslam & Shenoy, 2018, p. 202). This highlights a shift in views of what constitutes organisational value for future generations from one solely concerned with economic growth to a society that has growing expectations of organisational ethics, and responsibility to secure sustainability.

However, there is also doubt about changing our business approach from Friedman's perspective. Raworth published *Doughnut Economics* in 2017, and it has become the cause of much discussion in many forums. Raworth appeared in The Rest is Politics 'Leading' podcast with Alistair Campbell and Rory Stewart in June 2023. One of Raworth's main points is that the goal of constant growth is alarming and that we should seek to 'thrive' as opposed to grow. This supports moving the onus away from economic responsibilities as the basis for business and this move is reflected in the amended process of business/organisation responsibility as presented in Figure 8.2.

However, this change is a challenge to the economic and political systems of most countries and Campbell and Stewart, while supporting the ideal, saw it as that (idealistic) and asked how a politician could frame these ideas. Indeed, in chancellors' speeches the aim is always to be productive, to grow GDP. Raworth says that GDP is an invented human measure and that we cannot have, for example, in the UK, 2.5 per cent GDP growth and manage our impact on the planet. She asks, 'in the context of today's social and ecological crises, how can this single, narrow metric still command such international attention?' (Raworth, 2017, p. 31). However, Rory Stewart raised the issue that the state costs so much in the UK that if we reduced GDP we could not afford our government, and politicians therefore will not and cannot challenge the growth mantra. Campbell argued that he cannot see this challenge to growth translating into political strategy and cannot see it working in a democracy. However, we have already argued that by acting ethically and sustainably there would be less of a need for state intervention, as public sector bodies are filling the gaps left by private sector and capitalism, and the economic and legal-first perspective has led to economic crises in the past (e.g. the 2008 global recession).

CHAPTER SUMMARY

While strategic thinkers must operate within the legal frameworks of the countries where they are active, focusing on ethical and sustainable practices inherently satisfies legal requirements and promotes responsible strategic thinking. Limiting strategic thinking to mere legal compliance may hinder sustainable and responsible business practices.

RECOMMENDED READING

Carroll, A.B. (1991) The pyramid of corporate social responsibility: Toward the moral management of organizational stakeholders. *Business Horizons,* 42.

Visser, W. (2011) The ages and stages of CSR: Towards the future with CSR 2.0. https://www.waynevisser.com/articles/the-ages-and-stages-of-csr.

REFERENCES

Ackoff, R.L. (1996) On learning and the systems that facilitate it. *Reflections*, 1, 14–24.

Banaji, M.R., Bazerman, M.H. & Chugh, D. (2003) How (un)ethical are you? *Harvard Business Review*, December.

Bateman, J. (2021) Why climate lawsuits are surging. Retrieved November 13, 2024, from https://www.bbc.com/future/article/20211207-the-legal-battle-against-climate-change.

BBC (2023) Nine breakthroughs for climate and nature in 2023 you may have missed. Retrieved November 13, 2024, from https://www.bbc.com/future/article/20231214-nine-breakthroughs-for-climate-and-nature-in-2023-you-may-have-missed.

Bennett, N. & Lemoine, G.J. (2014) What VUCA really means for you. *Harvard Business Review*, January/February.

Campbell, A. & Stewart, R. (2023) Kate Raworth: Doughnut economics and thriving in balance (No. 22). *Leading*. Acast. https://shows.acast.com/leading/episodes/6482091e18995900l1aaaf07.

Carroll, A.B. (1991) The pyramid of corporate social responsibility: Toward the moral management of organizational stakeholders. *Business Horizons*, 42.

Clayton, J. & Espiner, T. (2023) Amazon: US accuses online giant of illegal monopoly. BBC News. Retrieved November 13, 2024, from https://www.bbc.co.uk/news/business-66920137#:~:text=US%20regulators%20have%20sued%20Amazon%2C%20alleging%20that%20the,strategies%22%20to%20push%20up%20prices%20and%20stifle%20competition.

Crane, A., Matten, D. & Spence, L. (Eds.) (2014) *Corporate Social Responsibility: Readings and Cases in a Global Context*. Abingdon, Oxon: Routledge.

Dean, J. (2020) *The Good Glow: Charity and the Symbolic Power of Doing Good*. Bristol: Policy Press.

Den Boer, M.G.W. (1998) Steamy windows: Transparency and openness in justice and home affairs. In V. Deckmyn & I. Thomson (Eds.), *Openness and Transparency In the European Union* (pp. 91–105). European Institute of Public Administration.

Dess, G.G., McNamara, G., Eisner, A.B. & Lee, S-H. (2019) *Strategic Management: Text & Cases* (9th ed.). London: McGraw Hill Education.

EC (European Commission) (2024) Regulation on deforestation-free products – European Commission. Retrieved November 13, 2024, from https://environment.ec.europa.eu/topics/forests/deforestation/regulation-deforestation-free-products_en.

Farenthold, D. (2016) Trump boasts about his philanthropy. But his giving falls short of his words, *The Washington Post*, October 29. www.washingtonpost.com/politics/trump-boasts-of-hisphilanthropy-but-his-giving-falls-short-of-his-words/2016/10/29/b3c03106-9ac7-11e6-a0ed-ab0774c1eaa5_story.html.

Ferguson, D. (2020) Worker exploitation in UK clothing supply chains. Insight. House of Commons Library. Retrieved November 12, 2024 from https://commonslibrary.parliament.uk/worker-exploitation-in-uk-clothing-supply-chains/worker exploitation in UK clothing supply chains.

Flynn, N. & Asquer, A. (2024) *Public Sector Management* (8th ed.). London: Sage.

Friedman, M. (1970) The social responsibility of business is to increase its profits. *New York Times Magazine*, September 13, 122–126.

The Guardian (2023) Shell to face human rights claims in the UK over chronic oil pollution in Niger Delta. Retrieved November 14, 2024, from https://www.theguardian.com/business/2023/nov/23/shell-to-face-human-rights-claims-uk-over-chronic-oil-spills-niger-delta. .

Haslam, S. & Shenoy, B. (2018) *Strategic Decision Making: A discovery-led Approach to Critical Choices in Turbulent Times*. London: Kogan Page.

Henry, A.E. (2021) *Understanding Strategic Management* (4th ed.). Oxford: Oxford University Press.

Higgins, K. (2015) *Economic Growth and Sustainability: Systems Thinking for a Complex World*. London: Academic Press.

Journal of Philanthropy and Marketing (2023) Overview. Retrieved February 6, 2024, from https://onlinelibrary.wiley.com/page/journal/26911361/homepage/productinformation.html.

Kline, J.M. (2010) *Ethics for International Business: Decision Making in a Global Political Economy* (2nd ed.). Abingdon, Oxon: Routledge.

Laasch, O. (2024) *Principles of Business & Management: Practising Ethics, Responsibility, Sustainability*. Thousand Oaks, CA: Sage.

Lauwo, S.G., Egbon, O., Denedo, M. & Ejiogu, A.R. (2023) Counter-conducting environmental injustices and (un)accountability: Ken Saro-Wiwa's accounts of the Ogoni's struggle for emancipation. *Accounting, Auditing & Accountability Journal*, 36(6), 1637–1664.

McCallum, S. (2023) Meta: Facebook owner fined €1.2bn for mishandling data. BBC News. Retrieved November 26, 2024, from https://www.bbc.co.uk/news/technology-65669839#:~:text=Facebook%27s%20owner%2C%20Meta%2C%20has%20been%20fined%20%E2%82%AC1.2bn%20%28%C2%A31bn%29,the%20EU%27s%20General%20Data%20Protection%20Regulation%20privacy%20law.

Meijer, A. (2013), Understanding the complex dynamics of transparency. *Public Administration Review*, 73, 429–439. https://doi.org/10.1111/puar.12032.

Neugebauer, F., Figge, F. & Hahn, T. (2015) Planned or emergent strategy making? Exploring the formation of corporate sustainability strategies. *Business Strategy and the Environment*, 25(5), 323–336.

Rawls, J. (1971) *Theory of Justice*. Cambridge, MA: Belknap Press of Harvard University Press.

Raworth, K. (2017) *Doughnut Economics: Seven Ways to Think LIke a 21st Century Economist*. New York; Random House Business Books.

Rousseau, D.M. (1995) *Psychological Contracts in Organizations, Understanding Written and Unwritten Agreements*. London: Sage.

Schnebel, E. & Bienert, M.A. (2004) Implementing ethics in business organizations. *Journal of Business Ethics*, 53, 203–211.

Scott, N. (2014) Boardroom revolution. *Director*, November 1.

Senge, P.M. (1997) THE FIFTH DISCIPLINE. *Measuring Business Excellence*, 1(3), 46–51. https://doi.org/10.1108/eb025496.

SOMO (2024) Shell's reckless divestment from Niger Delta. Retrieved November 14, 2024, from https://www.somo.nl/shells-reckless-divestment-from-niger-delta/.

Svensson, G. & Wood, G. (2008) A model of business ethics. *Journal of Business Ethics*, 77, 303–322. Doi:10.1007/s10551-007-9351-2.

UNEP (UN Environmental Programme) (2017) About Ogoniland. UNEP – an environmental programme. Retrieved November 14, 2024, from https://www.unep.org/topics/disasters-and-conflicts/country-presence/nigeria/about-ogoniland.

Visser, W. (2011) The ages and stages of CSR: Towards the future with CSR 2.0. https://www.waynevisser.com/articles/the-ages-and-stages-of-csr.

WCED (World Commission on Environment and Development) (1987) *Our Common Future. The Report of the World Commission on Environment and Development: Chapter 2: Towards Sustainable Development.* Retrieved August 18, 2014, from http://www.un-documents.net/ocf-02.htm.

WCED (World Commission on Environment and Development) (1991) *Our Common Future.* Oxford: Oxford University Press.

Wheeler, D., Fabig, H. & Boele, R. (2002) Paradoxes and dilemmas for stakeholder responsive firms in the extractive sector: Lessons from the case of Shell and the Ogoni. *Journal of Business Ethics*, 39, 297–318.

CHAPTER 9

Embedding the Environment in Strategic Thinking

Caroline Linhares and Jo Watts

CHAPTER OUTLINE

This chapter sets out the challenges and opportunities for strategic thinking in relation to the environment. There is widespread agreement that decreasing natural resources, the destructive outcomes of extreme weather events, and the related loss of biodiversity have significant organisational and societal implications. Our response to this is arguably the principal challenge of our time. Global society and international frameworks such as the United Nations Global Compact and Sustainable Development Goals frame the new ways of thinking about how to respond to environmental challenges.

In this context, organisations need to rapidly adapt to consider how they foster collective and personal action that balances, restricts, or compensates for the propensity of organisations to degrade the environment. For some organisations the climate crisis presents opportunity; for others the scope for action is challenging, potentially spanning complex business units and supply chains. Strategic thinking in relation to the environment raises questions about how organisations are navigating and approaching the exhaustive needs and expectations of stakeholders, including the planet. Strategic intervention means rapidly rethinking relationships with the natural environment to secure a sustainable future within a pressing time horizon.

Narrow neoliberal notions of competitive advantage in this context limit the capacity of organisations to think and operate systemically to account for more than wealth creation and financial stability. This chapter highlights the strategic approaches that reimagine value emphasising the interrelated nature of the economic, social, and ecological impact of organisations, looking at the UN Global Compact, Circular Economy and Doughnut Economics.

DOI: 10.4324/9781003475545-9

We foreground cases that illustrate how strategic thinking is limiting the harmful effects of the environmental impact of business, setting the pace for change and innovative thinking. We highlight initiatives that educate and foster agency to limit the potential for individual and organisational denial or inertia. In doing so we cue how others might catalyse and orient their strategic thinking in a range of organisational systems and contexts.

KEY POINTS

- Climate change is a reality that organisations have contributed to and strategic thinkers in those organisations can have an influence on reducing its impact.
- There are several international agreements and guidelines with which organisations should comply to reduce the impact of climate change.
- Three frameworks or guidelines – UN Global Compact, Circular Economy, and Doughnut Economics – offer ideas for embedding the environment in strategic thinking.
- Many organisations have successfully followed approaches that examine and remodel their purpose, networks, governance, ownership, and finance to reflect environmental responsibility.

THE CONTEXT: THE ENVIRONMENT, GLOBAL SOCIETY, AND INTERNATIONAL AGREEMENTS

As introduced in Chapter 1, sustainability is broadly concerned with meeting 'the needs of the present without compromising the ability of future generations to meet their own needs' (WCED, 1987, p. 43). In other words, sustainability is about meeting the needs of all, including future generations, within the limits of the planet (Raworth, 2017). Regrettably, scientists warn that many planetary boundaries have already crossed the limits within which humanity can safely operate (Rockström et al., 2009; Steffen et al., 2015). One of the planetary boundaries that has already overshot its safe operating limits is the concentration of greenhouse gases in the atmosphere, the main driver of climate change.

Climate change is defined as long-term changes in climate patterns resulting from an increase in the Earth's average temperature (UN, n.d.). The increase in temperature is caused by the excessive concentration of heat-trapping greenhouse gases (GHG) around the globe. Climate change impacts on the environment and global society in many ways. Changes in climate patterns affect the balance of ecosystems that support life on Earth. They cause extreme weather events, resulting in floods in some regions and drought in others. Climate change also impacts on livelihoods and access to health, food, water, and social equity (IPCC, 2018).

Climate change can be both human and naturally driven. Nonetheless, climate experts agree that human activities have been the main driver of climate change since the 1800s, and the industrial revolution (UN, n.d.) is seen as a major cause. Human activities that contribute to climate change include burning fossil fuels like coal, oil, and gas, and are intrinsically linked to organisations. Recognising that environmental degradation is induced by humans means recognising that there is a need to change the way in which humanity (and organisations) operate to reverse that environmental degradation.

International agreements have played a crucial role in placing the environment on the business agenda. Table 9.1 shows the key events in tackling climate change. An important milestone in this trajectory was the United Nations Framework Convention on Climate Change (UNFCCC), an international treaty signed in 1992 by 154 countries. The UNFCCC can be considered as a global recognition that climate change is caused by humanity and requires global cooperation to be tackled. Signatories to the UNFCCC, which by 2024 had been signed by 197 countries, committed to reducing atmospheric concentrations of greenhouse gases. The signatories meet annually to assess progress on these commitments (known as the Conference of the Parties or COP). During the 21st

TABLE 9.1 International Key Events to Tackle Climate Change

Year	Key events
1987	Publication of the UN World Commission on Environment and Development (WCED) commissioned report known as the Brundtland Report (Brundtland, 1987), which defines that sustainable development meets 'the needs of the present without compromising the ability of future generations to meet their own needs'.
1988	Establishment of the UN Intergovernmental Panel on Climate Change (UNIPCC), which provides objective and comprehensive scientific information on human-induced climate change.
1990	Adoption of the Montreal Protocol, which regulates the production and consumption of ozone-depleting substances (ODS).
1992	Adoption of the UN Framework Convention on Climate Change (UNFCCC), which recognised that climate change is caused by humanity, and requires global cooperation to be tackled.
1997	Adoption of the Kyoto Protocol, signed by parties agreeing on emission targets (superseded by the 2015 Paris Agreement).
2002	Millennium Development Goals (MDGs), 8 goals set for 2015 agreed to by 189 countries and all the world's leading development institutions. Replaced by the Sustainable Development Goals (SDGs).
2015	Sustainable Development Goals (SDGs), 17 goals to be achieved by 2030 agreed by 191 countries.
2015	Paris Agreement, signed by 193 countries agreeing on emissions reduction and long-term global temperature targets.

Conference of the Parties (COP-21), held in Paris in 2015, concrete targets for emissions reduction and long-term global temperature levels were agreed. These targets have been adopted by 196 countries in a legally binding treaty which became known as the Paris Agreement. The Paris Agreement sets a goal to keep the rise in mean global temperature to well below 2°C compared to pre-industrial levels, while making significant efforts to limit the increase to 1.5 °C (UNFCC, 2018). By 2024, the increase in the Earth's average temperature was nearly 1.3°C compared to the second half of the nineteenth century (Global Warming Index, n.d.)

The year 2015 was also marked by the launch of the UN 2030 Agenda, which sets forth 17 Sustainable Development Goals (SDGs) (as shown in Chapter 6) and 169 related targets as a framework for achieving sustainable development. The SDGs stimulate action across the three dimensions of sustainable development: the economic, social, and environmental (UN, n.d.), and provide a shared framework for business as well as civil society, governments, and international bodies to work together. The goals more closely aligned to the environmental dimension focus on issues of clean water and sanitation (SDG 6), affordable and clean energy (SDG 7), sustainable cities and communities (SDG 11), responsible production and consumption (SDG 12), climate action (SDG 13), life below water (SDG 14), and life on land (SDG 15).

WHERE ARE WE NOW?

Despite the large-scale adoption of the Paris Agreement, progress made towards achieving its goals has so far been scarce. Since the adoption of the agreement, signatories have continued to meet at the UN Climate Change Conference of the Parties (COP) annually (except for 2020 due to the Covid-19 pandemic) with the aim of reviewing the implementation of the commitments and adopting decisions to advance progress. The first 'global stocktake', concluded in 2023 at the COP28, showed that we are not on track to limit global warming to 1.5 degrees Celsius; if all national targets are fully implemented, we will have limited a predicted increase of 4 degrees to 2.1 to 2.8 degrees Celsius (UNFCC, n.d.). This means that more ambitious targets and concrete actions are needed to avoid increased temperatures (to note that, as of the time of writing, 2024 was the hottest year on record) and the related issues from floods, fires, and biodiversity loss. The 2023 stocktake showed insufficient progress not only in mitigation efforts (reducing emissions) but also in adaption (increasing resilience), particularly in supporting vulnerable nations, the world's most adversely affected by a changing climate despite being the ones that contribute less to climate change and environmental degradation.

THE RELATIONSHIP BETWEEN ENVIRONMENT AND BUSINESS

There is a perspective that a trade-off exists between sustainability and businesses' interests (i.e. profit-making). Another viewpoint is that there is a business case for sustainability, centred around the risks associated with unsustainable business models as well as the opportunities related to embracing sustainability. We argue that organisations depend on a living planet to exist just as much as they need a social licence to operate. Businesses and the environment are interdependent, and they cannot be separated.

Businesses' Impact on the Environment

Businesses impact on the environment in the following ways:

- **Greenhouse gas emissions**: Perhaps the most obvious impact and the main driver of climate change. The widespread awareness of international accords such as the Paris Agreement has contributed to society's attentiveness to this issue. Businesses are responsible for most of human-induced greenhouse gas emissions, which can be either direct emissions (those emitted from an organisation's premises or directly associated with their processes) or indirect emissions (those emitted by others when making or consuming products and services purchased or sold by an organisation). Climate change impacts on the balance of ecosystems leading to other environmental issues.
- **Biodiversity loss**: Biodiversity, short for biological diversity, refers to the variety of life (both animal and plant) on Earth or in a given habitat, and it sustains stability and resilience of ecosystems (Rockström et al., 2009). Through land occupation and associated habitat degradation, organisations contribute to biodiversity loss. Other drivers of biodiversity loss linked to businesses' operations include pollution, over-exploitation, and water overconsumption.
- **Issues of water quality**: Through water discharges if these are not treated appropriately (Laine et al., 2021), water quality can be impacted.
- **Chemical pollution and the release of toxic substances into the biosphere**: through poor waste management.

Businesses' Dependence on the Environment

All organisations are dependent on environmental resources. In addition, some businesses depend on particular resources to operate. The fishing industry relies on freshwater to enable fish to flourish. Freshwater is also the raw material for businesses in the food and beverage industry. Water availability is also crucial for many production processes, such as cooling methods (Laine et al., 2021). These resources rely on resilient ecosystems supported by biodiversity. A multi-faceted example would be agriculture, which depends on various resources as well as their interactions. Pollinator loss is in fact an example of interdependency: monocropping, the agricultural practice of growing a single crop in the same land, reduces the natural habitats of many species, leading to the decline of pollinators on which these same crops and agricultural practices are often dependent (Atkins & Atkins, 2016).

The Risks Associated with Environmental Degradation

Besides resource dependency, businesses also need to consider the risks associated with environmental degradation:

- **Physical risks**: Such as flooding or droughts caused by extreme weather events. These events may disrupt organisations even if they are not directly impacted by them, as they can impact partners across the supply chain, displace employees and damage essential infrastructure, including roads and energy supply (Laine et al., 2021).
- **Regulatory risks**: In order to meet targets, set in international agreements, governments have been introducing (or considering introducing) new regulations that require companies to change their practices, use more efficient processes, cleaner materials, disclose more information, and pay carbon taxes. The increase in environmental cases against organisations is noted in Chapter 8.
- **Reputational risks**: Accidents leaking harmful substances into freshwater, for example, can lead to a reputational crisis. Being associated with other companies implicated in environmental disasters can also be detrimental. These incidents can lead to loss of legitimacy, an organisation's licence to operate conferred by society (Deegan, 2002). A notable example would be BP's accident in the Gulf of Mexico in 2010. A rig operated by BP exploded, killing 11 people and causing an oil spill that threatened the lives of animals and plants and the livelihood of local communities. The accident became the largest oil spill in the history of the petroleum industry and it cost BP large sums in fines, clean-up costs, and damage reparations. The company also invested in presenting itself as a sustainable business, setting sustainability objectives and producing sustainability reports stating its sustainability commitments.

Risks and Opportunities

Managing the risks associated with environmental issues discussed above is in the long-term interest of organisations. A case for business sustainability also envisages opportunities that arise from global efforts to adapt and mitigate climate change. For example, the Taskforce on Climate-related Financial Disclosures (TCFD, n.d.) presumes that these efforts create cost-saving opportunities for organisations through adopting more efficient resources and processes and shifting to clean energy sources. Other opportunities identified include the development of new products and services, access to new markets, and building resilience along the supply chain. These opportunities are discussed further in Chapter 5, where Bottom of the Pyramid approaches and Frugal Innovations are featured.

EMBEDDING THE ENVIRONMENT IN STRATEGIC THINKING: TRANSFORMATIVE STRATEGY-MAKING

Organisations do not need to be the problem; they can be part of the solution. While the negative impact of businesses on the environment is evident, blaming companies is not productive. Where organisations collaborate with wider society to achieve ethical, responsible, and sustainable business, the effect is enhanced. Many initiatives and models have emerged as frameworks for new ways of doing business for a sustainable future and these can be considered as 'Transformative Strategy-making'.

Approaches to transformative strategy-making demonstrate a shift from the linear to the complex, the competitive to the connected, and from a degenerative focus on growth to sufficiency. These ideas shape sustainable environmental strategy-making. This goes further than meeting net zero targets or initiating recycling schemes to limit the impact of greenhouse gas levels accumulated through, for example, waste fashion. More radical approaches are needed, and the challenge is to design strategy that regenerates and replenishes, which also means engaging stakeholders to focus on long-term goals as well as (or rather than) short-term wins.

UN Global Compact

The Global Compact, a UN initiative launched in 2000, calls on organisations to become part of the solution, changing the narrative from one of culpability to one of cooperation. Companies that sign up to the UN Global Compact (UNGC) commit to aligning their strategy and operations to universal principles on the environment, human rights, labour and anti-corruption, and to produce a 'Communication on Progress' report annually. The initiative supports participating companies by providing access to four forms of engagement: connecting (access to events and conferences and local networks), learning (access to guidance and tools, training, peer learning groups, and accelerators), leading (through think labs and policy advocacy activities), and communicating (building credibility by communicating progress) (UN, 2024). Unfortunately, critics argue that the voluntary nature and the lack of monitoring and enforcement of the UNGC allow companies to enjoy the reputational benefits from membership without necessarily making meaningful changes to their human rights and/or environmental practices (see e.g. Berliner & Prakash, 2015).

Circular Economy

The Circular Economy is an alternative to the linear 'take-make-use-waste' economic model, in which humans extract resources from nature (take), process these resources into products (make), consume and/or use these products (use), and then dispose of them (waste). In contrast, in a Circular Economy, materials are kept in circulation through processes of repairing, reusing, refurbishing, recycling, and remanufacturing (Ellen Macarthur Foundation, 2022). A Circular Economy is not just about recycling – it is a model of production and consumption where products are designed to last longer, consumers buy less, reuse, repair, repurpose, resell, share goods and services. At the end of the product's life, materials are reused in manufacturing processes. A linear economy is unsustainable not only because most of the resources we take are not renewable but also because nature cannot assimilate all the waste we produce. Currently, more than 92 per cent of resources extracted from nature are wasted (Circle Economy, 2019). Some economies and businesses have made strides in creating more circular processes.

Strategic Thinking for Sufficiency

Bocken et al. (2016, p. 42) talk about 'a fundamental shift from over-consumption towards a more sufficiency-orientated view of consumption and production described as a "sufficiency economy"'. This means designing, manufacturing, and selling products and services for sufficiency: goods that are kept, loved, renewed, and repaired as well as implementing nudging behaviours to encourage consumers to make 'greener' choices (Thaler & Sunstein, 2008, p. 5).

There are **strategies to slow loops** or slow resource consumption (e.g. designing long-life products) and **strategies to close loops** so that disposal feeds into the creation of a new product (circular design, reuse of goods, and recycling of materials) (Bocken et al., 2016).

Strategies to Slow Loops

- **Sharing**: Provide the capability or services to satisfy user needs without needing to own physical products.
  - Examples: Car sharing, tuxedo hire, clothing rental, leasing phones.
- **Long-life products**: Design products that are reliable and durable and that require a low/slow replacement system.
  - Example: Miele's products purportedly last for 20 years which is more than double the life of other washing machines. In terms of financial sustainability, value creation is supported by product longevity and the associated income from the servicing and repair of appliances (Bocken & Short, 2016).
- **Product life extension**: Products and services designed for durability, upgradability, service, warranties, and reparability and a non-consumerist approach to marketing and sales (e.g. no sales commissions).
  - Example: Patagonia's 'Common Threads' campaign encourages customers to repair or reuse the product they purchase. This is further underpinned by their 2011 marketing campaign 'DON'T BUY THIS JACKET', emphasising the environmental 'bankruptcy' caused by over-consumption (Patagonia, 2011). Thus, strategic thinking connects with external stakeholders to achieve transformational goals. Marketing and labelling can be exploited by organisations to raise consumer awareness and support the decision to purchase sustainable goods (Singh et al., 2023).
- **Standardisation and compatibility**: Products with parts or interfaces that fit other products.
  - Example: Electric charging points demonstrate the need to close loops by limiting the need for car owners to use multiple chargers and promote wider use and adoption of electric vehicles, Shared standards across the globe leads to compatibility in the design and manufacturing of charging stations (EEHE, 2024).
- **Dis- and reassembly**: Products and/or their parts can be dis- and reassembled easily to increase future use and component reuse.
  - Example: Cycling helmets are typically made in such a way that complex disassembly sees them in landfill. The Myelin cycling helmet is purposefully designed

to use as few components as possible with interlocking parts that hold the helmet in place. Consequently, the materials used can more readily separated and reused/recycled (Museum of Design in Plastics, 2023). Dis- and reassembly fits with strategies for both slow and closed loop product design.

Strategies to Close Loops

- **Exploit the residual value of resources**: Collection and sourcing of otherwise 'wasted' materials or resources to turn these into new forms of value.
  - Examples: Interface collects and supplies fishing nets as a raw material for carpets, and RecycleBank provides customers with reward points for recycling and other environmentally benign activities. Toast Brewing uses excess bakery bread to replace 25 per cent of the malted barley in their beers. Gazelle and many other companies offer consumers cash for electronics and sell refurbished electronics or cash for DVDs, books, and clothing. Clothing return initiatives (e.g. H&M, M&S, Shwopping). Rubies In the Rubble uses waste fruit and vegetables to create chutneys and ketchups.
- **Design for a biological cycle**: Products of consumption with safe and healthy materials.
  - Examples: Some food byproducts such as the shells of nuts can be composted, releasing nutrients such as nitrogen into the soil and help regenerate land. In turn, land can be used to grow other renewable products such as cotton (Ellen MacArthur Foundation, 2022).

Doughnut Economics

Another transformative model is Kate Raworth's Doughnut Economics. Raworth (2017) calls for a radical change in the global economic mindset. The concept, introduced in the economist's Oxfam Discussion Paper (Raworth, 2017) and further refined in her internationally best-selling book *Doughnut Economics: Seven Ways to Think Like a 21st-century Economist* (Raworth, 2017), offers a holistic approach for economic thinking in the twenty-first century. The idea is that, to change the way we do business and achieve a sustainable future, we need to rethink our economies and change the systems within which businesses operate. The Doughnut represents a new framework for economic theory and practice which is aligned with the SDGs and fit for the twenty-first century. Its name derives from its shape, which contains two concentric rings: the inner ring represents a social foundation (the needs of all, building on the SDGs and universal principles of human rights); the outer ring represents an ecological ceiling (the means of the planet, built upon the planetary boundaries described earlier in this chapter). The space between these two rings, shaped like a doughnut, represents a safe operating space for humanity. That is, a space where no one falls short on their basic needs and where no ecological limits are overshot (see Figure 9.1). In response to the wide-ranging interest in her book, Raworth co-founded the Doughnut Economics Action Lab (DEAL) (https://doughnuteconomics.org/). The work of the lab offers guidance and

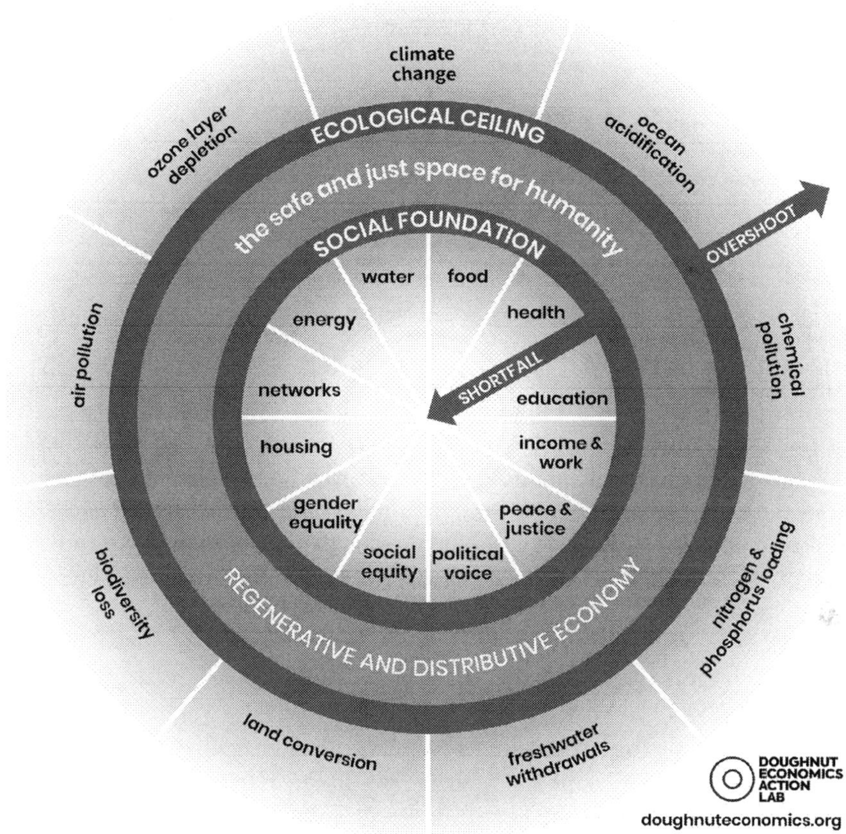

FIGURE 9.1 The Doughnut of Social and Planetary Boundaries
Kate Raworth and Christian Guthier (CC-BY-SA 4.0)

support to organisations, governments, cities, and change-makers at large to implement the Doughnut in practice.

Raworth's (2017) Doughnut encourages a shift in economics thinking to a model that pursues human prosperity rather than economic growth. For organisations, this means embodying value creation to meet the needs and expectations of all stakeholders, including the planet, as opposed to wealth accumulation. This view resonates with the notion of Corporate Social Responsibility (CSR) evolved in the 1960s and further explored by Carroll (1979, 1991). In his seminal work, Carroll (1991) questions early views that a corporation's sole responsibility was to provide a maximum financial return to shareholders and argues that corporations hold not only economical but also legal, ethical, and philanthropical responsibilities, which are presented as a CSR Pyramid. Thirty years on, Carroll (2021) reflects on the developments of CSR and the shift towards the use of the term 'sustainability', which seemed to better encapsulate the idea that businesses have social and environmental responsibilities for both the present and the future. Carroll

(2021) ponders that we are moving to an era that transcends greed and towards an age of collective responsibility. Carroll's CSR Pyramid is used as the basis to develop a new sustainable framework for business in Chapter 8.

The Seven Principles of Doughnut Economics

Doughnut Economics offers a holistic framework which is grounded on seven underlying principles of economic thinking.

Changing 'the goal' is the first of these seven (new) ways of thinking. In a broad sense, this principle refers to pursuing economies that thrive whether or not they grow, instead of pursuing an ever-growing national output, the infamous Gross Domestic Product (GDP). Economic growth does not necessarily lead to prosperity for all; thus a holistic framework indicating that an economy (whether local or global) meets the needs of all without overshooting planetary boundaries would be a more appropriate measure of progress and development. Raworth (2017) proposes that the new goal should be to move into the Doughnut's safe and just space, to thrive in balance between social foundation and the ecological ceiling. *For strategic thinkers, this principle calls for performance measurement that encompasses financial, environmental, and social performance.*

The second principle underlying the Doughnut requires **a change in 'the big picture' of the economy**. Raworth (2017) proposes the notion of an embedded economy, moving away from the idea of a self-contained market. An embedded economic model recognises that the economy is embedded in society, while human society is embedded in the living world, dependent upon the planetary boundaries. Within the economy itself, an embedded economy recognises that there are four ways in which we provision for our needs and wants: the market (price-based exchange), the state, the household (including unpaid but essential work), and the commons (where communities co-produce goods and services). Finally, an embedded economy recognises that there are financial flows moving across all these different forms of provisions. *For strategic thinkers, this principle calls for societal needs and wants to be equally valued.*

The third principle refers **to nurturing human nature**. Raworth (2017) calls for a move away from an economic model which assumes that human beings are a rational economic man to one that acknowledges humans as social and adaptable beings. Existing economic models assume that human beings are self-interested, with fixed preferences (i.e. are not influenced by advertising, only informed by it), isolated (i.e. independent from preferences and actions of others), calculating, and dominant (over nature and the rest of the living world). Raworth (2017) calls for models which recognise that human beings exhibit social reciprocity, have fluid values, are interdependent (upon one another), approximating rather than calculating, and dependent upon the environment. A rational economic man values competition over collaboration, but collaboration is essential if we are to build a sustainable future. *For strategic thinkers, the third principle of the Doughnut recognises the need to nurture the best of human nature so that we can collaborate and develop the skills and values that will enable us to live well together with over 8 billion people in the twenty-first century.* As an example of such strategic thinking, Rethink Glasgow is a purpose-oriented organisation working *to create a green and connected city, with co-created digital forums* to contribute ideas to a climate action plan. Towards the end of 2023, some 1,300 suggestions had been integrated into the city's plan. Such initiatives chime with Liedtka's (1998) collaboration through dialogue and Nonaka and Zhu's (2012) multiple perspectives.

The fourth principle of Doughnut Economics is concerned with **systems thinking**. It calls for refuting the ideas rooted in nineteenth-century mechanical equilibrium, such as the notion of equilibrium of supply and demand. Instead, twenty-first-century economic thinking opens up to a dynamic and ever-evolving complex system. *For strategic thinkers, this means recognising the interrelatedness of all things and the need to reach out and adapt. This is considered in chapters 1 and 10.*

The fifth and sixth principles of the Doughnut urge us to **design economies and business models that are distributive rather than divisive, and regenerative rather than degenerative**. Raworth (2017) refers to the twentieth-century Kuznets Curve, which implies that as countries get richer first inequality will increase but then it will decrease. This notion, which has underpinned twentieth-century economic thinking, results in a web of institutions that concentrate wealth and power in the hands of few. In the twenty-first century we should design models that are distributive instead. *For strategic thinkers, this means rethinking ownership models.* Different models that rethink the traditional profit-maximising shareholder logic have emerged over the past few decades. One example is Lush, a UK-based cosmetics company, which embarked on an Employee Ownership model in 2017. The company is 10 per cent owned by employees through the Employee Benefit Trust, whose board is composed of two company-appointed trustees, two employee-elected trustees and one independent trustee (Lush, n.d.). This distributive ownership model is reflected across all aspects of the organisation – with a stated ethos of 'happy people making happy soap' – the company's ethical standards include using vegetarian and animal testing-free ingredients, a stated pledge to equity and fair wages for staff, and a stated commitment to transparency and to paying the right amount of taxes in all countries where the company operates. Lush also has targets and policies around environmental impact, including fair trading with suppliers, making naked products, minimising use of packaging, and using recycled materials and renewable energy.

A regenerative design is aligned with the concept of Circular Economy discussed earlier in this chapter. Raworth (2017) refers to the 1990s Kuznets Environment Curve, which implies that, as countries get richer, first pollution will increase but then it will decrease. Alluding to global systems breakdowns, Raworth (2017) shows that these dynamics do not hold. Financial meltdowns are a result of financial systems designed to endlessly expand. Climate and ecological breakdown are a result of a system of energy and material use of endless expansion. *For strategic thinkers, this means designing economies and models that are regenerative rather than degenerative, running economies on solar and other renewable energy, and adopting models where waste from one process is input for another.*

Meyer-Emerick (2012) highlights the city of Cleveland, Ohio where in 2009, following a protracted period of industrial decline linked to the demise of steel and heavy industry, action was taken to involve around 700 stakeholders – representative citizens – in participatory summits using Appreciative Inquiry (see Chapter 6). These structured forums created the questions and context, often focusing on set themes such as local food, transportation, water, and engaged citizens in envisioning a new sustainable economy and environment (Bartuneck & Balogun, 2022). Underpinned by the United Nations Sustainable Development Goals, "development that meets the needs of the present without compromising the ability of future generations to meet their own needs." a non-profit body was formed to create a large number of sustainability initiatives. (Meyer-Emerick, 2012, p.53). Amongst other initiatives spawned by the project was the emergence of local farming initiatives supported by the collaborative efforts of statutory services, business, government leaders and volunteers (Bartunek & Balogun, 2022). Such efforts to convene citizens are not responsible for change; it is citizens and organisations that deliver on the ideas generated. Nonetheless, they provide a forum to set the context and provide a catalyst for change.

The Doughnut Economics Lab shares insights around other regenerative practice. In Europe, Amsterdam and Brussels are cities actively applying the 'Doughnut Economics' framework with coalitions from government, industry, and other partners shaping sustainable urban development, supported by teams of government, industry, and research partner initiatives.

- **Amsterdam Donut Coalitie**: Funded by Amsterdam University of Applied Sciences until the end of 2021. The team involved one full-time and one part-time member, collaborating with researchers, students, and freelancers. It has strong support from Marieke van Doorninck, Amsterdam's Deputy Mayor for Spatial Development and Sustainability.
- **Brussels Donut**: Managed by the association Confluences, this consortium includes the Doughnut Economics Action Lab (DEAL) as a formal member. The project, supported by Brussels' regional government and Economic Transition Minister Barbara Trachte, is funded for nine months. The six-member team includes a project manager, economic researchers, co-creation specialists, and participation experts, all focused on creating collaborative, sustainable economic models.

These projects illustrate how Doughnut Economics can be adapted to local contexts, with multi-sector teams advancing sustainability and economic resilience in their cities. For interested strategic thinkers, a participative toolkit for urban regeneration designed by the Doughnut Action Lab can be found at https://doughnuteconomics.org/tools/doughnut-for-urban-development-a-toolkit, and at https://doughnuteconomics.org/tools/doughnut-for-urban-development-manual-and-tools.

The seventh principle refers to **rethinking economic growth**, recognising that ever-rising growth is unsustainable. In the same way that economies strive for ever growing GDP, companies are under constant pressure to deliver growth in sales, market share, and profits. The idea of becoming agnostic about growth may be one of the most challenging for strategic thinking. This principle points to the limitations of natural resources. There is a general understanding that society would need three earths to sustain life as we know it. In other words, we cannot sustain the use of resources at the rates we currently do. *For strategic thinkers, this means examining their value proposition to decide when something is enough.*

Raworth's (2017) seven principles are conceptually seen as a catalyst for new approaches, cues for strategic thinking that underpin strategy-making at an international, global, and regional level.

The Doughnut Economics Action Lab

The Doughnut Economics Action Lab sets out a tool to transform business and embed the environment in strategy. Doughnut Design encourages business to suspend practicality and the concept of business as usual by exploring ambitious ideas, broader stakeholders, long-term focus, and a culture of courage (see Figure 9.2).

The tool consists of five key themes oriented around purpose, networks, governance, ownership and finance.

PURPOSE

- Is the business for consumption at scale or do quality and values matter?
- Freudenreich et al. (2020) stress the need to consider multiple stakeholders and the mutual relationships between them and businesses. They argue that 'stakeholders are both recipients and (co-)creators of value in joint value creation processes' (p. 4).

Example: Manos Del Uruguay (https://manos.uy/our-story 2024), was set up by friends in 1968 responding to the challenges and lack of opportunities faced by women. Their business began by selling items made and produced by women across the country to empower and develop. Moreover, inherent in their purpose and the items they create

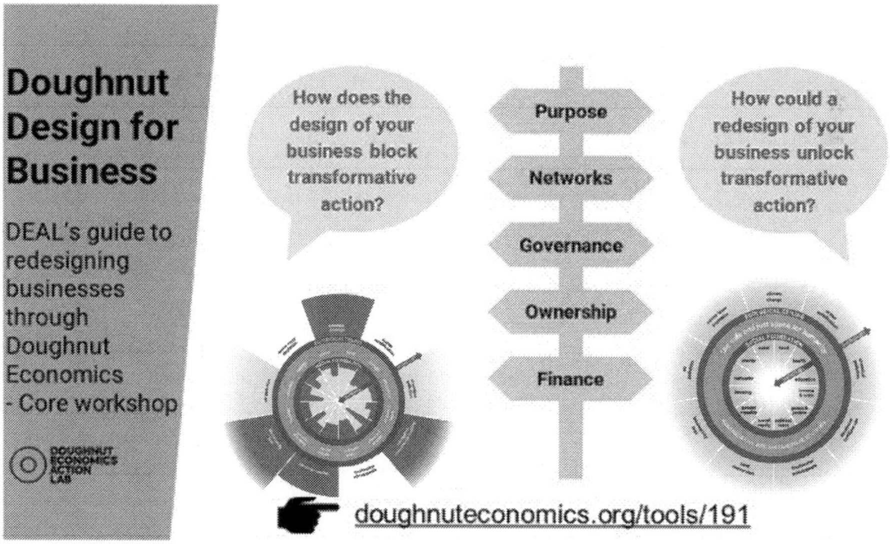

FIGURE 9.2 Doughnut Design for Business
Derived from DEAL (doughnuteconomics.org)

are the traditions where makers respect the use of their land and craft as opposed to making goods en masse and as cheaply as possible.

Example: German Business El Puente (https://www.el-puente.de/) is a leading fair-trade advocate working with small producers offering financial flexibility, board seats and co-ownership. In partnership with co-owners, the organisation adopts five standards that underpin business design including purposes, operations, revenue, the reinvestment of surplus revenue and legal structures / financing driven by a long-term purpose.

NETWORKS

- Strategy-making with networks recognises the significance of relations and commitment to consumers, suppliers and governments. Freudenreich et al., (2020) set out the importance of working across multiple relationships and organisations with a view to reciprocity to create joint value. Trust, relationships, and collaborative exchange are emphasised.
- Relationships matter. Children, for example, are arguably key moderators influencing parent and carers either through direct communication or simply their presence, making parents more conscious or mindful (Singh et al., 2023). The ripple effect of a child's school plastic recycling project can provide a catalyst to shaping the mindset of a parent in their role in packing or manufacturing products.
- The theme of relationships and networks also foregrounds the importance of business as an advocate and activist, challenging governments rather than seeking favourable tax arrangements (see Chapter 3 for the Strategic Thinker's Guide to Politics).
- For strategy-makers, collaboration within and among networks of educators, public and private sector organisations, and consumers can understand habits and the factors that influence environmental protection and action (Bamberg, 2003; Momberg at al., 2017)
- There is an issue with involving consumers, though! Notably, consumers tend to be blinkered to the effects of their consumption. Typically, consumers underestimate the environmental consequences of meat consumption while overestimating the impact of plastic reuse and recycling. Meat consumption in the industrialised world is argued to be crucial to meeting environmental targets (Kwansy et al., 2022). Combining messages that couple environmental and personal health appeals to consumers seems to be a more effective way of communicating impact in order to shift consumption habits (Cordts et al., 2014; Verain et al., 2017).

Example: Although the company faces current challenges, The Body Shop provides a strong exemplar of business activism in the late 1980s and early 1990s. The company sought to raise awareness with their 'Stop the Burning Campaign' as they engaged with consumers and suppliers. See https://www.thebodyshop.com/en-gb/about-us/activism/our-activist-foundations/a/a00065.

Example: In the city of Sheffield, local universities have partnered with households across the city and the local council to raise awareness of food waste. Through the scheme, consumers were provided with resources such as compost bins and biodegradable food-collection bags to collect and dispose of food waste. Through collaboration, the pilot highlighted the messiness of food waste collection to underscore the challenges for some households in collecting the waste and, for the council, the opportunities and limitations of a large-scale roll-out of the scheme (Jones et al., 2023).

GOVERNANCE

- Which stakeholders should be represented at the board?
- How should decisions map social, environmental, and financial goals?

Example: Riversimple, a hydrocarbon car company based in Wales, is not only innovative in product design but also in the configuration of its governance model. The business corporate structure is designed to include the environment, customers, the community, staff, and commercial partners who represent the perspectives of stakeholders to inform business goals, priorities, and decision-making.

Example: Faith in Nature, a UK cosmetics company, has appointed two external board members representing environmental groups, the Earth Centre and Lawyers for Nature, to shape the business agenda as part of the legal structure and board.

OWNERSHIP

- Ownership reflects the concentration of power across business and organisations. From the perspective of the Doughnut, the notion of ownership challenges organisations to share power more equally among those who contribute or co-create value.
- Deep design concentrates on ownership and financial structure among stakeholders, including clients, suppliers, and stakeholders, involving the whole system in decision-making structures as well as setting organisational purpose.
- This can help bring humanity within the realms of the Doughnut. Focusing attention on issues of regeneration, including environmental sustainability.

Example: Gripple, a manufacturing company operating in Sheffield, the UK, has introduced employee ownership models to gain employee commitment to shape the direction and focus of the business.

Example: At Patagonia shares are divided between two classes of shareholders. One class holds the dividend rights but not voting rights. The other class gets the voting rights but none of the dividends. In this way the unique ownership model avoids conflating profit with purpose.

FINANCE

- What is expected in terms of demand, transformation, reinvestment, and investors' expectations of return on investment.
- A short-term view around growth can limit regenerative and distributive strategies.

Example: The Eden Project invests back into the Eden Trust to support strategy-making through collaboration that promotes communication and activism in science, arts, technology, and commerce as part of a 'constituency for change'.

The following case studies show application of the Doughnut Economics Lab factors of Purpose, Networks, Governance, Ownership, and Finance.

CASE STUDY 9.1

FoodCycle

https://foodcycle.org.uk/

Purpose

FoodCycle was established by Kevin Cheung, a former LSE student who was concerned about food waste. FoodCycle was an adapted model of a similar project in the United States, Campus Kitchen, cooking waste food for local communities. The initial aim of the project was to bring together volunteers, surplus food, and free kitchen space to create nutritious food for people affected by food poverty and social isolation. The organisation's listed purpose now is to connect people, support mental well-being and reduce loneliness, nourish the hungry, promote sustainably, and inspire change. The project delivers on six of the UN SDGS: No Poverty, Zero Hunger, Good Health and Well-being, Reduced Inequalities, Responsible Consumption, and Climate Action.

Networks

As well as addressing issues of food waste and food poverty, FoodCycle worked with industry, large retailers such as Sainsburys, and government to raise awareness and engage business in action. According to Cheung this was difficult at the start of the project, but he persistently highlighted to the food industry that it would be more cost-effective to keep surplus food overnight and have volunteers collect it for free the following morning. As well as building networks with governments and business the projects also created communities among volunteers and diners. Corporate partners include financial institutions, retailers, other non-profit organisations, and R&D business.

Governance

As a charity, FoodCycle is governed by the CEO in partnership with a trustee board responsible for the assets and activities of the organisation and who hold the management to account in their leadership. They bring skills and expertise in areas such as food waste and surplus food redistribution, equality and diversity and social justice. As well as trustees, patrons and ambassadors share their influence and support to the project. These include restaurateurs, television personalities, and media professionals. The project creates an Annual Impact Report to highlight its yearly achievements and to set out future strategic plans.

Ownership

Not for profit.

Finance

The project was developed with funding from UnLtd UK (https://www.unltd.org.uk/), a foundation for social entrepreneurs and free office space from MyBnk (https://www.mybnk.org/). This helped support the development of organisational structures and secure the long-term financial sufficiency models based on a blend of funding and fundraising. Recent awards include a top prize $75,000 charity challenge award from the Janus Henderson foundation.

Social Impact Report 2023 (https://foodcycle.org.uk/wp-content/uploads/2024/05/Foodcycle-Impact-Report-2023-FINAL-medium.pdf)

CASE STUDY 9.2

Toast Brewing

www.toastale.com/about-us

Purpose

Toast Brewing's mission is to 'brew great beers and spread big ideas that can change the world'. The company was founded in 2016 with the purpose of brewing beer using surplus bread that would otherwise go to waste. Toast Brewing buys excess bakery bread and uses it to replace 25 per cent of the malted barley in its beers.

Networks

The company works in partnership with established breweries, but under its own licence and using its own ingredients and recipes. Toast Brewing supports charities such as Feedback (www.feedbackglobal.org) who work with governments, businesses, and society to promote behavioural change and to create innovative solutions to tackle food waste. Other charities include Rainforest Trust UK, Soil Heroes Foundation, and various food redistribution groups such as Food For All and Alchemic Kitchen.

Governance

Designed to create a positive impact, the company's decision-making is guided by its people-centred values. The company became a certified B Corp in 2018 and its commitment to employees and other stakeholders is written into its Articles of Association.

Ownership

Social enterprise with employee ownership.

Finance

All distributable profits go to charities, particularly those dedicated to the food system. Impact Report 2022(https://www.toastbrewing.com/uploads/files/1680220058TOASTALEIMPACTREPORT2022.pdf)

CASE STUDY 9.3

Hockerton Housing Project

https://www.hockertonhousingproject.org.uk

Purpose

Hockerton Housing Project, based in Nottinghamshire, is a community of sustainable homes. The project combines a business based on a cooperative model which offers business advice on sustainable living with a self-sufficient housing community. The overarching aim of the project is to live by example and operate as a catalyst for change towards ecologically sound and sustainable ways of living. The houses were designed by green architects Professor Brenda Vale and Dr Robert Vale. The focus of the housing was to practise low carbon living through renewable energy, the water system, food grown on site, and the communits transport practices.

Networks

The network originally comprised Nick Martin, a landowner and builder, along with family members and friends. The project has links with Suma Wholefoods who provide food to the community, as well as education networks to shape knowledge around sustainable housing projects and communities and educational establishments. The project has acted as a 'focal point for policy-makers' as exemplars of sustainable innovation 'cited in policy documents as recommending change to UK energy building regulations because of climate change' (Lovell, 2013, p. 18).

Governance

Hockerton Housing Project is run by a group of directors elected by shareholders, each has one vote, regardless of the number of shares they hold. This governance structure reflects a lack of hierarchy around wealth generation. Governance is set out in planning agreements and a 999-year lease. There are conditions associated with governance such as limited use of fossil fuelled cars and a commitment from each adult that they will contribute 300 hours' work per year to the project.

Ownership

Hockerton operates a shared ownership/cooperative model. Families own their own homes but share resources such as food and water.

Finance

The project initially struggled with financing as traditional lenders are unwilling to finance self-funded ecological schemes. However, two institutions who specifically focus on unique sustainably projects were able to help with the start-up of the project. The Co-operative bank provided early loans; these were later transformed into mortgages with the Ecology Building Society. Members of the group also invested in the project through personal financial means. A finance subgroup was also established, providing reports for members of the cooperative about the position of equity. This was supported by internal contracts and shared funding to complete the work.

CHAPTER SUMMARY

This chapter has shown that environmental degradation and the threat of climate change are challenging issues that require global cooperation to be tackled. Despite large-scale adoption of international agreements committing to limiting global warming, evidence shows that we are not on track to achieve global targets and more needs to be done. While this task can seem daunting, businesses and organisations are questioning their purpose and actions using several criteria to redesign for a more sustainable future. Strategic thinkers are invited to:

- Recognise the interdependent relationship between the environment and their organisation.
- Recognise that environmentally sustainable action offers opportunities such as cost savings for organisations through adopting more efficient resources and processes and shifting to clean energy sources, and the development of new products and services.
- Use the tools and guidance that are available (UN Global Impact, Circular Economy, Strategic Thinking for Sufficiency, and Doughnut Economics), and that have been used by others to think differently, and re-examine and guide their business or organisation's strategic direction.

If everyone does something, the intentions of the international agreements may be achieved.

RECOMMENDED READING

Explore the intention and resources of the Doughnut Economics Lab (https://doughnuteconomics.org/).

Explore the Ellen Mac Arthur Foundation site for resources (https://www.ellenmacarthurfoundation.org/).

Stahel, W.R. (2019) *The Circular Economy Guide.* A User´s Guide. London: Routledge.

REFERENCES

Atkins, J. & Atkins, B. (Eds) (2016) *The Business of Bees: An Integrated Approach to Bee Decline and Corporate Responsibility.* Sheffield: Greenleaf Publishing.

Bamberg, S. (2003) How does environmental concern influence specific environmentally related behaviors? A new answer to an old question. *Journal of Environmental Psychology*, 23(1), 21–32.

Bartunek, J.M. & Balogun, J. (2022) Context and how it matters: Mobilizing spaces for organization-community sustainable change. *Strategic Organization*, 20(4), 832-845.

Berliner, D. & Prakash, A. (2015) 'Bluewashing' the Firm? Voluntary regulations, program design, and member compliance with the United Nations Global Compact. *Policy Studies Journal*, 43(1), 115–138.

Bocken, N.M.P. & Short, S.W. (2016) Towards a sufficiency-driven business model: Experiences and opportunities, *Environmental Innovation and Societal Transitions*, 18, 41–61, ISSN 2210-4224. https://doi.org/10.1016/j.eist.2015.07.010.

Bocken, N.M., De Pauw, I., Bakker, C. & Van Der Grinten, B. (2016) Product design and business model strategies for a circular economy. *Journal of Industrial and Production Engineering*, 33(5), 308–320.

Brundtland, G.H. (1987) Report of the World Commission on Environment and Development: Our Common Future. UN-Document A/42/427. Retrieved November 28, 2024, from https://sustainabledevelopment.un.org/content/documents/5987our-common-future.pdf.

Carroll, A.B. (1979) A three-dimensional conceptual model of Corporate Social Performance. *The Academy of Management Review*, 4(4), 497.

Carroll, A.B. (1991) The pyramid of corporate social responsibility: Toward the moral management of organizational stakeholders. *Business Horizons*, 34, 39–48.

Carroll, A.B. (2021) Corporate social responsibility: Perspectives on the CSR construct's development and future. *Business & Society*, 60(6), 1258–1278.

Circle Economy (2019) The circularity gap report – Closing the circularity gap in a 9% world. *Circle Economy, Amsterdam*. Retrieved November 28, 2024, from https://circulareconomy.europa.eu/platform/sites/default/files/circularity_gap_report_2019.pdf.

Cordts, A., Nitzko, S. & Spiller, A. (2014) Consumer response to negative information on meat consumption in Germany. *International Food and Agribusiness Management Review*, 17, 83–106.

DEAL (The Doughnut Economics Action Lab) (2024) https://doughnuteconomics.org/.
Deegan, C. (2002) Introduction: The legitimising effect of social and environmental disclosures – A theoretical foundation. *Accounting, Auditing & Accountability Journal*, 15(3), 282–311. doi: 10.1108/09513570210435852.
EEHE (Electrics and Electronics in Hybrid and Electric Vehicles) (2024) FAQs. Standardization for future electronic systems. Retrieved November 5, 2024, from https://eehe.de/en/standardization-for-future-charging-systems-and-its-influence-on-vehicle-systems/.
Ellen MacArthur Foundation (2022) Circulate products and materials. Retrieved November 5, 2024, from https://www.ellenmacarthurfoundation.org/circulate-products-and-materials.
Freudenreich, B., Lüdeke-Freund, F. & Schaltegger, S. (2020) A stakeholder theory perspective on business models: Value creation for sustainability. *Journal of Business Ethics*, 166(1), 3–18.
Global Warming Index (n.d.) Retrieved November 11, 2024, from https://www.globalwarmingindex.org/.
IPCC (2018) *Global Warming of 1.5°C. An IPCC Special Report on the impacts of global warming of 1.5°C above pre-industrial levels and related global greenhouse gas emission pathways, in the context of strengthening the global response to the threat of climate change, sustainable development, and efforts to eradicate poverty* [V. Masson-Delmotte P. Zhai, H-O. Pörtner, D. Roberts, J. Skea, P.R. Shukla, A. Pirani, W. Moufouma-Okia, C. Péan, R. Pidcock, S. Connors, J.B.R. Matthews, Y. Chen, X. Zhou, M.I. Gomis, E. Lonnoy, T. Maycock, M. Tignor, & T. Waterfield (Eds.)].
Jones, S., Singh, P. & Dean, D. (2023) To bin or not to bin. *Journal of Customer Behavior*, 22 (1–2), 68–77.
Kwansy, T., Dobernig, K. & Riefler, P. (2022) Towards reduced meat consumption: A systematic literature review of intervention effectiveness, 2001–2019. *Appetite*, 168, 105739.
Laine, M., Tregidga, H. & Unerman, J. (2021) *Sustainability Accounting and Accountability* (3rd ed.). Abingdon, Oxon: Taylor & Francis Group.
Liedtka, J.M. (1998) Linking strategic thinking with strategic planning. *Strategy & Leadership*, 4.
Lovell, H. (2013) Discourse and innovation journeys: The case of low energy housing in the UK. In F. Geels, M. Hekkert & S. Jacobsson (Eds.) (2011) *The Dynamics of Sustainable Innovation Journeys* (1st ed.) (pp. 93–112). Abingdon, Oxon: Routledge. https://doi.org/10.4324/9781315873435.
Lush (n.d.) Who we are. Retrieved November 26, 2024, from https://weare.lush.com/lush-life/our-company/who-we-are/#:~:text=Lush%20is%2010%25%20Employee%20Owned%20and%20our%20people,of%20previous%20mail%20order%20business%20Cosmetics%20To%20Go.
Meyer-Emerick, N. (2012). Sustainable Cleveland 2019: Designing a green economic future using the appreciative inquiry summit process. *Public Works Management & Policy*, 17(1), 52–67.

Momberg, D., Jacobs, B. & Sonnenberg, N. (2012) The role of environmental knowledge in young female consumers' evaluation and selection of apparel in South Africa. *International Journal of Consumer Studies*, 36(4), 408–415.

Museum of Design in Plastics (2023) Blog Post, *Design for Disassembly*. Retrieved November 5, 2024, from https://www.modip.ac.uk/blog/2023/06/design-disassembly.

Nonaka, I. & Zhu, Z. (2012) *Pragmatic Strategy: Eastern Wisdom, Global Success*. Cambridge: Cambridge University Press.

Patagonia (2011) Don't Buy This Jacket, Black Friday and the *New York Times*. https://www.patagonia.com/stories/dont-buy-this-jacket-black-friday-and-the-new-york-times/story-18615.html?msockid=0051ecdfb59b64110b81f82ab4e16550.

Raworth, K. (2017). *Doughnut Economics: Seven Ways to Think Like a 21st Century Economist*. London: Penguin Random House.

Rockström, J. (2015) A 'perfect' agreement in Paris is not essential. *Nature*, 527, 411. https://doi.org/10.1038/527411a.

Rockström, J., Steffen, W., Noone, K., Persson, A., … (2009) Planetary boundaries: Exploring the safe operating space for humanity. *Ecology and Society*, 14(2), 32. http://www.ecologyandsociety.org/vol14/iss2/art32/.

Singh, A., Taneja, S., Zhu, Y., Jiang, H., Luthra, S. & Kumar, A. (2022) Hey, did you see that label? It's sustainable! Understanding the role of sustainable labelling in shaping sustainable purchase behaviour for sustainable development. *Business Strategy and the Environment*, 31(7), 2820–2838. https://doi.org/10.1002/bse.3049.

Steffen, W., Richardson, K., Rockström, J., Cornell, S.E., … (2015) Planetary boundaries: Guiding human development on a changing planet. *Science*, 347(6223). doi: https://doi.org/10.1126/science.1259855.

TCFD (n.d.) Taskforce on Climate-related Financial Disclosures.

Thaler, R.H. & Sunstein, C.R. (2008) *Nudge: Improving Decisions About Health, Wealth, and Happiness*. London: Yale University Press.

UNFCC (United Nations Framework Convention on Climate Change) (2018) *The Paris Agreement*. Retrieved November 11, 2024, from https://unfccc.int/documents/184656.

UN (United Nations) (n.d.). What is climate change? Retrieved November 11, 2024, from https://www.un.org/en/climatechange/what-is-climate-change.

UN (United Nations) (2024) The United Nations Global Compact. https://unglobalcompact.org/.

Verain, M.C., Sijtsema, S.J., Dagevos, H. & Antonides, G. (2017) Attribute segmentation and communication effects on healthy and sustainable consumer diet intentions. *Sustainability*, 9(5), 743.

WCED (World Commission on Environment and Development) (1987) *Our Common Future. The Report of the World Commission on Environment and Development*. Chapter 2: Towards sustainable development. Retrieved August 18, 2014, from http://www.un-documents.net/ocf-02.htm.

CHAPTER 10

A Systems View Toolkit for Responsible Strategic Thinking

Olivia Ramsbottom

CHAPTER OUTLINE

This chapter first describes a systems view way of thinking. It then presents a toolkit for responsible strategic thinking for business and society with reference to the content of the previous chapters.

By a toolkit we mean a set of resources and skills to enable you to better face the challenges of the complex environment of which we are all part. This book constitutes your main resource, a set of ideas and examples for you to draw on. This chapter presents a toolkit in diagrammatic form and considers the skills you need to practise, and the questions you need to ask, as a strategic thinker.

This chapter moves from a consideration of the strategic thinker as an individual at the heart of the system, to their role as part of the organisation or business, and then to their role as part of society/life, and here we take tips from chapters 3 to 9's examination of the political, economic, social, technological, legal, and environmental to guide you as to how to think differently and with a systems view.

Strategic thinkers are in a unique position, in their roles at the centre of society and life, to make a difference by making what might seem small decisions on larger issues, to change the way we do things, and potentially change the future of society and life to elicit a fairer future. Here are some suggestions of how to do this.

DOI: 10.4324/9781003475545-10

A SYSTEMS VIEW

This book has developed strands from other ideas, among them pragmatic strategy (Nonaka & Zhu, 2012), strategic thinking (Liedtka, 1998), doughnut thinking (Raworth, 2017), and the sustainable mindset (Ritz & Rimanoczy, 2021). A common strand throughout these theories is that we must take a systems view (Forrester, 1971; Beer, 1973; Senge, 1997; Sterman, 2002; Higgins, 2015).

A systems view means that we need to have a grasp of:

- The bigger picture (Haslam & Shenoy, 2018) meaning the wider environment (from a business, social, *and* an ecological perspective)
- The environment's dynamism (Raworth, 2017)
- The complex interconnections among ecology, society, and economy (Edwards, 2005)
- The way our lives are inextricably entwined with all – the actions of the individual extend beyond the boundary of his or her position (Higgins, 2015).

In systems thinking, all is interconnected in a dynamic web of relations: relations with the world, relations with the mind, relations with others (Nonaka & Zhu, 2012, p. 171). Consider the world as a network of cogs, levers, pulleys, and feedback loops. Action in one area will cause change and impact in another area. You need to trace the actions to understand the full impact of your decisions. As all is interconnected, the system will need to evolve and change too and our interactions with it can be redesigned (Meadows, cited in Raworth, 2017) to create an adequate response for our new world.

Throughout this book we have seen the pressures to look at the world differently and there is wider consensus that a new way of thinking is required. Raworth might ask us to start from scratch (Schumpeter, 1954; Raworth, 2017). A true grounded theory (Glaser & Strauss, 1967) is unfortunately unlikely for many reasons. We personally are the product of our experiences and strategy-making is the product of many works and theories that have gone before. Our system is also the product of thousands of years of development. We can however do our best to be creative. To think what we could, would, and should do given a blank sheet. Of course knowing the errors we have made (and Nonaka and Zhu (2012) do a good job of highlighting the weaknesses in strategy-making as of that time, post-2008 recession) can also be helpful in avoiding them in future. Raworth (2017) rethinks economics, and in this book we take up the baton and try to rethink strategy-making. Echoing Raworth, it's:

> not about finding the correct (model) (because it doesn't exist), it's about choosing or creating one that best serves our purpose, reflecting the context we face, the values we hold, and the aims we have. As humanity's context, values and aims continually evolve, so too should be the way that we envision the economy.
>
> *(Raworth, 2017, p. 22)*

As Raworth addresses the economy, we address strategic thinking and attempt to chip away at the conventional view from our direction to provide a 'compelling alternative frame' (Raworth, 2017, p. 22).

It is evident that some theories have been overlooked in favour of the dominant power in society at certain times. For example, Raworth (2017) highlights that original theories and approaches to economics were more about provision for all and sustaining society and later switched to acquisition of wealth. Meadows (1970s to 1990s), Senge (1997), Higgins (2015), Raworth (2017), Ritz and Rimanoczy (2021), to name but a few, have been dissenting voices from the developed dominant economic theory, but they were not listened to and Raworth's views have been labelled as idealistic, as radical approaches are hard for incumbents (the existing political and economic system, to say nothing of businesses who lobby governments for favour) to stomach. Similarly, we have overlooked more complex ways of looking at strategy (Liedtka's work dates to the 1990s) in preference for a simplistic, rational approach. There have been times where the status quo has been challenged, for example, following the crisis in 2008 (Nonaka & Zhu, 2012), but things returned to 'normal', as the established systemic issues meant that it was hard to challenge the neoliberal capitalist world order.

In this book we have examined the world through a systems perspective, recognising that all is interconnected, from us, to management concepts, to our organisations, and with external trends and influences. Here we propose a toolkit that incorporates the view of the strategic thinker at the heart of a system of which they are a part and on which they will and should have impact (Figure 10.1). It offers some ways to deal best with that system.

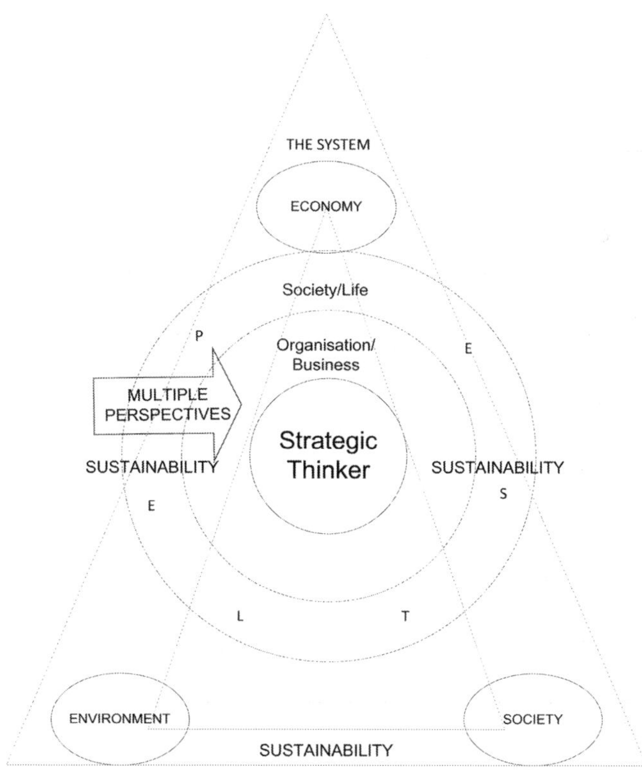

FIGURE 10.1 A Systems View: the Strategic Thinker at the centre of Responsible Strategic Thinking

A TOOLKIT FOR RESPONSIBLE STRATEGIC THINKING FOR BUSINESS AND SOCIETY

Strategic Thinker (Self)

The strategic thinker is at the heart of responsible strategic thinking (Figure 10.2). They will be the ones to redesign the system because 'markets do not correct themselves, industries do not have a purpose, firms do not make decisions, *humans_*do' (Nonaka & Zhu, 2012, p. 290). 'It is individuals who think strategically, not organizations' (Liedtka, 1998, p. 120).

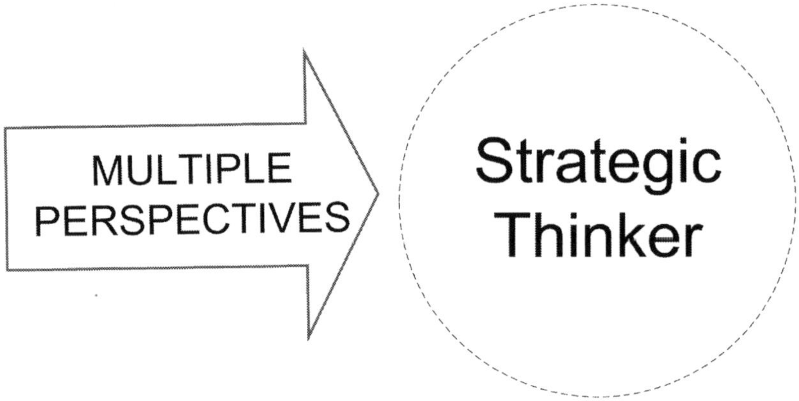

FIGURE 10.2 The Strategic Thinker

First, a strategic thinker must look to their own skills of strategic thinking, combining strategic management and strategic leadership into strategic thinking.

Strategic Management

Plan, organise, command, coordinate, control, guide towards goals, use resources, process, be efficient, be effective, budget, order, structure, implement, problem-solve, organise, be impersonal, be passive, balance, compromise, conserve, regulate, direct, be rational, consult, persist, be tough-minded, be analytical, deliberate, be authoritative, stabilise, task-driven, dominated by the mind, action.

+

Strategic Leadership

Develop a vision, produce change, communicate, create coalitions, motivate, engage, satisfy, build recognition, self-esteem, be personal, be active, create excitement, have empathy, understand and give meaning, search out opportunities, encourage, involve, dominated by the soul, be passionate, be creative, be flexible, inspire, innovate, be courageous, be imaginative, be experimental, be independent, reflection.

=

Strategic Thinking

But the strategic thinker is part of a bigger system, and we know that we struggle to think beyond our personal existence, beyond the short-term, and we find it difficult to deal with complexity. Thinking outside of our individual unit and insular entity requires us to challenge our mental models (Forrester, 1971; Beer, 1973; Sterman, 2002; Higgins, 2015; Haslam & Shenoy, 2018) and step outside of our natural tendency for selfish egoism (Higgins, 2015) and our tendency to think of the near, the short-term, and the responsive (Forrester, 1971; Sterman, 2002; Raworth, 2017). It is impossible to not be human, but strategic thinkers must consider their relationship with their management and leadership function and the whole system objectively. They must overcome their self-interest and bias and step outside of their natural short-term view to cater for their stakeholders. This takes emotional and spiritual intelligence (Ritz & Rimanoczy, 2021), imposition of the veil of ignorance to achieve a higher viewpoint (Rawls, 1971), understanding (Nonaka & Zhu, 2012), and the collection of multiple perspectives.

CASE STUDY 10.1

Personal Contribution to Strategic Thinking

Jayne Sowerby-Warrington is the Founder, Director of Kudos Leadership Solutions Ltd and was a previous Senior Leader at Lincolnshire County Council, and here considers her personal contribution to strategic thinking and the importance of collaboration.

Jayne questions the wisdom of a leader 'stepping outside of themselves' (with the intention of being objective) as she firmly believes that a leader needs to be authentic, and arguably that means bringing the subjective into the workplace. She expects and needs herself and her team members to be the best versions of themselves and for her: 'Coming to work pretending you're something you're not, will not work.' Each person brings a different skillset to the team. For Jayne, the authenticity element is important and working in an environment where you can be authentic, and your colleagues embrace and harness that, is very important. She agrees that you cannot be personally biased to the detriment of the work you do, but work is personal, and people should bring their personal values and personalities to work. She wants people on the team who care about what they're doing. Leaders need to be emotionally intelligent and self-aware. 'You've got to be aware of how you're coming across, how your emotions can affect others. You know what's right, what's wrong? You've just got to have those basic principles.' Jayne also sees the value of reflection, regularly assessing how far her and the team have progressed towards their goals. Finally, leadership for her is 'about the connecting with people. It's about creating an environment that brings the best out of others. Being a strategic thinker isn't about locking yourself in a room with your own kind thinking about what to do in isolation of the rest of the organisation. It is about going getting out there, finding out what stakeholders want and need and trying to design a collaborative solution around that. It's also important for colleagues to recognise where they are within that strategy as well, where they fit, where they can add value and know their purpose.'

Organisation

The strategic thinker is at the heart of an organisation (Figure 10.3). Without the organisation, the strategic thinker's role would not exist and the strategic thinker's role is to maintain the business (sustainably). The organisation is the supporting context (Liedtka, 1998) and the beneficiary of the strategic thinker's activities. The two are interdependent. To honour this relationship, the strategic thinker must understand the organisation, the organisation's internal resources and capabilities, and its purpose and culture. The planning tools discussed in Chapter 2 are good foundations for strategic thinking and Figure 10.4 represents the inclusion of vision, mission, and values statements in our strategic thinking.

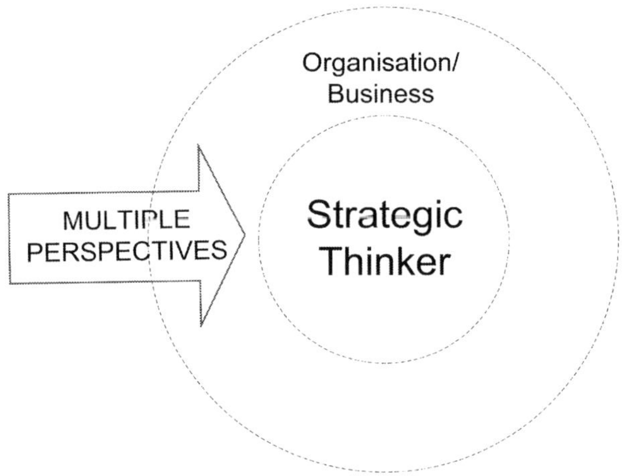

FIGURE 10.3 The Strategic Thinker and their Relationship with the Organisation/Business

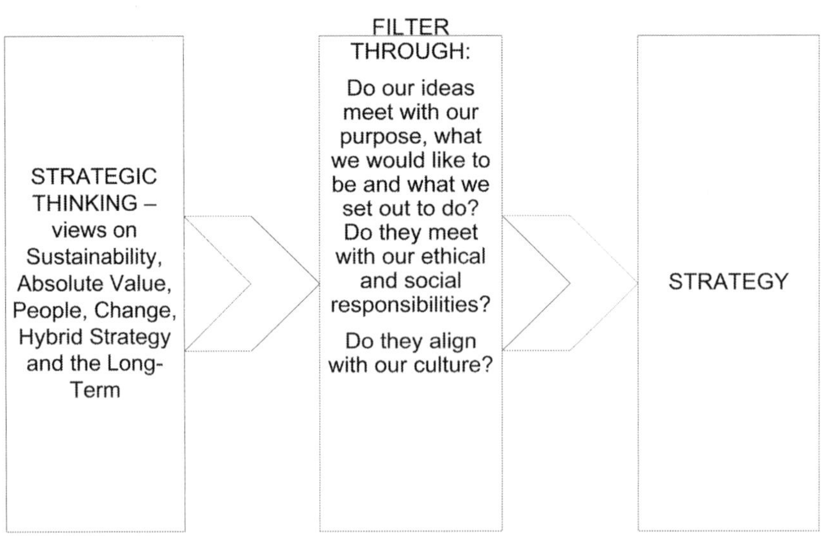

FIGURE 10.4 The Strategic Thinker Filters Decisions through the Core Ideas of the Organisation

The Activities of a Responsible Strategic Thinker

So far, given our model for responsible strategic thinking, you need to do the following to be a responsible strategic thinker:

- Take a systems approach – recognise that all is interconnected
- Understand your role at the heart of the process
- Use your people to provide multiple perspectives – talk, collect views
- Use the appropriate tools to understand your organisation's position, role, and intentions.

Society/Life

In turn, the organisation is impacted by what is going on in society/life and this environment has changed, continues to change, and is complex. We saw in Chapter 1 how terms that defined strategy-making previously are no longer valid and established that strategy-making in contemporary society needs to be sustainable, hold absolute value, respond to people and change, and be hybrid and long-term (Figures 10.5 and 10.6).

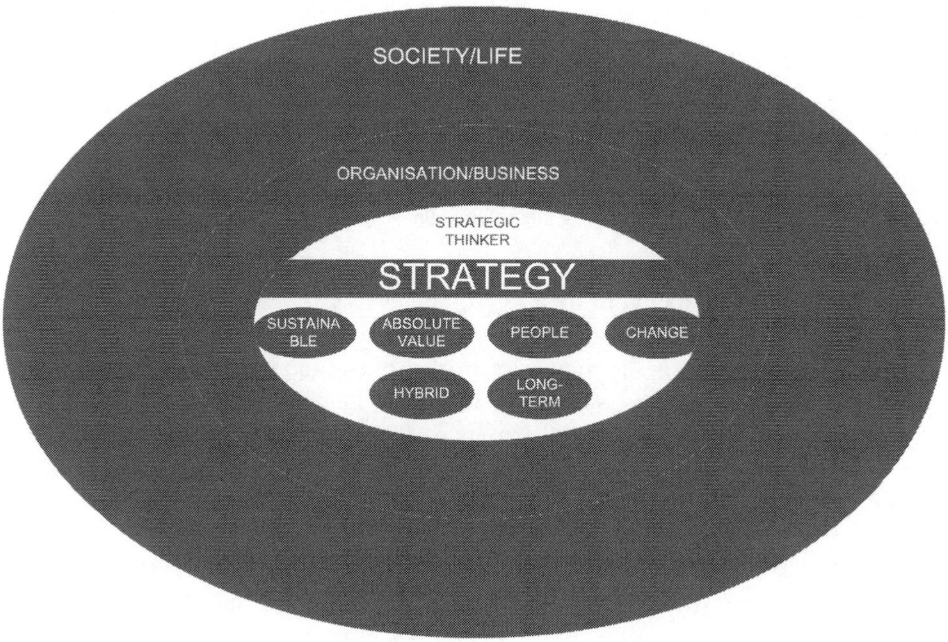

FIGURE 10.5 The Characteristics of Strategy-Making in Strategic Thinking

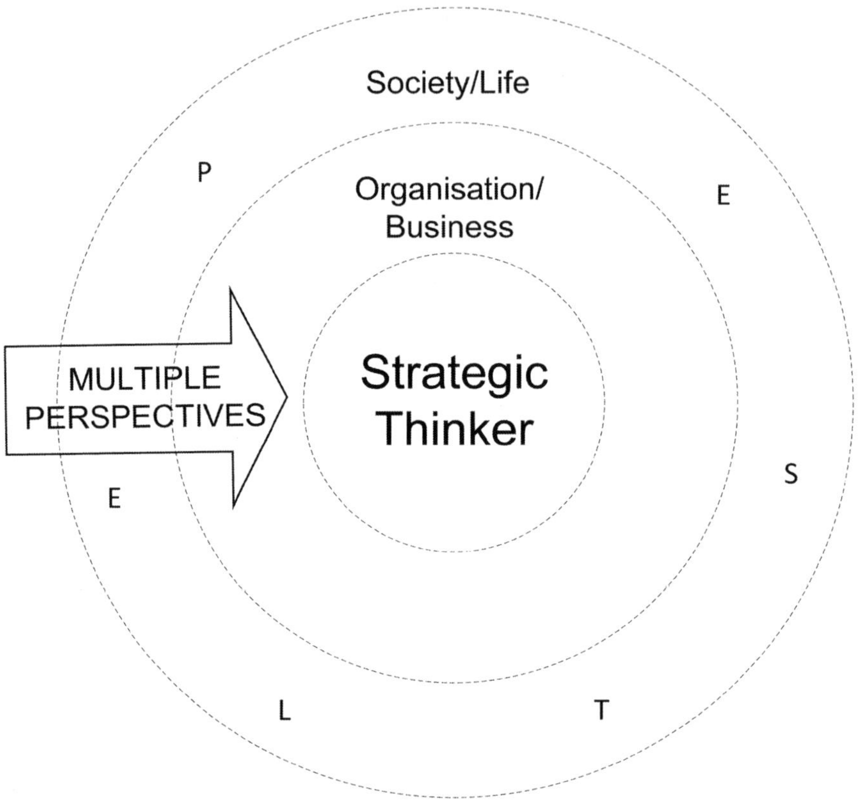

FIGURE 10.6 The Strategic Thinker's Relationship with Society/Life

To maintain ourselves and our organisation in society/life we need to respond to the influences and changes in society: find innovative ways to respond to society's evolution and complexity with changes to management theory and to the ways we do business.

Methods developed for past situations should not be expected to be applicable now (Beer, 1973; Raworth, 2017) and rather than a new way of operating being 'idealistic', as Raworth's Doughnut Economics was labelled, expecting established methods to be suitable is *unrealistic* and 'inadequate for dealing with our overpopulated, globally interconnected world' (Capra & Luisi, 2014).

As with the strategic thinker/organisational interdependency, the organisation and the strategic thinker's existence is interdependent with society/life, and the same approach to strategy-making incorporating multiple stakeholder perspectives holds firm.

There are permeable membranes between the strategic thinker, their organisation, and society/life. The lack of balance between the economic, social, and environmental parts of the system has led to serious detrimental impacts on society and the environment. We can no longer accept this for many reasons, but most pressing and most public is the climate crisis that will lead to increasingly serious environmental disasters which will impact on our and future generations' ability to live, full stop. In conjunction with this imminent threat to life are the impacts on humans' opportunities to live life *well* caused by a lack of respect for social sustainability from businesses and organisations.

Strategic thinkers need to be conscious of the external factors that have an impact on them and their organisations and respond accordingly.

The Activities of a Responsible Systems Strategic Thinker

From our chapters we take the following guides for responsible strategic thinking interacting with society/life.

POLITICAL

- **Clarify goals:** Organisations must ensure that their lobbying and advocacy goals align with their broader mission and objectives.
- **Strategy versus initiatives:** Focus on long-term strategy while balancing the need to respond to short-term opportunities and initiatives.
- **Context and timing:** Stay informed on political and environmental changes, recognising that while organisations cannot always shape the broader narrative (e.g. international votes and referenda), they can influence policy implementation.
- **Structure of advocacy:** Decide whether lobbying will be in-house, through dedicated teams, or outsourced to agencies, considering the specific needs and size of the organisation.
- **Key skills:** Effective lobbying requires skills in communication, diplomacy, relationship-building, and the ability to leverage evidence to shape policy narratives.
- **Networking:** Building and maintaining a strong network is essential. This often involves cultivating relationships with key policy-makers and influencers at various levels.
- **Global-national-local focus:** Advocacy priorities will differ based on an organisation's scope. Multinationals may focus on global/national, while smaller groups may emphasise local impact.
- **Insider versus outsider dynamics:** Organisations must navigate the balance between being external advocates or trusted partners in policy co-design, especially in larger, more connected sectors.

ECONOMIC

- **Balance short-term and long-term goals**: Combine profit maximisation with a focus on sustainability and social responsibility to remain competitive while addressing evolving societal demands.
- **Adopt adaptive strategies**: Use neoclassical tools for immediate market response, while integrating institutional insights to anticipate regulatory and societal changes for long-term flexibility.

- **Enhance organisational resilience**: Build resilience by anticipating external shocks and proactively aligning business practices with social norms and stakeholder expectations.
- **Prioritise ethical and inclusive decision-making**: Balance financial goals with ethical considerations to enhance corporate reputation, stakeholder trust, and long-term sustainability.
- **Leverage quantitative and qualitative insights**: Use quantitative data for performance analysis, while incorporating qualitative insights to ensure that strategies align with cultural, social, and institutional contexts.
- **Foster innovation and collaboration**: Encourage collaboration with stakeholders and external institutions to drive innovation, while ensuring that these partnerships are efficient and value-driven using analytical tools.
- **Shift the focus to people (social responsibility) and environment (environmental responsibility)** and to enhanced stakeholder relationships away from a focus on competitors to achieve value.
- **Consider alternative economic approaches:** Bottom of the Pyramid approaches, frugal innovation, disruption, coopetition and social enterprise.

SOCIETAL

- **Adopt strategic systems thinking**: Take a holistic approach that considers the interconnectedness of organisations, society, and natural resources. Use systems thinking to address complex, 'wicked' societal challenges, broadening the problem space and expanding solution options.
- **Think ahead**: Integrate long-term thinking into strategic decisions, focusing on the impacts on future generations, social inequalities, and the fair allocation of resources. Prioritise justice and equity for disadvantaged groups.
- **Think differently**: Embrace responsible competitiveness where value is created for all stakeholders, not just through economic gain. Move away from traditional wealth-centred models to a broader societal and environmental perspective (e.g. Doughnut Economics).
- **Think in circles**: Shift from linear planning models to circular thinking, recognising that complex issues evolve as solutions are explored and implemented. Adapt strategies as new insights emerge from ongoing problem-solving.
- **Think in combination**: Merge strategic management with leadership, fostering dynamic thinking through intuition, dialogue, and co-production. Engage diverse stakeholders in decision-making, allowing for coopetition and collaborative resource sharing.
- **Engage stakeholders actively**: Involve all relevant stakeholders, including community groups and staff, in shaping decisions. Empower them through participatory approaches that challenge assumptions, redistribute power, and encourage collaboration.

- **Focus on continuous improvement**: Use tools like B-Corp certification and materiality assessments to ensure ongoing evaluation and improvement of social and environmental impact. Make decisions based on both financial and societal considerations, aiming for long-term, sustainable growth.
- **Embrace double materiality**: Consider both the internal and external impacts of business decisions, addressing not only short-term needs but also long-term societal challenges and environmental stewardship.

TECHNOLOGICAL

- **Proactively adapt security measures** to stay current with emerging threats.
- **Embrace change and disruption** with proactive and adaptive strategic thinking.
- **Be transparent and open**, diverse, empower user autonomy.
- **Follow the principles of fairness by design and incorporate human judgement** in the application of AI.

LEGAL

- **Act ethnically:** Follow all laws of the country and the business/organisational sphere of which you are a part but go further. Be objective. Be right, just, and fair in one's practices. Preserve and increase the legitimate options available to others.
- **Act sustainably:** Understand the impact of decisions on society and environment while pursuing economic success. Collaborate and cooperate to understand others' perspectives.
- **Economic performance:** Thrive and re-invest.

ENVIRONMENTAL

- Recognise the **interdependent relationship between the environment and your organisation.**
- Recognise that environmentally sustainable action offers opportunities such **as cost-saving for organisations through adopting more efficient resources and processes and shifting to clean energy sources, and the development of new products and services.**
- Use the tools and guidance that are available (**UN Global Compact, Circular Economy, strategic thinking for sufficiency, and Doughnut Economics**), and that have been used by others to think differently and re-examine and guide their business' or organisation's strategic direction.

Thinking Sustainably

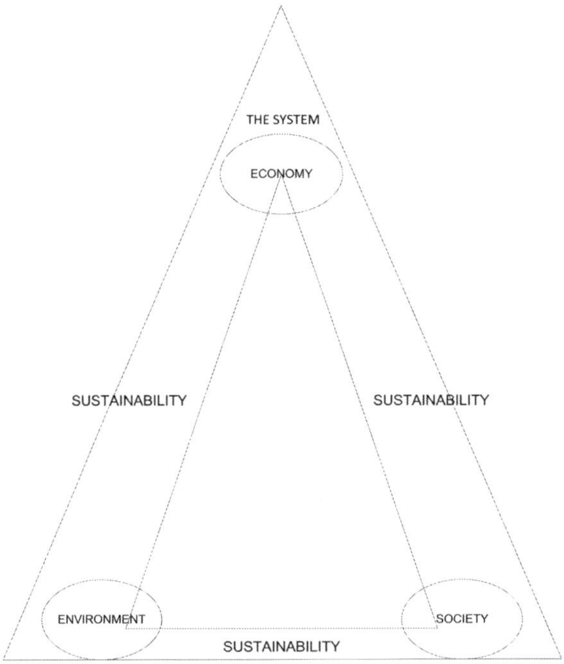

FIGURE 10.7 Applying the Principle of Sustainability

Finally in our model we redraw the pyramid of corporate social responsibility (Carroll, 1991) made up of economic, legal, ethical, and philanthropic responsibilities and combine it with other terms such as social purpose, conscious capitalism, adherence to the triple or quadruple bottom line, and most recently Environmental, Societal, and Governance (ESG) responsibilities (Figure 10.7). We incorporate Visser's (2011) theory of an organisation's age and stage of Corporate Social Responsibility (CSR) to reflect a responsible age of business and organisational practice, and we replace all these terms with 'sustainability' as we recognise, as detailed throughout this book, that sustainability implies an organisation's commitment to environmental, economic, and societal responsibilities and a sustainable approach naturally encompasses a philanthropic approach defined as giving, benevolence, welfare, altruism, prosocial behaviour, and 'doing good' (*Journal of Philanthropy and Marketing*, 2023) because a sustainable approach would make these activities *part* of a business or organisation's natural behaviour. A sustainable approach, given our definition of sustainability as 'intra- and intergenerational justice as well as ecological limitations' (WCED, 1987, cited in Neugebauer et al., 2015) and considering 'the needs of the present without compromising the ability of future generations to meet their own needs' (WCED, 1991, cited in Higgins, 2015, p. 2) also encompasses an ethical approach: 'the preservation and increase of legitimate options available to others as well as to oneself. Legitimate options are those that do not reduce the options available to others' (Ackoff, 1996). And an ethical approach assumes a higher responsibility than just doing what is legally required.

Our final model is shown in Figure 10.8.

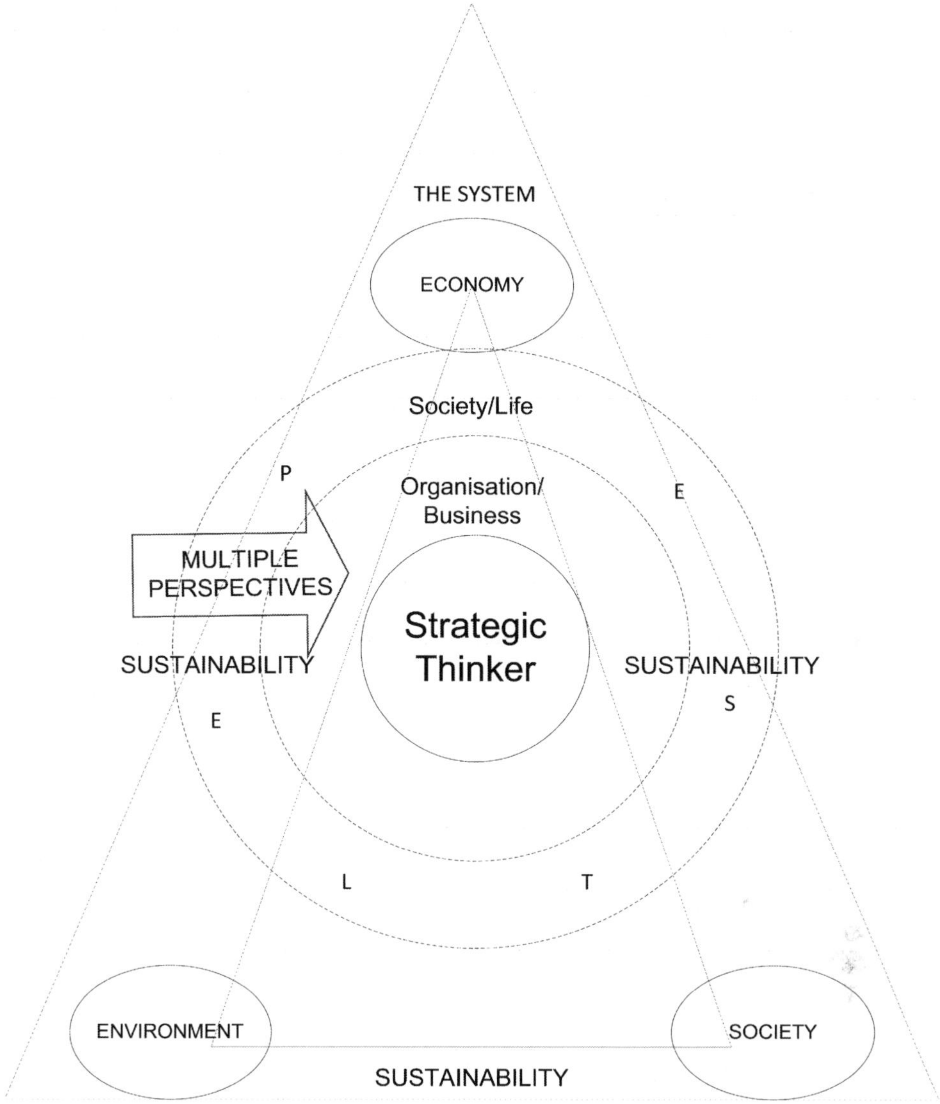

FIGURE 10.8 A Systems View: The Strategic Thinker at the Centre of Responsible Strategic Thinking

As a result of our re-examination of strategic thinking and strategy-making, we move from the actions, the doing, to the thinking, and ask the following questions when it comes to strategy-making.

The Questions a Responsible Sustainable Systems Strategic Thinker Must Ask

1. Who do we need to involve?
2. What and who can help me with my decision-making?
3. What is our organisation's overall intention?
4. What value are we seeking?
5. What factors are impacting us from the following areas: political, economic, social, technological, legal, and environmental?
6. What do we know? What don't we know? What do we think we know? How can we reduce the unknowns?
7. What can we do to impact the following areas: political, economic, social, technological, legal, and environmental?
8. Can we think differently and do something different to what we have done before?
9. How will this strategy *improve* the situation of the organisation, the society, the world?
10. How will this decision *damage* the situation of the organisation, the society, the world?
11. Is this immoral?
12. Is this right?
13. What will change?
14. What will our legacy be?

CHAPTER SUMMARY

This chapter introduces a systems-thinking approach and provides a toolkit for responsible strategic thinking, drawing on the insights from earlier chapters. The toolkit offers resources to help individuals navigate the complex environment of business and society. It emphasises the role of the strategic thinker, first as an individual within the system, then as part of an organisation, and finally as a member of society/life. By incorporating lessons from political, economic, social, technological, legal, and environmental considerations (chapters 3 to 9), the toolkit guides strategic thinkers on how to approach decision-making with a broader, interconnected perspective.

The toolkit outlines key activities and questions for responsible strategic thinkers to consider when formulating and implementing strategy. It highlights the unique position of strategic thinkers, who, by making informed decisions, could influence broader societal change and help create a fairer future.

RECOMMENDED READING

Higgins, K. (2015). *Economic Growth and Sustainability: Systems Thinking for a Complex World*. London: Academic Press.

REFERENCES

Ackoff, R.L. (1996) On learning and the systems that facilitate it. *Reflections*, 1, 14–24.

Beer, S. (1973) *Designing Freedom*. The text of six radio broadcasts given in the autumn of 1973 as the thirteenth series of Massey Lectures, Canadian Broadcasting Corporation. Retrieved February 22, 2024, from https://systemsorienteddesign.net/wp-content/uploads/2022/10/Designing-Freedom_Staford-Beer.pdf.

Capra, F. & Luisi, P.L. (2014) *The Systems View of Life: A Unifying Vision*. Cambridge: Cambridge University Press.

Carroll, A.B. (1991, July/August) The pyramid of corporate social responsibility: Toward the moral management of organizational stakeholders. *Business Horizons*, 42.

Edwards, A. (2005) *The Sustainability Revolution: Portrait of a Paradigm Shift*. Gabriola Island, BC: New Society Publishers.

Forrester, J. (1971) Counterintuitive behavior of social systems. *Technology Review*, 73(3), 52–68.

Glaser, B.G. & Strauss, A.L. (1967) *The Discovery of Grounded Theory*. Chicago, IL: Aldine.

Haslam, S. & Shenoy, B. (2018) *Strategic Decision Making: A Discovery-led Approach to Critical Choices in Turbulent Times*. London: Kogan Page.

Higgins, K. (2015) *Economic Growth and Sustainability: Systems Thinking for a Complex World*. London: Academic Press.

Journal of Philanthropy and Marketing (2023) Overview. Retrieved February 6, 2024, from https://onlinelibrary.wiley.com/page/journal/26911361/homepage/productinformation.html.

Liedtka, J.M. (1998) Strategic thinking: Can it be taught? *Long Range Planning*, February.

Neugebauer, F., Figge, F. & Hahn, T. (2015) Planned or emergent strategy making? Exploring the formation of corporate sustainability strategies. *Business Strategy and the Environment*, 25(5), 323–336.

Nonaka, I. & Zhu, Z. (2012) *Pragmatic Strategy: Eastern Wisdom, Global Success*. Cambridge: Cambridge University Press.

Rawls, J. (1971) *Theory of Justice*. Cambridge, MA: Belknap Press of Harvard University Press.

Raworth, K. (2017) *Doughnut Economics: Seven Ways to Think Like a 21st Century Economist*. New York: Random House Business Books.

Ritz, A.A. & Rimanoczy, I. (Eds) (2021) *Sustainability Mindset and Transformative Leadership: A Multidisciplinary Perspective*. Basingstoke: Palgrave Macmillan.

Schumpeter, J. (1954) *History of Economic Analysis*. Oxford: Oxford University Press.

Senge, P.M. (1997) THE FIFTH DISCIPLINE. *Measuring Business Excellence,* 1(3), 46–51. https://doi.org/10.1108/eb025496.
Sterman, J.D. (2002) All models are wrong: Reflections on becoming a systems scientist. *System Dynamics Review,* 18(4), 501–531. https://doi.org/10.1002/sdr.261.
Visser, W. (2011) The ages and stages of CSR: Towards the future with CSR 2.0. https://www.waynevisser.com/articles/the-ages-and-stages-of-csr.

Index

Pages in **bold** refer to tables
Names of businesses/organisations used as examples are underlined.

Kolibri 360 GmbH
Ferdinand-Jühlke-Straße 7
99095 Erfurt, Deutschland
produktsicherheit@kolibri360.de